A Reading of Hegel's
Phenomenology of Spirit

A Reading of Hegel's
Phenomenology of Spirit

QUENTIN LAUER, S.J.

New York
Fordham University Press
1976

Printed in the United States of America

Contents

Contents

A Reading of Hegel's
Phenomenology of Spirit

Introduction

PROSAIC AS THE TITLE to this volume may appear to be, considerable care and reflection went into the selection of it, out of concern to say exactly what the book is, and what it is not. It is not likely that at the present stage of philosophical interest in the Hegelian enterprise any serious objections will be raised to the appearance of still another book on Hegel—not even to another book on his *Phenomenology of Spirit.* No one can honestly say that too much has been written on this most seminal and most difficult thinker; if anything, too little has been written. It is important to know from the outset, however, just what sort of book this purports to be, just what it seeks to accomplish. A rather simple answer to that question is that the present work intends to facilitate in some way the well-nigh impossible task of reading Hegel's *Phenomenology* for the first time.[1] It is in no way intended as a substitute for a reading of Hegel's own words, nor to make unnecessary subsequent readings. The author hopes, however, in some degree to spare others the tortures he himself had to go through in coming to terms with the intricacies both of Hegel's thought and of the language in which he expresses that thought.

What I am, then—with considerable trepidation—here presenting is "a reading of Hegel's *Phenomenology of Spirit*," no more and no less. This means that it is, first of all, *a* reading. I do not in any way claim that it is the *only* reading possible, not even that it is the *best* reading. I do claim, however, that it is a legitimate way to read this milestone in the history of Western thought and that even those who disagree with this interpretation— no one should merely agree with it—will find their own interpretation facilitated, if only negatively, by this reading.[2] In a conversation with the present author some years ago, Martin Heidegger, then at the age of 62, said, "I began to read Aristotle when I was 16; I have now reached the point where I can *begin* to understand Aristotle." I myself began reading "the Aristotle of modern times" only 25 years ago; I think I am *beginning* to understand him.

What is here presented is, secondly, a *reading* of Hegel's *Phenomenology.* It is not, therefore, an erudite *commentary* in the manner of Hyppolite,[3] nor a genial *discussion* of the issues raised by Hegel, the sort of thing which

[1] "Pushed to the extreme we come up against the paradox of the impossibility of a first reading of a work of systematic philosophy" (Conrad Boey, s.j., *L'Aliénation dans la Phénoménologie de l'Esprit* [Paris: Desclée De Brouwer, 1970], p. 34).

[2] I can only hope that, having had the inadequacies (or inaccuracies) of the present reading pointed out, I shall be able to remedy them in the future.

[3] Jean Hyppolite, *Genèse et structure de la Phénoménologie de l'Esprit de Hegel* (Paris: Aubier, 1946). See also his translation of the *Phenomenology: La Phénoménologie de l'Esprit,* 2 vols. (Paris: Aubier, 1939, 1941).

has been carried off so felicitously by Loewenberg.[4] I acknowledge an enormous debt to both Hyppolite and Loewenberg, but I am not trying to do what they did. I am indebted, too, to numerous other studies on Hegel—some of which I have cited and some of which I have not—but my purpose is different from that of any of them.[5] My purpose has caused me to follow Hegel's text very closely—too closely, I am sure, for some tastes—letting Hegel dictate my own order of presentation, allowing only one major break with Hegel's own order, that of reading the Preface as epilogue rather than as prologue. Even the examples and metaphors are for the most part Hegel's own, used not only with a view to illumining his text and not another, but also in order to avoid saying what Hegel himself is not saying.

In this connection it might be well to point out that I have rarely found it necessary to take issue explicitly with other interpretations.[6] Apart from the fact that disputing interpretations is not the purpose of this book, those who are familiar with other interpretations will recognize the differences without having them pointed out; those who are not will be spared remarks which are but a profession of critical acumen and do not facilitate the reading of Hegel's own text. The text is always there as a check on interpretation. It might also be argued that this presentation is not adequately critical of Hegel—as though, so to speak, he were above criticism. In answer to this I can say only that criticism is as valid as the interpretation on which it is based and that my own experience of Hegel criticism is that it is, more often than not, based on an interpretation which a more careful reading of the text—and context—can render suspect. If Hegel is saying what I say he is, let the critical acumen of the reader go into action; if he is not, my own criticisms would be valueless.

It might seem at this point otiose to add that, thirdly, this is a reading of

---

[4] J. Loewenberg, *Hegel's Phenomenology: Dialogues on the Life of the Mind* (La Salle, Ill.: Open Court, 1965).

[5] Of those that have been cited—reference will be given when we meet them—the following can be said. Loewenberg unquestionably contributes greatly to an understanding of what is going on in the *Phenomenology*, particularly in its first three chapters—as does Charles Taylor in his brilliant article, "The Opening Arguments of the *Phenomenology*," in Alasdair MacIntyre's collection of critical essays, *Hegel* (New York: Doubleday, 1972)—and thus facilitates a first reading. He is somewhat less helpful, however, in enabling us either to unravel the complexities of the actual text or to come to terms with Hegel's manner of presentation. Hyppolite stands, so to speak, at the other end of the spectrum. His is perhaps the most erudite *complete* commentary on the *Phenomenology* yet written. But it is so thoroughly involved in the complexities of the text and in identifying the positions to which Hegel alludes that it becomes at times more complex than Hegel's own text. At these times we must turn to Hegel in order to understand Hyppolite. Others, like Findlay, Kaufmann, N. Hartmann, Seeberger, etc., comment on the *Phenomenology* in the course of presenting Hegel's system as a whole. They give us many valuable hints toward a reading of the *Phenomenology* but need to be complemented by a more detailed reading of the whole. Still others, like Kojève, Wahl, Labarrière, Boey, Gauvin, Pöggeler, Metzke, and the authors of the articles in MacIntyre's *Hegel*, are of great service in helping us to understand this or that aspect of Hegel's project but do not eliminate the need for a more complete reading.

[6] Similarly, with a view to avoiding confusion over the issues with which Hegel is concerned, little effort has been made to compare his endeavor with those of our contemporaries. It is a task I leave to others.

Hegel's Phenomenology, but it does seem important to stress that the reading is concerned not merely with a *book* but with Hegel's *phenomenological enterprise*, which is not that of any other "phenomenologist," be he Husserl, Heidegger, Merleau-Ponty, or Sartre. This is not to say that there are not similarities—and certainly complementarities—in all these "phenomenologies," [7] but it is to say that the key concept of the Hegelian phenomenology is unlike the key concept of any of the others mentioned and that, thus, Hegel's phenomenology has dimensions which the others simply do not have, and, perhaps, vice versa. In the Husserlian phenomenology, for example, the key concept is the "intentionality" of consciousness—all consciousness is consciousness-of, and a rigorous examination of consciousness will deliver the very essence not only of consciousness but also of that *of which* it is consciousness. In Hegel's phenomenology, on the other hand, the key concept is that the appearing of being, an appearing which is essential to the very being of being, is necessarily appearing-to. Thus, appearing-to and being-conscious-of (consciousness, *Bewusstsein*) are but two sides of the same coin— or, better, two aspects of one and the same movement. Appearing is no more a *state of being* proper to an object than being conscious is a *mental state* proper to a subject. More than that, the activity of experiencing, which for Hegel is essentially a spiritual activity and includes analysis, synthesis, inference—what Dewey calls the "stretching of experience"—is not to be separated from reality's activity of self-revelation. Consciousness simply is not the activity of mind on a matter foreign to it. By the same token, inseparable from consciousness is all that being-conscious-of implies with regard to the identity of consciousness and self-consciousness: the integrality of being conscious of one's own self and of other selves, the inseparability of an adequate consciousness of self and a consciousness of God, the inevitability of a concretely universalized subjectivity, which is spirit, if the universality of objectivity is to make any rational sense whatever. For Hegel, then, phenomeno-logy is a logic of appearing, a logic of implication, like any other logic, even though not of the formal entailment with which logicians and mathematicians are familiar. It would be saying too much, of course, to claim that the implications of phenomenological logic impose themselves with the same rigorous necessity as the entailments of formal logic, but it makes eminent good sense to withhold any judgment about their manifesting no necessity at all until Hegel's phenomenological investigation has unfolded before us.[8] There can be no question that the dialectical movement is easier to follow, even to accept, in its earlier stages. At this point, perhaps, one can but take it on faith that the effort to follow it, even without accepting it, in its later stages will prove rewarding.

It will be impossible, however, to follow the movement of Hegel's phenomenological dialectic in either its earlier or its later stages if the book is

---

[7] See Quentin Lauer, s.j., "Phenomenology: Hegel and Husserl," *Beyond Epistemology: New Studies in the Philosophy of Hegel*, ed. Frederick G. Weiss (The Hague: Nijhoff, 1974), pp. 174–96.

[8] "In all these dialectical transitions there is no entailment in the formal logical sense, and yet no stringing together of random observations" (J. N. Findlay, "The Contemporary Relevance of Hegel," in MacIntyre, *Hegel*, p. 11).

not read from beginning to end as a phenomenology of *Spirit*. It is true, of course, that the work was initially entitled "Science of the Experiencing of Consciousness," [9] and it seems to have been Hegel's original intention to present just such a "science." That this should have become a "Phenomenology of Spirit," however, was inevitable, not merely in the sense that the initial investigation turns out to be that—by the very "logic" of conscious activity—but also in the sense that Hegel is convinced from the beginning that the odyssey he describes is a "spiritual" one; that consciousness, if permitted to reveal itself, will reveal itself at every level as a "spiritual," as opposed to "natural," activity. When is knowledge (the culmination of experience) truly knowledge? When it is thoroughly spiritual; when consciousness is all *activity* and in no sense a *being-acted-upon*. In no sense, of course, does this mean that the "spiritual" is opposed to the "natural" as the supernatural to the natural; rather it is the opposition of autonomous *action* to elicited *reaction*.

Hegel's *Phenomenology of Spirit*, then, can be legitimately looked upon as his thoroughgoingly anti-naturalist epistemology, provided we do not interpret that last term in a narrowly cognitive sense. This does not mean that Hegel determines in some antecedent way—as do Hume and Kant— what are to count as the essential characteristics of knowing and then accepts as knowing only what manifests these characteristics. His procedure, rather, is strictly "phenomenological," in the precise sense that even on the assumption that knowing initially appears as, seemingly, a function of "nature," [10] it can never find satisfaction in itself so long as it is merely that—in fact, so long as it is that at all. It should be noted here, by way of warning, that nothing could be further from the truth than to see in the Hegelian contrast of "nature" and "spirit" the expression of some sort of "mind–body" dualism. Such a dualism was simply no concern of Hegel's— except to the extent that he repudiated the Cartesian version of it. The distinction of "spiritual" from "natural" functions does not bespeak separate *sources* of these functions; fundamentally it is a distinction between the essential repetitiveness and predictability of the natural and the essential

[9] The German *Erfahrung*, like the English "experience," can have both the rather static, objective connotation of a category covering whatever can be called *an* experience (or experience in general) or the more dynamic, subjective connotation of the *process* of experiencing. It is abundantly clear that Hegel employs the term primarily in this second way. This still leaves unclear, grammatically at least, whether in the "science of the experiencing of consciousness" the "of consciousness" is to be taken as an objective or a subjective genitive—experiencing consciousness, or consciousness experiencing. It is safe to say that both connotations are present, since for Hegel consciousness in experiencing has as its ultimate object itself experiencing.

[10] It must be confessed that Hegel's use of the term "nature" can be highly ambiguous. For the most part it signifies what is *not* spirit, i.e., not self-active, the sum total of which constitutes the domain in which "natural science" is operative. Thus he will deny that there can possibly be a "natural science" of consciousness. Sometimes, however, the term is used to designate a specific nature, i.e., "human nature," and then it is opposed to spirit only *dialectically*, i.e., spirit is what nature is to *become*. At other times, "nature" is used as practically the equivalent of "essence," e.g., that it is man's "essential nature" to be "spirit"—not *merely* "nature."

creativity and novelty of the spiritual. Both are "rational," but not in the same way.

It should be made clear that none of this constitutes a shift in focus on the part of Hegel. Consciousness in the process of a development which is "essential" to it, in the sense that if it does not develop it ceases to be consciousness,[11] becomes aware that it must progressively divest itself of all modes of operation proper to nature—the latter's essential repetitiveness and, hence, predictability—and thus become what it truly is.[12] This "divesting itself" is seen to be necessary because at any stage along the way consciousness is inadequate to its own object, an object which progressively reveals that it is *more* than the respective "mode" of consciousness takes it to be, and it reveals this to consciousness itself, which, then, forces itself to move on.[13]

As Hegel himself does in his Introduction, one could, of course, predict that such a process cannot stop until there are no more dimensions of the object to be revealed—until it is "absolute," and until there are no more inadequacies in the awareness of the object—when consciousness itself is "absolute." It should come as no surprise, then—even though the reader may not *want* to go along with him—that, having begun at all, Hegel will not stop until the object of consciousness has no more hidden crannies of itself to reveal, until as object it is "absolute," and until consciousness of this object has no more inadequacies, no more dependence on what is outside itself, until consciousness too is "absolute." For Hegel, however, there is only *one* "absolute," i.e., Spirit. The result, then, is inevitable: spirit's total consciousness of its total self; but Hegel is also convinced that he has not by some spiritual sleight of hand set up this result from the beginning. He simply invites us to follow the process as it unfolds and to judge for ourselves if the whole process does not reveal its own inevitability.[14] If it does, then at the end of the *Phenomenology* we shall know what knowing in the full sense is, and the unfolding of what is known in the full sense, the "system" of philosophy, can begin.

It would be vain for anyone—least of all the present author—to pretend that any or all of this is easy to follow, still less, easy to accept. The purpose of the present volume is to contribute in some measure to the fol-

[11] Ruth Marcus has given a good definition of what is "essential" in this sense. "Essences," she tells us, are "dispositional properties of a very special kind; if an object had such a property and ceased to have it, it would have ceased to exist or it would have changed into something else" ("Essential Attribution," *The Journal of Philosophy*, 68, No. 7 [April 8, 1971], 202).

[12] What consciousness "truly" is is what it is *an sich*. In the *process* of becoming conscious of this, it is what it is *für sich*. When it is fully conscious of all that it "truly" is, it is what it is *an- und für sich*.

[13] Ultimately this will mean that human experience will have to be more than "empirical" if it is to remain true to itself. Remaining inextricably rooted in experience, phenomenology reveals that the merely "empirical" is but truncated experience.

[14] To put this "transcendentally," so to speak, Hegel will submit the observable fact of consciousness (whatever its *explanation* may be) to an *examination* (self-examination), which ultimately—and progressively—reveals what kind of activity it must be if it is to make sense.

lowing, not in any measure to persuade to acceptance. Even though to "follow" means to "make sense out of," it need not entail making that sense one's own. What constitutes the greatest obstacle to following Hegel, of course, is the method, a method which Hegel claims is dictated by the subject matter itself, since the movement of the method is identical with the movement of the subject matter. With what sort of "necessity" does each step along the way entail the step which follows it? Even granting that all the steps described make good sense, what compels us to acknowledge that Hegel's order of entailment makes equally good sense? What criterion (criteria) is (are) there for determining that the list of steps is in the final count complete? That no step has been left out? Such questions will occupy us in the course of this study, when and where they become issues.[15] There is, however, another hurdle to be leaped before we can even confront the obstacle of the method, even though, it might be said, the method itself creates this preliminary hurdle. It is the problem of Hegel's language, his frequently undecipherable style, his indefensible liberties with grammar, his almost uncontrollable terminology.

HEGEL'S LANGUAGE

In a draft for a letter to his friend Voss, composed in 1805, Hegel speaks of his own philosophical task as that of "teaching philosophy to speak German." [16] There are, it is true, not a few Germans (and others) who dispute that Hegel was successful in his efforts; but there seems little room for dispute that one must make Hegel speak English in order to present his thought to an English-speaking public, not only because to many an adequate command of German, to say nothing of Hegel's German, is not available, but, more importantly, because a philosophy which is expressible only in one language necessarily lacks the universalism which makes it worthy of the august title "philosophy." What is more, to those of us who are convinced, as I am, that English itself is a supremely philosophical language, particularly for the expression of *dynamic* concepts, Hegel *must* be made to speak English, however tortuous that English, as was Hegel's German, may turn out to be. I venture even to say that a test of his philosophy's via-

15 "The difficulty of this work is not the approach required in order to get into it, not getting used to the style and the concepts which are admittedly often employed in an unusual sense; nor is it appropriating the contents. Rather, it is sticking with the method here spread out before us, sticking with this thought process right up to the last page. To this sort of following there is no introduction" (G. W. F. Hegel, "Einleitung des Herausgebers," *Phänomenologie des Geistes*, ed. Johannes Hoffmeister, 6th ed. [Hamburg: Meiner, 1952], p. vi). Truly, the problem of method cannot be treated in an Introduction.

16 "Luther made the Bible and you have made Homer speak German. This is the greatest gift which can be given to a people; for a people remains barbaric and fails to see the excellence it knows as its own true property as long as it does not come to know it in its own language. If you wish to forget these two examples, I still want to say of my own efforts that I will try to teach philosophy to speak German. If it ultimately comes to do that, then it will be infinitely more difficult to give triviality the appearance of profound speech" (*Briefe von und an Hegel*, ed. Johannes Hoffmeister, 4 vols. [Hamburg: Meiner, 1952], I 99–100).

bility is precisely its capacity to speak English. This should not be interpreted to mean, however, that I would have Hegel speak an English which
is formalized in such a way that it is not geared to handle the issues with
which he was involved and, thus, dismisses them as not significant issues.
It would be as vain to make Hegel speak a language acceptable to many of
our contemporaries as it would have been to make Nietzsche speak a German acceptable to philosophers in the Germany of his day.

The English which Hegel must speak, then, is not a literal translation
of his German (would that translations were even literal!), nor one which
can be "formalized" and thus made hopelessly abstract, nor yet one which
cleans up his style, grammar, and terminology in such a way as to deform
his thought. With all this, however, if Hegel is to be made to speak English,
it must be an English which is still recognizable as English, which does not
violate the genius of the language—any more than Hegel's German violated
the genius of that language.[17]

In attempting, then, to remain faithful both to Hegel's thought and
to the English language, one is faced with three problems—whether as
translator or as commentator—and one can honestly expect only a measure
of success in solving all three. The first is the problem of Hegel's style: to
unravel its intricacies in one's own reading in such a way as not to fail to
recognize that its very involutedness is for the most part integral to the
dialectical movement of the thought, even though there are times when one
legitimately has to wonder whether things have to be so complicated. Frequently the style is ponderous, but frequently, too, one overcomes that
ponderosity only at the risk of obscuring rather than clarifying the thought.
So much by way of excuse for the many ponderous (alas, even tedious) pages
which follow. Hegel is unquestionably repetitious, but it would be risky to
suppose that such repetitiousness is without reason. One can try to modify
the repetition, but not at the expense of the emphasis that repetition affords. More often than not Hegel's is like the repetitiousness of a piano
sonata: the trained ear can catch the variations, where they are present,
or it can recognize that a theme repeated after the introduction of a counter
theme is not simply the same; the original theme, even if repeated verbatim,
gains a depth, a richness, an intensity, even a meaning it did not have before; it is more response than restatement. In either case repetition is integral to the overall movement of the whole piece. With regard to Hegel's
repetitiveness a new danger sets in. Impatience is almost inevitable; one has

17 "Because Hegel sought to overcome—without in any way being a purist—the
alienated academic language of philosophy, because he injected into the foreign terms
and artificial expressions of that language the concepts of ordinary thinking, he succeeded
in introducing the speculative spirit of his native language into the speculative movement
of philosophizing, thus recapturing what had been the natural accompaniment (*Mitgift*)
of the incipient philosophizing of the Greeks. The ideal of his method, promoting a
process in which concepts move forward toward ever greater differentiation and concretization, at the same time continued to be oriented toward a clinging to and being
guided by the logical instinct of the language. In Hegel's view also, the presentation of
philosophy can never free itself completely from the propositional form and the appearance of a predicative structure given with that form" (Hans Georg Gadamer, *Hegels
Dialektik* [Tübingen: Mohr, 1971], p. 28–29).

a temptation to pass on too quickly—and no one, perhaps, can completely succeed in avoiding that. But if one hurries over a single sentence on a single page of Hegel's text, one cannot be sure of having comprehended what Hegel is saying. Almost as frequently as Hegel's style is ponderous it is also highly poetic, abounding in metaphors which do not seem to be contributing directly to the flow of the thought. One can be tempted to "demythologize" the poetical language, even going so far as to substitute handy abstract schemata of *a*'s, *b*'s, and *c*'s (plus a few *x*'s, *y*'s, and *z*'s), and the result is—not Hegel! Finally, the style suffers from the customary untranslatableness of so much philosophical German—three times compounded. One may have to read one sentence five times simply in order to understand what it is saying and still be unable to translate it into anything but barbaric English. This can explain not only the sometimes insufferably involved translations but also the large number of quotes contained in the text which follows. Hegel must frequently be allowed to speak for himself if we are to be sure that it is Hegel speaking.[18]

Perhaps the most constant obstacle to an understanding of Hegel, even for a German audience, is the Hegelian use (or misuse) of grammar. Perhaps the simplest way to treat the problem of Hegel's grammar is to say that what he had to say was beyond the capacity of ordinary grammar to handle.[19] We might put it this way: if a condition for philosophy's speaking German be that it speak an ungrammatical German (or a condition of Hegel's speaking English that it be an ungrammatical English), then so be it. Is it for grammar to tell philosophical thought how it must restrict itself, or for philosophical thought to tell grammar that it needs stretching? The problem, however, does not lie precisely there. It is not difficult to understand that the ordinary predicative proposition, expressed in terms of the copula "is," cannot express "speculative" truth. It is not even difficult to understand that when Hegel says "the particular *is* the universal," "the finite *is* the infinite," "the contingent *is* the necessary," he is not *attributing* any one of these predicates to any one of these subjects but rather seeking to express a *movement* of self-manifestation in which no subject is all that it is except by passing over to its seeming opposite, the predicate. We can, if reminded often enough, read any proposition this way. But to read page after page

---

18 Because no one is ever satisfied with someone else's translation of Hegel, all the translations are my own. The first of the page numbers inserted in parentheses into the text, then, refers to the Hoffmeister edition of Hegel's *Phänomenologie des Geistes*. But since some readers may also want to consult a complete English translation of the text, I have added, in the same parentheses, references to the corresponding page in Baillie's translation (*The Phenomenology of Mind*, trans. J. B. Baillie [New York: Humanities Press, 1949]). Although, at times, the passages may be scarcely recognizable as the same, I trust that these double references will be helpful, without making the format too unaesthetic. Only rarely will it be necessary to take issue with another translation—primarily to illustrate how what *could* be a legitimate translation of the words can miss the philosophical sense of what is being said.

19 "Hegel's language violates ordinary grammar only because it has to speak of the unheard-of, with which traditional grammar cannot come to terms" (Ernst Bloch, *Subjekt–Objekt: Erläuterungen zu Hegel* [Berlin: Aufbau-Verlag, 1952], p. 15).

constantly keeping in mind that the propositional form is not saying what we expect it to say is not easy.

By the same token, it is not too difficult to understand Hegel's claim that the conceptual movement of coming to grips with reality is the same as the movement of reality in revealing itself if we can remember the "key" notion that the objective movement of self-revelation *is* the subjective movement of being-conscious-of, but the burden of sustaining this kind of awareness is not light. Only if we do sustain it, however, can we make sense out of Hegel's contention that his "idealism" is in no sense "unrealistic," even though it must constantly transform the *real* into the *ideal*.[20] Nothing could be more erroneous than to conceive of Hegel's philosophy as an "idealism" for which there is no "reality" outside consciousness,[21] unless it be, perhaps, the error of thinking that for Hegel reality somehow "impresses" itself— presumably in the mode of causal efficacy [22]—on consciousness. For those whose epistemology sees things "out there" impressing themselves on sense-consciousness and thought subsequently conceptualizing these same "things," it can make little sense to say that reality is conceptual—still less sense to say that "reality is concept." If, however, one sees reality as a primordial unity ("substance") which is only implicitly (*an sich*) articulated and differentiated, whose articulation in conception is at the same time its self-articulation (*für sich*), ultimately resulting in a subsequent unity of "idea," wherein the being (*Sein*) of reality and the consciousness (*Bewusst-sein*) of reality are identified (*an- und für sich*), one can at least follow the movement Hegel describes. If conceptual thought is to grasp reality as it is, it can do so not because reality "impresses" itself on thought in some indescribable manner, but only because conceptual thinking re-produces, re-creates, reality. Conceptual thought, however, can do this only if reality itself is *basically* concept, i.e., if concept is the *ground* of reality. Just as concept, then—thought as process—is the ground of re-created reality, so concept is the ground of created reality; and the discovery of one ground is the dis-

20 Cf. John Dewey: "Knowledge is not a distortion or perversion which confers upon *its* subject-matter traits which *do* not belong to it, but is an act which confers on non-cognitive material traits which *did* not belong to it" (quoted in *The Philosophy of John Dewey*, ed. John J. McDermott, 2 vols. [New York: Putnam, 1973], I 318).

21 One reason for this error is the persistent tendency to translate the Hegelian *Wirklichkeit* by "reality," when it should be translated as "actuality." There is a great difference between saying that the "real" is not fully "actual" until it has been actualized in consciousness and saying that outside consciousness it is not "real." Cf. G. W. F. Hegel, *Enzyklopädie der philosophischen Wissenschaften*, edd. Friedhelm Nicolin and Otto Pöggeler, 6th ed. (Leipzig: Meiner, 1959), No. 6, where Hegel explains that in its "being" (*Sein*) reality has *Dasein* or *Existenz* but not *Wirklichkeit*. Only in "consciousness" (*Bewusst-sein*) does it have "actuality."

22 To grasp objects as the locus of causal properties which explain why the consciousness of these objects is what it is, for Hegel, not "false" in the sense that it is utterly to be repudiated. It is false only in the sense that it is an inadequate view, the view which is treated in his third chapter, "Force and Understanding," and which must give way to a more adequate view. In the more adequate view, that of reason, the "forces" which understanding infers as being located in objects are seen to be part and parcel of the structure of objectivity only because they are part and parcel of the dialectical structure of conceiving objects.

covery of the other. It is for this reason that the *Logic* is "the presentation of God as he is in his eternal essence, before the creation of the world or of a single finite spirit." [23] Concept is at one and the same time the process of thought comprehending reality and the process of reality revealing itself to thought. Re-creation, then, is the concretization of reality in the inner movement of thought.

For Hegel, reality *is* the content of thought—without it, thought would not be truly thought; but it is a content which thought re-creates for itself in such a way that it gradually becomes aware that in being conscious of reality it is conscious of its own re-creation of reality, a condition for which is that the structure of thought and the structure of reality be the same: concept. It is in the *Phenomenology of Spirit* that consciousness discovers this identity of (dynamic) structure; it is in the *Science of Logic* that consciousness capitalizes on this by articulating the structure of thought-reality.[24] It is, finally, in the philosophies of nature and of spirit, that the logical structure which culminates in the absolute Idea is seen to embrace the totality of reality in its concreteness. Small wonder, then, that ordinary grammar lags far behind in its efforts to express such a conceptual framework.

Although the commentator (or translator) will not succeed in making Hegel speak English until he has come to terms with this conceptual framework and has found an English adequate to express it, having done so his troubles are not yet over. It would be convenient if one could elaborate a terminology in which there would be a consistent, one-to-one correspondence between the terms Hegel employs and the English terms used to translate them. But apart from the fact that such slavish consistency would make a travesty of any translation—words in any language are susceptible of many shades of meaning determinable only in the context in which they are used—it would be particularly catastrophic to attempt this in interpreting Hegel. Sometimes, it is true, Hegel is extremely careful in his choice of terms, and one has to exercise equal care in selecting as exact an equivalent as possible, always remembering, of course, that every language contains terms for which there is no exact equivalent in another language. Sometimes, on the other hand, Hegel is—or seems to be—extremely careless in his employment of terms, and one must have a wide variety of English terms to choose from in attempting to get at just what he is saying, always running the risk that the choice will be, or will seem to be, arbitrary.[25] Nor is it easy to determine what device to employ in handling this difficulty. For

23 G. W. F. Hegel, *Wissenschaft der Logik*, ed. Georg Lasson, 2 vols. (Leipzig: Meiner, 1963), I 31.

24 Another way of putting this would be to say that the *Phenomenology* describes the movement of consciousness *toward* reason (completely self-conscious spirit), whereas the "system" (of which the *Logic* is the first stage) describes the movement *of* reason—in plumbing its own depths.

25 A display model of such a term is the German *Vorstellung*. To it sometimes Hegel attaches a very precise meaning, which is at best indifferently rendered by the English "representation." At other times the meaning of the term is so utterly vague that one almost has to toss a coin in determining what English term to use for it. This term, in particular, will come up for further discussion, when the occasion arises.

the most part, where my own choice of an English equivalent is more obviously subject to dispute, I have included Hegel's own term in parentheses. Unquestionably there will be instances where I should have done this and have not. For this I can only apologize; the format is cumbersome enough as it is. Nor need this Introduction be made more tedious than it is by giving examples here; there will be examples enough along the way.

In my commenting on the difficulties of making Hegel "speak English"—not to be separated from the difficulties the reader will have even when Hegel does speak English—one significant difficulty for the reader has up to this point been brushed aside: the difficulty of understanding why a "reading" of Hegel's *Phenomenology* should have turned out to be so long—at a time when books are supposed to be short if they are to be read. To that, of course, one might answer by paraphrasing Kant and saying that many a book would be not nearly so long if it were not so short, which would then raise a question as to how this one can do justice to Hegel without being longer than it is. To the first question I can only reply that a full-scale reading of Hegel's text could not have been shorter; to the second, that this reading is not intended to dispense the interested student from becoming acquainted with a rapidly growing body of literature on the *Phenomenology of Spirit* alone, where it is hoped he will find answers to some of the questions this "reading" raises.[26]

SUMMARY OF THE WHOLE

At the risk, now, of making even this Introduction too long, I should like to present here a synoptic view of the whole which may serve to preserve the overall unity amid the seeming meanderings of what is to follow.

1. *Hegel's Introduction.* In his own Introduction to the text, Hegel makes abundantly clear that what he hopes to do is to enable the human mind to come to a realization of what it does when it knows. This means both a resolute refusal to decide ahead of time what knowledge must be—based on the model of some acknowledged "science"—thus forcing all knowing, including philosophical, into this Procrustean bed, and the antecedent rejection of any suggestion that knowledge is at its richest when the knower "does" nothing, is only acted upon. To accomplish his task, then, Hegel

---

26 Another difficulty which plagues the reader of Hegel, but which could be handled in a "reading" of this kind only at the risk of encumbering the text unduly, is Hegel's tendency to allude to positions, philosophers, historic illustrations, or contemporary problems, without naming names. Ideally one should like to be able to identify all such allusions; practically this could obscure rather than illumine the reading. "Of course, the reader is meant to grasp the structure of the whole, and the serious reader, who alone is of any interest to the author, is certain to recognize familiar faces at every turn, usually in unfamiliar surroundings; but not every detail is put in mainly for the reader's sake, for his instruction and the promotion of knowledge. A great deal is there because it happened just then to be of interest to the writer, and he was wondering where it belonged, how best to place it—how to fashion a cosmos of the totality of his cultural experience without suppressing anything that seemed to matter" (Walter Kaufmann, *Hegel* [New York: Doubleday, 1965], p. 137).

will simply allow the indisputable phenomenon of consciousness to follow out its own implications until there are no more implications to follow out. This will make sense, of course, only if consciousness is in some sense of the term "necessitated" to move beyond any of the stages along the way of its development, until there is no longer any "beyond," until the correspondence between the mind's conceiving and its object's being is total. As stated in the Introduction, however, the goal of the *Phenomenology* is not to determine *what* the mind knows, only what *knowing* is in the fullest sense of the term; the "phenomenon" being examined is the phenomenon of knowing. Before going through the process, which is the whole of the *Phenomenology*, there is no telling either *whether* the goal can be attained (although a *fear* that it cannot be attained is an obstacle to attaining it) or what it will involve *if* it is attained. Of one thing, however, Hegel is certain from the beginning: there can be no criterion outside knowing— outside the process of coming to know—for the validity of the knowing. If we are to follow him, we must be content to let the process validate itself.

II. *Sense Certainty*. It is with an absolutely minimal form of consciousness that the process begins, a form which *appears* to be foolproof because consciousness is not permitted to introduce any distortion into the presentation of its object. Sensation, then, is most certain of its object because it apprehends that object with utmost immediacy. In fact, however, it soon finds out that its certainty is utterly empty since it cannot say of what it is certain, and that its immediacy is utterly illusory since unless the subject sensing confer meaning there is no meaning to what it does say. This sort of consciousness may or may not be a "natural" function; the point is that not only can it not be satisfied with its own apprehension of its object, it must *negate* whatever satisfaction it *appeared* to have and move on to a more adequate stage. At the very first stage of the process, then, the mainspring of dialectical movement is revealed. It will not always be as clearly revealed as it is here, but it will always be the same. It consists in (*a*) the unsatisfactoriness of the respective mode of consciousness (for its own content), and (*b*) its being pointed in the direction it must take if that unsatisfactoriness is to be overcome; the very negation of inadequacy will be an affirmation of what is more adequate.

III. *Perception*. The negation of immediacy on the first level of consciousness is already the introduction of reflection. If consciousness does not reflect on itself, on what it itself contributes to the apprehension of its object, it is condemned to remain caught up in the illusion of a worthless certainty. What is more, the movement from direct apprehension to reflection, which Hume had interpreted to be a move *away from* reality, is seen to be a move *toward* reality. Perception reveals that a mere apprehending of *things* is an impossibility; consciousness *of* things is an interacting *with* things, or it is nothing. Regarding itself, however, perception reveals something more: that it cannot hold on to the particulars which confront it without the mediation of universal concepts; objects are objects only to the extent that they have distinguishing "properties," and these are universal. Thus the negating–affirming movement of the dialectic continues.

IV. *Force and Understanding.* Charles Taylor has pointed out very perceptively [27] that Hegel's argument here is quite "transcendental." The awareness of the inadequacy of a mode of experience is at the same time an awareness of what is required if the experience is to be more adequate. That we do have experiences is undeniable. In this chapter it is revealed that we could not have the experiences we do have, i.e., of objects with universal properties, did not the experience include something in the objects which causes them to be experienced the way they are. To experience objects in this way is the work of "understanding," that mode of consciousness which at once *grasps* the universality perception is incapable of handling and *infers* the explanation of this on the model of Newtonian "forces" attributed to the things perceived. That these forces are *attributed* to things, however, reveals the inadequacy of understanding as a mode of consciousness pretending to the lofty title of knowledge. The forces which understanding imputes are its own products, and consciousness can come to terms with this only if it becomes consciousness of itself, which it cannot do if all it is is understanding.

V. *Self-Consciousness.* At this point in the dialectical movement a rather subtle switch takes place. Kant had pointed out that all awareness contains an element of self-awareness, an awareness that it is the same self which is the subject of its whole series of experiences. Fichte and Schelling had capitalized on this insight by making self-awareness the very heart of all awareness. Phenomenologically speaking, however, Hegel is not satisfied with this insight; it does not explain either how consciousness, having experienced the unsatisfactoriness of mere understanding, is forced to turn back on itself to examine its own activity in producing objects of which it is aware, or how the turning back is effected. Neither a concomitant awareness of an identical self in a series of experiences, à la Kant, nor a blatant affirmation that awareness and self-awareness have to be the same if awareness is to make sense, à la Fichte and Schelling, is satisfactory. What turns consciousness in on itself? This is where the shift occurs; consciousness will not turn in on itself if all it is is cognitive; therefore, only if consciousness is also appetitive will it turn back to itself effectively. Ostensibly, appetite is directed toward the cognized object of consciousness; but when it is *human* consciousness, what it recognizes is that the object of appetition is somehow itself. It is through appetition that the human self *begins* to recognize itself as a self, as the source of its own conscious activity, with all that implies. The dialectical movement begins to change in another sense: it becomes a series of attempts to reject the full implications of self-recognition, i.e., the thor-

27 See his "Opening Arguments," in MacIntyre, *Hegel*, p. 160. There is a brief summary of this argumentation in Taylor's *Hegel* (London: Cambridge University Press, 1975), pp. 140–47. The entire section on the *Phenomenology* (pp. 127–221) affords a good, compact overall view.

oughgoing responsibility of the self for its own activities. Autonomy is not only hard to come by; it is hard to accept. When the dialectic of consciousness becomes the dialectic of self-consciousness, the social and historical dimensions of the dialectic become inescapable, and the movement progressively bursts the bonds of the relatively simple formula of implication exhibited in the first three chapters. As a slave consciousness over against a master consciousness, consciousness will not affirm its autonomy at all; safeguarding life is too important. As stoic or skeptic consciousness it will affirm its autonomy, but only the empty autonomy of abstract thought or sheer negation. As the "unhappy consciousness" it will affirm that its slavery is not slavery at all; it is simply putting autonomy where it belongs, in God.

vi. *Reason*. Although the mainspring of the dialectical movement continues to consist in the negation of satisfaction in each successive mode of consciousness, which negation is equivalently the affirmation of the next stage in the development, with the debacle of the unhappy consciousness the inevitability both of the successive implications and of the order of these implications becomes progressively more difficult to follow. What the movement loses in cohesiveness, however, it gains in richness. With the advent of an awareness, inchoate as it may be, that only if the self of which consciousness is aware is an integral self, not looking elsewhere for a confirmation of the validity of its activities, consciousness begins to become self-conscious reason. In tune with the marvelous advances of scientific reasoning since the Renaissance and with the all-too-confident faith in reason of the Enlightenment, this insistence on the autonomy of reason has initially in view the reason of each individual—not forgetting, right from the start, that only if it is generalizable will it make ultimate sense. If reason is truly reason, it must (*a*) be totally responsible for its own activity, (*b*) recognize that what it knows to be the case must be so for any and all reason, and (*c*) be conscious that its own mode of knowing must characterize reason wherever it is to be found. The dialectic of reason, then, recounts a series of attempts to universalize the singularity of individual reason, each attempt in its own way a dead-end street, down each of which consciousness must go if it is ever to emerge conscious of its own thoroughgoing autonomy.

It would exceed the bounds of an Introduction to go through in any detail the steps scientific reason takes in attempting to find its own true self. Roughly, the overall movement is divided into three types of rational inquiry, each of which has its historical counterpart, even though the order of exposition could scarcely be called historically sequential. (1) The stage of empirical observation, where reason examines nature—nature in general, anorganic nature, and organic nature—hoping to find there the *model* of its own structure, but finding only structures of which its own mode of observation is the source. This prompts it to apply the same method of observation, relatively successful in the sciences of nature, to itself, from which emerges either a set of logical and psychological laws which are in fact not susceptible to empirical observation, or types of pseudo-science—physiognomy and phrenology—which serve to demonstrate by their own futility that the behavior of self-conscious reason cannot be discovered in what is empirically observable. (2) The stage of examining what is clearly the work of reason itself, i.e., the regulation of behavior, but which on the merely individual level can universalize itself only in self-contradictory ways: hedonism, which results in slavery to irrational necessity; utopian reformism, which ends in the singularity of self-enclosed conceit; ascetic virtue, which runs afoul of a course of events over which it has no control. (3) The stage of an incurable individualism which will willy-nilly lift itself by its own bootstraps into universality: by attributing to self-conscious reason the kind of universality which belongs only to an animal species; by enacting laws of behavior whose universality is dependent on their being without determinate content; or by finding in itself the universal norm for judging existing laws of behavior. The result of all this is a realization that general laws, whether of nature, consciousness itself, or moral behavior, can have neither their source nor their criterion in merely individual reason.

VII. *Spirit*. Even though the title alone, *Phenomenology of Spirit*, could make it clear that in Hegel's view the examination of consciousness could not be complete short of a thoroughgoing spiritualization of its activities, only a careful following of the movement thus far described could make it clear that the activity of self-conscious reason on the individual level could not be adequately spiritual. The movement of consciousness doubting its own adequacy and consequently negating its inadequacy goes on. Individual reason was not wrong in realizing that reason is most recognizable as reason in the regulation of moral behavior; it was wrong in imagining to itself that on the merely individual level it could come up with laws which can legitimately be regarded as universal norms of moral behavior. Only laws whose source is in some identifiable sense universal could do that. That the first example Hegel finds of a "universal" source of universal norms of moral behavior proves to be most unsatisfactory should cause no surprise; its function is to point the direction the dialectical movement must take. The example he finds is in the ethical [28] norms of a people—specifically

[28] The term *sittlich* (with its cognate *Sittlichkeit*) will occupy us more at length when we come to it in the text. Only two remarks seem to be called for here. (1) The German *Sitte*, whose root meaning is "custom"—as is that of the Greek ἔθος (ἦθος) and of the Latin *mos*, from which "ethics" and "morals" derive—does not indicate that "ethical" behavior is merely "customary" behavior. It simply indicates that its source is a sort of collective wisdom of a people, not consciously enacted law. *Sittlichkeit* is made up of "the laws and institutions of a social, cultural, and legal nature that inform the life of a people" (R. Schacht, "Hegel on Freedom," in MacIntyre, *Hegel*, p. 316). (2) Some confusion is introduced by the fact that in the *Phenomenology*, *Sittlichkeit* (ethical norms grounded in immemorial custom) is presented as preparatory to *Moralität* (ethical norms grounded in authentic moral reason), whereas in the *Philosophy of Right*, *Moralität* is presented as preparatory to *Sittlichkeit*. The meaning is simply not the same; there is an antecedent *Sittlichkeit* grounded in the not-thoroughly-rational customs of a people, and a consequent *Sittlichkeit* grounded in the integral, rational system of the state (however much one might want to dispute the "rationality" of Hegel's "state"). Nothing but confusion can result from remarks such as that of Walter Kaufmann ("The Young Hegel and Religion," in MacIntyre, *Hegel*, p. 91) that Hegel "repudiates" *Moralität* but accepts as a "higher type" *Sittlichkeit*.

the ancient Greeks, for an illustration of which Hegel turns not to historical fact but to the imaginative account found in Sophocles' *Antigone*. What
is exemplified here is the existence of norms governing the lives of a whole
people, norms whose origin cannot be traced. As universal both in its
source, the "spirit" of a people, and in its binding force on the whole people, *Sittlichkeit* is a sort of model of the "spiritual." The problem is that
in the Greek situation—and presumably in any similar situation—there
are *two* universal laws of behavior, the one "divine," regulating the actions
of the members of the family, the other "human," regulating the actions of
the citizens of the nation. The laws are not thoroughly integrated with each
other, because their source is not thoroughly integrated moral reason; [29]
and yet as laws they do not conflict with each other, since they are concerned with different duties. They can, however, produce conflict in human
consciousness, either in one consciousness faced with conflicting demands
or in two consciousnesses, each aware of a duty which conflicts with the
other's. From this situation there is no rational exit; all alike are ultimately
swallowed up in impersonal fate, where spirit is not recognizable at all.
The solution could seem to be found in the legal situation of the Roman
Empire, where there is only one source of law which both is equally binding on all and itself establishes the equality of all. The equality it establishes, however, is imposed on each and all from without. Each and all are
what they are, and who they are, by being recognized as such by the law.
In one sense this is the work of "universal reason," but it is a universal in
no way reconciled with individual reason and, therefore, not spirit.

   With the demise of the Roman Empire, the possibility of remedying this
impersonal situation would seem to open up with the progressive development of a "culture" (*Bildung*), which is at once "universal," in that it characterizes a people, an age, even a state of the world, and at the same time
individual in that each individual consciously "cultivates" himself. For the
first time, we might say, the human spirit stands off from itself—"alienates"
itself—and "works on itself" (*bildet sich*). In doing this, however, it must
come up with an activity which is purely its own, completely uninfluenced
by what is outside itself. Ideally, it would seem, we are getting close to
what Hegel has been looking for all along, the complete autonomy of the
rational spirit. If the price paid for autonomy, however, is emptiness, not
much has been gained. Hegel, then, sees "culture" of the kind he describes
culminating in the decadent reign of Louis XIV, where spirit (*esprit*) is
manifested more in the capacity to *speak* cleverly than to *think* profoundly.

   The ramifications of this complex section cannot be unraveled in an
Introduction, but the upshot of the whole thing is a relinquishing of empty
"culture" and a concentration on what consciousness can be confident is
peculiarly its own. Not strangely, however, what is peculiarly its own turns
out to be twofold, each contradicting the other and each equally vapid. On
the one hand, there results the "pure faith" of a pietism which is satisfied
with itself precisely because it has no grounds for what it holds. On the

---

29 There is a hint here, not to my knowledge picked up by commentators, that only
a reason which is at once "divine" and "human" will be thoroughly integrated.

other, there results the rationalism of "pure insight," which is rational only in the very negative sense that it is *not* anything else. By rejecting authority, tradition, faith, causal metaphysics, it has eliminated all influences from without but is left with only its empty self to look-into. For the tyranny of outside influence, it has substituted the tyranny of a ratiocination divorced from any roots in reality. This sort of thing Hegel finds best illustrated in the "Enlightenment" which, by burlesquing all faith and labeling it "superstition," deceives itself into thinking that it itself is "rational." The Enlightenment, however, does make a contribution to the onward march of spirit; it sets up the ideal—which it itself cannot realize—of the thoroughly autonomous human individual. The French Revolution, which takes up the Enlightenment ideal and seeks to construct a rational political society rooted in the ideal of the rationally autonomous individual, carries the movement a step further, but it turns the ideal into that of an "absolute" (unlimited) freedom which culminates in the "Terror," the folly of indiscriminate destruction.

One would expect Hegel to turn from the "Terror" to the reign of Napoleon, whom he had earlier characterized as "the World-Soul . . . riding a white horse," [30] but by the time he wrote the *Phenomenology* Hegel had become thoroughly disappointed with Napoleon. Instead, then, he turns to the world of non-politics, to the world of Kant and his "moral view of the world," where the true spirit, as morally responsible spirit, would seem to be most authentically conscious of what it is to be spirit. Here again, however, consciousness striving toward spirit runs into an obstacle. The Kantian "categorical imperative" with its concomitant "duty" would seem to manifest the reconciliation of individuality and universality Hegel has been looking for, but it does so only at the expense of getting nothing done. To be effective, duty must be specified, but as specified it ceases to be "pure duty." The dilemma, then, is either the universality of "pure duty," where nothing gets done, or the practicality of concrete action, where "duties" are multiplied *ad infinitum* without being able to be derived from "pure duty" at all. The result is a number of "subterfuges" designed to hold the particular and the universal together but without success. The last subterfuge of all is a "conscience," which is sufficient to itself and therefore autonomous, but which is incapable of demonstrating that it has any roots in reason. More than that, conscience tends to trail off into the quasi-religious "beautiful soul" which is beautiful only because it has a sort of inside track with God and safeguards its purity only by not dirtying its hands in an activity which is bound to have something unworthy about it.

VIII. *Religion.* Along the line in the *Phenomenology*, religious themes have cropped up—in the dialectic of the "unhappy consciousness," in the subterranean religious consciousness of the *Antigone*, in the empty faith of pietism and of the "superstition" against which the Enlightenment rages, and in the quietistic attitude of the "beautiful soul." There is at least a

30 *Briefe,* I 120.

hint in all this that for Hegel religion is ultimately going to find its rightful place in the overall movement. It does, in the slowly maturing realization that the human spirit will find itself only if concomitantly it finds the
divine Spirit. All along the tortuous path of the *Phenomenology* the mode
of consciousness which at any given stage is under scrutiny reveals itself to
itself as inadequate to its own object, and as consciousness moves to ever
greater degrees of adequacy, its object, too, moves forward, always, so to
speak, a step ahead of consciousness. At the end of the chapter on "Spirit,"
the moral spirit has gone as far as it can go, and still it must reach out to
an object which evades its grasp, an object which itself has no limitations.
Strictly speaking, along the path which consciousness has been traveling up
to this point, however meticulously it may have followed out the implications of each of its modes, it could not attain to a grasp of this limitless,
unconditioned, "absolute" object. Once more, as at the turn from consciousness to self-consciousness, a switch is required, and religious consciousness is just such a switch. Religious consciousness is not merely the inevitable phenomenological sequel to the consciousness of the moral spirit.
It has a series of manifestations all its own—its own "phenomenology"—
beginning with the most primitive awareness of a vague cosmic force and
terminating in a highly developed awareness of—even union with—the in-
tensely personal God of the Judaeo-Christian tradition. But in moving
through the various stages of awareness of a divine dimension in reality—
from *cosmic* force to *life* force to man-made representation, from representation in the motionless product of human art to the art work in which
human performance plays a part to the work of poetic (dramatic) art which
the human spirit infuses with divine meaning, and finally from the religion
in which God reveals himself through words spoken by others to that in
which he himself enters into human history to that in which as Spirit he
inhabits the human community—it is always human consciousness (self-
consciousness) in the process of recognizing that its consciousness of God and
its consciousness of itself are one and the same consciousness. The divine
and the human (God and man) are *not* identical, but the thoroughgoing
consciousness of one is the thoroughgoing consciousness of the other.

ix. *Absolute Knowing.* Because on the level of religious consciousness, no
matter how sophisticated, the identity of the divine-human consciousness is
not achieved—the forms in which God is "represented" stand in the way—
a final step in the odyssey of the human spirit is necessary. As Hegel sees
it,[31] the ultimate step in human self-consciousness is the infinitizing of that
consciousness such that not only does its content (object) know no limits,
neither does the consciousness itself. Only a consciousness which knows

---

[31] Much ink has been spilled over the question of whether in the move from "Religion"
to "Absolute Knowing" Hegel has effectively suppressed religion, allowing it to be
swallowed up in pure thought. Apart from the fact that the Hegelian *Aufhebung* is
never simply destructive of what is *aufgehoben*, we might say that in the *Aufhebung* of
religion what is "transcended" is a religious consciousness which is *only* religious—one is
reminded of Bonhoeffer's ideal of "religionless Christianity."

God as Spirit knows itself as spirit, which is but another way of saying that only the spirit which knows itself and God in one act of knowing truly knows. The *Phenomenology of Spirit* has revealed that short of knowing itself and God with the same knowledge as that with which God knows himself, consciousness does not truly *know* in the full sense of the term. Human self-knowing—and, therefore, knowing at all—is defined by divine self-knowing. Short of knowing God human knowing is still partially non-knowing; short of a knowing which is itself divine, human knowing does not know God.

The "phenomenological" journey has come to an end, but like every end it is only a beginning, and this in two senses. (1) The discovery of what *knowing* is is the beginning of the possibility of explicating *what* knowing *knows* (the "system"). (2) Absolute knowing is an end not in the sense that the phenomenological movement is finished, but in the sense that it is the culmination of that movement, gathering the whole movement up into itself, and somehow recapitulating that movement as it moves on to explicate its own knowing in the Hegelian system—which Hegel is convinced is not *his* but *philosophy*'s system.

x. *Preface.* It is truly difficult to decide whether the Preface to the *Phenomenology of Spirit* should be read as prologue or epilogue. Probably as both: once at the beginning, because in it the whole journey to be traveled is charted in panoramic fashion; once at the end, because the journey already traveled both illuminates the details of the panorama and is illuminated by the connection drawn in the Preface between the phenomenological and the entire systematic enterprise. It might, of course, be objected that the decision to treat of Hegel's Preface only at the end of the present volume is at once an arbitrary one and one which runs the risk of distorting the picture of what Hegel is trying to do in the *Phenomenology.* If by "arbitrary" is meant "having no reason" or "having no good reason," I think it possible to advance reasons that make the choice at least intelligible. If, on the other hand, "arbitrary" means "not having a good enough reason," the first objection shades over into the second; namely, that there are better reasons for retaining Hegel's own order, since only thus can we see the whole in the way Hegel wished us to see it when he published his *Phenomenology.* It is admittedly true that Hegel's purpose in attaching the Preface to the already completed work was not merely to show in retrospect where the phenomenological path had led but also to point out in prospect where it was to lead. It is also true that Hegel's method, particularly in the Introduction and in the early chapters, is more intelligible to a reader who is already familiar with the larger picture presented in the Preface. It may, in addition, very well be true that the Hegel of 1806, who had not yet established himself as Germany's outstanding philosopher, felt the need of initially presenting to his readers a global overview of where he was going. I nevertheless think that today's readers who, one can hope, are not being initiated into Hegel's thought by reading the extraordinarily difficult *Phenomenology*—with its extraordinarily difficult **Preface**—can profitably wait for the global overview, which will introduce them to the system as a whole, until the detailed exposition has set all the pieces in place in their proper order. The reader who still prefers to follow Hegel's own order can, of course, read the last chapter of this book first.

In any event, the Preface stands off from the rest and views retrospectively the totality of the process from incipient consciousness to "scientific" knowing. Nowhere is the integrality of the whole process expressed more forcefully than in the Preface; nowhere else is it made so clear that the only criterion for judging the adequacy of the process is the process itself. If, in fact, the process does issue in a knowledge of what knowing in the full sense is, then at the end we *do* know that the process has been adequate. Hegel, however, wants more than that: in an age in which doubts had been raised as to whether "philosophical" knowing is "knowing" at all, he comes up with the claim that *only* philosophical knowing is "scientific" in the full sense—because only philosophical knowing both knows the absolute and is itself absolute. This does not entail either the elimination or the degradation of other forms of knowing; it does mean that all knowing—whether the partial knowing of the stages along the way or the "exact" knowing of the positive sciences and mathematics, or the "factual" knowing of history— is knowing to the degree that it approaches the comprehensive grasp of objectivity in the "concept," in which being and thought coalesce in one movement. This, in turn, makes no sense unless the being which is known is itself primarily not "substance" but "subject," i.e., equally the source of the movement in which it is known as is the "knower." Most important of all, perhaps, knowing has revealed itself not to be a standing-off from reality, manipulating it, so to speak, with the aid of static abstractions, fragmenting it in order to make it more manageable, more predictable. The primordial unity of objectivity, "substance," it is true, is destined to remain unfathomable, to have only its surface scratched by "scientific" inquiry, if it does not articulate itself in being thought—and here abstraction is necessary—but unless it re-integrates itself in the *conceptual* movement, it will have been put apart never to come together again.

The philosophical task is not easy; one who expects it to be should not even begin it. It is, however, says Hegel, a rewarding one, and those who would reap its rewards must approach it by going through the phenomenological course here described.

———————

One final word. None of this will be even remotely intelligible unless it is seen against the background of the model of "practical" knowing, adumbrated by Kant in his *Critique of Practical Reason* and more metaphysically fleshed out in his *Critique of Judgment*, exploited by Fichte in both his *Theory of Science* and his *Theory of Morals*, romanticized by Schelling in his remarkable insight into the affinity of the theoretical and aesthetic view, and finally spelled out by Hegel in the *Phenomenology of Spirit*. Hence the centrality of both the moral and the religious spirit in the journey through integral human experience. Not since Plato, one might say, has anyone stressed the primacy of the "idea"—of ought-to-be-ness over is-ness—as did Hegel.[32] Not even Plato, one might add, emphasized as did Hegel the "conceptual" pathway from is-ness to ought-to-be-ness, from being to idea. No one, it should be further added, will make sense of the vast enterprise in which this passage takes place, who has not come to terms with the *Phenomenology of Spirit*.

[32] It is precisely for this reason that it is important to translate *wirklich* by "actual" and not by "real." What is *real* is not by that very fact *actual*; it is *actual* only when it measures up to its *idea*, its ought-to-be-ness, and only conceptual thought can determine that. See Walter Kaufmann, "The Hegel Myth and Its Method," in MacIntyre, *Hegel*, p. 37. It should be further noted, in this connection, that the *real*, for Hegel, does not correspond to its *idea* as to an abstract ideal, but rather as to the concrete goal of its striving, of its development.

1

Hegel's Introduction

ACCORDING TO Henry Harris, in his absorbingly interesting account of the early years of Hegel's development,[1] those years were dominated by Hegel's consciousness of a vocation to be a professional scholar and educator who would hold up to his own people the ideal of a religion of truly virtuous living and thus bring about a social metamorphosis. Initially, then, Hegel's ideal was a religious one; but gradually he came to the realization that the elaboration of this ideal demanded the articulation of political ideas, and by 1801, when he began his career as a university professor at Jena, Hegel had discovered that neither religious nor political ideas could stand against the test of experience without the rigorous underpinning of systematic philosophical thinking. By 1805, when he began working on his *Phenomenology*, which was destined to be his first major philosophical work, he had already to a great extent sketched out in his mind—and to some extent on paper—what the philosophical system was to be. It might, then, come as a surprise that in his Introduction to the *Phenomenology* he should ask the question which no previous philosopher had asked quite so explicitly: how can we start philosophizing at all? Later, in his *Science of Logic*, which was already projected before he began the *Phenomenology*, Hegel would begin its first book, "The Doctrine of Being," with the question "Womit muss der Anfang der Wissenschaft gemacht werden?" This latter question, however, is not nearly so devastating as the one with which he introduces the *Phenomenology*. Once the fact of rational knowing has been established, one can quite legitimately ask for the inevitable starting point in the elaboration of that knowing, and one can equally legitimately state that since the object of thinking is, at the very least, being, we can begin there, and then systematically work out all the implications of that first object of thought—or, to be more Hegelian, let the implications work themselves out. But this sort of beginning still leaves unanswered the question as to how one can begin philosophizing at all, which can surely seem a strange question, coming as it does from the pen of one who had been philosophizing for quite some time. The predicament into which Hegel was thus plunging himself might well seem to parallel that of the centipede of fable:

> The centipede was happy quite, until the frog in fun
> Asked, 'which leg comes after which?'
> This raised his mind to such a pitch,

[1] *Hegel's Development: Toward the Sunlight* (Oxford: Clarendon, 1972).

He lay distracted in a ditch,
Considering how to run.[2]

Hegel's *Phenomenology of Spirit*, then, is his testimony that he did not lie "distracted in a ditch." Nor did he, like Hume, make the initial decision that knowing is to be defined as the mental possession of that which is incontrovertibly true, which led Hume to the inevitable conclusion that since the only incontrovertible truths we possess are tautologies and matters of fact, philosophizing is really a waste of time. Hegel simply rejects all attempts to set up an antecedent critical apparatus for determining what is or what is not to be called knowing, as doomed never to get off the ground. Thus, Hegel's question about how to begin boils down, really, to something like: let us begin, but let us make sure that we begin at the beginning—neither before it nor after it. This will require two things: (*a*) the elimination of false starts, and (*b*) the recognition that every beginning is the beginning of a process which reveals itself for what it is only as it processes.

Thus, just as the Preface to the *Phenomenology* stands off, so to speak, from the work which has been accomplished and reflects on its significance for the total philosophical enterprise, so the Introduction is an integral part of the work *to be* accomplished. Here he looks at the problem to be solved: how are we to get to the point where philosophical thinking can justifiably be called "scientific"? That such an inquiry cannot *begin* with a determination of what conditions are to be fulfilled, if it is to be scientific, is fairly obvious: the determination of such conditions can be only the *result* not the *beginning* of a philosophical inquiry—even though the working out of a total philosophical "system" cannot begin until the results of this investigation are in.

Here, it might be argued, Hegel has us going around in circles—if he is not going around in circles himself. He knows from the beginning that he is looking for "science," but he does not know what science is. How can he know what he is looking for when he does not know what what he is looking for is? Apart from the fact that Plato seems to have handled that argument pretty well a good many centuries before Hegel—or the arguer—came on the scene, the argument misses the point. Hegel knew very well what the term "science" meant—or, perhaps, what it was getting to mean, ever since the Renaissance—and so did his contemporaries. The point was to determine whether philosophical knowing could aspire to be the kind of knowing which could justifiably be called scientific, which, Hegel claimed, could not be done by taking some acknowledged science as a model, deriving from it a definition of what science must be, and then seeing whether philosophy corresponds with that definition. What he will do, rather, is to begin philosophizing—that is why it is important to begin right—to see whether the process itself ultimately reveals what it is for philosophy to be

2 That the parallel is not too farfetched is evidenced by Hegel's own quips about those who seek to validate knowing before doing any, likening them to those who would learn to swim before entrusting themselves to the water, or to those who would unravel the mysteries of digestion before eating.

scientific. That this may also reveal what any scientific thinking must be need not be a presupposition of the investigation.

At this point, perhaps, it will not be out of order to digress briefly to consider the story of the term "science." The English term is employed to translate the German term *Wissenschaft*, but it is not quite adequate to the task —any more than the Latin *scientia* is an adequate translation of the Greek ἐπιστήμη. It is true that the German suffix *-schaft*, like the Latin *-tia*, is used to turn the concrete into the abstract, but it does more than that.[3] This is particularly true when the suffix is coupled with the infinitive of an active verb, yielding the meaning: the perfection, the totality, the process, the accomplishment, of the activity signified by the verb. If, then, we take *wissen* as the strongest German word signifying "know," to know in the strict sense,[4] *Wissenschaft* will mean the perfection of knowing in this strict sense, the sum total of such knowing, the state of having this kind of knowledge, or the process of accomplishing this knowing. It can also mean any discipline which is characterized by this kind of knowing or the framework within which this knowing is assured.

When we reach the end of the *Phenomenology*, we shall find that the knowing which characterizes philosophy and which makes it to be a science is "absolute knowing," which requires that the subject knowing as well as the object known be absolute. That the term "absolute" poses as many problems as the term "science," if not more, may readily be acknowledged; we shall return to it later.

Short of science, then, any knowing is at once knowing and not knowing, i.e., relative knowing. In the sense that science is knowing without any admixture of not knowing, it is absolute knowing. But if it is true to say that knowing cannot be satisfactory if it does have this admixture of not knowing, then it must also be true to say that, ideally at least, any knowing must have as its goal absolute knowing, a knowing which is totally the *activity* of the knower. Similarly, if the goal is absolute knowing, then the object of all knowing is ultimately the absolute object. This is not to say, however, that to know absolutely is to know everything—the concept is not quantitative at all—rather, it is to say that knowing is an *acting*, not a *being acted upon*, and that short of an "absolute" object the knowing will be at least partially a being acted upon. The implications of this cannot be spelled out here. As Hegel says in another context, "The history of philosophy is the history of the discovery of thoughts about the absolute which is its object." [5] At the beginning of the process, then, it is necessary to eliminate any notions of knowing (knowledge) which would obviously render impossible the grasp

[3] See Hennig Brinkmann, *Studien zur Geschichte der deutschen Sprache und Literatur.* I. *Sprache* (Düsseldorf: Schwann, 1965), pp. 388–89.

[4] The claim that the *Wissen* of *Wissenschaft* is knowing in the strongest sense should not be taken to conflict with what is said of *Erkennen* (cf. *infra,* pp. 278, 283). *Wissen,* it is true, is susceptible of a more generic and, therefore, weaker meaning, which is not true of *Erkennen;* but the highest degree of knowing, in which the *Phenomenology* culminates, is *Wissen,* and as *Wissenschaft* it is science in the fullest sense.

[5] *Enzyklopädie,* No. 13. See Georg Lukacs, *Der junge Hegel* (Zurich & Vienna: Europa, 1948), p. 556.

of the absolute—without prejudicing the issue by saying that some particular notion of knowing does, indeed, make it possible. If knowing is an activity of the knowing subject, an activity whose function it is to unite the knower with the object known, it is well to make sure that by coming between the knower and the known it does not serve more effectively to separate than to unite them. Thus, if knowing is conceived of as some sort of "instrument" which the subject employs to master the absolute, the subject runs the risk of contributing something which distorts the object and which the subject cannot get rid of without being back at the starting gate: with no knowledge at all. The problem here might be rendered somewhat more intelligible if we substitute "concept formation" for "knowing," where the concepts are considered as a *means* of grasping the object. Hegel himself puts it in these terms when, in a letter to Niethammer,[6] he criticizes Fries: "His pure general logic begins (in the system): 'The first means employed by the understanding in *thinking* are concepts,' as though chewing food and swallowing it were simply a means to eating, as though the understanding did a lot of other things besides thinking." The concept is not a means employed in order to grasp; it is the very activity of grasping the object— not that that gets us very far at this point, but it keeps us from going off on a tangent which will get us nowhere. Another tangent to be avoided is that of looking upon the activity in question—thinking, conceiving—on the analogy of a lens *through* which the object is more accurately seen. Once more the operative notion runs the risk of distorting rather than clarifying the object, and there is no way of checking what it does.

Perhaps what it all comes down to is a certain timidity in regard to the whole question of knowledge. The naïve position simply sees the whole question of knowledge as a matter of an object out there which a subject knows and in so doing knows that it is the way it is known. Hume's epistemology had pretty effectively dashed the hopes of getting any satisfaction from that kind of naïveté, and now those who, with Kant, have seen the necessity of finding a guarantee of knowing on the side of the subject are anxious to avoid any mistake which would ultimately land them back in naïve realism. But, says Hegel, perhaps the initial mistake is precisely this fear of making a mistake, which turns out to be a fear of taking a long hard look at what is to be looked at. One could, of course, say with Kant that knowing exactly what the subject contributes to the act of knowing permits us to eliminate that and be left with pure objectivity. Provided, of course, that the whole business is not contributed by the subject, in which case, when it is eliminated the subject is left with—nothing.

REALITY AND APPEARANCE

Here we are faced with one of the most difficult concepts Hegel has bequeathed to us, yet one without which neither the *Phenomenology* nor the rest of Hegel's philosophizing can be intelligible to us. Taking its cue from Plato, the entire Western philosophic tradition—with, perhaps, the excep-

[6] October 10, 1811; *Briefe*, I 389.

tion of Berkeley, whose individualistic subjectivism Hegel repudiated—had taken for granted that there is a clear distinction between reality and its appearance. This distinction did not necessarily entail that the way reality appears does *not* correspond with the way reality is, but it did bring it about that a quite significant part of the philosophical enterprise was devoted to the effort to guarantee that human thinking could somehow overcome the *possible* deceptiveness of appearances, beginning with Plato's endeavors to bypass appearances and culminating in Kant's contention that the best we can do is make the most of appearances and let reality as it is be what it may. With Fichte and Schelling the effort becomes that of guaranteeing the consciousness of reality by identifying it with consciousness of the Ego, which needs no guarantee other than itself.

Now, Hegel was not about to deny that there is a reality distinct from any individual subject who grasps it in thought. Nor will he deny that appearances can be deceptive—the whole of the *Phenomenology* is a prolonged effort to overcome one by one the erroneous certainties consciousness finds satisfaction in with regard to reality. What Hegel does deny is that the appearing which reality does is nothing more than the subjective activity of the individual consciousness which is aware of it. That reality is available only in its appearing, he grants. He grants, too, that appearing is always to a subject. What he will seek to do, however, is to identify appearing—as the self-manifestation of reality [7]—and being-conscious-of reality, which he obviously cannot do if consciousness is no more than it is naïvely taken to be. Our difficulties are increased here by the fact that we have nothing better than the term "consciousness" to translate the highly nuanced German *Bewusstsein*, which carries the meaning of the being which reality has when subjects are conscious of it. What Hegel will try to do, then, is to identify the appearing of reality (subjective genitive) with the consciousness of reality (objective genitive)—a long process, which will culminate only when the subject–object dichotomy has been broken down completely, where the knowing of reality will not be partially a not knowing.

If the initial fear of making a mistake, the fear that consciousness is not quite adequate to the task it faces, is permitted to have its way, however, the culmination will never be achieved: "In fact, this anxiety has to turn into the conviction that the whole beginning, for consciousness to attain through knowledge to that which is in itself, is in its conception nonsensical, and that between knowledge and the absolute there falls a screen which definitively keeps them apart" (p. 63/131). Thus, only a phenomenology which is resolutely bold has any chance of succeeding, one which does not mistrust but comes to terms with the very fullness of appearing.

One could wish, of course, that Hegel had not introduced so early in the game such an uncompromising term as "the absolute." It may even be that the choice of such a term is unfortunate (as might also be said regarding the subsequent use of such terms as "infinity" or "necessity") and that some

[7] In the *Logic* he will say that it is the essence of being to appear. See Part II of *Logik*, "Das Wesen" ("The Doctrine of Essence," in A. V. Miller's translation, *Hegel's Science of Logic* [New York: Humanities Press, 1969]).

other term would be more convenient. Still, apart from what further meaning the term may take on as the theme develops, it seems safe to say that at
this point "the absolute" need not mean more than "that beyond which
one need not (and cannot) go for truth." In any event, since the partially
true is only relatively true, and since it does not make a great deal of sense
to speak of "relatively" with no reference to "absolutely," there does seem
to be warrant for the term. Thus, when Hegel speaks of an "absolutely
true" (p. 65/133), he is not saying that there is some other kind of true, at
least not in the fullest sense of the word. Used adjectively or adverbially,
then, the term simply means "in the fullest sense of the word." If the adjective and the adverb make sense, so, it would seem, should the noun. If
Hegel says (as he does in the Preface) "there is truth only in the absolute,"
we might try saying "there is truth short of the absolute," or "what is not
absolutely true is true nevertheless," to see whether that makes better sense.
On the other hand, if we accept the term "absolute," we may well have
found the key to the whole of the *Phenomenology*, whose question then becomes "what content of consciousness can justifiably be called 'absolute'?"
We shall be less surprised at the answer if we do. The goal Hegel sets for
himself at the beginning is a state "where it [knowing] no longer needs to go
beyond itself, where it finds itself, and the concept corresponds to the object,
and the object to the concept" (p. 69/137–38). There is no guaranteeing at
the beginning that the goal will be attained, but if it is not, the quest for
knowledge has been futile. What Hegel is asking us to do is to turn our
thinking around in such a way that when we come to the end we shall see
that the goal has been attained. It is worth a try. This means that right
from the beginning of the *Phenomenology* Hegel knows where he wants to
go—and not merely because he has already been there—but there is nothing
wrong in that, so long as he is willing to wait to see whether the path he has
chosen really gets him there. Only if it does get him there, however, will
the rest of his philosophizing, his "system," make any sense. As late as
May 1, 1807, he was still wondering: "I am curious as to what you have to
say regarding the idea of this first part, which is properly the Introduction—
since I have not gone past . . . introducing." [8]

The "path" which Hegel chose has also been called a "ladder" [9] he sets up
to enable us to climb to a summit where knowing is, in fact, absolute or
scientific. The image is a good one—as long as the movement of climbing is
seen as continuous—since it is rather more obvious in the case of a ladder
than of a path that if one stops anywhere between the bottom and the top
one is nowhere, and that getting to the top is what makes sense out of the
ladder at all. The rungs of the ladder are successive 'appearings" (*Erschein-
ungen*, phenomena) of the genuine knowing which is at the top. To be
satisfied with any one of these is to rest in "mere appearance" (*Schein*,
illusion) and to lose whatever truth they do contain. At the same time, however, no rung can simply be dispensed with or cast aside; they must be *used*
for getting to the top.

8 *Briefe*, I 159–62.
9 Lukacs, *Der junge Hegel*, p. 566.

If, then, what is at the top is science, the very first rung is the appearance of science which, Hegel tells us, is the beginning of science (p. 66/134), which is to say that apparent knowing is already a form of knowing which contains within itself the capacity to develop. It will not develop, however, unless it becomes more than the *mere* appearance (*Schein*) of knowing by turning against (climbing up from) what is merely apparent in it—and this requires that it *use* the appearance, not merely get rid of it. Thus, it will at one and the same time *negate* the first step and *make use* of it to climb higher. It will be seen to be not true knowing, but negating it will preserve whatever is relatively true in it. "Natural consciousness [being-conscious] will show itself to be a mere conception (*Begriff*) [10] of knowing, or not real knowing. Since, however, this consciousness is convinced immediately that it is real knowing, the path it takes will have for it negative significance, and what is the realization of the mere conception will rather count for that conception as the loss of itself, since along this path it loses its truth" (p. 67/135). Negation, then, becomes not merely the condition but more significantly the propelling force toward a more genuine knowing, a more adequate grasp of truth. Knowing is a process constantly oriented toward and moving to better knowing. "The process of knowing seems rather to be such that what is directly apprehended as true is always seen by the reflective thought, which occurs as the experience is continued, to be merely a partial truth." [11]

This is an introduction to knowing and to truth in the literal sense of the word, not a procedure which tells the beginner what scientific knowledge and truth are, but one which sets him on the path which leads to both. To do this, the procedure must make the unscientific consciousness dissatisfied with itself, make it reject what it took for granted, lift itself (climb) from one unsatisfactory level to a more satisfactory one (not yet, of course, completely satisfactory). One cannot but be reminded of the procedure Socrates employed in trying to get his interlocutors to relinquish their cherished certainties in order to move upward to more satisfying truth. There is, however, an important difference: Hegel is not concerned with getting the consciousness which is at this incipient level of knowing merely to doubt its certainties; he seeks to bring about "conscious insight into the untruth of apparent knowing" (p. 67/136).

At this point, once again, it is necessary to issue a few cautions as to what is not taking place. Since the ongoing process of consciousness reveals to itself the untruth of its initial position, it might seem requisite to look outside the process for some means of guaranteeing its validity, particularly since the "knowing" in question only "appears" to be knowing. But Hegel will have none of this; an external guarantee would be no guarantee at all; the process has started, and he is convinced that it has its own built-in guaran-

---

10 More than once Hegel introduces a note of ambiguity into his text by employing the same term, *Begriff*, to designate now the *mere* concept of something, a sort of embryonic stage in the process of coming to know comprehensively, now the fully developed, comprehensive grasp of reality in all its objectivity, its "idea."

11 Wolfhart Pannenberg, *The Idea of God and Human Freedom* (Philadelphia: Westminster, 1973), p. 94.

tee that faithfulness to it will find it adequately self-corrective. "Hegel accepts the standard inherent in apparent knowledge," [12] which is to say it needs no help from outside either to point out or to remedy its inadequacies. Nor is the answer an enduring skepticism, which would cling to a one-sided negative attitude, which makes no positive contribution—even though as an attitude to be overcome in its turn, skepticism itself is a necessary step along the way. Finally, and perhaps most significantly, since the temptation is so great, error is not to be avoided simply by concentrating on what the ego *means*, in which it can make no mistake; to be certain of what one means (intends) is no guarantee that one is knowing at all. To give up a position which one holds on the basis of authority and to substitute for it one which one holds on the basis of one's own convictions—without going through the process of substantiating those convictions in the only way Hegel thinks possible—is to substitute one form of irrationality for another. "Still, when holding something to be so on the basis of authority is turned into holding it to be so on the basis of one's own convictions, the content held is not necessarily changed in such a way that truth takes the place of error" (p. 68/136). What is at issue is a questioning of customary notions (*Vorstellungen*), no matter what their source. It might be noted, of course, that one can quite conceivably find adequate grounds for holding exactly what one previously held on inadequate grounds; the force of negation need not affect the content of what is held to be true, only its truth. This will be seen to be particularly important in the transition from religious consciousness to absolute knowing, both of which have the identical content, the absolute.[13]

The contention, then, is that to be conscious at all is to be involved in a process wherein consciousness finds itself logically necessitated [14] to go beyond itself, thus denying itself the satisfaction of holding its own position to be true. More than that, the process cannot stop; consciousness can allow itself no rest as it passes successively from one state of inadequacy to the next, more adequate but still not completely adequate. What we have called forms of being inadequately conscious Hegel calls "forms of non-real consciousness." The important point is that if consciousness is ever to be adequate (*a*) the transition from one form to the next must be necessary, and (*b*) the total process must be such that it is seen by consciousness to be complete; no step which is necessary to the completeness of the process can be left out. This is, in fact, the goal at which the process aims from the very beginning. The completeness aimed at will be seen to have been achieved *if* the progression is seen to be necessary, *and* the transition from one form of consciousness to another is seen to be equally necessary. "The completeness of the forms of non-real consciousness will itself result from the neces-

12 Loewenberg, *Hegel's Phenomenology*, p. 13.

13 Quentin Lauer, s.j., "Hegel on the Identity of Content in Religion and Philosophy," *Hegel and the Philosophy of Religion*, ed. Darrell E. Christensen (The Hague: Nijhoff, 1970), pp. 261–78.

14 It should be obvious that the necessity is logical and not psychological. Not only *can* consciousness remain satisfied that its inadequate grasp is adequate, it frequently *does*.

sity of both progression and interconnection" (p. 68/137). This means, of course, that the negation propelling consciousness from one form to another cannot be merely negative; the rejection of one form must coincide with the introduction of another—and precisely in the order which Hegel describes.[15]

All this, however, leaves us facing three very serious problems if Hegel's phenomenological procedure (a "logic" of the interrelationship of phenomena) is to make sense. (1) What can "necessary" and "necessarily" mean in this context? As has been seen, it can scarcely be psychological necessity; and, as will be seen, it cannot be some sort of necessity of temporal sequence. It can only mean, then, the necessity of logical implications. But what can that mean, when it is phenomena implying each other? (2) Why must the order be the order which Hegel describes and not some other, so long as the series is complete? This question is not thoroughly distinct from the first, since a strictly logical necessity of implication would also dictate the order of progression, but if the meaning of "necessity" is somehow modified, it does become a distinct question. (3) Can the process, even at the end, be seen to have been complete without some antecedent criterion as to what will count as completeness? Hegel himself seems to justify this last question by his remark: "This presentation, seen (vorgestellt) as a position which science takes (ein Verhalten der Wissenschaft) toward knowing as it appears and as an investigation and testing of the reality of knowing (des Erkennens), seems incapable of taking place without some sort of presupposition which is laid down as a basic criterion" (p. 70/139).

These objections are serious, and it does not seem that we shall find a satisfactory answer in the statement that the Phenomenology of Spirit is Hegel's intellectual autobiography, even though to a large extent it is precisely that. There is no question that Hegel does universalize and thus speaks not merely for himself but for consciousness as such. At the end of the Phenomenology we shall see that consciousness, as Spirit, has reached the absolute standpoint where it will remain throughout Hegel's Science of Logic; but we may still experience some difficulty convincing ourselves that we know how he got there, or that he was justified in getting there. In any event, we have to take a long hard look at the above three questions before we go on, even though it may well be true, as Hegel says in his Preface, that only the process itself will show itself to have been justified.[16]

(1) What do the terms "necessary" and "necessity" mean when employed by Hegel in his Phenomenology? It should not be amiss, in beginning our "long hard look" at this question, to consider two fairly typical ways of not

---

[15] In order to highlight the dynamic interrelationship of steps in the dialectical process, Hegel employs the technical term "moment" to designate them. It should be noted—although little confusion would result from not doing so—that Hegel employs two almost identical terms for "moment." Das Moment (Hegel seems to have coined the neuter himself) designates the dialectical "moment" in a process of development, indicating the kind of relationship involved, and is the more frequent. Der Moment has the normal temporal meaning and need not have dialectical overtones. Even without the article, the context (even in English) will supply the meaning. In general one can say that what "element" or "factor" is in a static context, "moment" is in a dynamic context.

[16] Preface, p. 19/80.

answering the question, i.e., of dismissing it. In his commentary on the Preface to the *Phenomenology*, Walter Kaufmann notes, "Hegel often uses 'necessary' quite illicitly as the negation of 'utterly arbitrary.' " [17] If all this means is that Hegel does not employ the term the way a contemporary mathematician or formal logician would understand it, it is quite correct, but rather trivial. If it means that whatever is not "utterly arbitrary" is therefore "necessary," it cannot hold water—or if it can, Hegel's *Phenomenology* cannot. It is quite clear that when Hegel speaks of negation as "determinate," he means more than that the positive result which follows upon such a negation is merely not arbitrary; there is an awareness that what follows *has to* follow: "With this, then, a new form has immediately emerged, and in the negation the transition has been made, whereby inevitably (*von selbst*) progress through the complete series of forms results" (p. 69/137). As Henry Harris interprets this, Hegel is talking about "a sequence in which the breakdown of each form of consciousness leaves the germ of the next one as its natural residue." [18] It may very well be that the German term *notwendig* does not mean "necessary" in the strictest sense but rather something like "needed"; but it is clear that Hegel sees consciousness as justified in concluding that this is the way it has to be—no alternatives, even though the alternatives might not be "utterly arbitrary."

Another non-answer to the question—although it is more attractive and has more going for it than Kaufmann's—is John Findlay's: "A study of Hegel's dialectical practice will show, further, that in spite of anything he may *say* regarding their necessary, scientific character, his transitions are only necessary and inevitable in the rather indefinite sense in which there is necessity and inevitability in a work of art." [19] That the *Phenomenology*— and, indeed, Hegel's entire "system"—reveals many of the traits we look for in a work of art rather than the compact logical argumentation which most of us look for in a work of philosophy cannot be denied, but Findlay seems to weaken the force of the *Phenomenology* beyond the acceptable limit. Nor does he redeem this when he subsequently says quite correctly, "To look for absolute rigour in the Dialectic is to ignore the illumination it *has* for the sake of some quasi-mathematical interconnection which it does not and cannot possess." [20]

What we have to look for, then, is something between strict mathematical necessity which, Hegel himself notes (as do Aristotle, Whitehead, and many others), would not suit philosophy at all, since it is the work of understanding and not of reason, and a vague sort of necessity which is not necessity at all. [21] The necessity of which Hegel speaks is the necessity proper to the

17 *Hegel*, p. 371. Kaufmann simply compounds the felony when, in his article "Young Hegel and Religion" (in MacIntyre, *Hegel*, p. 96), he speaks of "necessary" as a "synonym of 'natural' and an antonym of 'arbitrary,' " which comes down to saying that when Hegel says "necessary" he is "giving some reasons for a development."

18 *Hegel's Development*, p. 321.

19 *The Philosophy of Hegel: An Introduction and Re-examination* (New York: Collier, 1962), p. 71.

20 *Ibid.*

21 See *infra*, pp. 291–92, on the distinction between "understanding" and "reason."

"inner movement" of the contents of consciousness, and it is the same sort of necessity as that with which his *Logic* is concerned: "The exposition of the only possible true method of philosophical science takes place in the treatment of logic itself; for the method is consciousness of the form of inner self-movement proper to its content. In the *Phenomenology of Spirit* I have put forth an example of this method with regard to a concrete object, consciousness." [22] Perhaps we should not call this "necessity"—neither here nor in the *Logic*—any more than we call the necessity proper to Plato's ἐπιστήμη necessity in the formal logical sense. At the very least, however, Hegel is saying: "If consciousness looks at itself as long and as hard as I want it to, I guarantee that this is what it will see; and when it sees it, the seeing will be scientific knowledge." Perhaps we shall not see this, but what we do see will make the looking worthwhile.

What we need, perhaps, is something akin to, but stronger than, Findlay's notion of artistic necessity. In the contemplation of a great work of art—a statue, a painting, a poem, a symphony—there is an awareness on the part of one who with taste looks long and hard that "nothing else will do"; each detail *demands* each other detail. It would be difficult (impossible) for the observer to formulate reasons *why* the details are demanded, but the details reveal themselves as "necessary" to the long, hard look. The same "necessity," Hegel is convinced, will reveal itself to the one who looks long and hard at the phenomenon of consciousness as it reveals itself. The only criterion of necessity, however, is the process of self-revelation itself.

(2) What justifies the order of implication which Hegel presents? If we are to take his word for it, there is only one way to do a phenomenology of consciousness—which inevitably becomes a phenomenology of spirit, when it becomes clear that consciousness is but *one* manifestation of spirit—and that is the way Hegel himself does it. In trying to answer this question, it might be well to note at the outset that there are, in fact, two orders of implications, which may or may not turn out to be identifiable. There is the order of what might be called "phenomenological" implication which is manifested in the passage from chapter to chapter—particularly the first three chapters, "Sense Certainty," "Perception," and "Force and Understanding." It is not too difficult to see a logic here governing the order of phenomenal manifestation; but it becomes somewhat more difficult to follow this order when, beginning with "Self-Consciousness" and its subdivisions, "Domination and Servitude," "Stoicism and Skepticism," and "Unhappy Consciousness," Hegel reaches back into his vast store of erudition and finds concrete pegs, so to speak, on which to hang the forms of consciousness he is seeking to elucidate. With this is introduced the order of "historical" implication, and this raises a host of problems. First of all, the order is not historical in the ordinary sense of either chronological sequence or cause–effect relationship. Even though Hegel employs the *names* of historical attitudes in seeking to describe the process of consciousness, the description could be quite intelligible without them. Secondly, once Hegel has made the transition from "Self-Consciousness" to "Reason," he himself

[22] *Logik*, I 35.

jumps back and forth in time in such a way that it simply will not do to look for chronological sequence. Thirdly, as Hyppolite has noted so well, although one can detect an historical order of development *within* the particular moments of the overall development, it is less easy to see the same sort of order in the transition from moment to moment.[23] This problem becomes even more complex when we come to the sections on Spirit, where it is no longer a question of individual development, but of the development of concrete totalities,[24] where the individual ego ceases to be merely individual and becomes representative of the human condition.[25] This, incidentally, is the reason why a number of scholars, taking their cue from Häring,[26] have felt that when Hegel reached Chapter 5 ("Reason"), he abandoned his original project of a "Science of the Experience of Consciousness" and began to write an entirely new "Phenomenology of Spirit."

Be all this as it may, we are left with the problem of making sense out of the order Hegel does present—and, while we are at it, of accounting for certain significant historical omissions (e.g., the Reformation) from the series of forms of consciousness. It does make a certain amount of sense to say with Hyppolite that the itinerary Hegel is describing is his own which, in the process, takes on universal significance,[27] but we cannot simply leave it there. It would seem rather that, just as in the *Lectures on the History of Philosophy* Hegel followed the history of philosophy in such a way that he eventually saw his own *Logic* emerging from it and, then, returned to the history to consider it in the light of the *Logic*, so too in the *Phenomenology* his knowledge of history brought him to see the development of consciousness (Spirit) in a certain way (we can find confirmation of this in his *Lectures on the Philosophy of History*), which, in turn, enabled him to re-read history in the light of the *Phenomenology*. That he could find historical instances for each moment in this development he was convinced; that the order in which he presented these instances should be strictly chronological did not too much concern him.

(3) This brings us to the final question which plagues us from the beginning: "Can Hegel engage us in such a process without antecedently adopting a criterion which will enable us to say what will count as 'completeness' at the end of the process?" An answer to this question is at least partially given in the answer to question two. If one looks at the history of philosophy from Thales to Hegel (perhaps even to Heidegger), one can see that, whatever else "truth" may have *meant* to various philosophers, it will be *attained* only when the thinking of being is entirely adequate to the being which is thought, i.e., when being is adequately *known*. This it will not be, so long as some further step is necessary for knowing to be called knowing in the fullest sense, which is another way of saying that it will not be genuine knowing so long as it is conditional, only when it is "absolute." Thus, Hegel could very well begin with the conviction that the only ac-

23 *Genèse et structure*, pp. 39–40.
24 *Ibid.*, pp. 40–41.
25 See *ibid.*, p. 44.
26 See *infra*, pp. 125–26 and n. 3.
27 *Genèse et structure*, pp. 50–51.

ceptable end of the process would be "absolute knowing," or he could begin with the conviction that knowing could be absolute only when it knows "the absolute." Before the process is completed that conviction can only be a conviction, a *faith* in reason. *If* the process does, in fact, terminate in a knowledge of knowing which leaves no further questions to be asked, Hegel has his criterion right there. Whether he does precisely that remains to be seen; whether, having done it, he can then move on to an explication of what knowing knows is not the *Phenomenology*'s task to prove. It is the *Logic* which tells us that he has chosen the only method which could have succeeded.[28] It is the *Logic* which will also tell us what more we can make of it.

CONSCIOUSNESS AS PROCESS

It is time, now, to get back to the process as explicated in the Introduction, a process which turns out to be the method which consciousness imposes on itself by remaining true to itself—essentially a method of successively destroying its satisfaction in any position short of a position which can legitimately be satisfactory—a kind of protracted self-torture: "Consciousness, then, suffers at its own hands this violence, of spoiling its own limited satisfaction" (p. 69/138). In the course of this, consciousness will recognize that the suffering it imposes on itself will demand a movement from its own particular self to the universal (p. 70/138–39). But it has to begin far from that.

What consciousness will be trying to do in the *Phenomenology* is to find out the truth about consciousness, i.e., when is consciousness really true, and not merely partially so? To do this, it must watch consciousness in operation, to see not only what it does but also what the logic of its doing demands that it do next. This is by no means the self-consciousness, which we meet for the first time in Chapter 3; it is the consciousness of the philosopher (Hegel; ourselves, if we follow him) standing off and observing consciousness in operation. It is not, however, the consciousness of the philosopher telling consciousness what it *ought* to be doing; it is the consciousness of the philosopher watching consciousness discover within itself an inner movement which is its own justification. The stance is not an easy one to maintain, for, although the philosopher wants to stand off to observe consciousness in operation, the only consciousness he can observe at this point is his own—no others are available to him—and he has not yet found grounds for universalizing his own.

What the *Phenomenology* sets out to do, then, is to find out "the truth of knowing," i.e., just when is knowing truly knowing. Its first object is what *appears* to be an act of knowing. In order to handle this, its first object, the observing consciousness (of the philosopher) immediately—and uncritically—makes a distinction between itself as knowing and the object as known. This is but another way of saying that what is known is what it is in itself, what has a being (*Sein*) of its own, in itself, and also has a kind

28 *Logik*, I 35.

of being in the consciousness (*Bewusst-sein*) which is had of it. Thus, since
the being of the object is available to us only in consciousness, we look for
what the object, i.e., knowing, is in itself but find only what it is *for us*. We
do not want to determine merely what we *think* knowledge is but what it
really is, but the only criterion for determining this is *in us*. If the object
with which we are concerned is, as a matter of fact, outside of us, a criterion
in us would certainly seem to be inadequate. Since the only being which
this object, knowing, can have is in us, however, the criterion, too, can only
be in us. The point which Hegel is somewhat laboriously making is that in
every case of objectivity there is nowhere else for the criterion of that objectivity to be but in us and that, in the case of knowing as an object, it is
quite legitimate that the criterion should be in us. If it can ultimately be
established that the knowing in us is knowing in the full sense of the word,
then the objectivity of that knowing will have been established, and the
criterion for that objectivity will be in the knowing itself, which is in us.
With regard to other objects of consciousness, it might be argued that what
they are in themselves is altered by their being for us in consciousness; but
this is not arguable in regard to that object, knowing, whose very being is
to be for us.

In one sense there is nothing terribly new here, although the tortured
analysis may set our heads spinning: objects are available to us in concepts,
and we want to find out if there is some way of guaranteeing that the object
thus made available is indeed the object as it is—without interference, in
itself. But since Kant had made it doubtful that the object—or "thing"—
could ever be available to us as it is in itself, Hegel sets out to show that
there is one object, knowing, which is available to us as it is in itself, even
though not adequately at the beginning of the process, and that the adequacy
of this consciousness may permit consciousness to move on to ever greater
objective adequacy, provided that the true being of an object (of objectivity)
can be shown to be the being it has in us. The way to do this is to turn our
ordinary, naïve way of looking at things around.

Ordinarily we not only break up the activity of knowing into that in
which an object is conceived, the concept, and the object or the being conceived, we also look upon the being as that to which the concept must
correspond if it is to be true. "If we call the *knowing* the *concept*, and the
being (*Wesen*) [29] or the *true*, on the other hand, that which is or the *object*,
then the test (*Prüfung*) consists in seeing whether the concept corresponds
to the object" (p. 71/140). We can, however, look at it the other way around
and consider the concept as object, whose true being is precisely the being it
has for consciousness—the way, it would seem, Plato saw it; then the concept would become the measure of the object, of its objectivity. "If, however,
we call the *being* (*Wesen*) or the *object's* in-itself *the concept* and in the opposite way understand by *object* the concept (*ihn*) as *object*, i.e., the way

[29] Although the term *Wesen* is ordinarily translated "essence," there is ample justification for translating it in certain contexts as "being." This latter meaning need not be
confused with the "being" which translates *Sein*, since this last retains a strong verb
force.

the object is *for another*, then the test consists in seeing whether the object corresponds to the concept" (p. 71/140–41). This would mean that the true being of the object is its being conceived, since apart from being conceived it is not an object. Now, Hegel maintains that both ways of looking at the matter come to the same, since the only way of comparing object and concept is in the concept, where alone the object is available for comparison. This, once more, is particularly true if the object under investigation is the very nature of knowing, the phenomenon with which the whole of the *Phenomenology* is concerned. "It is easy to see that both come to the same. What is essential, however, is that, throughout the entire investigation, we hold fast to this: that these two moments, *concept and object*, are contained in the knowing we are investigating and, thus, we do not need to bring criteria with us and to apply *our own* [private] conjectures (*Einfälle*) and thoughts in the investigation. By leaving these out we attain to a consideration of the matter (*die Sache*) as it is *in* and *for itself*" (pp. 71–72/141). The content of consciousness, then, is the object as concept, which contains within itself all that is necessary to validate it, since nothing external to it could possibly validate it. Consciousness tests itself, and as we, the observers of consciousness, look on, we see (progressively) a "consciousness of what is the true for it and a consciousness of its knowing it" (p. 72/141). At this point, of course, it can scarcely seem satisfactory that this is simply asserted. An Introduction can do no more than this; Hegel is convinced that if we stay with him we shall see that the process does, in fact, justify itself or, as he says in the Preface, his view "must justify itself by the presentation of the system" (p. 19/80). The main point of the whole contention is that the inner movement of the knowing process is one and the same with the inner movement of the object known, which is to say that in the consistently sustained *experience* of the object the object reveals itself more and more as what it truly is. Only in plumbing the depths of what it is *for us* shall we ever attain to what it is *in itself*. "This *dialectical* movement which consciousness exercises (*ausübt*) on itself, on its object as well as on its knowing, *insofar* as out of this *the new true object emerges*, is properly what is called experience" (p. 73/142). If we add to this, as Hegel does in the *Encyclopedia*, that "whatever is in consciousness at all is experienced," [30] we can say that every object of consciousness is subject to this dialectical movement of progressive self-revelation.

At long last we come to Hegel's solution to the problem raised at the beginning of the Introduction. If knowing is either an instrument with which or a medium through which the object is made available to consciousness, then the object is altered by this contact with what is other than itself, and the subject cannot be sure that the object is available to him as it is in itself. This is the problem which Kant solved by simply admitting that this identity of consciousness with the thing-in-itself is not to be achieved, and which Schelling solved by simply asserting an identity without working it out. Hegel, on the other hand, recognizes an *othering* of being in conscious-

[30] *Enzyklopädie*, No. 8.

ness, but denies that this *otherness* is foreign to it; it is the essential self-othering whereby the object of consciousness becomes what it really is. What consciousness first took to be its object changes itself as the consciousness of it changes; it becomes *other*, and the other it becomes is the *true* object. "Consciousness knows something, and this object is the being (*Wesen*) or the *in-itself*" (p. 73/142)—*what* is known has its own being (*Sein*). "It is, however, also the *in-itself* for consciousness; and with this comes in the ambivalence of what is true" (p. 73/142)—the being-for-consciousness is as true as the being-in-itself because it is the same being. "We see that consciousness now has two objects: one, the first *in-itself*; the second, the *being-for-consciousness* of this *in-itself*" (p. 73/142)—thus, it is the *in-itself* which is for-consciousness, but only embryonically. "At first the latter seems to be merely the reflection of consciousness on itself, a representation (*Vorstellung*),[31] not of an object but only of its own knowing of the former" (p. 73/142–43)—the second consciousness *seems* to be twice removed from the object. "But, as was shown earlier, in this [seeming representation] the first object alters itself for consciousness (*ihm*); it ceases to be the *in-itself* and becomes such that it is only *in-itself for consciousness (für es)*" (p. 73/143)—what seems to be an alteration imposed by consciousness is seen to be the in-itself changing into what it more truly is. "The result, however, is this: The *being-for-consciousness of this in-itself* is its being true, which is to say, it is the *being (Wesen)* or the *object* of consciousness" (p. 73/143)—it is the true object which changes, thus becoming more true. "This new object contains the nullity (*Nichtigkeit*) of the first; it is the experience had (*gemachte*) of it" (p. 73/143)—the dialectical self-alteration of the object and the dialectical experience of it are the same.

There can be no question that Hegel makes here a rather astounding claim; a claim, however, on which depends the intelligibility of absolutely everything which follows.[32] The whole thing becomes even more complicated when we recall that consciousness is constantly seen under two aspects, consciousness as observing and consciousness as being observed (the philosopher—*uns*—observing what goes on in being-conscious). The *observing*

[31] Where *Vorstellung* has the meaning not only of "representation" in the ordinary sense, but also of "representative" in the sense of another's "standing for," "taking the place of."

[32] It might not be amiss to point out here that the above passage contains the key to an understandable misunderstanding in John Smith's review of the present author's *Hegel's Idea of Philosophy* in *Thought*, 47, No. 186 (Autumn 1972), 470–71. Says Smith: "Lauer, however, seems to think that for Hegel there are 'classes [*Gattungen*] in nature, only to the extent that man (spirit, thought) thinks nature' (p. 85 n.), and he stresses the point several times. But Hegel explicitly denies this in his *Philosophy of Nature* (*Encycl.* 246) where he maintains that we cannot regard *Gattungen* and *Klassen* as 'subjective additions' introduced by thought precisely because these forms and kinds are 'substantial.'" It is, in fact, my claim that Hegel denies in the very text which Smith cites precisely what he denies in the Introduction to the *Phenomenology*: that what is true of the object of consciousness cannot be a "subjective addition" imposed by consciousness; it *becomes* true of the object, however, when the object is thought (experienced), when the "substantial" is articulated.

consciousness, then, can be aware of what occurs in the *observed* consciousness, without the latter's being aware of the same. "The emergence of the new object" is a "necessity," and it "takes place without consciousness' knowing it." "It is for us, so to speak, but behind its back" (p. 74/144). As consciousness progresses, it becomes aware of this new object; but when it is caught up in the process of experiencing its object, it does not take time out to reflect on what is going on; "we phenomenologists" do. "Of necessity (*dadurch*) there enters into its movement a moment of *being-in-itself* or *for-us* which does not present itself for the consciousness engaged in experiencing; still, the *content* of what comes across (emerges) (*entsteht*) to us is *for that consciousness* (*für es*), and only we grasp [33] what is formal, the pure emergence of the object; *for that consciousness* what has emerged is there only as object, *for us* it is there at the same time as movement and coming to be" (p. 74/144).

Whatever "necessity" is to mean in the present context—certainly more than "not utterly arbitrary"—it is that which guarantees that not only the end result will be science, but that the way leading to the result will also be science, since unless the whole process is scientific, neither will the result.[34] The whole, then, is a "science of the experience of consciousness" (p. 74/144).

It is difficult to say with certainty whether "the experience of consciousness" is to be taken as an objective or a subjective genitive. If the former, the science in question would have as its object "consciousness as experienced"; if the latter, the object would be "consciousness as experiencing." It is probably both, even though the fact that the "science" ultimately became a "phenomenology of the Spirit," wherein the *Gestalten des Bewusstseins* become *Gestalten des Geistes*, would favor the subjective genitive. In any event, the very last sentence of the Introduction would seem to indicate, contra Häring, that from the very beginning Hegel was aware that his investigation was going to lead him into the complexities of developing Spirit; he did not change his mind in the middle of the book. He tells us here that somewhere along the line not only *observing consciousness* but also *observed consciousness* will come to the realization of all that its progressive experiencing involves; and when it does, the "science of spirit" will be its own. "In propelling itself forward to its true existence, consciousness will arrive at a point where it puts aside its illusory appearance (*Schein*) of being burdened with something foreign (*Fremdartiges*), which is only for it as something other, or at a point where the appearance (*Erscheinung*) will equal being (*Wesen*), and precisely at this point its presentation will be identified with what is properly speaking the science of spirit; and finally,

[33] The German here reads *wir begreifen nur*, which should mean "we grasp only," but the context makes it clear that the "only" modifies "we."

[34] A remark of John Dewey's seems apropos here: "The layman takes certain conclusions that get into circulation to be science. But the scientific inquirer knows that they constitute science only in connection with the methods by which they were reached" (in McDermott, *Philosophy of John Dewey*, II 631).

because it itself will have grasped this, its being (*Wesen*), it will show forth (*bezeichnen*) the nature of absolute knowing itself" (p. 75/145).[35]

Having finished this Introduction, which in the text is surprisingly brief,[36] Hegel is ready to launch into the tracing of consciousness in its progress— a progress which, to the uninitiated, may well look like meandering. If he has convinced us that we can justifiably begin the examination with an absolutely minimal form of consciousness—which, because it is conscious- ness at all, is a form of "knowing"—convinced us that this form of con- sciousness will reveal what is needed (*notwendig*) to make it more complete, the Introduction will have accomplished its task. Without at this point prejudicing the issue as to the "necessity" of either the first or any further implications (transitions), we can simply try to follow along the path Hegel traces out for us to see how much is revealed to us in the process.

---

[35] If this passage alone is not enough to show that Häring's thesis cannot hold water, Pöggeler and others have taken great pains to show that, although Hegel had plenty of time to let us know that he had changed his mind during the writing of the *Phenome- nology*, he in fact treated it as a unit on four separate later occasions: (1) in a letter (to Schelling) dated May 1, 1807 (cited in n. 8); (2) in the first volume of the *Science of Logic* (p. 29), published in 1812; (3) in the *Encyclopedia*, No. 25, published in 1817; (4) and in the revision of the *Logic*, which he began in 1831, shortly before he died.

[36] It might be added that in our own text not only the chapter on Hegel's Introduction but also the next two chapters are "surprisingly brief." That they are is the result of a decision to be brief. No part of Hegel's *Phenomenology* has been commented on more extensively—and perceptively—than the Introduction and the first two chapters. It did not seem necessary to go over in detail what has been so frequently treated elsewhere.

2

Sense Certainty

HAVING DISCUSSED in his Introduction the very possibility of beginning a scientific philosophy at all, Hegel now gets down to work and begins, at the only point, he is convinced, at which one can begin: with an examination of what is an absolutely minimal thinking or knowing, the most direct possible form of consciousness. He has already told us that if we are going to find out what scientific thinking is and then do it, we cannot start out with science full blown, nor can we prior to any scientific thinking whatever determine what science is going to have to be. If there appears to be knowing at all, then the appearing itself is at least an embryonic knowing, and with this we can legitimately begin, as long as we remember that the beginning of any process makes sense only in terms of the whole process. There is a sense, then, in which beginning where he does can be legitimated only when the process has come to completion, and we can look back to see that it was indeed correct to begin where we did.

It might of course be argued that to begin with sensation is too obvious a move to need discussion; both Plato and Aristotle had made it clear centuries earlier that one either begins with sensation or one does not begin at all—and no one thereafter seriously disputed what they said. Strictly speaking, however, Hegel does not begin with sensation; nor is the first chapter of his *Phenomenology* entitled "Sensation." The title of the chapter, which the translation "Sense Certainty" renders as well as English can, is "Sinnliche Gewissheit," where the operative term is the noun *Gewissheit* (certainty), and the term *sinnliche* (sensible) is an adjective modifying that noun. What Hegel is talking about, then, is "certainty" and of its destruction as a condition for moving forward toward truth. In doing this Hegel accomplishes two things: he provides a quite obvious and not likely to be disputed starting point in the kind of certainty we have regarding the object of sensation; and he serves notice that the whole book is going to be a book about certainties—or, better, about the progressive destruction of certainties until we reach a point where certainty and truth coincide. It should be fairly obvious that certainty, a subjective attitude, serves little purpose unless what we are certain of is true. What is not so obvious—what Hegel says is rarely obvious, even though it may seem so—is that certainty, any certainty, does in fact serve an important, even though negative, purpose. The kind of certainty we experience on the level of sense quickly cancels itself out—as will a host of other certainties along the way—but the result of the canceling will be not merely negative; it will not only *clear the way*, but also *pave the way*, for a more adequate grasp of truth, which in turn will *give way* to a still more adequate grasp, until finally the grasp is totally adequate, i.e., "absolute."

Before plunging into what Hegel actually says in this chapter, it might be well to issue a caution. Although it is true that Hegel's vast historical erudition makes his work fairly bristle with allusions, one should be slow to conclude just what is being alluded to. In some cases, of course, Hegel tells us; in others there are sufficient indications to justify identifying an allusion; in a great many, however, there are not. One suspects in many instances that Hegel himself need not have been sure to what historical position he was alluding or that he was alluding to an amalgam of positions. In any event, the assurance with which many writers identify Hegel's allusions can at best give evidence of their own erudition; at worst it can confuse the issue. Thus, when Hyppolite—following Purpus [1]—claims that in this chapter Hegel has the Greeks, primarily Plato, in mind,[2] he may well be correct—if it matters—but if we fail to recognize Hume and the British empiricists at the same time, we shall have been led astray.[3] More important still, we shall do better in reading Hegel to take what he says on its own merits; he is difficult, but intelligible, and departing from his text rarely adds to that intelligibility.[4]

In seeking to allow Hegel's text to unravel itself before us, we should recall, as was mentioned above, that Hegel is not instituting an investigation of *sensation* but rather examining the kind of *thinking* which finds in sensation an adequate source of certainty regarding sensation's object. The case is made quite simply both for its adequacy as a starting point and for its adequacy as consciousness of its object. It is adequate as a starting point— in fact it is the only possible starting point—because as consciousness it is most direct, most "immediate"; in it nothing comes between consciousness and its object. Since no change is effected, there is nothing to separate the thinking which conceives, appropriates (*Begreifen*) the object from the sense activity which apprehends (*Auffassen*) it (p. 79/149).[5] Clearly, then,

[1] Wilhelm Purpus, *Die Dialektik der sinnlichen Gewissheit bei Hegel* (Nuremberg: Seitz, 1905).

[2] *Genèse et structure*, p. 84.

[3] In this connection, Charles Taylor's remark ("Opening Arguments," in MacIntyre, *Hegel*, p. 160) is very much to the point. "The notion of consciousness with which Hegel starts his dialectical critique is one he calls 'sense certainty.' This is a view of our awareness of the world according to which it is at its fullest and richest when we simply open our senses, as it were, to the world and receive whatever impressions come our way, prior to any activity of the mind, in particular conceptual activity." The reference, quite clearly, is to Hume.

[4] Cf. Pierre-Jean Labarrière, *Structures et mouvement dialectique dans la Phénoménologie de l'Esprit de Hegel* (Paris: Aubier-Montaigne, 1968), p. 29: "The underlying postulate is that an understanding of the work does not require any antecedent knowledge and that it itself provides, in the necessity which animates it, the key to its own elucidation (*déchiffrement*). In order to penetrate into it, consciousness need only be that naïve consciousness which Hegel first places before us, in its certitude at once the richest and the poorest."

[5] As Charles Taylor has shown so clearly, however ("Opening Arguments," in MacIntyre, *Hegel*, pp. 151–88), the whole force of the argumentation in the first three chapters

the activity with which Hegel is concerned from the start is thinking, manifest in its most characteristic act of "conceiving" *(Begreifen)*. The claim is that the thinking itself is immediate, because in the conceiving nothing has been *added* to the apprehending; its object acquires an ideal structure without ceasing to be immediate.[6] By the same token, not only is it the most immediate form of consciousness, "in addition it appears *(erscheint)* as the *most true*, for it has not yet left anything out of its object but has it before itself in all its completeness" (p. 79/149). No addition, no subtraction; therefore perfect.

This, quite obviously, is a far cry from claiming that there can be human sensation in isolation, or even from saying that there are those who do so claim. The claim being investigated is that there is a cognitive activity which *does* nothing to the object of sensation and yet *has* that object in all its richness and its truth. The point to be investigated, then, is: if, by an effort of thought, we isolate the object of sense from all that thought subsequently does to it, what in fact do we have? "Sense certitude is a first state in which consciousness takes no account of having done anything whatever to acquire knowledge regarding its object." [7] This is what might be called "pure empiricism," or what Dewey calls "a spectator theory of knowledge," [8] and Hegel is at pains to have us look at it carefully to see if it can hold water.

Here the importance of the distinction between the observed consciousness *(für sich)* and the observing consciousness *(für uns)* immediately becomes evident. They may very well be one and the same consciousness functioning in two ways; but consciousness in the grip of its conviction that sensation renders its object adequately present must be looked at, not in order to tell it that it is wrong but in order to see whether it can consistently hold on to that conviction. "We," observing consciousness, see that it is not justified in its conviction. Are we also going to see it disappointed with its own conviction? Hegel is convinced that we shall, but consciousness itself is not going to give up without a struggle. "The interchange of positions regarding the meaning and validity of sensory awareness constitutes the contrapuntal pattern upon which the comedy of the situation chiefly depends: the positions advanced in the face of opposition turn out to be progressively unstable and hence untenable." [9] It is as though the observed and observing consciousnesses were engaged in dialogue in which the observer *tells* the observed nothing, but by raising objections brings the observed to doubt *(zweifeln)*, indeed to despair of *(verzweifeln)* its own certainties.

is directed toward a rejection of any conception of consciousness, even on the level of sensation, as a mere passive acceptance of stimuli impressed from without. The only adequate activity of consciousness is conception *(Begreifen)*, but even the reception *(Auffassen)* of stimuli associated with sensation is a beginning of the autonomous activity of conception.

6 Cf. Henri Niel, *De la Médiation dans la philosophie de Hegel* (Paris: Aubier, 1945), p. 95.

7 Charles Andler, "Le Fondement du Savoir dans la *Phénoménologie de l'Esprit* de Hegel," *Revue de Métaphysique et de Morale*, 38 (1931), 321.

8 McDermott, *Philosophy of John Dewey*, II 370.

9 Loewenberg, *Hegel's Phenomenology*, p. 24.

Let *us* look once more at the immediate certainty which is so rich in the completeness with which its object is present to it. We shall see that it is neither "rich" nor "immediate," but we must watch the observed consciousness become aware of this. If the "we" in question are also already philosophers, we can also see that "what the senses deliver must, then, be rationally tested and non-sensibly understood." [10] But how did we ever get to be philosophers if we had to get over the conviction that sense certainty is indeed adequate before we could do so? It is all very well for us to say that the richest of certainties turns out to be the poorest and most abstract of truths, saying of its object no more than "is" and thus containing "only the being of the thing" (p. 79/149), which is pretty empty truth, but how does our own consciousness become an awareness of this? We have to remember that, at this stage of the game, the consciousness in question is supremely individual and has nothing but its own resources to rely on. If it simply looks at the sort of object with which it is faced, a sensible object, it would seem quite justified in holding that the most adequate—most true—form of consciousness for the presentation of this object as it really is is the one which corresponds to it most exactly, i.e., sensation, and it seems nonsensical to claim that some other form of consciousness presents it better—more truly.

But Hegel says precisely that: he says that because sensation is immediate and, therefore, not a movement, it is not experience, which alone can come to terms with the rich complexity of even a sensible object. "This is a hard saying, and who can bear it?" [11] It certainly seems to be saying that unless consciousness goes beyond what is given to it the given is not, in fact, given —which would justify Husserl's conviction that Hegel was a "constructionist" and not a "phenomenologist" at all. What Hegel actually is saying, however, is, first, that unless consciousness sees what is necessarily implied in the givenness of its initial object it is not adequate to that object; and, second, that what is necessarily implied is not "immediately" given.

"Immediate" consciousness in sensation, then, is one in which "I, *this I*, am *certain* of *this* thing (*Sache*), not because *I* developed myself as consciousness thereby and put thought in motion in a variety of ways" (p. 79/149). But precisely because "this I" did not develop itself in being conscious, the *Sache* does not manifest to it any of its rich variety (pp. 79–80/149–50). For this sort of immediacy to be consistent, both consciousness and its object must be isolated: "Consciousness is *I* and no more,[12] a pure *this*; the *isolated individual* [subject] knows a pure this, or *the isolated individual* [object]" (p. 80/150). Once more, it should be emphasized that there is no question of isolating sensation from thought, as though the former could take place without the latter; rather, it is a question of determining just

10 Block, *Subjekt–Objekt*, p. 111.

11 Cf. Theodor W. Adorno, *Drei Studien zu Hegel* (Frankfurt: Suhrkamp, 1963), p. 72: "The specific difficulty of beginning is not to be passed over in silence. The notion of experience has in the schools which employ it emphatically, those in the Humean tradition, the very character of immediacy as its criterion, immediacy to the subject. Experience is supposed to mean what is immediately there, immediately given, as though clean of any contribution of thought and, therefore, non-deceiving."

12 See *Enzyklopädie*, No. 20, Zusatz: "The I, therefore, is thinking as subject."

how adequate consciousness can be to its object if we leave out of consideration the contribution of thought, if we think of it as "immediate." Thought,
Hegel will ultimately say, neither adds to nor subtracts from the object; the
activity of thought in determining the object is indistinguishable from the
activity of the object in determining itself.

By the same token, those who claim that Hegel illegitimately introduces
here the question of "expressing" the content of sensation have missed the
point. If one wishes to be satisfied with nothing but the mere "being" of
the object of sensation, one can dispense with either thought or expression,
but that is an empty satisfaction, as empty as "being." Where what is sought
is the "truth" of the object, the object as it truly (really) is, there thought
is essential, and a thought which cannot be expressed is an empty thought.
Thus, the "mere being" which is supposed to "constitute" and "express the
essence (*Wesen*) of sense certainty" (p. 80/150) does not get the job done; it
simply leaves out too much; it is abstract, not concrete, as the proponents
of sensation would have it.[13] If consciousness is forced to face the implications of its own content, it will inevitably come to the realization that the
fullness and richness of that content is simply not available to it on the level
of sensory immediacy.

If we seem to be belaboring the point here—or if Hegel does—he assures us that we have to do here not only with "this pure immediacy but
with a *model (Beispiel)* of the same" (p. 80/150); a model which will reveal
what consciousness must do as long as it is only immediate, on any level. It
is a model we shall have to keep before us throughout the *Phenomenology*.
Out of this model of immediacy, in fact, arises the very first distinction
which makes it possible for consciousness effectively to look into itself, to
see itself as it first appears, i.e., as separated into subject and object—*"this
as I* and *this as object"* (p. 80/150). "We," the observing consciousness, are
aware that neither the I nor the object is immediate, since they are correlatives, neither of which makes sense without the other. "If *we* reflect on this
distinction, it becomes clear that neither the one nor the other is merely
immediate in sense certainty; rather, they are at the same time as *mediated*;
I have certainty *through* another, namely, the thing *(Sache)*; and the thing
too is in the certainty *through* another, namely, through I" (p. 80/150).
Furthermore, *we* do not *make* the distinction between the immediate and
the mediated; we *find* it in the sense certainty itself (p. 80/150–51). For the
observed consciousness itself to find it requires a bit more doing.

The "doing" begins with another distinction which consciousness *makes*—
based on the distinction between subject and object—a distinction between
what is "essential" and what "inessential" in the relationship of subject
and object. Looking at the matter naïvely, one is certainly tempted to say
that "that which simply is immediately" has a different status from "the
knowledge had of it" (p. 80/151), since the object is what it is independ-

---

[13] "For Hegel the concrete is not the feeling or the intuition of the concrete opposed
to discursive thought; it is the result of an elaboration, of a reflective winning back of a
content which sense consciousness, which believes itself so rich and so full, in fact always
allows to escape" (Hyppolite, *Phénoménologie*, I vii).

ently of being known, whereas the knowing is what it is only because of the object—if the object *is not* the way knowing takes it to be, there is no knowing, but there is still the object (p. 81/151). The object, then, is "essential," and the consciousness of it "inessential."

Strangely enough, this distinction, however inadequate it may be as a distinction, contributes mightily to the downfall of sense certainty. Granting the distinction for the moment, one can look at sense certainty and ask: is the object, in fact, there the way it essentially is? The rather obvious answer is, "this" object "before me," "here" and "now," is, of course, the object as it is essentially. Nothing could be simpler (p. 81/151). The matter would seem to be settled, yet even the empiricist consciousness must feel a bit uneasy; it has tipped its hand by using too many unclarified terms. "*Just what is this?*" (p. 81/151). What is *here*? What is *now*?

THE FUNCTION OF NEGATION

At this point one can get the impression—and many critics have—that Hegel is trying to dazzle us with some sort of linguistic sleight of hand. If to the question "What is now?" he says, the answer given is "now is night," *we* (observers) tell *you* (observed) to write it down. That will not affect its truth. But tomorrow, when it is day, the statement will not be true any longer. How can that which becomes untrue be true in the first place? The writing-it-down bit can seem to be a trick, but it is not. Hegel is not saying that a true "now" becomes untrue in another "now"—we ought to presume that he is not being that nonsensical. What he is saying, rather, is that since "now" is true in both cases, the term "now" is too ambiguous to give any positive information about the object in question. "The truth written down," he says, "has become empty" (p. 81/151). In the sense that an "empty" truth is no truth at all, then, the truth of the "now" is untrue; which is not to say that today it is untrue in the same sense that yesterday it was true— as "empty" it is not "true" at any time, and a "now" which is immediate is empty. "The now which is night is *held on to* (*aufbewahrt*—note the play on "wahr," i.e., true), i.e., it is treated as what it is given out to be, as something which is (*Seiendes*), but it shows itself to be rather something which is not (*ein Nichtseiendes*)" (p. 81/151–52); now *is* now only to the extent that it is for a subject who designates it as such, and apart from such a subject it is meaningless.

We have to remember, of course, that for Hegel negation is never merely negative; its function is not *to cancel out* but *to put in opposition to*. Thus, the "non-being" of the "now" is its opposition to another "now." This means that the term which was employed to designate the immediate is itself not immediate but mediated and, therefore, cannot do the job. If "now" is equally applicable to any time I choose to designate, it is indifferent; it is *universally* applicable. "Something so simple, which, through negation, is neither this nor that, a not-this and equally indifferent to being this as well as that, we call a *universal*" (p. 82/152). Suddenly sense certainty finds itself with a universal on its hands: "In fact, then, the universal is the true in sense certainty" (p. 82/152).

The "pure empiricist" may still think that Hegel is practicing linguistic sleight of hand, but he must confess that Hegel (or the empiricist's own consciousness, if he has been following the argument) compels him to re-group his forces. While he is doing so, however, Hegel will continue. His concern, after all, is not to embarrass the empiricist but to keep conscious-ness looking at itself until it finds itself, which demands not only that it admit to not finding itself in sense certainty but also that it *do* find in sense certainty the key to what the next move must be.

What has been discovered in the first attempt to express sense certainty in words describing its content is that words whose primary function is to convey the speaker's meaning to another can also serve to make the speaker realize that there is more to what he intends than he thought there was. His language, in fact, which necessarily employs universal terms, speaks truer than his intending does if he seeks to confine his meaning to the purely individual. Having discovered that his language expresses universally what he was certain he had grasped in its individuality, he is on the point of realizing that only if he grasps his object in its universality, which the senses cannot do, has he grasped it truly.[14] Only much later will he realize that not only the object but also the grasping must be universalized, but now at least he is on the path which leads to that further realization. "Language is, however, as we see, the truer; in it we ourselves immediately contradict our intending (*Meinung*), and because the universal is the true in sense certainty [i.e., it is the true reality of the object the senses present], and language ex-presses only this true, then it is utterly impossible that we can ever enun-ciate the sensible being we intend [i.e., say it the way the senses intend it]" (p. 82/152).[15]

Sensory awareness is limited, then, to the here and now, but "here," as well as "now," are susceptible of such an infinite variety of contents that, by themselves (i.e., unmediated), they are of little help in coming to terms with the content of sensory awareness. The point is that just as "now" is meaningful only as related to another "now" which it negates and "here" is what it is only because it is not "there," so neither has meaning except in relation to a subject for whom here and now are. In this connection the

---

14 Cf. *Enzyklopädie*, No. 20, Zusatz: "Because *language* is the work of thought, nothing can be said in it which is not universal."

15 Because we are completely at the mercy of the limitations of the English language, we simply have no way of conveying either the nuances or the wordplay contained in the single German verb *meinen* (along with its cognates). We have, it is true, three English words which translate *meinen*, i.e., "intend," "mean," and "signify" (although this last more frequently translates *bedeuten*), but neither singly nor all together can they do the job adequately. The ambiguities of the term "intend" are too patent, as are the limita-tions of "mean" and "signify." Add to this that the German *meinen* resembles *mein* ("mine," "what refers to me alone") and, therefore, in Hegel's use of it it has overtones of purely individual (and arbitrary) subjectivity, and the problem of translation becomes insoluble. One is tempted simply to borrow the German term, but that would only add to the confusion. Instead we shall, each time we translate the term, add the German in parentheses. This may help, as long as the reader remembers that, for Hegel, the senses intend (*meinen*) in a way peculiarly their own, i.e., are directed purely to the individuality with which they are in contact.

suspicion might be raised [16] that Hegel is taking advantage of an unpardon-
able solecism in trying to get his point across. If when he asks "What is
now?" "What is here?" the answer is "now is night" or "here is a tree," one
might complain that he is confusing the issue by using the terms "now"
and "here" as though they were subjects of propositions, when in fact they
are adverbs, and the accurate expressions are "It is now night" and "What
is here is a tree." It is true, of course, that Hegel habitually employs grammar in a most unusual way, but he does not engage in solecisms. There may
be better ways of speaking, but what he is saying is "When I say 'now' I am
referring to a particular time, night" and "when I say 'here' I am referring
to what is before me, a tree." What is important is that "now" and "here"
of themselves do not refer to a particular time or a particular object; *I make*
them refer to what they refer. They have meaning (content) through the
mediation of a subject who gives them meaning. All that is left of "here"
and "now," then, is *the meaning we give (unsere Meinung)*" (p. 82/153).

This, then, brings about a reversal of roles in regard to the essential and
the inessential. It is no longer the object which is essential and the knowing
of it the inessential; what is essential is what one *means*, and the object is
not essentially an object until it is *meant*: the essence lies "in the object as
my (meinem) object, or in the *meaning (Meinen)* of it" (p. 83/153). Sense
certainty is certainty after all, the certainty of what I mean; my knowledge
will be true if I know what I *mean*, even if there is no object out there
corresponding to my meaning. This certainty is not affected by the former
conclusion that the truth of sense certainty is the universal, since the universal is the work of the subject who means it.

What has actually taken place is not so much a reversal of roles as a
getting completely off the track, since the certainty is no longer sensory at
all, but is the work of thought. Still, if this certainty is as immediate as
sensory awareness was claimed to be, the subject adding or subtracting
nothing in meaning the object or in being certain of what he means in
meaning it, we are still engaged in the same issue of immediacy. If the
"here" and "now" I mean are the true "here" and "now" and are pinpointed
(individualized) by my meaning them, what could be more immediate? But
the price to be paid for this immediacy is a retreat into a solipsism which
refutes itself, not because it is arbitrary but because the I it posits is that
and only that, an I without content, i.e., not a self, a not yet determinate
object of consciousness, equally applicable to any I and thus remaining a
universal, indifferent to and, therefore, empty of any content (p. 83/154).

Since neither the object side nor the subject side of sense certainty can
establish its claim to be essential, it must now be taken as a unified whole
whose reality does not reside in either one of its parts: "As a result we
come to the point of positing as its essence the *whole* of sense certainty and
not merely a moment of it as happened in both cases, where first the object
over against the I and then the I were supposed to be its reality" (p. 84/155).
Even though neither the object nor the subject turned out to be as im-

---

16 It has been, by Werner Becker in his *Hegels Begriff der Dialektik* (Stuttgart: Kohlhammer, 1969), pp. 114–16.

mediate as this sort of empirical consciousness successively claimed them to be, the whole thing can be called immediate because it needs nothing beyond itself to complete it; it can be quite satisfied with itself. "Thus, it is only the whole sense certainty itself which is convinced of itself as immediacy and thereby eliminates all the opposition which was present in the previous situation" (p. 84/155). This, however, turns out to be not just a form of solipsism; it is the utter solipsism of an I which is "pure intuiting" (*reines Anschauen*) (p. 84/155). This sort of intuiting makes no comparisons, it doesn't speak, it just *points*; it cannot be wrong (p. 85/156).

What we now have Loewenberg calls "gesticulating immediacy," [17] which is an arresting expression but seems to say either too much or too little: too much, if it implies that one can with a bodily gesture point out a "now" as well as a "here"; too little, if it fails to take into account the phenomenon of focusing attention as a kind of "pointing." In addition, it leaves out of account the one *to whom* something is being pointed out, which would seem, since this is a solipsistic position, to be consciousness itself—as it observes itself. Be that as it may, Loewenberg recognizes the incongruity and untenability of intuitive "positing": "How point to an intuited datum without freezing the intuition entertaining it?" [18] What Hegel is doing is casting doubt on the possibility of focusing attention in this exclusive way on the datum of sensation without the focusing's becoming more than "immediate intuition."

EMPIRICAL IMMEDIACY

We can profitably watch the movement as Hegel describes it. (1) I, this pure intuiting consciousness, point out (focus attention on) a "now" which in the very pointing turns out *to have been*; time refuses to stand still. (2) Therefore I affirm that the "now" *was*. (3) What *was*, however, *is not*, so I eliminate the *was* and turn up with a "now" which is not instantaneous and, therefore, not immediate: "Both the now and the pointing out of the now are so constituted that neither the now nor the pointing out of the now is something immediate and simple but rather a movement which has different moments in it" (p. 85/156–57). Any attempt to isolate a "now," whether by speaking about it or by "pointing" to it, is doomed to failure, not only because the term is too general for the task but also because any "now" turns out to be a succession of "nows." Even the isolating "gesture" is a movement corresponding to the designated succession. "Consequently, then, pointing out is itself the movement which expresses what the now in truth is, namely, a result or a multiplicity of interconnected nows, and the pointing is the experiencing that now is a *universal*" (p. 86/157). It should be noted here that Hegel has unobtrusively substituted his own notion of "universal" as *process* for the abstract universal, which is merely a general meaning covering a multiplicity of instances. The Hegelian "universal," of which both the "now" and the experiencing of it are examples,

[17] *Hegel's Phenomenology*, p. 34.
[18] *Ibid.*, p. 35.

does not merely unite a multiplicity under one heading; it is the union of an interrelated multiplicity. It applies to place as well as to time; a multiplicity of "heres" is similarly united in the dialectical process of experiencing "here." Sense certainty, then, which initially presented itself as the isolating of a "this-here-now" object, has turned out to be a process of experiencing an object which is also a process. "It is clear that the dialectic of sense certainty is nothing other than the simple story of its movement or of its experience, and sense certainty itself no other than simply this story" (p. 86/158). What is more, says Hegel, *we* (observers) are not telling this "story"; experience itself, if *we* look at it carefully, tells us *its* story. "The analysis of sense-certainty, the supreme example of cognitive immediacy, is simply the 'story,' as Hegel calls it, of its own inner development or of the implications of its experience made articulate." [19]

We should remember that throughout this discussion what is being investigated is "naïve consciousness," as the awareness of a something which is taken to be external to the consciousness of it. What has come out of the investigation thus far is that sense consciousness does not get at the true being of external things (p. 87/158). The conclusion, of course, is not startlingly new, but the smugness of the empiricists made it necessary to revive an old one. More importantly, the revival was accomplished on the empiricists' own grounds; experience has been permitted to tell its own story, and the story it tells is both an old one and a new one. An old one, because what it tells us is that the truth of sense consciousness, which is universal, is not to be found on the level of sense at all, but only on the level of reflection. A new one, because the telling is the inner dialectic of the senses' own development. For Hegel sensation does not present a content which thought subsequently works on; sensation is the beginning of a *process* which will refuse to stop short of being completely satisfied that it is adequate to its content.

The advocates of sense certainty, however, do not give in without a fight. What counts, after all, are practical consequences. Hegel can cast all the doubts he wants on our ability to get at the true reality of external things, but we can still stick our knives and forks into them (or bang our heads against them). This, says Hegel, is a retreat to the Eleusinian mysteries of Ceres and Bacchus—bypassing even the ancient Greek philosophers—where disputes about the "true reality" of bread and wine are solved by eating the bread and drinking the wine. Who cares about your doubts? This, however, is responding to doubt (*Zweifeln*) not with certainty but with despair (*Verzweifeln*). "Even the beasts are not excluded from this wisdom—rather, they show that they are profoundly initiated in it. They do not stand still in the face of sensible things [regarding them] as being in themselves. Rather, despairing of this reality and completely certain of their nullity, without further ado they set to to chew them up; and the whole of nature celebrates, as they do, the revelation of these mysteries, which teach what the truth of sensible things is" (pp. 87–88/159). Unquestionably a rather heavy-handed way of disposing of the kind of skepticism in which empiricism

[19] *Ibid.*, pp. 38–39.

culminates, but it does make the point graphically that blind trust in the "being" of the sensible ends in despair of knowing the sensible. Even the brutes know what to do with that kind of despair.

What it all comes down to is that those who make claims for the accuracy of what the senses deliver cannot *say* what they *mean* (*meinen*). They *mean* (*meinen*) something out there, completely individualized, only a *this*, but language cannot *say* the this. In fact the proponents of sense certainty do not say it, either. They speak, says Hegel, of "real (*wirkliche*) things, of *external* or *sensible objects*, of *absolutely individual beings*, etc." (p. 88/160), which is about as vague as one can get and serves to pinpoint nothing. "If no more is said of something than that it is a *real thing*, an *external object*, then it is expressed most universally, and what is expressed is much rather its similarity to and not its distinctness from everything else" (p. 88/160). Not only is every "thing" susceptible of being called "one individual thing," so is every piece of paper (or whatever) susceptible of being called "this piece."

What is needed, then, is not a grasp of reality which isolates this or that sense datum but one which recognizes the interrelatedness of a multiplicity of aspects. Any "this" will exhibit a multiplicity of interrelated sense data which must be grasped precisely in their interrelatedness if the "this" is to be nailed down. To grasp the sensible reality in this way is to grasp it as it truly is—to perceive it.[20] When I point to a "here" which is at once many "heres" together, a "universal," [21] "I grasp it the way it in truth is and, instead of knowing an immediate, I *perceive* (*nehme ich wahr*)" (p. 89/160). This, Hegel claims, is not a transition which we philosophers make in treating the cognitive process; it is a transition which consciousness makes in uncovering the implications of its own position.

By this time the reader may well have the impression that we have been unconscionably long-winded in presenting what Hegel himself dispatched much more tersely. But apart from the fact that one cannot dispatch briefly anything Hegel says, a certain amount of prolixity is required because in his first chapter Hegel is setting the stage for much that is to follow. The dialectical movement of Sense Certainty and the transition to Perception constitute, so to speak, the model not only for the subsequent dialectics to be described but also for the overall movement of the *Phenomenology*. More than that, the implications of what is discovered here are very wide ranging and will leave their mark on what we are to see later. The impossibility of expressing (thinking) the immediate or the merely individual will provide the cue for an understanding of the "abstractness" Hegel finds in all immediacy and mere individuality—particularly individual subjec-

---

[20] Once more we are faced with a play on words which simply cannot be rendered in English. The German *wahrnehmen* and *Wahrnehmung* are quite accurately translated "perceive" and "perception"; that is what a German *means* when he uses the terms. The term *wahrnehmen*, however, is composed of the adverb *wahr* (truly) and the verb *nehmen* (grasp). What Hegel is saying, then, is that to *perceive* a sense object is to *grasp it truly*, which is to say, to get at its truth not merely at what it *seems* to be to the senses.

[21] A universal in the Hegelian sense of an interrelated multiplicity, whose unity is not simply that of abstract classification.

tivity—and of the thought process as a process of constant concretization. The impossibility of merely *meaning (meinen)* the universal, on the other hand, will enable us to understand gradually what Hegel means by "universal" and to recognize that the very possibility of a genuine scientific knowing depends on a subjectivity which is as universal as objectivity. Finally, once we have passed the first three chapters of the *Phenomenology*, we may have difficulty in disengaging ourselves from the workings of successive dialectical stages in order to see each one as a "moment" in one large dialectical movement—a difficulty which is only increased when we read most of Hegel's commentators. Only by constantly returning to the beginning to see how all that follows is, in fact, implied here can we retain the sense of unity of the whole.

What the first chapter has accomplished is to shatter the empiricist dream, to show how "unreal" is the attitude which hopes to attain to science while remaining satisfied with a content which is given in sensation. What is crucial to the shattering of this dream is the realization that it is not sufficient that the content *given* in sensation be elaborated in thought—every empiricist admits that—but that in sensation the content is not even wholly given. It is only progressively given as the *Phenomenology* moves on.

3

Perception

ALTHOUGH IT IS TRUE to say that the *Phenomenology of Spirit* is Hegel's presentation of his own spiritual itinerary for a journey which begins with the barest fact of minimal consciousness and continues without pause until the ideal of authentic philosophical knowing—"science"—has been attained, it is equally true that, like anyone else, Hegel does not write a book *in order to* find out how to arrive at his goal. He is describing a journey which he has already made, whose tortuous windings have already been traversed. Nevertheless, he does not take his stand at the goal and then write a book to tell us what we must do to join him at the goal. Rather, he invites us to join him as he retraces the journey step by step and, in the process, discovers that there are aspects of the journey which take on an importance and an amplitude of which he need not have been aware in making the journey for the first time.[1] That is what "science" is all about, seeing all that has to be seen if the journey is to be continuous and complete; that is what makes the book grow in an unanticipated way as he writes it. With each successive step he makes he must retain an awareness of the significance of the step (or steps) he has already made and take care not to lose what has been gained in making them. Thus, although he cannot move at all without negating the adequacy of each step, neither can he lose sight of the contribution each step makes to the overall journey.

We who make the journey with him, then, must be able to see just what has and what has not been negated as we pass from step to step. At the point where we are now, we can see that to be certain of what is immediately given to the senses is not justified, because the senses are given more than they can handle; the singularity of what is given is belied by the universality of its import. What is denied, then, is neither the givenness nor the immediacy of the sense datum, but rather that either its givenness or its immediacy is a cause for rejoicing; neither has the cognitive adequacy it pretends to have. In fact both cry out for a forward movement which will supply what they lack; immediacy cries for the mediation needed to explicate it, and givenness cries for a comprehension which will grasp the "more" which is given—that it be grasped in its truth, *wahr-genommen*.

In making this move Hegel in no way states that there are those who deny that the move need be made; it is, in fact, a move which "sound com-

---

[1] It is, in fact, characteristic of the spiritual journey Hegel describes—or, perhaps, of any genuinely philosophical itinerary—that it must be traveled repeatedly if its true significance is to be grasped.

mon sense" *(der gesunde Menschenverstand)* demands. What he does deny, however, is that those who make the move and are quite satisfied with having made it are aware of what the move implies, either in regard to the inadequacy of what preceded it or in regard to its own eventual inadequacy. Once more, the technique is that of taking a long hard look at the consciousness which has made this move, not only that *we* may observe its inadequacy but that we may see the uneasiness experienced by the consciousness which has reached only this stage.

The subtitle of the chapter, "The Thing and Deception," gives the key to what is going on. Consciousness has become aware that what is present to it on the level of sense is not a mere sense datum—or even a congeries of sense data—but a "thing" exhibiting a number of sensible qualities, and consciousness is haunted by the possibility—or likelihood—of "deception" in regard to this "thing." To say "thing," of course, is to say what is almost as indeterminate as "being"; it is so all-inclusive that it says no-thing. We might, for the sake of being more contemporary, change "thing" to "percept," but in so doing we gain nothing in determinateness. The question is whether there is any way the object of perception, which is seemingly more determinate than the object of sensation, can become more determinate *in* perception. To answer that, we shall have to find out exactly how much more is in perception than in sensation.

PERCEPTION AND REFLECTION

We begin to differentiate perception from sensation when we recognize that the objects of sensation, insofar as it is "immediate," are unrelated sense data—if they were related they would be mediated—whereas perception grasps these same sense data as related to one and the same object, or "thing," and thus as determining it. To what extent perception grasps them as related to each other and to what extent they determine the "thing" to be this particular thing remain to be seen. What is important to note at this point is that perception immediately reveals itself as a more complex way of knowing.[2] We must remember, however, that it reveals this complexity not merely to *us* but also to the perceiver, which it can do only if the awareness of the perceiver has ceased to be directed exclusively to objects "out there" and has become an awareness of awareness, or reflection.

Here it is that the distinction between "for us" *(für uns,* observing consciousness) and "for itself" *(für sich,* observed consciousness) begins to take on a complexity which can well prove baffling as we move forward in the *Phenomenology.*[3] As a distinction between what we are aware of in regard to the consciousness we observe and what the latter consciousness is aware of in regard to itself, it is simple enough. When, however, "for us" and "in

2 "Defunct in the form in which it is made to appear initially, sense-certainty survives as an indispensable element in a more complex way of knowing—namely, in that of perception" (Loewenberg, *Hegel's Phenomenology,* p. 41).

3 Cf. Joseph Gauvin, "Le 'Für uns' dans la *Phénoménologie de l'Esprit,*" *Archives de Philosophie,* 33, No. 4 (December 1970), 829–54.

itself" *(an sich)* are identified, as they consistently are, and when "for it-self" is applied not only to consciousness but also to the object of which it is conscious, things become complicated indeed. The *we* in question, "we philosophers," enjoy a privileged position; we observe what is implicit in consciousness, both in its activity and in its content, before consciousness itself does. Now, what something is implicitly it is "in itself," i.e., the im-plications are there, even if they are not explicitly grasped. Thus, when we grasp what is implicit at any level of consciousness, "we" are aware of what consciousness is "in itself," but the consciousness in question is not (the "in itself" is "for us" but not "for consciousness"). It does not yet have reflective awareness of what is true of itself—its truth is "for another" *(us)*, not "for itself." [4] Later we shall see that, because "for itself" means inde-pendent, i.e., on its own and not in reference to something else, the object (percept) as viewed by itself, not in reference to another object, is also spoken of as "for itself," [5] which complicates the issue even further.

For the moment, however, we can simply return to the implications of sense certainty of which we philosophers were aware and of which experi-encing consciousness becomes aware through its own frustration, in such a way that it *necessarily* moves forward to perception. Having been forced to recognize that its object which presented itself as singular is in truth univer-sal, and is, without further mediation, any and every "this-here-now," con-sciousness also found that it could not take refuge in its own "intending" *(Meinen)*, since simply as intending, that too could not be pinned down and was seen to be equally universal. What it must now find—or develop into—is a form of consciousness which is adequate to this emerging univer-sality. Not only do we see this universality as a principle operative in con-sciousness, but we see that consciousness must become aware of it as neces-sary: "That principle *has arisen in our consciousness (ist uns entstanden)*, and hence the apprehension proper to perception *(Aufnehmen der Wahr-nehmung)* is no longer an apparent apprehension *(ein erscheinendes Auf-nehmen)*, like that of sense certainty, but a necessary one" (p. 89/162). As a result, what on the former level was simply an incidental distinction between the sense datum and the activity of sensing—between passive reception and active grasping—now shows itself to be inevitable in the kind of conscious-ness in question, the perceiving *of* a percept. "With the advent of this principle the two moments, which on the level of appearing merely happen to be separated *(herausfallen)*, have come into being together; the one, namely, the movement of pointing out, the other, the same movement but as something simple; the former the *perceiving*, the latter the *object* [per-cept]" (p. 89/162).

It is, of course, true that the universal is an abstraction [6]—there is uni-

4 Cf. Baillie's note at this point, pp. 162–63.

5 "By itself" might resolve the ambiguity in English, but Hegel reserves *bei sich* (literally, "with itself") for the much greater dignity of designating thought when it is completely autonomous, the activity of completely autonomous spirit, i.e., "absolute knowing."

6 Hegel is here speaking of the formal or abstract universal, properly the object of "understanding," not of the concrete universal which is properly the object of "reason."

versality only in the abstract—but it is an abstraction essential to perception. That the universal should present itself in terms of a subject perceiving
and an object perceived is not essential; it is an attempt to come to grips
with what is essential. "For us, or in itself, the universal as principle is the
essence of the perception, and over against this abstraction the moments distinguished, the perceiving and the percept, are *inessential*" (p. 89/162–63).
If, of course, we take the two as simply an articulation of the universal, then
both together constitute what is essential. If, on the other hand, we take
them as opposites related to each other, then what is universal and therefore essential—at least at this stage of the game—is the percept (pp. 89–90/
163).[7] Because, then, the essence of perception is to be looked for in the
percept, we must look carefully at the percept to see how it presents itself.
When we do, we find that what sense awareness grasped as a congeries of
sensible qualities, each isolated from the other, has turned out to be a
"thing," to which all the sensible qualities belong—in isolation they are
not, strictly speaking, objects of *knowledge* at all. "The richness of sense
knowledge belongs to perception and not to immediate certainty, where
this richness played only an incidental role." [8] Mere sense awareness simply
cannot get at the multiplicity of distinct qualities belonging to one and
the same thing. "The reason is that only perception has negation, distinction or multiplicity belonging to its essence" (p. 90/163). Essentially, then,
the percept is *"the thing with many properties"* (p. 90/163).[9] In grasping
its object truly (*wahr-nehmen*), then, perception puts the sensible qualities
present to sense where they *belong*, in the percept, since properties are essentially properties *of something*. The singularity of the sense datum—the
"this"—has been negated, but the negation has not simply canceled it out;
it has retained it by raising it to a higher cognitive level, that of the universal.[10] The "this-here-now" of sense certainty quickly manifested its cog-

[7] "At this stage of the game" because, as will become evident in the course of the
Phenomenology, for Hegel only a universal subject can be adequate to a universal object.
In the process, however, "universal" will have taken on concrete significance, as the totality
of interrelatedness becomes manifest.

[8] *Das Beiherspielende war.* Once more the untranslatable play on words is obvious and
significant. In the chapter on Sense Certainty, we were told that the movement involved
was an "example" (*Beispiel*) of dialectical movement. Because it is but a minimal example,
however, the richness of its content plays no important part in it, only an "incidental"
one (*das Beiherspielende*). It only *seemed* to be rich.

[9] It seems clear that the only correct translation of the term *Eigenschaft*—at least in
the *Phenomenology*—is "property." (1) It is the exact, literal meaning of the word compounded of *eigen* ("own" or "proper") and *-schaft* which adds the notion "state of being";
(2) it indicates that the quality in question "belongs to," "is owned by," "is the property
of," the object perceived—is not *attributed* to it from outside. It should be emphasized,
however, that the term here does not have the technical meaning given to it by traditional
logic, where a "property" is inseparable from an "essence" and belongs to it exclusively.
That Hegel is playing on this stricter meaning should be clear, too. The percipient is
out to pinpoint this particular percept, not merely the class to which it belongs. Even
though the properties of the class are properties of the individual, no individual exclusively *owns* properties. What was supposed to be an *Eigenschaft* turns out to be a
Gemeinschaft (common to many, both individuals and classes).

[10] Without going into a disquisition on the Hegelian *Aufhebung*, which has been
adequately treated by almost every commentator, we need only point out that its three
characteristics, negation, retention, and lifting-up, are admirably illustrated here.

nitive inadequacy. By negating the "this-here-now" of separate particularities, perception has done away with both separateness and particularity, retained them as united universals, and raised them to the higher level of properties of a thing—negation of particularity of content is not negation of content. "Through the negation of the *this*, the sensible itself is still present (*vor-handen*), not, however, as it was supposed to be in immediate certainty, i.e., as the intended singular (*das gemeinte Einzelne*), but rather as universal, as that which will determine itself [11] as a property" (p. 90/163).

What has now surfaced in the investigation is an object which is the way it is, not because it is intended (*gemeint*) in a particular way, but because it manifests a number of properties which are its own. The properties, however, are universal both because they are to be found in every object of this kind and because each can be found elsewhere not in conjunction with the others; since they do not imply each other, they are indifferent, independent, in relation to each other—a congeries not a cohesion. Precisely because their relationship to each other is one of independence, they are *common* properties. Thus, although in fact they are united in the object under consideration, they do not serve to particularize it. The "thing" of which they are the "properties" is just as universal as they are—whether the object be a totally generic "this thing" or a very specific "this grain of salt" makes no difference—and as that which unites them, it is distinct from each and every one of them; not that the "thing" can dispense with any of its "properties," but it cannot be identified with any or all of them.[12]

In the object perceived, then, we note: (*a*) it is a universal "thing," (*b*) each of its "properties" is universal, and (*c*) each is a "property" of this "thing" without affecting each other—the "thing" is this and "also" this and "also" this, etc. "Thus the *also* in question is the pure universal itself, or the medium, the *thingness* which in this manner gathers them together" (p. 91/165). Perceptive consciousness is now, it would seem, in a somewhat unsatisfactory position. Its claim is to grasp a very determinate object, but if the properties manifested by the object are simply independent (*unabhängig*) of each other, they are indeterminate; they do not determine the object to be this and no other. Only as "distinct" (*unterschieden*) from, and therefore related to, each other can they be determinate and therefore determining. They identify this and only this "thing" only if they are inextricably bound up with each other, and perception, Hegel insists, cannot tell us that they are, precisely because, as perception and only perception, it is in need of further mediation. If perception is to live up to its claim of solving the

11 Somewhat surreptitiously Hegel has here introduced the notion of what is objective "determining itself," as opposed to being determined by the subject who objectifies. This means more than that the "property" which determines the object pertains properly to the object; it means that in *being perceived* the object is actively determining itself to be *what it is perceived as*. This is crucial for the whole of the *Phenomenology*: the cognitive grasp by the subject and the self-revelation of the object are constantly one and the same movement.

12 Hegel is very careful in the terminology he employs. The "properties" are "independent" (*unabhängig*) of each other and of the "thing" which unites them because they are not confined to this conjunction. The thing is "distinct" (*unterschieden*) from its "properties" because as *merely* uniting the many "properties" it has its own self-identity which is not constituted by the *congeries* of properties.

dilemmas of sense certainty, the "thing" perceived, the percept, ought to be the individual object of *this* act of perceiving. "Thing," however, is universal, as is "percept"—or, for that matter, "this grain of salt." Can perception individualize its object? It can grasp a congeries of "properties," but each of these is universal. The inextricable interrelationship of these "properties" might do it, but perception does not grasp this. Ultimately, if the individual is grasped at all—not merely ineffably intuited, which was the last unsatisfactory refuge of sense certainty—it must be grasped as an instance of a class of objects. But perception knows nothing of "instances" or "classes."

The example which Hegel uses to illustrate perception's predicament may seem unduly homely and trivial—as did Socrates' "cobblers and carpenters" to his fellow-Athenians—but it gets the job done. Who, after all, would doubt that he *perceives* "this grain of salt" precisely as it really is? So, let us examine the *perceiving* of this grain of salt; what does it tell us about its object? That it is an object of perception? But that is true of every object of perception and does not serve to distinguish this one. That it is hard, white, crystalline in shape, acrid to the taste? But each of these is true of many other objects of perception and cannot serve to identify a particular object,[13] except through the unique relationship they have to each other in this object. What is more, although on the level of perceiving, consciousness knows that the whole thing is white, hard, acrid, and crystalline, it cannot account for the way these qualities interpenetrate without affecting each other.

The conclusion would seem to be that consciousness still has a long way to go beyond perception before it "knows" even a single grain of salt, and Hegel's homely illustration has made its point. The Hegelian dialectic, however, is never that simple. It is not enough to know that perceiving is not knowing (Plato took care of that part of the argument long ago). Nor is it enough to know that there is a long road ahead—*if* there is any road at all. Consciousness must come to a realization of what is the next necessary step, and this it will do only after it has made a number of unsuccessful attempts to salvage perception. Dialectically speaking, it is the unsuccessful attempts which lead inexorably to the next step. If consciousness were to throw in the towel at this point, it would run the double risk (*a*) of not recognizing that perception is in fact an improvement over sense certainty and (*b*) of never attaining to its own "truth" at all.

It becomes necessary, then, to pause to examine just how much of its own truth perception has grasped. By recognizing that the determinants of its own reflection are part and parcel of its experience of reality, not distortions of it, consciousness has come to the realization that its object manifests a number of truths about itself which are true *of it* and not merely *attributed to it* from outside. (1) It is one "thing," distinct from other things; (2) it has a plurality of "properties" which, as combined in this one "thing,"

---

[13] It might be argued, of course, that only salt has this peculiar acrid taste and this peculiar crystalline form, but the first can be determined only by comparing many acts of perceiving, and the second only by a highly sophisticated scientific procedure, neither of which the act of perceiving has at its disposal.

are its congeries of properties not something else's; (3) these properties are both negative in relationship to each other (many properties of one thing, each property *not* the other) and negative in relation to the same property in other things (one property of many things, each thing *not* the other). It is not being said that on the level of perception consciousness can handle all this "truth" about its object; but this is what has to be handled, whether at the level of perception or on some higher level of consciousness.[14] For the moment consciousness will continue its efforts to handle all this on the level of perception.

When we turn to Hegel's own words at this point, we face the risk of confusing ourselves—and the issue—in an effort to disentangle them. "In the complexus of these moments the thing is complete as the true of perception [15]—to the extent that it is necessary to develop it here" (p. 92/165–66). There are further implications, but they must wait. The "thing" is (*a*) "the indifferent passive universality, the *also* of many properties, or, instead, of materials." [16] The "universality" here spoken of scarcely qualifies as a technical term, but if universality means simply "unity in multiplicity," then the unity of multiple qualities in one thing qualifies. In the first part of the *Parmenides* Plato considered this as at least part of the problem. (*b*) "It is the *negation*, likewise as simple, or the *one*, the exclusion of opposed properties." That the one "thing" in question "possesses" properties necessarily means that it excludes qualities opposed to these—at least at this level. If the grain of salt is white it is not black, if hard not soft, if acrid not sweet, if crystalline not spherical. As far as the "truth" of perception goes, contradictions are inadmissible. Finally, (*c*) "the thing is the many *properties* themselves, the joining together (*Beziehung*) of the two first moments; the negation as it joins itself (*sich bezieht*) [17] to the indifferent and spreads itself therein as a manifold of distinctions; the point of singularity in the medium of constancy (*Bestehens*) radiating into multiplicity" (p. 92/166). The language is picturesquely metaphorical, but it expresses quite clearly the culmination of the "thing's" presence to perceptive consciousness: the indifferent, unrelated presence of the many properties in the "thing" becomes through the intervention (mediation) of negation a cohesion of interrelated properties, all of which together constitute the determinate "thing." Merely as properties they are unrelated to each other and

14 As on the level of sense certainty, so here, consciousness reveals to itself what has to be handled, only to discover that it can do so only on a higher level. This will be true on every rung of that ladder of consciousness which is the *Phenomenology*.

15 At this point one might well find "the truth of perception" more congenial—as does Baillie in his translation—but Hegel employs the term *das Wahre*, and he does so for a reason; the "true" in the perception, i.e., its content, the "thing," is not the same as the abstract quality of its *being true*.

16 Today we could well be spared this reference to the "materials" (matters?) of the obsolete physics of Hegel's day. The point is that, in Hegel's view, it was a physics which attempted to stick to the level of perception and was, therefore, forced to resort to the subterfuge of explaining diverse properties of matter by composing it of subtly interpenetrating "materials"—"caloric," "magnetic," "electric," etc.

17 Ordinarily *Beziehung* is translated as "relation" and *beziehen* as "relate." Hegel, however, uses the term more etymologically as a "drawing together"—or "joining"—of relata. For "relation" (or "relationship") he uses *Verhältnis*.

can be grasped separately; as properties *of* the "thing" they are *related* to (joined with) each other to form a determinate unity (p. 92/166).

This, then, is the way the object of perception is constituted. If perception can grasp its object the way the object manifests itself, it will have come to terms with that object's "truth" (its reality). What follows is an attempt to "take" the object as it presents itself, without additions or subtractions which would deform it; the perceiver is looked upon as a spectator, no more than that. The question becomes: is perception by itself up to it? "Now that is the way the thing of perception is constituted (*beschaffen*); and the consciousness is determined as a perceiving consciousness, insofar as this thing is its object; it *merely* has *to take* (*nur zu nehmen*) the object and relate itself (*sich verhalten*) to it like pure reception (*Auffassen*); what results for consciousness from this is the true" (pp. 92–93/166)—hence *wahr-nehmen*. Having determined how the object is to be grasped if the grasp is to be "true," the dialectic of perception proceeds on two assumptions: (1) that *reception* is the key to accurate grasping; and (2) that perception is in fact reception, where the perceiving *does* nothing. If this is to be a dialectic *of* perception, however, the judgment of the validity of the two assumptions cannot depend on anything extrinsic to perception. Reception will have made it, if the "thing" continues to be "self-identical" (*sichselbstgleich*) in being received. What criterion, then, for the self-identity of the object is to be found *within* perceiving itself? Once more Hegel indulges in a play on words and posits as an intrinsic criterion for the reliability of perceiving–receiving the undeviating self-identity of the perceiving; if the percipient *always* perceives the object as exactly the same, he can be quite sure his perceiving is reliable. Manifestly this will not work: undeviating self-identity of perception might well be an undeviating mistake; and, in fact, perception never is undeviatingly self-identical. Conclusion: receptive perception is deceptive [18]—hence the subtitle of the chapter, "The Thing and Deception"; thing-perception is subject to deception. "Its criterion of truth, therefore, is self-identity, and its relation [to the object] is to be apprehended (*aufzufassen*) as identical with itself"—not unlike the criterion which naïve realism sets up for the validity of perception. "To the extent that a diversified content (*das Verschiedene*) is simultaneously present to this consciousness (*für es*), it is a joining of the diversified moments of its reception with each other" (p. 93/167). It may not add or subtract, but it does connect, and this is a *doing*. "When in this process of comparing [one apprehension with another], however, a discrepancy makes its appearance, this is an untruth not due to the object, since that is the self-identical, but to the perception" (p. 93/167). Receptive perception, then, is not immune to error, and the problem has not been solved.[19]

[18] For once English has an edge on German in the play-on-words department!

[19] It should be noted that according to this interpretation Hegel is not treating discrepancy as a hypothetical possibility but as an observed fact. The *Wenn* at the beginning

We now have to examine carefully just what the experience of perception reveals about itself; "Let us take a good look at what sort of experience consciousness has in its actual perceiving" (p. 93/167). To put it succinctly: consciousness becomes involved in contradictions, which it is unable to resolve.[20] *We*, of course, already know this, but consciousness must have it brought home to it. (1) The object apprehended presents itself to me as singular. (2) At the same time, however, I am aware of a universal property belonging to the object. Universality contradicts singularity and, therefore, my apprehension was *erroneous*. Because the property (*Eigenschaft*) is universal (common), the object is essentially not a unity but a "community" (*Gemeinschaft*). (3) Furthermore, I perceive the property as determinate, excluding its opposite. If that be the case, I was wrong to see the properties joined together in a "community." Simply apprehending properties as properties affords no way of connecting them with each other.[21] (4) The fact remains, however, that there are many properties of one object, clearly not excluding each other, and I was wrong to apprehend them as so doing. The question which this sort of apprehension is incapable of answering is put rather neatly by Loewenberg: "How then do universal qualities of which the percept presents a congeries rather than a cohesion become the specific properties assumed to constitute its particular thinghood?" [22]

To sum it all up: if perception is passive reception, then the series of contradictions attendant on such an assumption bring us back to our starting point in sense certainty. Once more only the isolated "property," and not the "thing" at all, is the object of perception. An isolated property, however, is neither a property nor determinate, since it is property (properly speaking) only as property of some one thing, and it is determinate only in being identified as related to (distinct from) others. What remains is the property as "sheer self-reference (*Sichaufsichselbstbeziehen*), simply sensible being as such, since it no longer possesses the character of negativity" (p. 94/168). What it is not is as important as what it is, if it is to be distinct. Furthermore, consciousness has lost contact with whatever true being its object has: "The consciousness for which there is now sensible being is nothing but an intending (*Meinen*), i.e., it has completely abandoned perceiving and has returned into itself" (p. 94/168).[23]

At this point Hegel reveals one of the most important characteristics of dialectical thinking—or of dialectical process in general. Going back to a previous position can never be an effective solution. Since any position is a

of the last sentence *could* be translated as "if"; we have translated it as "when." The very next sentence in the text seems to justify this.

20 Which, of course, is precisely what "sound common sense" does, and philosophers from Socrates to Hegel have been at pains to point this out.

21 Again, the difficulty is an ancient one: if sense perception is merely passive reception, and different senses apprehend the object differently (e.g., white, acrid, hard), what *unites* the differing aspects into *one* object? Not passive reception.

22 *Hegel's Phenomenology*, p. 44.

23 It should be emphasized that very early in the *Phenomenology* Hegel makes it abundantly clear that a consciousness which does not have the *real* as its object is simply empty; consciousness does not manufacture its objects, it makes them its own.

position in a dynamic process (i.e., not a "position"), it will with equal necessity demand that it be superseded and that the movement continue. We
must, then, go through the process once more, this time avoiding the dead-end
street down which passive receptiveness led us.[24] The alternative approach
is a "necessary" one, precisely because the first one failed; if a perception which in no way alters its object has proved futile, let us try a perception which *does* alter its object. "With regard to perceiving, consciousness
has, we have seen, gone through the experience that the result, what is
true of perceiving, is its dissolution (*Auflösung*) or a movement out of the
true [25] and into a reflection on itself" (p. 94/168). The attempt to locate the
"true" simply in the self-identity of the object had left consciousness saddled
with nothing but its own "intending" (*Meinen*). The time has come for
consciousness to look into itself to see whether the object is there more significantly than as a mere "intention" (*Meinung*). "With this it has been
made clear to consciousness how its perceiving is essentially constituted
(*beschaffen*), that it is not, namely, a sheer simple apprehension, but rather
that *in the very apprehending* consciousness has to be reflected back out of
the true and upon itself" (p. 94/168–69). This reflection does alter the true,
not in the sense that reflection distorts the true and makes it false, but in the
sense that it makes it more true by permitting it to reveal itself more fully.
Even more importantly, mere reception (apprehension), which *does* nothing, cannot correct itself; it is stuck with the object merely *as received*. Reflection can uncover the deception to which reception is prey and thus correct it.[26] "The orientation (*Verhalten*) of consciousness now to be considered
is, then, so constituted that it no longer merely perceives but is also aware
of its reflection on [turning back to] itself, and by itself it separates this off
from simple apprehension" (p. 95/169). The "sound common sense" of mere
perception as merely receptive awareness becomes *involved in* contradictions
of which *we* are aware, but without reflecting on itself it can neither recognize them nor cope with them.

Once perceptive consciousness has turned its gaze upon itself, it can then
justifiably recognize that the seemingly contradictory aspects of the perceived object *are* due to the perceiving of it. "First, then, I become aware
of the thing as *one*, and I have to hold on to it in this true determinateness.
If in the movement of perceiving, anything contradicting this emerges, then
the emerging contradiction is to be recognized as my reflection" (p. 95/169).
This does not mean, however, that consciousness adds to, subtracts from,
or distorts, an object which in itself is statically self-identical. Rather, it

---

[24] Although it does not present any great difficulty here, one of the difficulties which
will crop up again and again in following the dialectical movement of the *Phenomenology*
is that it will repeatedly require going down one dead-end street after another. Not that
a process of elimination is necessarily arbitrary, but it is not easy to see that consciousness
imposes this process on itself. There will be times when we could wish that Hegel had
skipped a few of the dead-end streets.

[25] The "true" as equated with the self-identity of the object reflected in the self-
identity of the perceiving.

[26] Cf. *Logik*, "Doctrine of Essence," where "essence" and "essentialities" are available
only to reflection.

means that consciousness is a medium through which the object is enabled both to manifest contradictory aspects and to unite them in the unity of its own dynamic self-identity. Because we [27] have a variety of senses, we enable the object to manifest a variety of aspects which are in truth its own. "Thus, we are the *universal medium* wherein such moments detach themselves and are for themselves [independent]" (p. 95/170). This makes it possible to see that the thing's determination as one in no way contradicts the many determinations of its relationship to consciousness. "Because, then, we consider being determined as universal medium to be our reflection, we retain the self-identity and truth of the thing as being one" (p. 95/170).

If reflection were to stop here, however, we should still be faced with the irreconcilability of the way something is *in itself* and the way it is *for consciousness*.[28] Furthermore, since both the determinateness of properties and their unification in one thing have been recognized as the work of consciousness, it would be necessary to conclude that in themselves properties are indeterminate and things are, in fact, a mass of unrelated qualities. But here comes the turning point in the whole investigation. Because perception is also reflection, it can focus on the way things are in consciousness and recognize that only because they are the way they are can they be the way they are in consciousness. In themselves neither things nor properties are indeterminate, since to be indeterminate is not to be. If it is true to say that determination comes about through reflection, then it must be through reflection, i.e., by being related to consciousness, that they are determined. Better still, they determine themselves in our reflection. This is not really so difficult to accept if we are talking about sensible qualities—which is what we have to be talking about in relation to perception—since sensible qualities are actually fully what they are only when they are perceived. In a pitch black room where no eye can see, there are no colors; they become colors when they are seen; but when they are seen, they are the colors of colored objects. When the tree falls in the forest, there is no sound; it becomes sound when there is an ear to hear it, and then it is the sound of a falling tree. The "property" which a "thing" possesses it truly possesses, even if that property is fully real (determinate) only in relation to something else. "It is, then, in truth, the thing itself which is white and also cubic, also sharp tasting, etc., or the thing is the *also* or the *universal medium*, wherein the many properties are external to each other, without either touching each other or canceling each other out; and when the thing is so grasped, it is grasped truly" (p. 96/171). Aristotle had said the same thing somewhat more succinctly when he stated that "the sensible in act is the sensing in act." [29] On the level of sense the coming-to-be (actualiza-

---

27 In the present passage the "we" is the we of experiencing consciousness, not the "we" of the philosophical observers.

28 Not to be confused with the *in itself* of consciousness which is identified as *for us observers*.

29 *De Anima*, 3.2, 425B26–27. For a detailed discussion of Hegel's relation to Aristotle in this connection, see Frederick G. Weiss, *Hegel's Critique of Aristotle's Philosophy of Mind* (The Hague: Nijhoff, 1969).

tion) of the truth of the sensible and the coming-to-be (actualization) of the truth of the perceiving are identical. Hegel adds that only because perceiving invokes reflection is this true. Aristotle goes on to say that "the intelligible in act is also the intellect in act," [30] a statement to which Hegel will also subscribe. For Hegel this second statement will have momentous consequences, but only the elaborately articulated movement of the entire *Phenomenology* will reveal what those consequences are. For the moment we can stick with the consequences of the first statement, which are to reveal the direction the movement—of both consciousness and objects of consciousness—must take. At this point consciousness can say only that it is in truth aware of a thing (perceives it), that the thing in truth subsists (endures) as one thing, and that the many distinct properties it reveals to consciousness are in truth its properties. "The thing itself is the *enduring* (*Bestehen*) of the many distinct and independent properties" (p. 96/171).[31]

Gradually the lines of battle are being carefully drawn between those who would hold that the only reality there is is perceptible reality and Hegel, who will ultimately hold that reality, even the reality of what is perceived, is not adequately available to perception. We should not, however, make the mistake of thinking that Hegel is out to impugn perception —any more than that earlier he was out to impugn the functioning of the senses. Just as in the first chapter he did not attack the givenness of what is present to the senses but only the presumed certainty that the given was both immediately and adequately given, so in the present chapter he casts no doubt either on perceptible reality or on the perceiving of it but only on the contention that perception grasps all there is to grasp. He has taken a major step in this direction by showing that consciousness cannot be satisfied with what it perceives unless reflection on its perceiving is part and parcel of the perceiving itself. The employment of certain subterfuges on the part of his adversaries (real or hypothetical) would seem to indicate that they concede the necessity of reflection if perception is to give an account of itself, but they also contend that what is reflected on is wholly given in perception; the reflection in no way contributes to its givenness. Thus, the contention is, the simultaneous presence of *one* "thing" and *many* "properties" or of *independent* "properties" all perceived *at once* in no way argues that the perceiving has anything to do with bringing them together or that perceiving is anything more than passively *accepting* what is given. If this contention seems to involve contradictions, the contradictions can be explained away.

The subterfuges, which were apparently of interest to Hegel's contemporaries, may be of no interest to us today—other subterfuges can always be found—but they are of interest in typifying an attitude toward contradic-

---

[30] *De Anima*, 3.5, 430A20.
[31] The difference between "distinct" (*unterschieden*), i.e., "related," and "independent" (*unabhängig*), i.e., "unrelated" (see n. 12), should be recalled. What Hegel is saying here is that properties are at once related and unrelated, a "contradiction" which begins to make sense. Only later will consciousness recognize that even "independence" is a relationship, which rather softens the contradiction.

tion. Hegel seeks to impugn an attitude which when faced with contradiction will try either to show that there is no contradiction or to explain it away. Hegel, on the other hand, will strive to *resolve* contradictions—or, better still, allow them to resolve themselves. The former attitude is a concern that contradictions *not be*; the latter, that contradictions *not remain*.[32] Hegel, then, has shown that a perception which is no more than passive acceptance runs up against contradictions in what it accepts, contradictions it is powerless to resolve. The subterfuges are attempts to show that if you look at it the right way there are no contradictions. Thus, although it might *seem* contradictory to say that a grain of salt is all white and at the same time all crystalline, i.e., other than white, there is really no contradiction if we say "insofar as" it is white it is *not* crystalline, in which case the qualities become "materials," each of which is co-terminous with the "thing" and none of which interferes with another (pp. 96–97/171).

To our modern ears the subterfuge is too obviously weak to merit serious consideration. When, however, it is translated into "when I consider the whiteness of the grain of salt, I do not consider its crystallinity and thus do not become involved in contradiction," it takes on a more familiar ring—perception can handle everything provided it take things one at a time. But even in "taking" things one at a time, says Hegel, receptive–perceptive consciousness involves itself in contradictions. To see this let *us* look at what consciousness attributes to itself and what to the object in this procedure. We find that it alternates: when it *considers* only the unity, it attributes that unity to itself—its manner of accepting—and multiplicity to the object; when it *considers* only the multiplicity, it attributes the multiplicity to itself and unity to the object. What it comes down to is that both are responsible for both and that to consciousness' reflecting back on itself there corresponds a reflecting of the object back on itself. If this seems like turning the object into a subject, so be it; what it is saying is that the activity which we recognize as reflection on the part of the subject is an activity shared by the object, since the *appearing* of the object and the *grasping* of the subject are one and the same movement, involving reflection.[33] "Thus, by making this comparison consciousness finds that not only *its own* per-

---

32 See Bloch, *Subjekt–Objekt*, p. 117.

33 It is extremely important to note that Hegel's talk about the thing "reflecting back into itself," which constitutes the heart of the dialectic of perception, is not, as it might seem to some, double-talk. No one, it would seem, finds difficulty in admitting that it makes sense to say "the thing appears" to consciousness. It should be no more difficult to admit that when it appears it "manifests itself." Heidegger, incidentally, has devoted several pages to an explanation of how the term "phenomenon" (appearance) is derived from the present participle of the Greek verb in the middle voice (reflexive) φαινόμενον, which means "show itself" (*Sein und Zeit* [Tübingen: Niemeyer, 1953], pp. 28–31). Thus, just as consciousness "turns in on itself" when it reflects on its content, so too the content "turns in on itself" when it progressively reveals itself to reflecting consciousness. That the content of consciousness develop itself, and not merely be developed by consciousness, is crucial to the entire Hegelian dialectic. It is a concept, by the way, familiar enough to artistic creation. The artist is well aware that, as he works on his product, it in turn works on him—he "creates" it, and it "creates itself."

ceiving (*Nehmen des Wahren*) [34] the diverse moments (*Verschiedenheit*) of both *apprehending* and *returning into itself*, but, what is more, the true, the thing itself, manifest themselves in this twofold way. This constitutes a manifest experience that the thing *presents* itself *for the consciousness* apprehending it in a determinate way but *at the same time* deviates from that way of presenting itself and is *reflected back into itself*, or contains in itself a contrary truth" (p. 97/172). What is discovered in the reflection in which consciousness is engaged is attributed to the object as well as to consciousness. The movement which was previously parceled out between the thing and consciousness now becomes as a whole the movement of the thing: "The thing is *one*, reflected into itself; it is *for itself* but it is also *for another*; what is more, it is *something other* for itself *than it is* for the other" (p. 97/172). The "thing" perceived, then, is both itself and other than itself, not as contradicting itself but in a process of becoming all that it is, the unity of its for itself and its for another, both of which are determinations of itself.

Since the "insofar as" [35] of the first subterfuge proved not only trivial but futile, the defenders of the right of perception try another. This time, however, it is a different contradiction they want to get rid of, the contradiction of the thing's being both for itself and for another. As will readily be seen, if they can get rid of this contradiction, they will also get rid of any dialectical movement of becoming in the object, which will make Hegel's whole house of cards come toppling down. These not-so-imaginary interlocutors have consciousness saying "insofar as the thing is for itself it is not for another" (p. 97/172). What does it matter if this leaves consciousness in the skeptical position of saying that the thing itself is not the same as the thing for consciousness and thus that consciousness is effectively barred from access to the thing itself? They have rid themselves of the contradiction, and that is what counts. Shades of both Hume and Kant? Still, what the contention turns out to be saying is that "the thing for itself" *differs* from "the thing for consciousness," and "the thing for consciousness" *differs* from the "thing for itself," which means that the *difference* inheres in each, since, as Hegel sees it, to "differ" is to do something. But since what necessarily differentiates something from something else is its "essence" (what essentially identifies also essentially differentiates), the problem arises as to which of the two is the "essential" thing. This calls forth the most subtle subterfuge of all: since the "essential" being of the thing is quite obviously its being for itself, its being for another is "inessential." But since this being for another is necessary if there is to be perception at all, then its being for another is at once *inessential* and *necessary*—which would seem to be saying that the being of the thing in perceptive consciousness is *necessarily* inadequate to the thing itself, and the devotees of perception have refuted themselves.

Hegel, however, as we have seen before, is not nearly so interested in re-

---

[34] Once more the untranslatable play on words: *Wahrnehmen* (perceiving) is a *Nehmen des Wahren* (taking of the true).

[35] E.g., "insofar as the salt is white it is not crystalline."

futing adversaries—or making them refute themselves—as he is in permitting the implications of a position to unfold. If it is true to say that
the being for itself (independent being) of the object of perception is not
the same as its being for perception, the conclusion could, of course, be
that its being for consciousness simply is not its true, its essential, being.
But since that conclusion makes the process of knowing grind to a screech-
ing halt—any link missing in the chain will invalidate all that follows—
and since it is the very assumption that perception is adequate to itself
which forces that conclusion upon the holders of that assumption, Hegel
will have us look once more to see if the double being of the thing does not
force some other conclusion upon us. If, of course, the distinction between
"essential" and "necessary but inessential" is permitted to stand, there is
not much hope. If, on the other hand, "necessary" involves "essential,"
then what is being revealed here is that the relationship to consciousness
which is essential to the thing as percept is essential to the full (true) being
of the thing. Its being for itself, then, will not be its full being, and it will
develop into its full being—at this level, of course, only relatively full—
in being grasped in consciousness. What has happened is that the "absolute"
validity of perception and the "absolute" being of the thing for itself have
been revealed to be relative and not absolute.[36] The "true" being of the
"thing," then, will manifest itself only in the dialectical relationship of the
thing appearing and the consciousness grasping. Paradoxically enough, arriving at this conclusion has as a necessary condition that consciousness
posit both its perception and its percept as absolute, for it is in the collapse
of the absolute that the relative establishes its position. It will be necessary
to remember this at every level of the dialectic of the *Phenomenology*.[37]

In the dialectical movement of perception at the point where *we* now see
it, the absolute independence of the "thing" is abrogated and its "true"
being made manifest. "It is precisely through the *absolute character* and
what is opposed to it that the being for itself relates (*verhält*) itself to *others*
and is essentially only this *relating* (*Verhalten*). Relatedness (*Verhältnis*),
however, is the negation of its independence, and the thing collapses under
the weight of its essential property" (p. 99/174). It is now necessary to recognize that the thing is not what it essentially is except in consciousness.
"The necessary experience for consciousness," then, that its *being for itself*
which is "an absolute negation of *all* being-other" is in fact a negation
directed at itself, i.e., a *"superseding of itself,"* i.e., "to have its essence in
another" (p. 99/174). The *Aufhebung* of the being-for-itself of the percept
is classic: it is a negation (of independence), a retention (of content), and a
lifting-up (to a level of fuller being). It was accomplished because the distinction between "essential" and "necessary" could not hold water; it turned
out to be a purely verbal distinction. With the collapse of this distinction
the last subterfuge is dismissed, and it becomes necessary not to eliminate

36 "Absolute" here need mean no more than "not relative."
37 "No theme treated in the *Phenomenology*, to put the method's guiding principle in
the proverbial nutshell, can be revealed as relative unless first exhibited as absolute"
(Loewenberg, *Hegel's Phenomenology*, p. 50).

the contradiction in the double being of the thing but rather to recognize
that it is a fruitful contradiction which resolves itself. "With this disappears
the last *insofar as* which kept the being for itself and the being for another
separate. Rather the object is *from one and the same point of view the opposite of itself; for itself insofar as for another* and *for another insofar as
for itself*" (p. 99/175). Furthermore, both the for-itself and the for-another
are seen to be "inessential," because even together they do not express the
full being of the object; the movement must continue.

The result of all this is that the universality of the object of sense, which
mere sense awareness itself could not handle and which required the passage
to a higher level of awareness in perception, is now seen to be a universality
still *conditioned* by the sensible realm from which it was derived. The content of perception is a content drawn from sensation, the only content
which Kant would permit even his "concepts" to have. A universal such as
this is not truly self-identical but enjoys only a "universality *tainted by an
opposite,* which for this reason splits itself up into the extremes of singularity and universality, of the *one* of a plurality of properties, and of the *also*
of free materials" (p. 100/175). Even though consciousness now sees the
futility of such moves, it is still burdened with that which occasioned them,
the heterogeneity of its content. At the end of this dialectic, we can see that
the content of consciousness is a "*being for itself* linked to a *being for another*; but because both are essentially *in a unity,* what is now before us is
unconditioned absolute universality" (p. 100/175). Consciousness sees the
necessity of cutting the ties which bind it to the sensible conditions of its
object's universality, but when it has done this "for the first time it enters
truly into the realm of understanding" (p. 100/175). There the object of
both sensory and perceptive consciousness remains, but stripped of the
sensible conditions which prevent it from revealing itself in its true being.

As long as the sensible conditions remain, conditions of the "this-here-now
thing," the efforts of consciousness to get above them fritter away in empty
abstractions like singularity, universality, an essence joined with an inessential, or an inessential which is also necessary. "These are the powers
whose plaything perceiving consciousness, frequently called sound common
sense, is" (p. 101/176). Because in its attempts to philosophize "sound common sense" is at the mercy of such empty abstractions and verbal distinctions, it has a tendency to look upon philosophy as a waste of time, dealing
only with *entia rationis* (*Gedankendinge*). Hegel will insist, in fact, that
thought does deal with "thought-things"; it recognizes them for what they
are, permitting them to slough off their empty "sophistries" and appear as
the genuine determinations of reality. The point is that as "thought-things"
things reveal themselves as they really are—the thought of being is the
self-revelation of being.[38]

Perceptive consciousness has now reached the point of no return; its object has revealed itself to be universal with a universality which a "perceptive understanding" still enmeshed in sensory reception is powerless to grasp.

[38] Cf. *supra*, p. 65 and n. 33.

This universality is "unconditioned" or "absolute" in the sense that it is unqualifiedly universal, uncontaminated by the weight of singularizing materiality. The object has been so transformed—has so transformed itself —that it now shares the immateriality of a higher level of consciousness, true understanding. Consciousness must, so to speak, raise itself to the level of its own object, which it can do only as the consciousness whose proper task is the grasp of universality as such, i.e., understanding. In making this move consciousness will reveal to itself the folly of seeking to understand merely on the basis of perception, which causes it to waver, now attributing the deceptiveness of perception to itself, now to the illusoriness of things. On the level of understanding it will come to the realization that neither consciousness nor things need be illusory, because the "truth" of one will be the "truth" of the other—up to a point.

The meanderings of the dialectic of perception have indeed been complex; going back over them, however, one sees that they are not confusing if the salient points are kept in view. What had seemed to be certain on the level of immediacy attributed to sensory awareness have proved to be neither immediate nor certain. What are present to the senses have turned out to be "things" endowed with "properties," where the properties at one and the same time characterize things and manifest the things to consciousness. The "truth" of things which consciousness "grasps" (wahrnehmen) is constituted in the properties they manifest. If, however, perceiving (wahrnehmendes) consciousness is no more than a spectator receiving what is presented to it, the contradictoriness of a thing which presents itself as at once one (in itself) and multiple (for consciousness) is insoluble. If, on the other hand, it is the activity of perceiving consciousness which constitutes either the unity of the thing perceived or the multiplicity of the aspects under which it is perceived, there would seem to be a contradiction between the way things are in themselves and the way they are for consciousness— a contradiction which "spectator consciousness" cannot solve. Only if both "things" and their "properties" are at once self-constituting and constituted in consciousness, i.e., if their being as manifesting themselves to consciousness is inseparable from the activity of consciousness in grasping them, will either set of contradictions be resolved. Yet because the identity of self-manifestation and being grasped in consciousness can be realized only on a level of universality where the singularizing materiality in which sense is immersed has been eliminated, only the consciousness whose proper object is the "unconditioned universal," i.e., understanding, can grasp perception's true object.

4

Force and Understanding

TOWARD THE END of his chapter on Perception, Hegel rather unobtrusively introduces a notion which up to that point had not made its appearance and which serves both as a key to what has been going on and as an indication of the next move consciousness must make. What had throughout the chapter been presented as "perceiving" (*das Wahrnehmen*) or "perception" (*die Wahrnehmung*) at this point becomes "perceptive understanding" (*der wahrnehmende Verstand*). Because perception involves a reflection on both the activity and the content of sense awareness, it is not an activity which the senses alone can perform; because in the process of this reflection perception discovers that the "truth" of its object is that object's universality, perceptive consciousness involves a movement away from the sensible merely as sensible, and this movement is a function of understanding. Since, however, on the level of perception the universality of the object of consciousness is unable to sever its ties with the singularity of the sensible, and consciousness is thus faced with the insoluble paradoxes of unity in multiplicity and multiplicity in unity, consciousness must raise itself to a higher level, where universality is unfettered—which is but another way of saying that it is "unconditioned"—and this is the level of understanding properly speaking.

Here it seems necessary to pause briefly to consider the difficulties posed for the English-speaking reader when Hegel's term *Verstand* is translated by the English "understanding." Gustav Müller has pointed out more than once, most recently in a review of Henry Harris' *Hegel's Development: Toward the Sunlight*,[1] that it is the perpetuation of a nineteenth-century mistake to translate *Verstand* by "understanding" (or *Vernunft* by "reason"). " 'Verstand' in Hegel," he tells us, "is *always* 'reason' as defined by formal logic." There is no question that Müller is right; the "mistake" began, as William Wallace pointed out long before Müller,[2] with Coleridge. Be that as it may, we can scarcely be content with repeated circumlocutions, and since no single English term presents itself which can do justice to the mode of thinking which German philosophers since Kant and Jacobi have called *Verstand*,[3] it seems preferable to retain the term "un-

---

[1] *The Owl of Minerva*, 4, No. 3 (March 1973), 1.
[2] *Prolegomena to the Study of Hegel's Philosophy* (New York: Russell & Russell, 1968), p. 267.
[3] Cf. *ibid.*

derstanding" and let the sequel reveal what the term involves.[4] Among other advantages—granting the disadvantages—this will prevent us from following Wallace, in one of his rare lapses, where he refers to understanding as "the systematized and thorough exercise of what in England is called 'sound common sense.' "[5] This term, as we saw earlier, translates Hegel's *gesunder Menschenverstand*, which can be identified with *wahrnehmender Verstand*, not with *Verstand* in its strict and technical sense. As this present chapter unfolds we shall see that *Verstand* is indeed best instanced in the thinking proper to mathematics and the physical sciences.[6] This does not mean, however, that in the *Phenomenology* Hegel will present any exhaustive treatment of all that can be said of scientific understanding; his aim is to clarify it as a level of consciousness to be superseded.[7] It will be important to remember this when we come to Hegel's critique of scientific thinking.

With "understanding," then, consciousness has reached the level of *thoughts* necessarily provoked by the perception of *things*.[8] The thoughts it has come up with "it brings together only (*erst*) in the unconditionally universal" (p. 102/180). This we can call the conceptualization of the percept. Percepts do not explain themselves; nor does perception explain them. Consciousness now turns to concepts, which are its own products; not, however, simply as the work of consciousness but as revelatory of the true nature of things "out-there"—somehow the object of consciousness must explain itself, even its conceptualized self. Now, if it is conceptualized as "unconditionally universal," its universality is in no way affected by the conditions of sensibility, and understanding seeks in the object the suprasensible *more* which is responsible for its universality as conceptualized. Such a *more*, however, since it cannot be perceived, is in the interior of things, and can only be inferred. The concept becomes the tool which consciousness employs in trying to get at the heart of things. "This unconditioned universal, which is now the true object of consciousness, is still present to consciousness as *object*; consciousness has not yet comprehended its *concept* as *concept*" (p. 103/180). Consciousness looks on its concept as *having* an

[4] We shall, in Chapter 6, be forced to do the same sort of thing with regard to Hegel's *Vernunft*, whose translation as "reason" Müller finds equally painful.

[5] *Prolegomena*, p. 267.

[6] Hegel himself has contributed what might be called a technical definition of *Verstand*, which we now take the liberty of translating as "understanding": "Understanding is thinking determination in general, and it is a dwelling in determinations which have been thought. As objective understanding it contains the categories, the thought-determinations of being, which constitute the inner unity belonging to the multiplicity of intuitions and representations. It distinguishes essential from inessential and recognizes the necessity and laws of things" (*Philosophische Propädeutik*, ed. Hermann Glockner, Sämtliche Werke III [Stuttgart: Frommann, 1927], No. 164).

[7] "It must be borne in mind, however, that not the activity of understanding in general is what Hegel here presents but only a special application of it requisite for the resolution of the issues thus far precipitated" (Loewenberg, *Hegel's Phenomenology*, p. 59).

[8] The "necessity" here is quite obviously logical, not psychological or historical. To put it rather colloquially: "Consciousness must take this further step, or else." Loewenberg says it more eloquently: "The necessity, as observed before, is but dialectical, the necessity every persuasion is under to yield the palm of truth to a logical successor in which it becomes transfigured (*aufgehoben*)" (*ibid.*, p. 66).

object for it, not as *being* its object, and so it seeks to find what the concept reveals *about* its object. Because the concept is the concept *of* an object, consciousness can reflect on the concept and thus discover what the object is essentially.

What actually happens, however, is that consciousness does not *discover* an essence in its object; it *posits* an essence as explanatory of the conflicting aspects of the object as perceived.[9] What is thus *posited* is supposed to have objective reality, and with this supposition the dialectic of understanding begins. To anticipate just slightly, then, the overall movement of the dialectic will be a demonstration that the various "beings" which consciousness as understanding will find itself forced to posit in support of its initial supposition will turn out to be contradictory if they in turn are *supposed* to have objective reality. Ultimately, then, objective understanding, in which consciousness does not have itself as object, will have to yield to another form of consciousness which is capable of resolving the contradictions. It should be emphasized once more that in the Hegelian dialectic only if consciousness does in fact *suppose* that the *entia rationis* it posits do have objective reality can they reveal to consciousness that they are its own products and that it must look into itself if it is to find the explanation it seeks.

As far as understanding is concerned, the conceptualized object presents itself in understanding's concept; the object has been conceptualized, the consciousness of it has not, and hence consciousness does not recognize itself in the object presenting itself (p. 103/180). Therefore, it looks for what makes the object to be essentially this object, i.e., the essential unity of a multiplicity of aspects, the "essence" of the object, *in* the object. Having done this it finds that the untruth of both object and consciousness, which still persisted on the level of perception, has been *aufgehoben*. The result is that the "true" of the *Wahr-nehmen* is in the concept, but in a concept which is not yet *truly* concept, i.e., where consciousness is not yet *truly* concept, i.e., where consciousness is not yet truly *für sich*, independent. The essence it seeks is not seen to be its own work but is taken to be something it merely looks at (p. 103/181). Consciousness is, nevertheless, moving forward; it is effectively *conceiving* consciousness. It simply does not grasp what that implies, even though *we* who look on do. The experiencing consciousness does not yet know what its grasping of the object (conceiving) contributes to the being of the object; "the articulated object," which we have called the "unconditioned universal," "presents itself to consciousness as a being" (*ein Seiendes*) (p. 103/181), whose being (*Sein*) is for itself, which is posited as "the very same essence" which is for another, i.e., for consciousness (p. 104/181).

The identity here is not merely formal, in the sense that the object *is* the *way* it is conceived; the universal content too is one and the same. Still, since being *for itself* and being *for consciousness* seem to be two formalities of the same content, the unified content (object) is looked upon as having

---

9 This sort of "positing" is not necessarily illegitimate. It is the result of the sort of "transcendental thinking" which philosophers from Plato to Kant—and beyond—have employed. It is the merit of Kant to have recognized it precisely as "transcendental."

two moments, the moment of passivity in being conceived (being-for-another) and the moment of activity in presenting itself (for-itself). This looks as though the content in question is "on the one hand a universal medium of many subsisting materials, on the other a one reflected into itself, wherein the independence of the material has been canceled" (*vertilgt*) (p. 104/182), and we are back with Kant's sense manifold impressing itself in sensation, only to be united in the categories of understanding —unless consciousness can see the whole thing as essentially passage from one to the other. The essence then is seen as a manifold of elements (*Materien*), each in its being distinct from the others and each coterminous with the whole. In this case unity and multiplicity turn out to be the same in both the object out there and the object in consciousness: the unity of the one object *expanding* into a multiplicity of aspects being contracted into the unity of one concept. But this still leaves consciousness with the problem of finding in the object "out there" an explanation of the movement of expansion and contraction.

Here, it would seem, Hegel is imposing something on the explanation which consciousness is supposed to be giving itself. In his day there stood to hand a notion which was getting great mileage among scientists, the notion of "force" as residing in the physical realities they observed and explaining the activities of these realities. That consciousness should be seen as viewing some such force as explaining the movement whereby a "thing" becomes an object for consciousness seems at best an arbitrary procedure. Still, even granting the arbitrariness of the application, the notion does seem admirably suited to trigger a movement from the sensibility of diversified qualities in perception to the intelligibility of a unified essence in understanding.[10] Equally importantly it permits Hegel to renew a critique of contemporary scientific thinking which he had begun in his dissertation, "De orbitis planetarum,"[11] by pointing out the fallacy of positing the mental entities of a conceptual scheme as though they corresponded to real entities in things. "Force" is precisely one such mental entity, as is the distinction between "force" as a unified source and the multiple "aspects" it is supposed to effect. Science today has no difficulty recognizing that such terms as "thing," "force," "aspects," designate mental entities whose explanatory functions are limited to conceptual schemes, but such was not the case in Hegel's day. Thus, the sort of critique contained in "De orbitis planetarum" may well seem to us otiose; it was not so at the beginning of the nineteenth century. Nor should it be thought that Hegel is denying the reality of "forces"—any more than he is denying the reality of "things" or "aspects." What he is denying is the adequacy of either the terms or the concepts to explain reality.[12] The kind of explanation such mental entities

10 "The only way to explain the particular is to subsume it under some general concept. And force is precisely such a concept with the aid of which an object sensuously qualitied (to use this happy locution) may receive qualified intelligibility" (Loewenberg, *Hegel's Phenomenology*, p. 61).

11 Ed. Hermann Glockner, Sämtliche Werke I (Stuttgart: Frommann, 1927).

12 " 'Forces,' no less than 'things,' are terms of thought, names of reality indeed, but

give is of advantage only if the explanation is not imposed on reality from without—as Hegel claims is the procedure in both mathematics and the natural sciences.[13] What he seeks is a method which will permit reality to explain itself, from within, not on the basis of entities *posited in* it; but the quest for that method is the whole of the *Phenomenology*.

His purpose, then, in introducing the notion of "force" into the dialectic of understanding is not so much to analyze the notion itself as to lay bare the contradictions implicit in the act of positing such "forces" as explanatory.[14] What has in fact been posited, he tells us, is "only the concept of force not its reality" (p. 105/183); the only "being" such a force has is its being-for the consciousness which thinks it (p. 105/183). Hegel is, however, scrupulous to avoid in a "phenomenological" investigation any criticism of a notion based on a position of superior knowledge—the notion must be allowed to refute itself. But the notion of "force" will refute itself only if consciousness posits it as what it is not, as having an independent being [15] of its own responsible for the distinctions which follow from it. One might argue, of course, that consciousness is in no way necessitated to posit such an "independent being"—although one wonders whether it can be avoided without considerable sophistication—but Hegel is saying that *if* consciousness insists on looking for an explanation *in* the object "out there," it is only logical that it should have recourse to a "force" *in* the object.

If we are willing to go along with the contention that consciousness quite consistently passes from perception to understanding along the path of explanatory thinking, we can also go along with the contention that it posits "force" as an independent being, a unitary source of a variety of activities. This, however, immediately implies a distinction between the force and its activity, which latter also has a being of its own.[16] "The force as such or as drawn back into itself," i.e., as distinguished from its activity, "is thus for itself as an *exclusive one*, for which the unfolding of the materials is another *separately existing being (bestehendes Wesen)*" (p. 105/184). What has been posited is *one* independent force; but this has two aspects, its being and its activity. Each aspect, therefore, is posited as not the other, and consciousness itself has posited two entities (p. 106/184).

inadequate because due to an abstraction and leaving their correlatives out of sight— names of momentary elements seized in the flux and made with more or less success to indicate 'moments' and 'factors' or 'aspects' in the total sum and power of reality. Explanation by permanent and separate forces labours under the same disadvantage as that by things. Science, grown more self-critical, begins to see that in forces, etc., it has names and formulae which are not the full reality, but only useful (*if* useful) abstractions. Neither things nor forces, though called real, are so in the full sense" (Wallace, *Prolegomena*, pp. 152–53).

13 See Preface, p. 36/102.

14 "We should realize that Hegel does not analyze the notion of force itself but the act whereby consciousness thinks its object by means of this notion" (Niel, *De la Médiation*, p. 121).

15 The term Hegel uses here is "substance," but its meaning is scarcely technical.

16 The overtones of the traditional distinction between a "substance" and its "accidents" will not be lost on the reader. Nor, if one prefers, with Locke, to abandon "substance" and speak of "primary and secondary qualities" ("powers" = "forces") is one much better off.

This can be quite readily expressed in terms of perception. The percept, as we have seen, is one "thing." As presented to consciousness it manifests a multiplicity of "aspects." If a unified "force" is to be conceived of as explaining this phenomenon, its activity is that of *impressing* its various "aspects" on consciousness. It is just as logical, however—perhaps inevitable—to conceive of consciousness as exerting a "force" which *draws* the aspects out of the percept. One and the same movement is logically conceived in two distinct—not to say contradictory—ways. What is happening is that consciousness begins to see that it makes no sense to think of a multiplicity of aspects as *emanating* from a unitary force, *because* it makes just as much sense to think of the same multiplicity of aspects *being drawn* out by the activity of consciousness. The movement as it presented itself in the dialectic of perception was articulated in a number of notions which contradicted each other and thus canceled each other out. In understanding, the same movement is *objectified* in such a way that as emanating from a single force the various aspects *do not* contradict each other. This is accomplished, however, by positing the "force" as in the interior of things and, hence, as not the direct object of awareness. "The movement, which previously presented itself as the self-cancellation of contradictory concepts, then, has here *objective* form and is a movement of force, as a result of which the unconditionally universal emerges as *non-objective* or as *interior* to things" (p. 106/184–85).[17]

The force thus conceived at one end of the movement as having a being of its own distinct from the unfolding of the elements is seen as the source of that unfolding. Still, as a force whose only activity is thus to externalize itself, it makes no sense except as externalizing itself and, therefore, does so "necessarily." Furthermore, the "externalizing" makes no sense except as a going out *into* another and thus requires the other (the "soliciting" by that other) for what is "necessary" to the very externalizing. Now, since for Hegel what is necessary in this sense is "essential," [18] then the being of the other, consciousness, is essential to the very being of the force. Thus, the externalizing which was posited as other than the force itself has to be posited as the very essence of the force. "In fact, however, because it *necessarily* externalizes itself, it has what was posited as another essence in itself" (p. 106/185). Its outward movement becomes identified with its movement back into itself, and now the only "existence" it can be posited as having is that of "the medium of the unfolded elements" (p. 107/185), that wherein the multiple aspects have whatever being they have.

THE CONTRIBUTION OF CONSCIOUSNESS

What is gradually emerging is a relationship between consciousness and its "suprasensible" object in which the very attempt to posit the force as "out there" reveals that the activity of consciousness is as essential to the "ob-

17 The contradiction between "objective" and "non-objective" here is not quite the dialectical contradiction with which we are becoming familiar. It is the opposition of two senses of "objective."

18 See *supra*, p. 67.

jective" force as is the activity of the force to consciousness. Because this is so, it is seen that the force in question is simply a conceptual force; whatever reality it *may* have has no explanatory value. "Because, then, another is for it and it for another [they mutually define each other], the force has simply not yet emerged from its concept" (p. 107/186). There may be a "real" force, but it is not what consciousness is dealing with here. "Two forces, however, are simultaneously present. The concept of both, admittedly, is the same, but it has abandoned its unity and entered into duality" (p. 107/186). When consciousness tries to find satisfaction in this sort of conceptual explanation, it finds itself with two "independent forces," a soliciting and a solicited, each being what it is only because the other is; hence they are not "independent," which is patently contradictory. Once more consciousness contradicts itself and must move on.

In an effort to move on, the consciousness *we* are observing turns the simple distinction, which had proved inadequate, into a double distinction.[19] If we look at the concept of the movement which force, posited as real, is supposed to explain from the point of view of that concept's content, the distinction becomes that between the "force turned back into itself," having its own independent being, and force as "the medium of the materials," containing all the "aspects" which the activity of the former manifests (p. 108/187). From the point of view of the form of the concept, the force is seen in two distinct *ways*, as a force which acts when "solicited" and as the activity of "soliciting," i.e., from the angles of *passivity* and of *activity* (p. 108/187). Now, from the point of view of content the two concepts are distinct; they are not synonymous, they do not *say* the same things; and *we* can see it (p. 108/187). From the point of view of form, on the other hand, the moments of passivity and activity, which *look* even to *us* as though they are independent of each other, turn out to be not only essentially related to each other; they vanish into each other, i.e., they are meaningless outside a movement which is *designated* now one way, now the other (p. 109/188). What is more, the distinction between form and content vanishes—at least for *us*—because the distinction made from one point of view is seen to be identical with the distinction made from the other—both are different ways of *designating* one and the same (p. 109/188).

The members of the distinctions which have been made turn out to be related to each other not simply as opposites or correlatives which imply each other but as interwoven in such a way that the only being either has is its being "posited" by the other; the op-position of one to the other is precisely that, a *positing* by its opposite number.[20] Thus, the only being

19 One of the best known philosophical ploys in the effort to eliminate rather than to resolve (employ) contradictions is to multiply distinctions. In the dialectical movement all that does is to slow up the process—but no stone must be left unturned.

20 The play on words here is somewhat more subtle than those we have already seen. *Entgegensetzung* means "opposition"; *entgegengesetzt* means "opposed." The *Setzung* and the *setzen* in the two expressions can refer to the act of *positing* by consciousness; they can also refer to the members *opposing* each other. In characteristically Hegelian fashion the terms mean both; the opposites oppose each other, because they are *posited* by consciousness as opposites, and each *posits* the other in being opposed to it.

each has is its being posited by the other, or the *being* of both is the same, since only in the mutual positing is there any being at all—the being of each lies, so to speak, between them (p. 109/188). "Their essence is simply this, to be each through the other and immediately no longer to be what each thus is through the other, precisely in being that" (p. 109/188–89). A rather complicated way indeed of saying that for consciousness to break up the movement of force into an active and a passive moment, a "soliciting" and a "being solicited," is a waste of time, because what results is a difference which does not differentiate. The whole thing is put more simply and more succinctly in the *Jenenser Logik*, where Hegel tells us "The force itself is in truth the whole relationship, and it is a completely useless distinction to characterize (*bestimmen*) the relation as force and to oppose this to its exteriorization." [21] "The content and the form of the appearance are the same," [22] and thus the latter does not *explain* the former. It may be convenient for the purposes of natural science to make such mental distinctions, but that is *not* to enable reality to explain itself; it is to impose on it from without an explanation which does not explain.[23] The concept of force turns out to add nothing to the phenomenon it is calculated to explain. "Instead the concept of force takes its position (*erhält sich*) as the *essence* itself in its actualization (*Wirklichkeit*); the *force as actual* is simply and solely in the *externalization* which at the same time is nothing but its self-supersession" (p. 109/189). The force, then, which has been posited is not *that which* externalizes itself; it is the externalization, and its hiddenness within reality has been overcome.

Understanding, of course, may be correct in inferring the existence of force from the existence of its manifestations, but the truth of that inference is the *thought* of force, not its reality. "The truth of force, then, remains only the thought of it" (p. 110/189). But a necessity of thought on the level of understanding is not only not a necessity of reality; it is the replacement of an assumed reality by a reality of thought. "The realization of the force, therefore, is at the same time loss of reality" (p. 110/189); as essentially a mental being, it is essentially a non-real being. What is left is simply an "interior" of the thing which is but an object which understanding *has* and does not *discover* in reality—it is "its concept as concept" (p. 110/189).

What has happened is the following: the percept of perception has presented itself to consciousness as a composite of many qualities, each of which is universalized and thus exceeds the capacities of perception. Understanding comes to the rescue and takes the many qualities as the multiple activities of the percept, which make sense only if at the heart of the percept there is a force from which these activities flow. But even the flow of activi-

---

21 G. W. F. Hegel, *Jenenser Logik, Metaphysik, und Naturphilosophie*, ed. Georg Lasson (Hamburg: Meiner, 1967), p. 53.
22 *Ibid.*, p. 59.
23 Because all this is the work of thought not yet fully aware of what it is to be thought, Hegel treats this whole matter again at considerable length in the *Science of Logic*, II 144–55. It should be noted that in the *Logic* the treatment belongs to the second part of "objective logic," "The Doctrine of Essence."

ties from the assumed force can be conceived of only as a "play of forces" requisite to get the action going. Thus understanding infers what it does not directly experience. The argument is almost that of a common-sense scholasticism; since *agere sequitur esse* and *esse sequitur essentiam*, one is justified in arguing from *agere* to *esse* and from *esse* to *essentiam*. The whole thing, however, is the imposition of a thought pattern on reality, a syllogism in which reality itself plays no part. A perfectly valid thought pattern which *can be* useful in approaching reality is taken without justification to be descriptive of reality itself.

To get back to Hegel's own words: "Understanding, *by means of this play of forces, penetrates to the true background of things*" (p. 110/190). Midway between the "force" at the interior of things and the understanding which posits this force stands "the developed *being* of the force" which is for understanding only to the extent that it is *not* at the interior of the thing "out there," and so "for understanding itself this [developed being] is a vanishing" (p. 110/190). This play of forces, then, is negative in relation to the reality of force but positive in relation to the consciousness whose product the force, and hence the interior, becomes. "This play of forces, therefore, is the developed negative; but its truth is the positive, namely the *universal*, the object which is *in itself*" (p. 111/190). Penetrating through the movement of appearing, understanding *makes* for itself an "objective interior" (p. 111/190), but "making for itself" is conceptualizing, and the "interior" it thus conceptualizes is a concept—which understanding does not yet recognize as such. "For it, therefore, the interior is quite clearly a concept, but it does not yet know the nature of the concept" (p. 111/191). The only "out there" there is is a conceived "out there." The "true supra-sensible world" over against "the sensible world as appearing" is "on the other side" of the sensible; "beyond the vanishing this side is the enduring other side" (p. 111/191). The object of consciousness as *we* see it is now neither the external qualities of the thing nor the thing in its innermost being but the inference from one to the other: "With this *our object* is now the syllogism which has as its extremes the interior of things and the understanding and as its middle term the appearance" (p. 111/191). For consciousness—as opposed to *us*—the interior of things is simply beyond consciousness; it does not find itself in its object; nor is the object *in* consciousness (p. 112/191).

This sort of interior of things is empty—there just is not anything there —and those who say it cannot be known are quite right; but for the wrong reason. It is not that consciousness does not have the capacity to know it or that, so to speak, it hides itself from consciousness; there simply is not anything there to be known. Its unknowability, then, "is not due to the fact that reason [24] is too shortsighted, or limited, or whatever—nothing is yet

---

[24] It may come as a surprise that, in a chapter on "understanding" (*Verstand*), Hegel should without warning call it "reason" (*Vernunft*)—just as in the chapter on "perception" we suddenly find him calling that "perceptive understanding" (*wahrnehmender Verstand*). It should be remembered, however, that to speak of consciousness at all is to speak of reason which consciousness is to become. At this point, of course, the term is as vague as

known about that; we have not yet gone into it that deeply [25]—but rather from the simple nature of the case (*Sache*), because, that is, in the *empty* nothing is known, or, to put it from the opposite point of view, because it has been characterized as *beyond* consciousness" (p. 112/192). Consciousness simply cannot know what is not *in* consciousness, and nothing has as yet been said to explain how what is *outside* consciousness can be *in* consciousness.

One might, of course, wonder why so much build-up was necessary to get across what seems to be a fairly obvious point: to speak of knowing what is not an object of knowing is nonsense. Yet the point is not so obvious as it might seem. As Hegel sees it, consciousness is gradually coming to a realization that it is nonsensical to look for an explanation of what is *in* consciousness by an appeal to what is outside consciousness. What Hegel is *not* saying is that there is nothing outside consciousness *nor* that it cannot be known. What he is saying is that to talk of the *reality* of what is outside apart from the consciousness of it is to talk nonsense and that an *inference* from what is *in* to what is *outside* gets us nowhere, because what is "out there" cannot be the *source* of what is "in here." The conclusion will be that only consciousness can be the source of what is in consciousness—but the awareness of *how* that can be will be long in coming; whence the necessity of a *Phenomenology*.[26]

Another reason for the elaborate build-up, it would seem, is that "scientific" understanding, with its insistence on its kind of "objectivity," has not yet given up the ghost.[27] It still wants no evidence except that presented by the senses, and it still wants that evidence to tell it what reality is all about. Harried by Hegel, however, consciousness has reached a point where it must change its line of march—without changing its conviction that "objective" understanding holds the solution. Granted, then, that the suprasensible— call it "force"—is not the *source* of appearances; it is the *appearing* of appearances, as long as we recognize that appearing to the senses is not the whole appearing; "grasping" and "appearing," after all, have been identified (p. 113/193). What has disappeared is the existence of a number of particular forces "out there" whose interplay is responsible for the appearing of reality and thus for the grasp consciousness has of it. "Objectivity" still demands that the explanation be found "out there." "The result of all

is the term "knowing" (*Wissen*). That neither term has the fullness of meaning both will later have does not prohibit their use here.

25 We do not yet know what reason can or cannot do; reason itself has not yet told us. The gulf between Hegel and Kant begins to widen here. Kant needs a "critique" which will tell him ahead of time what the limits of reason are; Hegel will simply prepare the ground so that reason itself can tell us its limits—or lack thereof.

26 Hegel's complaint against both Fichte and Schelling was that, having realized the inadequacy of the Kantian formalism which merely permits consciousness to *work up* the materials presented to it, they came to the same conclusion regarding the content of consciousness, but then simply took off from there as though no further explanation were needed.

27 One is reminded that one hundred years later Husserl was to find that things had not changed much—except perhaps that by his time even the "psychologists" were insisting on this "objectivity"!

this is that every distinction of *particular forces*, which were supposed to be present and as such opposed to each other in the movement, disappears, since the forces depended solely on such a distinction" (p. 114/194). If couples of forces exist only because to posit one is to posit its op-posite, there are no couples. "The distinction of the forces, by the same token, collapses with those two into one" (p. 114/194). The explanation is still "force"—"out there"—but it is all one force for whose operations there are "laws." "This *distinction as a general one (als allgemeiner)* is, therefore, *what is single (Einfach)* [28] *in the play of forces itself*, what is true in its regard, and that is *the law of force*" (p. 114/195).

Scientific understanding is now where it wants to be. Admitting that "forces" are mental entities, abstractions which help understanding get at reality, but not themselves real, it now appeals to what are clearly realities, the "laws" which govern the real activities of real things. Understanding does not *impose* these laws on reality, it *discovers* them in reality, and they operate whether consciousness says so or not.[29] The victory has been snatched from Hegel's hands; if he speaks against the "objectivity" of "laws," he will be "unscientific," and that is a fate worse than death. Hegel even makes the case as strong as possible, which to those who know him makes it quite clear that he has an ace up his sleeve. "Now the *suprasensible* world is a *calm realm of laws*, obviously beyond the perceived world, since the latter presents the law only in the form of constant change. Even so, the former is *present* in the latter and is its immediately undisturbed [unchanging] image" (p. 115/195).

CRITIQUE OF SCIENTIFIC UNDERSTANDING

In what follows we should not make the mistake of thinking either that Hegel is downgrading the accomplishments of eighteenth-century science, or, in particular, those of Newton in the seventeenth—he was both familiar with them and enthusiastic about them—or that in presenting his somewhat primitive illustrations he is "doing" science. He is engaging in a critique of a perfectly legitimate kind of scientific thinking which either takes itself to be more than it is or thinks that there is nothing more. He begins by pointing out that the "calm realm of laws" is not adequate to the phenomenon it is supposed to explain. Even granted that the law is "present" in the appearance, there is more in the appearance than the law can account for. If consciousness considers *one* law and not law *as such*, then it covers too little. If it considers a multiplicity of laws, then the sort of determinateness which belongs to a single law becomes an indeterminate

28 Although the term *Einfach* is usually translated "simple," here the implied contrast is with *Zweifach* ("dual" or "double"), and "single" carries the sense better.

29 One of the "discoveries" which had fascinated scientists since the Renaissance, and whose implications were becoming more and more all-embracing in Hegel's time, was the *regula-rity in* nature itself which dispensed with the necessity of a divine *regula-tor* outside nature. The *regular*, then, were "laws," and the whole of nature was subject to them. Science had but to discover and formulate them—always running the risk, of course, of confusing the formula and the law.

multiplicity, i.e., if there is no one law which governs all laws (p. 115/196). If it does seek to group all laws under one, e.g., the law of universal gravitation, then this becomes *one indeterminate* law and says very little. It "expresses no further content than simply *the mere concept of law itself*" (p. 115/196), i.e., that nature is regular, which represents no determinate advance. Moreover, in the concept, its content "is posited as something which is" (p. 115/196). But since law conceived in this way is no more than a *description* of what is the case and not an *explanation of why* it is the case, it has no being "*out* there" of its own.[30] "Universal gravitation says only that *everything is constantly distinct from something else*" (p. 115/196). This is not to say that the law is invalid, only that its very universality makes it too indeterminate to be explanatory, the equivalent of "*all* reality is *in itself* subject to law" (p. 116/197)—a statement important enough, since it abolishes contingency in nature, but which does not get done the job understanding wants it to do. The general law becomes determinate only if we return to particular "forces" in things, but they have already been ruled out.[31] It is common enough, of course, to speak of "laws of nature," but they are in truth no more than the operations of nature translated into concept—a very *useful* concept indeed, but not a *reality* which *governs* nature. The problem of a law "out there" is actually the same as that of an "interior" of things *outside* consciousness. The concept of it would be the opposite of the law the concept posits as existing. "The pure concept of the law as universal attraction must be so taken in its true meaning *(Bedeutung)* that in it as absolutely *single* the *distinctions* which are present in the law as such must themselves *return into the interior as a single unity*; this unity is the inner *necessity* of the law" (p. 116/197). Thus, in being conceptualized that which is supposed to be single is multiplied: the law of gravity has to be expressed in terms of force, weight, time, and space; the law of electricity in terms of attraction and repulsion, or positive and negative, which are simply ways of *conceptualizing* what happens, not the way it *is*. Furthermore, the very necessity which is predicated of law is conceptual, not real. We might put it this way: necessity in relation to law can mean one of three things. (1) Necessity that there be law; but that is too indeterminate to explain anything, e.g., there must be a law governing the rate of acceleration of falling bodies, but that tells us nothing about the rate of acceleration. (2) Necessity that there be this law, e.g., that the rate of acceleration be a function of the square of the distance; but there is no

---

30. "Scientific laws, in short, merely provide us with an orderly *redescription* of the phenomena we wish them to explain, a conclusion platitudinous to us, but not so to the contemporaries of Hegel" (Findlay, *Philosophy of Hegel*, p. 92). We may, of course, at least partly have to thank Hegel that the conclusion is "platitudinous" to us.

31. "A simple association of ideas induces understanding to affirm that the whole movement of the real obeys a single law. Still, this objection of Hegel's does not mean that Newton's law is false. It means that this law is not an explanation. Understanding distinguishes *force* and *law*. Now, if the general manifestations of force, those to which it is confined by the constitution of time and space, deserve to be called laws, then *law* and *force* are the same thing. There is a difference *only* of terminology" (Andler, "Fondement du Savoir," 331).

reason why it could not be a function of the cube of the distance, there is only the *fact* that it isn't. (3) Necessity that given the law the behavior of things will be predictable, e.g., given the law of the rate of acceleration, bodies will fall at this rate, but that is reality necessitating the law, not vice versa.

In any event, either the distinctions without which the law cannot be expressed are distinctions which define each other, for example, "positive" and "negative" electricity, and definition is the work of understanding, not the work of electricity, or the separation of the phenomenon into its elements (parts), such as "time" and "space," "distance" and "velocity," is performed by understanding which then looks upon the elements as each *being* something (p. 118/199–200).[32] What it comes down to is that, since understanding necessarily deals in abstractions, it necessarily holds itself off from the reality to which those abstractions are supposed to give it access.[33] What understanding has taken apart, of course, it can put together again, but both the taking apart and the putting together take place in understanding itself, and the reality with which it is concerned is left untouched; neither the distinctions made nor the synthesis effected is demanded by the reality in question.[34] Granted that both distinctions and synthesis are required by the very concept of law, since "the distinction is not a distinction proper to the matter in question" (p. 119/200), law becomes a mental *mode* of explanation which enables science to *manipulate* reality, not to *comprehend* (*begreifen*) it.

Once again it must be emphasized that none of the foregoing implies that scientific laws are invalid or that a knowledge of them is not significant. The question is whether the laws belong to "things" or only to the understanding which employs them: "In this tautological movement the understanding, as it turns out, sticks to the calm unity of its object, and the movement occurs within it, not in the object" (p. 119/201). Dialectically speaking, however, the recognition that both the distinctions made and the movement of their interaction are the work of understanding itself does not call for a simple return to unity, as though no distinction had been made. The distinctions have been made, but because they are in reality not distinctions, they are canceled out (*aufgehoben*), which is to say they are raised to a higher level of significance (p. 120/202); they tell us little about "things" but a great deal about the movement of consciousness: "Our consciousness, however, has gone from the interior of the object over to the other side of *understanding*, and there it finds the change" (p. 120/202). What was taken to be the "interior of things" is now seen to be the "concept of the understanding" (p. 120/202). The words are retained ("force," "law," "distinction"), but

32 See what Hegel has to say about mathematics in the Preface.

33 "Now, because the activity of understanding rests chiefly on the functions of abstraction and analysis, and because the abstract concepts it brings forth are its most important tools, the activity of understanding shows itself to be essentially an activity of separation and resolution. As will be shown in what follows, the purely formal joining activity of understanding can do nothing to change that" (Wilhelm Seeberger, *Hegel oder die Entwicklung des Geistes zur Freiheit* [Stuttgart: Klett, 1961], p. 292).

34 Cf. Wallace, *Prolegomena*, p. 269.

their reference changes. "The concept experiences,[35] then, that it is a law of appearing itself that distinctions which are not distinctions come about, or that what bears the same name [e.g., "force"] is self-repelling" (p. 120/202).[36] Force is real, and so is the concept of force, but force is not real in the way it is conceptualized, even though it is still called "force." "By the same token it experiences that the distinctions are only such as in truth are not distinctions, thus canceling themselves; which is to say what does not bear the same name is self-attracting" (p. 120/202).

No one can pretend that this is particularly attractive language or that, for our contemporary ears, it is the best way of saying what is to be said. It does, however, illustrate graphically the character of the Hegelian dialectic and distinguish it sharply from the Kantian dialectic. For Kant, the function of dialectic is to uncover illusions for what they are, thus enabling us to avoid them. For Hegel, the function of dialectic is to permit illusions to uncover themselves and, thus, correct themselves. The "concepts" of understanding, then, are quite useful as tools of "scientific" investigation but illusory tautologies if taken as revelatory of the true nature of reality. Still, they themselves reveal that they are illusory and in so doing reveal that they must become adequate concepts, which they ultimately will as thoroughgoing concepts of reason.

It might, of course, seem that having done so well thus far, these concepts are on the brink of becoming adequate concepts of reason—but that too is an illusion. For the moment, in fact, consciousness seems to be worse off than it was before: the "calm realm of laws" which was taken to be an "untroubled picture image" of the world of appearance, the latter's "essential" foundation, has turned out to be nothing of the kind. One world is now the *reversal* of the other. The opposition between the "world of the senses" and the "suprasensible world," i.e., the world of sense and the world of concept, is such that the one is the reverse of the other, *die verkehrte Welt* (p. 121/203),[37] since the relation of name to thing named need not be the same in each. As Hegel sees it, then, understanding has been pushed into a corner, where its own concepts are not faithful reproductions but reverse images of the world as "sound common sense" took it to be. In a letter to his friend van Ghert on December 18, 1812,[38] Hegel puts the matter clearly and succinctly: "To the uninitiated, speculative philosophy, as

35 We should more likely say, "in its conceiving, consciousness experiences," but Hegel avoids such substantive language and, hence, expresses it more dynamically.

36 *Das Gleichnamige*. Baillie mixes things up by translating this term as "what is self-same" and, a few lines later, *das Ungleichnamige* as "what is not self-same," thus blurring the linguistic play. What Hegel is trying to say is "what bears the same name turns out not to be the same thing" and "what bears a different name turns out to be the same thing."

37 It should be pointed out that in German the term *verkehrt* ("reversed," "turned-around") is not synonymous with *falsch* ("false"). When something is seen upside-down, or backwards, it is seen differently but not necessarily falsely. Upside-down and right-side-up can be two true ways of seeing something—but things do look different. A mirror-image is not a false image, but it does reverse all positions and can be *understood* as doing that.

38 *Briefe*, I 426.

regards its content, must simply seem to be the world reversed, contradicting all their habitual concepts and whatever else, according to so-called sound common sense, seemed to them valid." In the *Phenomenology* the treatment of this reversal of meanings is not only somewhat heavy-handed but also confusing, since it lumps together judgments about the physical and the moral world, the theoretical and the practical. It is easy enough to see that the distinction makes sense on both levels if all it is is a distinction between what is the case and what seems to be the case. It goes deeper than that, however, but the complexity not only of Hegel's style but also of his illustrations makes it difficult to see just how much deeper.

The whole analysis begins as an analysis of language about these two "worlds": things designated by the same word in both are different, and things designated by different words are the same. "According to the law of this reverse world, then, that which in the first has the *same name* is [in the second] *not the same* [thing], and what in the second is not the same [thing] is [in the first] likewise *not the same* [thing] [as what has the same name], or it becomes the *same* as itself" (p. 122/203–204). There can be no question that this language is intolerably involuted. What Hegel is trying to show, however, is that, on the assumption of two worlds, of reality and of appearance, words risk losing their univocal meanings—"sweet" can mean "sour," "sour" can mean "sweet"—and consciousness has fallen into a hole it cannot get out of, on the level of understanding; its language— and its concepts, too—have become arbitrary. More importantly, however, under the cover of this rigmarole the dialectic is at work. Only if consciousness recognizes that the "sweet" is also "not sweet," etc., i.e., that speculative thinking cannot be satisfied with merely univocal terms, can it get out of the hole where understanding put it; but this it is powerless to do if all it is is understanding. This is particularly true, because understanding represents the reversed suprasensible world by means of sensible qualities. Of course, the intelligibility of sweetness is not the same as the sensibility of sweetness (any more than the intelligibility of a circle is the same as the sensibility of a poker chip), but this is lost on a thinking which employs only "representations," which is what the "concepts" of understanding are (p. 123/205–206), simply inadequate tools.

None of this means, incidentally, that the "suprasensible world" is simply the "sensible world" reversed; the fact that non-sensible determinations such as "revenge" and "punishment," "good" and "evil," figure in the reversal should make that clear. Rather, it means that a suprasensible world whose intelligible determinations are no more than abstractions from the sensible is a reversal of itself, since its abstractions have not been intelligibly concretized so that it can justifiably be called "the true world." There is nothing in the mere understanding of the concepts sweet and sour, or revenge and punishment, which can guarantee the stabilization of their meaning; they can "mean" what the subject wants them to mean—and we are back, merely on a higher level, with *das blosse Meinen* of "sense certainty." This becomes clearer when the determinations in question belong to the practical, moral order. What is it, says Hegel, which makes an act of revenge evil and one of punishment good if what is done to the culprit in both instances is the same? That, however, would simply mean that one and the same act, sensibly apprehended, would in one case be evil because its purpose is to satisfy the frustrations of the injured party and in the other case would be good because its purpose is to be of moral profit to the criminal —the difference would be in the "intention" of the one acting. The whole point is that, in Hegel's view, we are not dealing with one and the same content and with differences which are attributable only to the attitude of a subject. The intelligible goodness or badness of an act must be contained in the act itself, not merely in the good or bad intention of the one performing it.

Once again, one wonders whether Hegel had to be quite so complicated in his mode of expression. He is dealing with a *kind* of thinking which inevitably comes up against the *kind* of contradiction he illustrates. The question is whether consciousness is to throw up its hands in the face of such contradictions, push them off by opting for one side over the other, or *think* them through in such a way as to resolve them. It is as though Hegel were saying to us: "The contradictions are inevitable; do not try to run away from them, but make something of them." It is not as though opposite positions simply presented alternatives between which a choice is to be made; rather, they are positions which involve each other in such a way that neither makes sense except in relation to the other. Thus, neither is the "suprasensible world" simply the reversal of the sensible nor is the "reversed world" simply not the "true world." The reversal is ultimately indispensable to the intelligibility of any real world, thus entering into its truth. Only if partial truths refuse to allow themselves to be fixed in such a way that they seem to be the whole truth is there any chance of coming to terms with the whole truth at all. Dialectical opposition is essential to the process of thought, since to conceive at all is to "posit" (*setzen*), and every "position" (*Setzung*) implies its "op-posite" (*Entgegengesetztes*), without which it is not conceivable. "For in the distinction which is intrinsic the opposite is not merely *one of two*—that would be a *being* and not an op-posite—it is the op-posite of an op-posite, or its other is immediately present in itself" (p. 124/206).[39] To put it another way, any insistence on one position to the exclusion of its opposite not only risks falsification; it is false by virtue of its very onesidedness. Not only can insistence on what is itself good *lead to* evil consequences; it is itself evil if the insistence is one-sided.[40]

Although we have already seen, both in the dialectic of sense certainty

[39] Those who are familiar with the Fichtean dialectic will see that here Hegel is making good use of it, even though he is critical of Fichte for having failed to exploit it.

[40] Apropos of Hegel's own illustration of revenge and punishment Hans Gadamer has put this very succinctly. "The good *is* the evil. We cannot understand Hegel literally enough. 'Summum jus—summa iniuria' ('The greatest right is the greatest wrong') means: abstract justice *is* the reverse, i.e., it not only leads to injustice but is itself supreme injustice. We are too accustomed to read speculative propositions as though in them one subject served as a basis to which merely another characteristic were assigned" (*Hegels Dialektik*, p. 45).

and in that of perception, that the inadequacy of both does not consist in their inability to accomplish what they are geared to accomplish but rather in the unjustified satisfaction consciousness had that they accomplish all that needs to be accomplished, the point is made so powerfully and so clearly in the examination of understanding that this section becomes a key to the grasp of all further movement in the *Phenomenology*. The abstract analyses proper to understanding had by Hegel's time proved so successful in mathematics and the physical sciences that it was not at all unusual for mathematicians and scientists to be convinced that they had attained to knowledge in the strictest sense. Not only was Hegel convinced that they were wrong; he was convinced that if understanding were faithful it would find that the very analyses to which it owed its success were obstacles to all but a very partial and limited grasp of reality. Because the analyses it makes are extrinsic to the reality analysed, they do not permit that reality to unfold itself in its infinite richness for consciousness; rather, they promote an abstract intelligibility (a "suprasensible world") which is the "reverse" of the intelligibility of a self-unfolding concrete reality—and "objective" understanding of itself turns out to be another dead-end street. "Thus, the suprasensible world which is the inverted has at the same time overreached the other and has that other in itself" (p. 124/207). The only intelligibility it will recognize is that proper to its own abstractions which have replaced reality. "This world is for itself the inverted, i.e., it is the reversal of itself; it is itself and its opposite in one unity" (p. 124/207). It has come to the realization that there is nowhere to look but in itself for whatever intelligibility is to be found. "Only in this way is distinction *intrinsic*, or distinction *in itself*, or *an infinity*" (p. 124/207). For consciousness to do this is to break through the limitations imposed upon it by an objectivity supposed to be outside itself. As we saw before, the *appearing* of reality and the *grasp* of reality in consciousness are one and the same movement; now consciousness becomes aware that it "has taken all the moments of the appearing into its own interior" (p. 124/207); it embraces in itself *all* the op-positions it has discovered and thus knows no limitations, is "infinite" (p. 125/207–208). Having lost all hope of finding the "essence" of its world outside itself, consciousness must look for its world within itself.

What is important in all this is the realization that philosophical knowing will get nowhere if it seeks to bypass scientific understanding.[41] Thus, what at first looks like an out and out critique of understanding as a mode of consciousness turns out to be a recognition of this sort of understanding as an absolutely indispensable stage on the march toward a knowing which is "absolute." As we shall see, when consciousness reaches its final stage of "absolute knowing," it will look back to find that every stage along the way

[41] That Hegel repeatedly insists on the importance of empirical science if the philosophical "Idea" is not to be an empty abstraction may not be too obvious to readers of the *Phenomenology*—especially to first readers. Even a cursory reading of his "Philosophy of Nature," however, and, even more strikingly, his "Philosophy of Objective Spirit," in the *Encyclopedia*, should be sufficient to make his appreciation of the empirical obvious. "Absolute knowing" may know *that* reality must correspond to the "Idea" which Logic has seen as the only rational framework; it is still true that only an empirical observation of reality will evidence this correspondence.

has been indispensable, not only as a rung on the ladder to be stepped over but also as one which must remain in place if knowing is not to lose its foundation, its contact with reality. In particular it will see, what *we* are beginning to see here, that it will have to take into account the accomplishments of scientific understanding or else fall victim to the very emptiness it sought to overcome. If consciousness stops at understanding, as Hegel says it did for Kant, it still has something to be proud of; if it tries to leave understanding out of the picture it has nothing.[42]

Still, if all consciousness achieves is what understanding with its sciences makes possible, too much has been left out. Scientific understanding is like dissection, it is incompatible with life; its abstract analyses destroy life, and only the synthetic activity of reason can revitalize dead objectivity. This synthesizing function of reason, its "concept," as opposed to the abstract concept of understanding, knows no limits and in this sense is "infinite" in its comprehensiveness.[43] "This simple infinity, or the absolute concept, is to be called the simple essence of life, the soul of the world, the universal blood which is omnipresent, neither disturbed nor interrupted by any distinction" (p. 125/208). It is the universal vitalizing force which animates the whole of reality.[44] "Instead it itself is all distinctions, just as its being transcended (*Aufgehobensein*) pulses within itself without moving itself, shaken to its depths without losing its calm" (p. 125/208). The language, admittedly, is poetic, but not more so than that of Aristotle when he describes an "unmoved mover," which at once transcends and is immanent to the whole living world of reality. For Hegel the world and reason are coextensive, because the only world there is is the world which reason comprehends. Of this he will say in the *Philosophy of Right* (fourteen years later), "Whatever is rational is actual; whatever is actual is rational." [45] At

42 Cf. *Dokumente zu Hegels Entwicklung,* ed. Johannes Hoffmeister (Stuttgart: Frommann, 1936), p. 364. "The understanding which, with the help of abstract generalization and the specific concepts of understanding, investigates the forces and laws of nature and, with its categories, for the first time makes possible the quantifying of phenomena has also the additional merit of having created the presuppositions for the development of natural sciences, mathematics, and technology, of which it itself is the constitutive moment. The notions and methods applied by these sciences and by technology are then also without exception the products of developed understanding, and inseparable from all of these is the sharp separation between subject and object. Hence, both the natural sciences and mathematics can quite justifiably be designated properly as sciences of the understanding, even though their validity, like that of understanding itself, is confined to the realm of the finite, within which they are certainly in a position to realize extraordinary accomplishments" (Seeberger, *Hegel,* pp. 302–303).

43 One might well wish that Hegel had employed some term other than "infinity" (*Unendlichkeit*) to designate this conceptual comprehensiveness, but it does serve to sharpen the contrast with the limited, partial grasp of understanding. As we shall see, the comprehensiveness Hegel envisions will demand not only that reality be grasped in the framework of an "infinity" of interrelationship but also that reason be correspondingly "infinite" in its grasp. This neither will be until both the object thought and the subject thinking are "absolute"—one and the same "absolute."

44 Consciousness is "infinite," as Dewey has remarked, because it is "the bond, the living union of all objects and events" (McDermott, *Philosophy of John Dewey,* I 118).

45 G. W. F. Hegel, *Grundlinien der Philosophie des Rechts,* ed. Johannes Hoffmeister (Hamburg: Meiner, 1955), p. 14.

this point in the *Phenomenology*, consciousness is only on the threshold of becoming aware that as reason it is all reality—because in its consciousness of all reality it directs itself (*bezieht sich*) only to itself (p. 125/208).

This is not to be understood as though reason were some higher "faculty" which takes up where understanding leaves off; it is what understanding *becomes* when it becomes aware that it must transcend itself if it is to be adequate to its own content. Understanding is inchoate reason.[46] The distinctions which understanding in its analytic function makes are, it is true, abstract; but the distinguishing it does becomes part and parcel of the movement of synthesis. The function of understanding, looked at in isolation, is the fixation of objectivity in categories, in formal concepts, thus fixing the opposition of one concept to the other. Reason, then, must unite (re-unite) what is thus separated and, in so doing, bring them back to their original truth (and unity) in the absolute, the infinite.[47] This is not to say, however, that when reason steps in, understanding is abandoned; rather, understanding ceases to be merely understanding by transcending itself (*sich aufhebt*) and thus, by consciously entering into itself (being faithful to itself), becomes more than itself, becomes reason. "The distinctions between *being torn asunder* (*Entzweiung*) and becoming identical with itself (*Sichselbstgleichwerden*), therefore, are by the same token simply *this movement of self-transcendence*. For, because the self-identical, which first has to tear itself asunder or become its contrary, is an abstraction or is *itself already* torn asunder, then its being torn asunder is thereby a transcending of what it is and thus the transcending of its torn-asunder condition" (p. 126/209). Analysis is necessary, but only for the sake of synthesis on a higher level.[48]

The awareness which understanding has now come to that the elements of analysis it initially thought it found in the reality analyzed are in fact its own doing is, as we said before, the *beginning* of reason. It is only a beginning, however, because now consciousness must undertake a detailed examination of itself, in order to find out what it is conscious of when it is conscious of itself, before it can become aware that to be conscious of any

---

[46] "From every point of view, therefore, we must avoid separating, as is commonly done, reason and understanding. If the concept is looked upon as non-rational, then, that must be looked upon, rather, as reason's incapacity to recognize itself in the concept. The determinate and absolute concept is the *condition* or, rather, *essential moment of reason*. It is the spiritualized (*begeistete*) form in which the finite, by means of the universality with which it relates itself to itself, ignites itself within itself, is posited as dialectical, and thus is the very beginning of the appearance of reason" (*Logik*, II 252).

[47] G. W. F. Hegel, "Differenz des Fichteschen und Schellingschen Systems der Philosophie," *Jenaer kritische Schriften*, edd. Hartmut Buchner and Otto Pöggeler (Hamburg: Meiner, 1968), p. 6.

[48] "The kind of thought characteristic of a formal deductive system is called by Hegel the thought of the Understanding, a thought characterized by great fixity and definiteness of notions, presuppositions and deductive procedures, as well as by an extreme stress on the distinctness and independence of one notion or principle from another. The understanding, we may say, cuts off the corners of our ideas, all the penumbra by which they shade into other ideas, or imply them without plainly including them; it also checks the tendency of our ideas and principles to shift and transform themselves into other ideas and principles when faced with unwanted cases or questions" (Findlay, *Philosophy of Hegel*, p. 57).

reality whatsoever is to be conscious of itself as reason. Having begun its attempted "explanation" of reality by positing forces and laws "out there," it has now come to the realization that forces and laws "out there" do not make sense. The only way left to turn is back upon itself. "The *explanation* of understanding constitutes at first only the description of what self-consciousness is" (pp. 126–27/210). Still, the consciousness which is just beginning to experience itself in this way is by no means aware of *what* it is going to find when it examines itself. "The consciousness of something other, of an object as such, is, it is true, necessarily self-consciousness, reflection on itself, consciousness of itself in its otherness" (p. 128/211). Consciousness must make itself its own object, but it is not yet aware that in so doing it will be uniting all its objects in the infinite complexity of this one object. "*We*," presumably, see what is coming; the experiencing consciousness does not. "Self-consciousness, however, has just become *for itself*, not yet *as a unity* with consciousness as such" (p. 128/212).

What consciousness will be finding out is that the only "interior" of reality there is is *in consciousness*, i.e., so to speak, "outside" reality. "It becomes clear that behind the so-called curtain which is supposed to hide the interior there is nothing to be seen if *we* ourselves do not go behind it, in order that by so doing we may see whether there is anything back there to be seen" (p. 129/212–13). Not until the entire explanation is transferred from "out there," which is nowhere, to "in here," which is everywhere, will there be authentic knowledge at all.[49]

The transition of understanding to reason, then, cannot be direct; it must pass through consciousness of self. Nor is the latter so simple as those might think who, having become aware *that* it must be done, choose to ignore *how* it is to be done. Self-consciousness is not merely a reflexive consciousness of consciousness which one can put into operation by simply wanting to. It is a consciousness of what it is to be a self, and that demands not only a deliberate effort to get rid of the "objective" obstacles which have accumulated along the way, but also a very elaborate process of development which will ultimately carry the self-consciousness of the individual far beyond itself, allowing it no rest until it is finally taken up in "Spirit." As we proceed, then, "it will turn out that the knowledge (*Erkennen*) of *what consciousness knows* (*weiss*) *when it knows* (*weiss*) *itself* will require still further ramifications. What follows will set these forth" (p. 129/213). Consciousness now knows where to turn; *we* know (vaguely) what it is to be looking for; neither *we* nor consciousness knows what it will find when it gets there—nor whether it can get there.

[49] "Thus, something which is *nothing* but an *interior* is by that very fact *only* an exterior. Inversely, something which is only an *exterior* is for that very reason *only* an interior. To put it another way: because the interior is characterized as *essence*, whereas the exterior is characterized as *being*, then insofar as a thing is only in its *essence*, for that very reason it is only an immediate *being*; or, a thing which merely *is* is for that very reason still nothing but in its *essence*. Exterior and interior constitute determinateness so posited that each of the determinations not only presupposes the other and goes over into it as into its own truth but also each, insofar as it is this truth of the other, remains *posited* as *determinateness* and points to the totality of both" (*Logik*, II 152).

5

Self-Consciousness

IF "WE" PHILOSOPHERS, who stand on the sidelines and watch consciousness in the initial stages of coming to be all that it is to be, can stop for a moment to reflect on what we have already seen, we shall recognize that, with Hegel's help, we have done more than simply observe the dialectical workings of a hypothetical "pure" consciousness as it becomes progressively aware of what is implied in its initial position. Much more importantly Hegel has been giving us a number of significant hints as to what will be going on if we continue to follow hm. Thus, when he speaks of the consciousness we have been observing as "natural" consciousness, he is not merely pointing out, as might any epistemologist, that such a consciousness is "naïve" in its assumptions; he is also telling us that such a consciousness is seen as a function of human "nature," not of human "spirit," and that it is, therefore, not genuinely human—nature is not enough.[1] It is not only for the late Hegel that man is essentially spirit; this is true also for the Hegel of the *Phenomenology*. Consciousness itself, however, as long as it is conscious only of "objects," does not see itself as spiritual; in fact, it does not see itself at all, because it does not *recognize* itself in what it sees. "We" who look on can *begin* to see what being conscious at all involves, even though the extent of that remains hidden from "us" too. "We," then, are beginning to see that any awareness of objects entails an awareness of the self's part in that awareness; consciousness itself is beginning to be aware of itself simply as a sort of center of reference for all its awareness. *What* it is to be this center of reference remains to be seen.

Hegel has also shown us in the initial dialectic of consciousness that a thoroughgoing phenomenology cannot rest content with recognizing dead-end streets for what they are and refusing to go down them; we must accompany consciousness down these dead ends to learn what it learns from them regarding the next move. As the *Phenomenology* progresses, not only will the dead ends become tantalizingly numerous, but we shall have to resist the temptation to skip any of them; each is necessary to the overall movement—they have to be *negated*, not *ignored*. In doing this we shall note, as we have already, that the phenomenological dead-end street is any "certainty" which is inadequate to its own content, or "truth." This will mean not only successively negating certainties for the sake of truth but also making sure not to lose the truth contained in each certainty. It is the fixity of certainty in

[1] Hegel is simply not a "naturalist"—a fact which Marx and Engels saw quite clearly, even though some of their followers do not.

regard to partial truth which is inimical to the unfolding of the whole truth. The relationship of truth and certainty, then, is one of mutual negation; to cling to any certainty along the way is to negate the truth it contains; to affirm the truth is to negate the certainty containing it. Along the way, however, as each certainty is negated, another arises to take its place, and this must be in turn negated if the movement is not to stop and become abortive, and it must be negated in such a way that no truth already attained is lost.

When Hegel, then, tells us at the end of the preceding chapter that the end result of the movement of mere objective consciousness, "for which the true was a thing other than itself," was the realization that the very consciousness of a thing makes sense only as identified with self-consciousness, which is thus the "truth" of all objective forms, he is quick to add that this says very little if self-consciousness does not contain *all* that mere consciousness truly contained (p. 128/212). Now, in the initial paragraphs of the present chapter Hegel will reiterate this in another way by showing that a mere recognition that consciousness must look into itself for the truth of what it formerly took to be outside itself will get nowhere if the *movement* is not accomplished whereby the return to itself is effected and if anything—except certainty—is lost in the process.

It is important to note, of course, that "in the previous modes of certainty" (p. 133/218) it is neither "we," the observing philosophers, nor consciousness reflecting, which *discovers* the inadequacy of these "modes of certainty"; it is the content itself—the "this," the "thing," the "inner" of reality—which, so to speak, bursts the bonds of the mode of consciousness supposed to contain it and presents itself not as an "in-itself" but only as "for another" (p. 133/218), with the result that "certainty is lost in truth" (p. 133/218). There is no way out of this unless the being-for-another of the object, i.e., its concept, itself becomes the object, an object which does in fact "correspond" to its concept—the concept of the concept,[2] an awareness of what consciousness *does* in being aware. "If we call *concept* the movement of knowing, and the *object* the knowing as unmoving unity, or as I, then we see that not only for us but also for the knowing itself the object corresponds to the concept" (p. 133/218). The I is at one and the same time the activity of conceiving and what is conceived; the for-itself and the for-another are one and the same: "I is both the content of the [cognitive] relationship (*Beziehung*) and the [activity of] relating (*Beziehen*) itself" (p. 134/219). The I "center of reference" and the "being aware" are not distinct.

In a very vague sort of way this identity of the I knowing and the content of the knowing can be called self-consciousness, at least in the sense of consciousness of consciousness; and, although this sort of self-consciousness tells us very little, nowhere else is truth to be sought: "With self-consciousness we have now entered into the domain where truth is at home" (p. 134/219). This, of course, is nothing more than what every idealist has recognized: if the gap between the subject and the object of cognition can be eliminated,

2 It should be clear that "concept" here is at the level attained in understanding, i.e., the abstractly universal grasp of a universal object.

then the element of contingency in the relationship can be eliminated too, and necessary knowledge becomes a reality. The question is whether the price which is paid for eliminating the gap is not too high, which it is if the knowing has been emptied of content. It is Hegel's contention at this point that the otherness of the object known has been eliminated, while the moments of the knowing have been retained: these moments are "the being proper to meaning (*Meinung*), the *singularity* with its opposed *universality* proper to perception, as well as the *empty interior* proper to understanding" (p. 134/219). Because these abstract distinctions which are not distinctions of being are placed within consciousness where they belong, they become moments of self-consciousness, and the "inverted world" of understanding becomes the true world of self-consciousness.

If, however, the return of consciousness to itself accomplishes only this, it accomplishes very little; the choice of one "world" over another does little to help knowledge if there remains the lingering suspicion that "out there" is a world which knowledge has not touched. To be aware that all awareness of objects is basically an awareness of being aware is at once too obvious to need emphasizing and too sterile to be of much help—unless it is the beginning of the gradual realization of *what* it is to be the subject of one's own awareness. Perhaps knowing a world which is presumably "out there" just does not make sense except in terms of knowing what knowing is, and that is inseparable from knowing what man *in* the world is, a knowing which begins when consciousness posits itself rather than an alien object as the object of its knowing. To many it can seem to be the most banal of utterances to state that all knowledge is ultimately self-knowledge—that is too obvious to need emphasizing. To say, on the other hand, that self-knowledge is ultimately all knowledge does not seem to meet the same welcome acquiescence, and Hegel is out to show not *that* the latter is the case but that if consciousness is true to itself it will inevitably come to the realization that self-knowledge is all knowledge. The real point, however, is what coming to this realization involves.[3]

It is at this point that it becomes particularly difficult to follow Hegel if the only translation we have for *Bewusstsein* is the English "consciousness" ("awareness" is no help either). The *Sein* of *Bewusst-sein* is originally taken as a mode of being other than the being of the object independently of its being *bewusst*. Even granting, then, that *Selbst-Bewusstsein* always accompanies *Bewusstsein* (Kant's "transcendental unity of apperception"), this position would hold that *Bewusstsein* and *Selbstbewusstsein* are not one and the same, because *self* and *other* are not one and the same. The idealist, however, will claim that the other as other cannot even be the object of *Bewusstsein*, except insofar as *Bewusstsein* is *Selbstbewusstsein*, which means

---

[3] In an earlier essay, "Der Geist des Christentums und sein Schicksal," Hegel had said: "The task is to think pure life [self-consciousness], to get rid of all deeds, everything which man was or will be. . . . Consciousness of pure life [pure self-consciousness] would be consciousness of what man is" (*Hegels theologische Jugendschriften*, ed. Hermann Nohl [Frankfurt: Minerva, 1966], p. 302. A partial translation is available in *Georg Wilhelm Friedrich Hegel: Early Theological Writings*, trans. T. M. Knox and Richard Kroner [Chicago: The University of Chicago Press, 1948]). This does not mean that what man *does* is not important, only that the *doing* is not other than the *being*.

that all knowledge of the other must be derivable from knowledge of the self.[4] Hegel will not deny this latter position; he will simply say that *Selbst*, too, cannot be the object of *Bewusstsein*, except as a *movement* of return to the self from the *posited* otherness of the other.

The danger is that in recognizing that "the return out of otherness" (p. 134/219) is necessary if knowledge is to be truly knowledge, the move is made so rapidly (immediately) that it is no move at all. Consciousness very simply distinguishes itself as object (static) from itself as subject (movement) and then immediately gets rid of the distinction: "Thus for consciousness the distinction as a being-other is *immediately* superseded" (p. 134/219). What this leaves, however, is the "motionless tautology of I am I," which is not self-consciousness at all because it has no determinate content; the I does not know what it is knowing when it knows "I," and from that nothing is derivable. An I completely withdrawn from a world of reality of which it is conscious has no resources within itself on which to draw. The "otherness" of this world, it is true, must disappear, but not all at once.[5] If self-consciousness is to have a content, the distinction between I-subject and I-object is necessary, but merely *positing* the distinction does not provide the content. Just as, on the level of mere consciousness, the moments of sensation, perception, and understanding presented not the reality (*Sein*) but only the appearance (*Erscheinung*) of knowledge, so here "the unity of self-consciousness with itself" (p. 134/220) is only the *phenomenon* not the reality of self-knowledge (p. 135/220).

Understanding, it turns out, was a dead-end street in a more profound sense than was initially evident. Not only was it unable to cope adequately with its own object; it was also the last step in the march of a consciousness whose relation to its object was only cognitive. In its merely cognitive relationship, it found no *means of negating* the otherness of its object and, therefore, no *means of moving* back to itself. If the consciousness of self, then, is to reach the genuinely cognitive level, we must look to some non-cognitive mode of consciousness for a solution to the dilemma; we must turn to what Loewenberg calls "a self-conscious posture below the cognitive level." [6] For consciousness to return to itself and simply relinquish the objective content it has thus far gained would scarcely be a fruitful move; it would, in fact, be the acme of sterility. The key to the return of consciousness to itself Hegel finds in a mode of consciousness which at once retains the objectivity of the object of cognition and aims at the elimination of its otherness, the relationship of "appetition" (*Begierde*).[7] In one sense it

4 Fichte's position.

5 "I" must return to itself, but it must find a *means* of getting there—in its relation to reality—if the return is to be *fruitful*.

6 *Hegel's Phenomenology*, p. 79. The term "below" at this juncture may seem prejudicial, but there is no reason to quibble about it.

7 The term *Begierde* has for the most part been translated "desire" (e.g., by Baillie) which, in this context, seems much too strong and overloaded with overtones. This is particularly true, since at this juncture Hegel uses the expression *Begierde überhaupt*, i.e., "*Begierde* in its broadest sense." George A. Kelly translates this as "appetition," which, in the light of the Aristotelian tradition to which Hegel is indebted, seems appropriate (see his article, "Notes on Hegel's 'Lordship and Bondage,'" in MacIntyre, *Hegel*, p. 205).

might seem too obvious to need mentioning that appetition is a relationship following upon cognition; in another it could seem arbitrary to make this relationship the link between objective consciousness and self-consciousness. If, however, we recall that for Hegel movement always demands negation, and that appetition is a mode of consciousness which does in fact aim at the assimilation and, thus, the gradual negation of its object, we can at least wait to see what Hegel is going to do with it.[8] What is more, if self-consciousness is to be more than an abstraction, posited but not realized, it must be *alive*, and, says Hegel, in the relationship of appetition the object, which in the cognitive relationship is distinct only as *posited*, "is something living" (*ist ein Lebendiges*) (p. 135/220); a vital relationship supplants the dead relationship of merely abstract cognition. This is important: for Hegel there is no such thing as disembodied consciousness. On the level of objective consciousness, it is true, there is no need to examine the sort of being who senses, perceives, understands; these are forms of conciousness which need not be referred to the subject who is conscious. When the subject, however, becomes the object of consciousness, it must reveal itself as a living, organic, human subject, and for this revelation the relationship of appetition is crucial. Appetition not only is the vital function which draws the subject back into itself from the object it contemplates; it also transforms contemplation into action, since only through action in relation to the object can appetition be satisfied. Appetition and action, then, conspire to reveal the subject to itself as a living being. More than that, human appetition will be revelatory of human consciousness as essentially self-consciousness in a way in which animal appetition—or mere appetition "as such" (*überhaupt*) —is not.

Now, just as in understanding we saw that distinction is a prelude to the unification of the distinguished, so here the unity of the concept which unites the distinctions of understanding in self-consciousness "*doubles* itself into the opposition of self-consciousness and life" (p. 135/221); to be alive and to be self-conscious are not synonymous. Self-consciousness is that in which the infinity of distinctions which make up the total interrelationship of objectivity are united: "The unity *for which* the infinite unity of distinctions is" (p. 135/221). Life, on the other hand, is initially at least the simple unity of a concept embracing all living without reference to any individual living being: "simply this unity itself, in such a way that it is not at the same time *for itself*" (p. 135/221), but also not as a merely abstract universal concept; life embraces everything living more than merely abstractly, it

---

8 "Consciousness of self is the truth of consciousness and is, then, a return of consciousness into itself away from otherness; and, as this return, it is a *movement*. But when consciousness of self is only the tautology of I = I, when otherness is immediately suppressed, consciousness of self has also suppressed within itself consciousness and is no longer movement; it is *then no longer consciousness of self*. Consequently, otherness is preserved, being for consciousness of self as the sensible and perceived world (first moment), but it is at the same time negated, and consciousness of self should be through this negation the movement of return to self. That is why Hegel says that here consciousness of self is *desire* (*Begierde*). The object of the desire still *is*, but as desired it is posited as *negative*" (Hyppolite, *Phénoménologie*, I 146–47n5).

concretizes the interrelationship of living beings.[9] The appetition, then, which is awakened by the presence of a sensible object in consciousness would seem to be simply another relationship of the subject to the sensible object. This, however, it only *seems* to be; actually it relates the subject to itself as a demand of life. One can, if one wishes, say that whatever is *alive* has "life," or is organic, or whatever generic term one chooses to employ—provided one realize that in so saying one says very little. "Life" has scant meaning apart from the *experience* of living, and that is not abstractly universalizable. Only a concept of life which concretely embraces the experience of living has meaning in the Hegelian sense. Such a concept is, in fact, concretely universal; it comprehends life as an organic totality.

If being conscious and being alive are not one and the same, which at this point they are not, they are over against each other, "independent" of each other, and the relation they have to each other is through "appetition," a conscious function which serves life. But since the true object of appetition is the self—as alive—and not the object of cognition, which in appetition "is marked with the *character of the negative*" (p. 135/221), in appetition one negates the *object* of appetition and in so doing affirms one's *self*. Self-consciousness, then, becomes a consciousness which has an independent self as its object (p. 135/221). Thus, the self as object of appetition is more than the self of which mere self-certainty is aware; the consciousness of "I" as a mere subject of awareness, the subjective "pole" of the cognitive relationship, is not the same as consciousness of "I" as a living being. This may seem vague enough, but, says Hegel, at this point we can afford to be this vague (p. 136/221); it suffices that consciousness has gained entry into the sphere of life.

More importantly, however, if, as was noted at the term of the dialectic of understanding, what consciousness finds in its experience of the objective world is itself, then the objective world is endowed with what consciousness now finds to be true of itself, i.e., vitality. The totality of interrelationships which is the world *over against* consciousness and at the same time the world *in* consciousness is a *vital* totality, whose "moments" are now to be investigated. What we shall find initially is the vitality of everything in motion, the impossibility of pinning anything down, what William James calls a "booming bustling confusion." It is as though everything had been cut loose from its moorings, and we look in vain for the distinguishing marks of all that seemed so familiar. To put it another way: understanding had by its neat distinctions fixed everything in its place; nothing was out of order. Now everything has been set in motion; by endowing its "world" with its own qualities, consciousness has deprived itself of the right to *impose* order on this apparent chaos; the world of self-consciousness must *sort itself out*. What we have essentially is the "infinity" of interrelationships, with which understanding could not cope, now presenting itself "as all distinctions *having been superseded*" (p. 136/221). If everything is in

[9] Life, as Loewenberg puts it (*Hegel's Phenomenology*, p. 82), is a first example of a concrete universal.

motion, then motion is a constant—filled with inconstancy. There are no fixed categories into which reality can be fitted willy-nilly; the unity of total motion is the unity of self-consciousness, the axis about which all rotates.

Spinoza's "substance" has reappeared, but now as a dynamic totality; it is "independence itself wherein the distinctions proper to motion have been resolved" (p. 136/221). It embraces time and space and, thus, all experience. It is the "universal medium" which understanding was seen to require, but not one in which distinctions are fixed and catalogued; rather, it is a "fluidity" in which distinctions are and are not distinctions, because as interrelations they flow into each other and thus are superseded. The reality which had been analyzed into the independent component parts of a universal whole is now brought together again in the supersession of the independence of *parts* in the mutual dependence of *members* of an organic totality. Still, as independent parts, they cannot be superseded "if they have no constancy" (p. 136/221). The constancy, however, is the "fluidity" itself, a constancy which is not a fixity, wherein everything is at once distinct from everything else, "for itself," and yet related to everything else, each determining all and all determining each. Gone is being as an abstract universal of which each being is merely an *instantiation*. In its place "is that single (*einfache*) fluid substance of pure movement into itself" (p. 136/222), "the *distinction* of whose members *from each other* consists as distinction in no other *determinateness* than the determinateness of the moments of an infinity or of pure movement" (p. 136/222). Thus, "beings" are distinct from and related to each other only as identified in one moving whole—not the abstract whole of the vague generalization "being," but the whole of a totality of interrelationships. If the task of sorting out the relationships is to be, ultimately, the *doing* of self-conscious reason, the preliminary chaos of total fluidity is necessary.

The language, it might well seem, is needlessly obscure, but the organicity it seeks to portray would be even more obscured if presented in the "clear" language of understanding. The independence of "parts" which is at the same time the interdependence of "members" would indeed be unintelligible unless their intelligibility is that of one united whole. This whole is at once one and multiple; only as both (*entzweit*) is it intelligible. It is consciousness, of course, which breaks up the totality into unity and multiplicity, and it is consciousness too which breaks down the duality of unity and multiplicity. "This independence of the mode of appearance (*Gestalt*) appears as *something determinate, for another*, since it is *something doubled*, the *supersession* of whose duality by the same token takes place through another" (p. 136/222). But since, as we have already seen, where consciousness of consciousness is in question, being-for-itself and being-for-another are identical, both the doubling and the transcending of the doubling are the work of the one–many whole, "since precisely the fluidity is the substance of the independent modes of appearing" (p. 136/222), i.e., they are independent only as inseparably united in total movement. "This substance, however, is infinite" (p. 136/222), in the sense that there is nothing outside it to limit it. The identity of what it is for-itself and what it is for-another is not merely posited, as it was initially; it has manifested itself—its very self-identity is its doubling "or the transcending of its being-for-itself" (p. 136/222). The world of consciousness, then, is the only world there is, and to be conscious of the world is to be conscious of consciousness, just as to be truly conscious of consciousness is to be conscious of its world. Much of the confusion here is due to the fact that Hegel anticipates what will become clear only in the light of the whole movement of the *Phenomenology*—whence the need, at the end, of a "Preface."

SELF-CONSCIOUSNESS AS PROCESS

At this point, it would seem, we must stop to take stock: what has emerged from the bewildering complexity Hegel has presented to us? The dead end of understanding consisted precisely in the abstract distinctions and generalizations it made but could not concretize because it stood off from its world and operated on it, so to speak, from outside. Its world was a suprasensible world, but because abstraction had cut this world loose from its moorings, there was no way of telling whether this world was right-side-up or upside down. Only a world endowed with the same capacities of differentiation which consciousness has could straighten itself out, i.e., engage in self-differentiation. Only where consciousness recognizes that the only world it has to deal with is the world which it finds in examining itself will this be possible. What is common to the world of consciousness and consciousness of this world is that both are instilled with life, and what one does the other does. In this sense, however, "life" too is but an abstract term applying to whatever is alive. Only as a *process* embracing both world and consciousness is life concrete. Life, then, is the process which unites consciousness and world; the task is no longer that of standing off from the world and cognizing it; the task is that of entering into the world and living its life. When consciousness does this, it ceases trying to control the world (manipulate it, as science does) and simply lets the world reveal itself.[10]

As a first moment in this movement, "substance" ceases to be, as it was for understanding, the abstract category within which distinctions are made, and it becomes infinite substance concretely embracing the totality of what is, whose distinctions are the organic interrelationship of all that is in both the static unity of space and the dynamic unity of time, ultimately the unity of life as process. "Life, which in the universal fluid medium is a *calm* separation of modes of appearing, turns, precisely by overcoming the anorganicity of abstract substance, into a movement of these same [modes], or it becomes life as *process*" (p. 137/223). The vague "fluidity" becomes other than itself in differentiating itself, and life comes alive in the living individual.

With this, another "inversion" takes place. In the "inverted world," consciousness came to the realization that the "suprasensible world" does not make sense except in relation to another suprasensible world which is the reverse (inverse) of the former. Thus, to the being-for-itself of the world is

10 There is a striking parallel between this and the "being-in-the-world," a having-to-do-with-the-world, as a preliminary to an articulated consciousness-of-the-world, which Heidegger and Merleau-Ponty have made familiar (cf. Taylor, "Opening Arguments," in MacIntyre, *Hegel*, pp. 182, 185).

essential its being-for-another (for consciousness). When the move is made to self-consciousness, this becomes a realization that the being-for-itself of the self, its life, makes sense only as essentially related to its being-for-another. Life which had seemed such an individual thing, universalized only in the vagueness of life in general, now makes sense only as part of a process which embraces all living. "The *unity* [of individuality] with itself, which it gives itself, is precisely the *fluidity* of the distinctions, or is the *universal resolution* of distinctions" (p. 137/223). The individual is individual only as over against other individuals, all in the one process which is life. Here again, just as in the "inverted world" of understanding it was seen that "immanent distinction" is self-differentiation of the object of consciousness, it is now seen that life is that process of "immanent distinction." So too, the "doubling" (*Entzweiung*) between the whole as one and the whole as multiple, a doubling which is transcended in interrelatedness, we now see as a multiplying, which begins as a "doubling" of living individuals, setting them over against each other in a relationship of complementarity without which the life process does not go on. "The single (*einfache*) substance of life, then, is the doubling of itself into modes of appearing and at the same time the resolution of these constant distinctions; and the resolution of the duality is itself a doubling or an articulation" (pp. 137–38/223).

We now see that the vaguely universal "life" which is shared by all living beings is more significantly a process which concretely embraces all. It is also a process in each individual who thereby shares in the universal process. Life, it is true, is actual only in living individuals, but living individuals are actual only as related to other living individuals. Life, then, is not simply a universal essence, nor is it any individual instantiation. It is not the process of instantiation, nor is it simply the sum total of living beings; "but the totality which develops itself, resolves the development, and in this movement maintains itself as single" (p. 138/224). This is the thoroughly interrelated totality.

The movement is a familiar one; it is on the level of life what the play of forces was on the level of abstract understanding. Beginning with an original unity, the movement expands in two moments of manifestation (*Gestaltung*) which are then reunited into a second unity—distinguishing in order to unite. The second unity, "a reflected unity," is not simply the same as the first; it is a unity articulated in consciousness. Thus, the first unity, the unity of universality, "does not exist" (*existiert nicht*) in its simple form; "rather, in this *result* life points to what is other than itself, namely to consciousness, for which it is as this unity, or as genus (*Gattung*)" (p. 138/224). Self-consciousness, then, which initially had only the pure "I" as its object, is now seen as the all-embracing genus, the constantly self-developing, self-enriching totality.

Up to this point "we," the philosophers, have seen what the development must be if consciousness is to make sense out of itself and, thus, out of its world. Now we have to look at consciousness to see how it experiences this same development. "In its experience, which is now to be observed, this

abstract object will for consciousness enrich itself and attain to the unfolding which we have seen in life" (p. 138/225). Not only, however, has consciousness not experienced this; its experience would seem to militate against
it. The individual consciousness—and this is the way consciousness "exists"
—has experienced life only as its own (natural existential solipsism). A
condition for its own self-certainty is that it negate the other; the very
positing of the ego is a negating of the non-ego. A condition, then, for
consciousness' being *certain* of itself as its own object is the nullifying of
the independence of any other object, and we are back with the relationship
of "appetition," which seeks to affirm the self by consuming the other
(p. 139/225). In terms of experience, however, this means experiencing the
independence of that other, since only what is can be canceled out. What is
more, self-consciousness simply as a form of consciousness is incapable of
canceling anything out; instead, the very attempt to do so affirms the reality
of the other, which is true also of the relationship of appetition. "Self-
consciousness, then, cannot by its negative orientation (*Beziehung*) cancel
the other out; instead, therefore, it produces it again, as does appetition"
(p. 139/225). In its essence, in fact, appetition is not the same as self-
consciousness, and so its canceling relationship to the independent object
must also be different. If its self-affirmation demands the negation of the
object, and the object is independent, then the object must negate itself.
But the only kind of object which can do that is another consciousness. In
other words, in affirming itself self-consciousness does not relate itself negatively to any and every object but only to such as can itself negate, i.e. another consciousness.

Very subtly now the object of appetition turns out not to be a thing at
all—it is not, for example, food which hunger wants; it is the satisfaction
which the consumption of food brings. Ultimately, then, life is the object
of appetition, and the kind of negation involved in this relationship of
appetition to life is either in the appetition itself, i.e., as distinct from self-
consciousness' determining what is otherwise indifferent, or it is in a sort
of universalizing of conscious life, as opposed to the life of any organism as
such. This last sort of life, however, is what is proper to self-consciousness,
and so the other which stands over against self-consciousness in negative
relation is another self-consciousness: "Self-consciousness attains its satisfaction only in another self-consciousness" (p. 139/226). We might note that
here, as in all previous dialectics, movement to a new level of awareness is
demanded by the destruction of satisfaction in mere self-certainty; if this
"certainty" is to become "true," another self is needed. The affirmation of
life which is essential to self-consciousness cannot be the affirmation of one's
own life alone.

We can now distinguish three "moments" in the movement of self-
consciousness. (1) There is the mere undifferentiated I of which consciousness is immediately aware by the very fact of being aware of any object; it is
I who am aware. (2) Where the object becomes an object of appetition, the
very appetition mediates a reflection of consciousness on itself as more than
a mere vague I, on a self negatively related to its object, a self which is the

true content of merely immediate *certainty* (p. 140/226). (3) This reflection reveals more than the one self of which consciousness is conscious, because there is for it an object which not only is independent as other than consciousness but posits its own independence by its negative relation to another; the kind of independence which belongs to this object of consciousness is the independence of self-consciousness, without which "independence" is actually meaningless. The result is another self-consciousness of which can be said all that is said of the initial self-consciousness: "it is for itself genus (*Gattung*), universal fluidity contained in its own separate self; it is a living self-consciousness" (p. 140/226).

For self-consciousness to be meaningful, it must be at once subject and object of its own concept. The object of a concept, however, is universal, and the mere I of which consciousness is initially certain is not even an object in this sense. As an object of appetition, on the other hand, the I is merely objective, in the sense of being independent of the subject, but it is not as such subject, only a "universal inerradicable (*unvertilgbare*) substance, the fluid, self-identical, essential reality" (p. 140/227), i.e., it is objectively but not subjectively universal. With this notion of subjective universality's corresponding to objective universality, we already have before us the concept of spirit, but as yet scarcely recognizable as such. Little more can be said of it at this point than that a self-consciousness such as this cannot be merely individual. Once more, we who look on can see that an objective universality which is no more than the product of an individual consciousness, for which universality is necessarily abstract, can in no significant sense pertain to self-consciousness. The consciousness which is experiencing itself, however, is merely on the threshold not only of realizing *that* self-consciousness has to be a unity of "different self-consciousnesses, each for itself . . . an *I* which is *we*, and a *we* which is *I*" (p. 140/227), but also of becoming just that, namely, spirit. Only as spirit will it be able to overcome, by reconciling, the sensible immediacy of empirical consciousness and the abstract universality of a suprasensible world "out there." "Only in the concept of spirit does consciousness find its turning point, enabling it to emerge from the multi-colored illusion of sensible immediacy and from the empty night of suprasensible remoteness and enter into the spiritual daylight of the present" (p. 140/227). But, once again, there is a long way to go— forward, not backward. Only in the forward movement will the almost intolerable complexities of this introductory section sort themselves out.

A. DOMINATION AND SERVITUDE [11]

Up to this point, the "phenomenology" in which Hegel has been engaging us has not been strictly speaking a "phenomenology of spirit." The con-

[11] Heretofore all subdivisions in the text have been my own, not Hegel's. From now on there will be two kinds of subdivisions: those which Hegel himself makes and those which I introduce. To keep them distinct my own subtitles will be bracketed; Hegel's will not. Occasionally, however—and this will be noted—Hegel's rather cumbersome subtitles will be re-worded. The whole present chapter heading, for example, is "The Truth of Self-Certainty," and the first subsection is entitled "Independence and Dependence of Self-Consciousness; Domination and Servitude."

sciousness we have been observing has been presumed to be merely natural, and in the Hegelian vocabulary the term "natural" is the diametric opposite of "spiritual." That is natural in man which is *given* by the fact that he is the kind of biological organism he is. In this sense consciousness is one of the functions of that organism—unique to it, of course—which can be examined the way any other natural function can be examined. There are, it is true, differences which appear right from the very beginning of the examination: consciousness has a relationship to its environment which is different from any relationship of an organism as such to its environment; it objectifies the environment; it makes the environment its own without consuming it; it can examine its own functions in a way in which no mere organism can; its development is more than merely organic. Nevertheless, up to the present it has not been observed to be doing other than "what comes naturally"; in observing itself it has not done anything to itself, any more than in merely observing its environment it does anything to that environment. When its relationship to its environment ceases to be one of mere objectification and becomes one of appetition, however, its relationship to itself changes too. In the realization that it could not find the truth of its objective world outside itself, it had turned back to itself and looked for that truth in a simple objectification of itself. It soon found out, however, that to have itself merely as an object was not to come to terms with itself as itself, since its own doing is not the doing proper to a mere object. It came to the further realization, then, that to objectify itself as its true self it had to do something *to* itself—but this it could not do all *by* itself. If it was, so to speak, to objectify selfness, it had to "selfify" objectivity, which is to say it had to have over against itself an object which was also a self.

Thus, unlike the Husserlian phenomenology of intersubjectivity which first discovers the self and then seeks to "constitute" a world of other selves, the Hegelian phenomenology finds that other selves are essential to the discovery of one's own self and that this "discovery" is actually a producing of oneself in relation to others. Just as, in the dialectic of understanding, the very concept of force was seen to make no sense except in the reduplication of forces as "soliciting" and "solicited" and in the relationship of these opposing forces, so now the very concept of self is seen to require a reduplication and a relationship of opposing selves. The Hegelian self, then, cannot be simply posited as an object of its own observation; it must produce itself by its own activity, and this it can do only through the mediating activity of other selves which, as selves, also require the same mediating activity. Only in a community of selves, then, is self-consciousness possible; but community is a "spiritual" not a "natural" framework, and "self-production" is a spiritual not a natural activity.

That Hegel should see the dialectic of self-consciousness as necessarily involving more than one consciousness of self would seem, then, to make a great deal of sense. That the initial stage of that dialectic should be expressed in terms of the relationship of a lord and a slave—or, more abstractly, of "domination and servitude"—however, can seem to the reader of only the *Phenomenology* somewhat arbitrary. There is no question that the dialectic as here described admirably illustrates the characteristic features of the dialectical relationship. Nor is there any question that, historically speaking, as Marx was to point out,[12] the dialectic Hegel presents admirably describes the passage from the primitive relationship of opposing human forces to the gradual civilization of man through his own activity. But Hegel is doing a "phenomenology" of human consciousness, and one can well ask whether the phenomenon of consciousness does in fact reveal precisely this kind of split and this kind of dialectical opposition. The explicit answer, it would seem, is to be found not in the *Phenomenology* but in the *Philosophy of Right*, where Hegel states that if man is only a being of *nature*, then it is perfectly *natural* that one man should be master and another slave; if the relationship of self-consciousness to self-consciousness is *natural*, slavery is the result.[13]

As Hegel sees it, to be conscious of self is to be conscious of being free; but since man is *by nature* neither free nor conscious of being free, he must become both in a process which begins by seeing freedom as nothing more than independence and independence as that which characterizes the self as negating the independence of another self. This sort of consciousness of independence, however, is scarcely a step beyond the unsupported self-affirmation which solipsistically ignores any other; it merely finds confirmation of its own self-affirmation in recognition by another. Still, as we saw before, if the self is object to another consciousness not as a self but only as a thing, its very thinghood is a dependence which negates its independence.[14] Thus, in isolation self-consciousness is no more than an abstract awareness of gathering all objectivity in itself, in the sense that there is no awareness

12 "The outstanding achievement of Hegel's *Phenomenology* and of its final outcome . . . is thus first that Hegel conceives the self-creation of man as a process, conceives objectification as loss of the object, as alienation and as transcendence of this alienation; that he thus grasps the essence of labor and comprehends objective man . . . as the outcome of man's own labor" (Karl Marx, cited in Kelly, "Hegel's 'Lordship and Bondage,'" in MacIntyre, *Hegel*, p. 190n2).

13 The whole passage bears quoting. "The alleged justification of *slavery* (with all its more precise foundations in physical force, capture in war, saving and preserving life, nourishing, education, welfare, the slave's own acceptance, etc.), as well as the justification of a *domination (Herrschaft)* as the simple fact that there is a master-class *(Herrenschaft)* and any *historical* view regarding the justice of masters having slaves is based on a point of view which sees man as nothing but a *being of nature* with *an existence* (to which likewise belongs arbitrariness) which does not correspond to the concept of man. The affirmation of the absolute injustice of slavery, on the other hand, clings to the *concept* of man as spirit, as free *in himself*, a concept which is one-sided to the extent that it sees man as *by nature* free, or, what comes to the same thing, takes as true the concept as such in its immediacy, not the idea. . . . The dialectic of the concept and the initially merely immediate concept of freedom brings about the *struggle for recognition* and the relation of *domination* and *servitude*" (No. 57, Zusatz). There follows a reference to the present section of the *Phenomenology* and to Nos. 430 and following of the *Encyclopedia*.

14 This is the sort of thing which makes Jean-Paul Sartre nervous (see "Le Regard," *L'Être et le néant* [Paris: Gallimard, 1949]). To be objectified in another's "look" is, for Sartre, to be transformed into a "thing" and thus to lose one's subjectivity. The very being of the other as a self, then, is a threat to one's own selfhood. For Hegel, on the other hand, the being of the other is so far from being a threat that it is dialectically necessary for one's self-revelation to oneself.

which is not awareness of the one self being aware. To be aware of more than that, however, the self must see the need of doubling itself; the self cannot be its own object if in the field of its objects there are no other selves. But if for the other self of which it is aware it is not a self but only a thing, all has been lost. The unity of self-consciousness must be at the same time a multiplicity of self-consciousnesses, or it is nothing at all; the multiplicity of selves must *recognize* each other as selves, or there is no unity at all: "The articulation of the concept of this spiritual unity in its doubling presents to us the movement of *recognition*" (p. 141/229). Unity in multiplicity is a demand not only of objectivity but also of subjectivity; and the relationship which binds the multiple into one is the relationship of mutual recognition.

Once again, however, it is "we" who see that; self-consciousness sees only the need of being its own individual self and of being recognized as such. Still, by the very fact that it looks to another individual for recognition, self-consciousness loses itself, i.e., its solipsistic certainty of itself. By the same token, however, in finding itself in the other, self-consciousness supersedes the other, as *nothing but* other. Still, at first the self-conscious individual face-to-face with another individual resists being in the other; with a Sartrean sort of self-assertion, it resents being an *object* for another, being robbed, so to speak, of its selfhood. Only gradually can it realize that mere self-assertion is self-defeating; if it remains where Sartre, in fact, leaves it, as resistance to the other, it is at the same time a stifling of the self. If, on the other hand, it is an overcoming of the otherness of the other, it turns out to be also an overcoming of the mere independence of the self, thus reaffirming the self on a higher level where relationship to another self is constitutive of selfhood. This has become the almost paradigmatic instance of the Hegelian "negation of negation" wherein the self returns to itself, leaving the other free and, thus, assuring its own freedom (p. 142/229–30).

Superficially all of this can look like the activity of one self-conscious individual in relation to another: initial self-affirmation, finding that this involves affirmation of another, negating the merely objectifying activity of the other, returning to itself enriched by the other's recognition of the self's selfhood, and a final self-affirmation which does not require overcoming the selfhood of the other. But none of this is possible without the cooperation of the other. Insofar as the movement described is that of consciousness to self-consciousness, it is one continuous movement, but it is a movement involving the activity of more than one consciousness; one consciousness cannot do to another consciousness what it does not do to itself—just as there is no physical *action* which does not involve a physical *reaction* (p. 142/230). In fact, Hegel tells us, the "play of forces" described in the dialectic of understanding is here being repeated on the level of consciousness; there "we" *observed* it, here consciousnesses are *experiencing* it: "What was for us in the former is here for the extremes themselves" (p. 142/230). In this comparison self-consciousness (a movement) corresponds to the simple concept of force. Understanding *conceptualizes* the latter as the relationship of opposing forces; consciousness *experiences* the former as the relationship of opposing consciousnesses. Each consciousness makes sense only as both for itself and for the other; each mediates the movement by which the other comes to itself, and the mediating activity is *recognition*. "Each is for the other the means whereby each mediates and binds itself to itself and whereby each is to itself and to the other an immediate being which is for itself and at the same time is thus for itself only through this mediation. They *recognize* themselves as *mutually recognizing each other*" (p. 143/231).

The question now is whether "we" philosophers can observe this movement in such a way as not to prescribe how it is to be spelled out but rather to let it spell itself out in its being experienced. We must try to observe "how the process of self-consciousness appears to self-consciousness" (p. 143/231).

It would unquestionably be arbitrary to say that the first conscious relationship which one human being has to another is that in which one *dominates* and the other is *enslaved*. In another place,[15] Hegel explicitly denies that it is the first relationship. It is, he says, a fundamental relationship, and it is a relationship of individuals, not to be confused with the general relationship of subjection to authority. It is interesting, in this connection, to note that in one of his earliest references to the relationship Hegel illustrates it by the example of Robinson Crusoe and Friday.[16] The point is that he sees the movement toward authentic self-consciousness beginning in a relationship of inequality between two individuals, where the recognition which self-consciousness demands is all one-sided: one recognizes, the other is recognized. What Hegel is *not* saying, incidentally, is that at the beginning of human development there are two kinds of individuals, the dominating type and the servile type; he is talking about a dialectic of self-consciousness and saying that there are two fundamental ways in which consciousness can face the issue of life.[17] Before facing the challenge of another consciousness, self-consciousness finds all the recognition it wants in itself. This does not mean that there is no other consciousness, simply that this other does not count; it is "inessential" (p. 143/231). If there is another, it is equally isolated, independent, self-contained; each is for the other, as Sartre would complain, simply an object; or, as Hegel has it, they walk onto the stage of life as "independent figures" (*Gestalten*) (p. 143/231) who do not see each other as selves. Each is certain of its own self, but neither has objectified itself, since to do that is to make oneself what one is for the other (p. 144/232). If there is to be self-objectification, it will be the work not merely of one but of both; each needs the other in order to be for itself the sort of object it is. Initially, however, the objectification effected by each is merely abstract, abstracted from the life of both. But if to abstract from

---

15 G. W. F. Hegel, *Schriften zur Politik und Rechtsphilosophie*, ed. Georg Lasson, 2nd ed. (Leipzig: Meiner, 1923), pp. 441–43.

16 *Dokumente zu Hegels Entwicklung*, p. 110.

17 This needs to be said, in view of the influence of the Kojève interpretation—and, in general, the Marxist interpretation—of what Hegel is doing here. It must be insisted that he is doing a *phenomenology* of consciousness, not a *history* of social development. One wonders whether the misinterpretations are not conscious and deliberate (cf. Kelly, "Hegel's 'Lordship and Bondage,'" in MacIntyre, *Hegel, passim*).

the life of another is to *negate* that life, another factor has entered into the initial relationship which pushes it a step forward: "Therein, however, is present also a second step, *an activity which affects the self,* since the former [negating] involves the risking of one's own life" (p. 144/232). There is, then, no self-affirmation without negating the life of the other, and there is no negating the life of another without risking one's own life. Life becomes, so to speak, the bone of contention between the two would-be selves, and the striving to impose recognition of one's self on the other becomes a life-and-death struggle. Either *self-assertion* has reference to the other as a self-conscious being or it remains static and cannot become *self-consciousness*; independence without relation to another of whom one is independent is meaningless, un-recognized.

Now, Hegel tells us, if one is so dependent on life as to be unable to risk it, there is no way of getting the recognition which makes independence meaningful.[18] Independence does not belong to an individual by the very fact of being an individual and being alive; the individual must struggle to *make* himself independent, and to struggle is to risk. "The individual who has not risked his life may well be recognized as a *person,* but he has not attained to the truth of this recognition as the recognition of an independent self-consciousness" (p. 144/233).[19] There is a very real sense in which to be alive merely biologically is not to be alive humanly, and this means that the merely biological (the given) must be negated if it is to become human; only by risking inauthentic life can one live authentically: "He who loses his life shall gain it."

If we remember, once again, that what Hegel is describing here is the dialectical progress of consciousness and neither the life-and-death struggle of primitive man nor the historical rise and fall of nations or social classes, we can see that there is a certain inevitability to this struggle for recognition and to the risk it involves. The self-certainty with which this whole thing began inevitably involves a kind of unilateral self-affirmation (we see it in children). This sort of self-affirmation inevitably runs up against the other, who simply by being another self-affirming being seems to be an obstacle to be overcome. This may reveal itself in nothing more dramatic than the tendency of some to affirm themselves by associating with inferiors —in age, talent, intelligence, strength, etc.—and in this way to do away with the obstacle to one's own self-affirmation; with results not unlike those

---

18 As an illustration on a larger scale, we might take the American Declaration of Independence. America did not become independent by declaring *itself* to be so, but only by risking its life and thus bringing about a *recognition* of its independence.

19 It may seem strange here that Hegel speaks of a "person" who is not an authentically self-conscious being. That is certainly not what we mean by "person." What Hegel refers to here is a person in the absolutely minimal sense of being recognized by law as capable of owning property (cf. *Enzyklopädie,* Nos. 488, 539; *infra,* "Legal Status," pp. 187–90). Such a "person" has done nothing to *win* recognition. One who *counts* as a person is something else again: "The fact that it is man . . . who is recognized as a person and counts as such legally is so little a matter of *nature* that it is rather only the product and result of the consciousness of the profoundest principle of the spirit and of the universality and development of this consciousness" (*Enzyklopädie,* No. 539).

described by Hegel in the remainder of the section.[20] Thus, when Hegel says that risking one's own life means *intending* the death of the other (p. 144/ 233), it is the death of the other's *self-consciousness* to which he refers, not to *natural* death—any more than Sartre wants to go around killing people, because by "looking at" him they negate his selfhood.

This becomes more evident in the sequel. If, says Hegel, in the struggle the death of the other actually ensues, nothing has been gained for self-consciousness. The other has been treated as a *thing*, and self-consciousness has regressed to the level of "natural" (thing) consciousness (p. 145/233). Getting rid of the other, then, is getting rid of another self-consciousness, and this cancels out the progress made in the doubling of self-consciousnesses, which means canceling out the movement which is one's own self-consciousness. For the dynamic relationship of opposed forces is substituted the dead unity of solipsistic isolation: "The mean collapses into a dead unity, which is separated into dead extremes, which merely are but are not op-posed to each other" (p. 145/234). "Rugged individualism" is bound to come a cropper. What has to be overcome is the negative relationship of individuals which is only *destructive*; and in its place must stand the relationship which is at once negative and *constructive* (we see both kinds in the relationship of parent to child, teacher to student, psychiatrist to patient, etc.). This is "the negation of consciousness which *cancels out* (*aufhebt*) in such a way that it *retains* and *preserves* what has been canceled, and, thus, survives its cancellation" (p. 145/234).

What has happened is that in the experience of consciousness which is self-consciousness is involved the realization that self-consciousness is nonsense if it is not that of a living being; life is essential to self-consciousness. Thus, to reflect on consciousness and leave life out of the picture is to have as an object "the simple I" (p. 145/234), an abstraction in need of mediation if it is to be concrete, and that mediation can be supplied only by another consciousness. The question remains open whether the mediation of a consciousness which is not also a self-consciousness is sufficient mediation. If another is conscious of me as a self but not of himself as the same, is my selfhood authentic?

[DEPENDENCE AND INDEPENDENCE]

It is at this point that two opposed "types of consciousness" (*Gestalten des Bewusstseins*) (p. 146/234) come to the fore. Face to face they are distinguished from each other by their attitude toward life. The attitude of one is *independence*; to have this consciousness "for itself" is essential, to be alive is not—given a choice between freedom and life it will choose freedom. The attitude of the other is dependence; to be alive is essential, and it is content to be conscious of the selfhood only of the other—given a choice of freedom and life it will choose life. The cast of the two-character drama is complete: on one side of the stage stands one for whom recogni-

---

20 Cf. Seeberger, *Hegel*, p. 412.

tion is so important that he will risk his life in order to gain recognition; on the other side stands the one for whom life is so important that he will forgo recognition in order to retain life—he will depend on the other for his life. The situation is classic: face to face in the conflict of life are, on the one hand, the master, and, on the other, the slave. If two who are willing to risk life face each other, there is struggle to the death of one, and in death there is no recognition. If two who are unwilling to risk life face each other, there is no action at all, no mediation. Where the master who is willing to negate his *animal* life in order to affirm his *human* life faces the slave who is willing to relinquish his *humanity* in order to preserve his *animality*, the process of self-realization can begin. The process, however, will not turn out to be what it initially seems to be.

The master, quite obviously, would seem to have the edge. His concept of selfhood has ceased to be that of the abstract, empty "I" and has been concretized in the recognition by another, a consciousness which is content merely to be, to relinquish *selfhood* for *thinghood*. It is in the master that selfhood is triumphant. But—and here again it is important to emphasize that Hegel is *not* writing social, political, or economic history—just what has the master gained? By acquiring a slave who will minister to his appetites, he has set up a whole network of relationships whose significance is to be worked out. Immediately he has a relationship to the *thing* which is the object of his appetite, for which he does not have to work, and a relationship to a "consciousness for which thinghood is the essential" (p. 146/ 235). Mediately, on the other hand, the master is related to the slave through the latter's desire to stay alive; the slave has relinquished the independence of selfhood in order to retain the independence of thinghood, i.e., since the slave has to continue to be if he is to be of any use to the master, his *being* is to that extent independent. But the master is also related to life through the slave, since his willingness to risk life would be fruitless, were there no slave to subjugate thereby. In subjugating the slave, however, the master also sets up a relationship between the slave and the thing the slave provides him.

At this point the master begins to lose ground. His own relationship to things is that of *enjoyment* only; he is a consumer. But he would not have anything to consume if the slave did not work. So, the master puts the slave in the position of working on things, of producing. Not only, then, does the slave come between the master and the things the latter enjoys; he also develops a relationship to things which is more significant than is the master's. The master is a *consumer*; the slave, a *producer*. The master becomes the representative of a consumer culture, which is no culture at all since it promotes no development. The slave becomes the representative of a producer culture, which is a culture precisely because it *cultivates*. The master has condemned himself to simply taking what is *given*, himself included; he has turned over to the slave the task of *negating* what is merely given, which is the task of creativity. The master *merely* negates; the slave negates significantly by transforming. Thus, the master "links himself thereby merely to the dependence of the thing and merely enjoys it; the independent aspect, on the other hand, he relinquishes to the slave, who works on the thing" (p. 147/236). The master has no future.[21]

There is no question that Hegel finds this aspect of the dialectic of self-consciousness illustrated in history—as he will even more explicitly as the overall dialectic moves on. Moreover one can readily see a parallel between the movement described here and the dialectic of freedom described in the *Philosophy of History*, which moves from a situation in which "only one is free" (the ancient Orient, where one was master and all the rest were slaves), through one in which "some are free" (Greece and Rome, where some were masters and some were slaves) to one where "all are free" (none is master and none is slave). It is still true, however, that there is a difference between doing a *phenomenology* of the development of consciousness and doing a history or even a philosophy of history. Hegel's *Phenomenology* is no more to be praised because it is good history than it is to be condemned because it is bad history. It simply is not history at all—even though it is *historical*. Thus, when at this point Hegel goes on to say that the master's domination is dependent on the slave's clinging to existence and that, therefore, what the master does to the slave in subjugating him the slave does to himself, we should beware of making Hegel say something he does not say. Since the relationship in question is one of consciousness and not one of physical forces, there has to be a sense in which what the master *takes away* (the slave's consciousness of "being for himself") the slave *gives away* (p. 147/236). Hegel is not saying, as Roger Garaudy,[22] and the Marxist tradition from which Garaudy draws his interpretation, would have him say, that it is the spirit of slavery in the slave which brings about the institution of slavery and not vice versa, which, Garaudy continues, leads to a glorification of war, a justification of slavery, and what not. Of course it is the institution of slavery which makes slaves and not the spirit of slavery which makes the institution—but Hegel is not talking about an "institution"; he is talking about what happens to the master-type of self-consciousness in the working out of this relationship.[23] It must be remem-

---

21 "The future belongs to the once-terrorized producer, progressively liberated by the spiritualized quality of his own labor, not to the seemingly omnipotent consumer, who treats both the servant and his product as dead things" (Kelly, "Hegel's 'Lordship and Bondage,'" in MacIntyre, *Hegel*, p. 193). It should be noted, however, that Kelly here takes issue with the over-simplified but influential interpretation of this dialectic by Kojève and his epigones.

22 Roger Garaudy, *Dieu est mort: Étude sur Hegel* (Paris: Presses Universitaires de France, 1962), pp. 228–29.

23 One might find more room for Garaudy's sort of caviling in the following passage from the *Philosophy of Right*: "To adhere to man's absolute freedom—one aspect of the matter—is *eo ipso* to condemn slavery. Yet if a man is a slave, his own will is responsible for his slavery, just as it is its will which is responsible if a people is subjugated. Hence, the wrong of slavery lies at the door not simply of enslavers or conquerors but of the slaves and the conquered themselves. Slavery occurs in man's transition from the state of nature to genuinely ethical conditions; it occurs in a world where a wrong is still right. At that stage wrong has validity and so is necessarily in place" (p. 239). Yet, this is *not* a "justification of slavery." It is simply a description of a state of affairs, a period of transition from nature to spirit, when men—both masters and slaves—have not, in fact, developed the consciousness that man is essentially free.

bered that the use of historical illustrations does not tie the dialectic of consciousness to historical institutions. "Slavery, in this sense, is not merely a *past* phenomenon; it recurs every time one prefers the security of one's own physical existence (comfort, etc.) to the affirmation of one's spirit—where fear wins out." [24]

The point, then, of Hegel's saying what he does say is that the kind of recognition the master has gained for himself by subjugating the slave is worthless, no recognition at all, because it comes from one who has abdicated his selfhood and makes the master dependent on dependence, which is the worst kind of loss of independence—it is the master's own abdication of selfhood.[25] The *thing* the master consumes depends on the slave; the *recognition* he gets depends on the slave; the master is worse off than the slave; doubly dependent he is condemned to stand still, not to develop. "Herein the inessential consciousness is for the master the object which constitutes the truth of his self-certainty" (p. 147/236). The master, as master of the slave, cannot move from his empty certainty of self to genuine self-consciousness; "he is, thus, not certain of truly being for himself; rather, his truth is the inessential consciousness and its inessential activity" (p. 147/237). As Loewenberg puts it quite aptly: "The relation between the lord and the persons subservient to his will is essentially unstable. . . . Crucial here is the contention that neither dependence nor independence can ever significantly appear as a relation altogether one-sided." [26] To be a master at all is self-defeating.[27]

Once more, then, as in the dialectic of understanding, an "inversion" occurs. Not only is the relationship of domination stagnant and, therefore, self-defeating, because the truth of this "independence" is to be found only in the non-independence of acknowledgment in an enslaved consciousness, and domination becomes its opposite; but also, we might say, the master becomes the slave of his own situation. He is, moreover, enslaved in a situation from which, as master, he cannot be liberated. If, on the other hand, the truth of the master's self-consciousness is in the slave, it will ultimately be the slave who can come to consciousness of what it is to be self-conscious, to be a self. Then, "servitude too will indeed in its working out turn out to be the opposite of what it is immediately; as consciousness *drawn back* into itself it will enter into itself and transform itself into true independence" (p. 148/237). Independence is not a state, it is a movement; and only the

24 Cf. Seeberger, *Hegel*, p. 417.
25 The examples in everyday life are all too obvious.
26 *Hegel's Phenomenology*, p. 88.
27 It is here that the one-sided socio-political interpretation which Kojève gives of this dialectic (and through it to the whole of the *Phenomenology*) becomes particularly insidious. The *Phenomenology of Spirit* ceases thereby to be a "phenomenology" at all; the "spirit" of man is lost in the shuffle. Cf. Kelly, "Hegel's 'Lordship and Bondage,'" in MacIntyre, *Hegel*, p. 196: "On the one hand Hegel is showing that mere political mastery or subjection cannot inaugurate the long adventure of history and freedom unless faculties of the subjective mind, necessarily present in all men, create the possibility and condition the result. On the other hand, it is clear that none of this is conceivable in a solipsistic universe." It is the Marxist *need* to make economic and political history "scientific," it would seem, which dictates Kojève's interpretation.

slave can move, because he engages in an activity which transforms. The master's very independence makes him unfree, since unmediated freedom is not freedom, not a process. The slave's dependence, on the other hand, will ultimately make him free through the mediation of that which he works on and transforms. From now on, then, the only process to be watched is the process of slave-consciousness.

Initially, it is true, servile consciousness has no other reality than what the master gives to it—the slave's role in life is the one assigned to him by the one who has subjugated him. But precisely in virtue of this role, he can *experience* what the master cannot. (1) The slave knows that, in fact, the master is dependent on him for whatever grasp on his own being (*Fürsichsein*) the master has (p. 148/237). (2) The slave's fear of death, the absolute master, has left nothing fixed or static within him; he is not stuck with the way things are, the given; he can be not only creative but also self-creative. "This pure universal movement, the absolute fluidification of all constancy, is, however, the simple essence of self-consciousness, absolute negativity, *pure* being-for-itself, which is *in* his consciousness as an accompaniment of that fear of death" (p. 148/237). The fear of death relieves him of any fear of change. (3) Nor is it merely a question of consciousness of possible change; the slave can bring about the change; by serving the master he has learned that; and because the consciousness of the slave is responsible for whatever objectivity the master's being-in-himself had, the slave can bring that about, too. "Being-for-self is not simply this abstract (*überhaupt*) universal dissolution [of the fixed], but by serving, the slave makes of it a *reality*" (p. 148/238). (4) Finally, the work he does has a spiritualizing effect on him and relieves him of dependence on his merely "natural existence" (p. 148/238). It is the work of spirit to transcend nature, and it is only the slave who does that.

Almost imperceptibly Hegel has brought us to the point where we see work as that which *makes* the difference (i.e., brings the difference about) between spiritual consciousness and merely natural consciousness: "Through work consciousness comes to itself" (p. 148/238). The master's relation to things, consuming them, is purely destructive, a non-mediating negation. The slave's is a relationship of construction, of development, negating the merely natural being of things by making them into products of human work. The thing is *aufgehoben* in the full sense of being negated (its being is changed), retained (it continues to be), and lifted up (it has the mark of man's spirit on it). "Work, on the contrary, is *restrained* appetition, *withheld* disappearance, or it *constructs*" (p. 149/238). Thus, work is not merely negative in relation to its object; it negates by forming (transforming); it objectifies not by abstracting but by making. In doing all this to the object, work also transforms the subject's consciousness of the object into a more authentic consciousness of itself. "This *negative* mean or formative *activity* is at the same time *singularity* or pure being-for-itself of the consciousness which in work now emerges from mere being-for-itself and into the element of the enduring" (p. 149/238); in what man makes he finds a prolongation of his being. "The consciousness which works arrives thereby to an insight into independent being *as itself*" (p. 149/238).

It seems safe to say that Hegel is the first philosopher to have stated explicitly that man's work is a significant contribution in the development of man's self-consciousness. To understand how this should be so, we must recall the first moment of self-consciousness in general, in which the fixity of the given is dissolved and all is set in motion, all is rendered fluid. The channeling of this fluidity is movement of consciousness realizing the universality of its competence. As this general movement begins to be concretized (actualized) in servile consciousness, then, the first moment was seen to be the *fear* which shook up the universal stability of the given, put everything in motion, rendered it fluid. Now it is work which "forms" (transforms) the given and thus by channeling the fluidity of the objective acts negatively on the first moment of fear. In this way the transforming of the world transforms the consciousness of the slave. "By the fact that it is *put into existence*, the form becomes for consciousness not something other than it, for the form is precisely its pure being-for-itself, which thus comes to be its truth" (p. 149/239). In this way consciousness finds itself in work; what the slave *makes* reveals to him what he *is*.

There are, then, three moments necessary, and universally necessary, to the "reflection" (turning back) of consciousness on itself: fear, service, and constructing (*bilden*) (p. 149/239). The negative moment of *fear* is required to dissolve all fixity; the moment of *obedient service* transforms chaotic activity into *work*, which effects the transformation (construction) of both reality and the consciousness of the slave.[28] "Without the discipline of obedient service fear remains merely formal and does not spread itself over the actuality of the being which consciousness experiences" (p. 149/239). By forcing him to work the master has done the slave a favor; he has made him discipline (channel) "the universal fluidity," which fear had brought in its wake. Without constructive work fear issues only in unproductive service; without initial fear the activity of "forming" will be undisciplined and arbitrary, culminating in no essential consciousness of self; and unless the fear is total (not just this or that anxiety), development will be just a hit-and-miss sort of thing—nothing can remain fixed if consciousness is to embrace the whole of objectivity. "To the extent that the entire content of its natural consciousness is not rendered unstable, consciousness *as such* (*an sich*) is fettered to some determinate being; its own mind (*der eigene Sinn*) is stubbornness (*Eigensinn*),[29] a freedom which still remains enslaved" (p. 150/240). If consciousness does not go through the stage of total enslavement to the absolute master (the fear of death), it will be at least partially the slave of its own arbitrariness. Only when fear has completely dissolved the fixity of its objectively *given* world can consciousness take over completely. The following two sections of this chapter detail a series of attempts to take over only partially.

Once more, as on the previous levels of development, the dialectic mani-

---

28 To put order into a chaotic world, consciousness looks to itself; awareness, however, is not an adequate ground for self-awareness as the locus of reality; creating reality is required.

29 The pun, quite obviously, is not reproducible in English. It is Hegel's way of saying that anything short of total self-reliance is irresponsible.

fests a pattern which is becoming familiar. It begins with *consciousness experiencing* a movement which *we* foresaw at the end of the previous dialectic. It ends with *our seeing* what further movement is to be experienced. What we have seen, consciousness must experience. We already know that any attempt on the part of consciousness to take over only partially and not completely is doomed to failure. Consciousness must go through the attempts to be partial so that, by experiencing failure, it may be forced forward.

B. FREEDOM OF SELF-CONSCIOUSNESS [30]

At the end of the dialectic of domination and servitude, which is historical only in the very vague sense that it illustrates two attitudes toward life in the concrete which can be verified in history, the situation of the master has been seen to be without any future—his "independence" can never become genuine freedom. The consciousness, then, which can assert itself only by dominating another has been effectively eliminated from the developmental process; it is essentially stagnant. The slave, on the other hand, who has been forced by the master to work, has thereby acquired two instruments, so to speak, which will make progress possible: the *work* itself which enables him to transform nature, to put the mark of human spirit upon it, and the *discipline* which will enable him in working to transform himself, to become what he is not yet, i.e., free.

Freedom, however, is self-possession, and as one who is just about to emerge from being possessed by another, the slave is neither conscious of just what steps he must take nor quite ready to take the steps when their necessity is revealed to him. Instead he makes a series of attempts to assert his freedom, attempts which will prove to be inadequate precisely because they fall short of a concrete self-creation which alone can *produce* what is not *given*.

Still face to face with another who is stronger than he, one who has achieved independence by risking his life, the slave who has preferred slavery to the risk of life sees as his only way out a declaration of independence—a declaration, however, which he makes only to himself. He has his work, it is true, which enables him to impose form on the material with which he works, but so long as this is but a piecemeal transformation of at one time this and at another that he builds up skills but builds up in himself no universal competence in relation to the totality of reality over against him. The only consciousness he has of himself is of being the subject who does the work; what the work does to distinguish and develop him he is not conscious of. He must become conscious that, while remaining one and the same subject, he is the one who makes himself into what he is to be. "This self-consciousness, then, does not become an I which in its singleness truly differentiates itself or which in this absolute differentiation

[30] The full title of this subsection is "Freedom of Self-Consciousness; Stoicism, Skepticism, and the Unhappy Consciousness."

remains identical with itself" (p. 151/242). There is constancy, and there is change, but the I cannot get them together.

a) Stoicism

As long as consciousness remains servile, the only consciousness it has of itself is the consciousness the master has of it; it sees itself through the master's eyes, its only objective being is the role *assigned* to it.[31] There is, thus, a separation between "*itself* as an autonomous object and this object as object of a consciousness which makes it its own being" (p. 151/242). All this split consciousness can do is withdraw into itself, seeking refuge in what is clearly its own, its thinking. "We" who look on, however, see that in *thinking* the form (*Form*) which work *produces*, consciousness has brought forth a form (*Gestalt*) all its own of self-consciousness, one not imposed on it by what is outside itself. The slave's work is for the master, but his thinking is free; the product of the former is for another, of the latter for himself. His is now "a consciousness whose being is to be its own infinity or the pure movement of consciousness, a consciousness which *thinks* or is free self-consciousness" (p. 151/242). As a *thinking* being he is free.

For the first time since the beginning of the *Phenomenology*, we begin to grasp the significance of the concept in the march toward the fulfillment of consciousness in self-consciousness. To think, says Hegel, is to conceive, to bring forth one's object from oneself, not to have it given to one; and the concept which is brought forth is not other than the conceiving—process and product are identical (p. 152/243). When consciousness represents something to itself, it has to remind itself, "this [representation] is mine"; when it conceives it is conscious that "the concept is immediately *my* concept" (p. 152/243); it is clearly not adventitious. At least to this extent, then, consciousness is free; the responsibility for its concept is its own; the *Sein* of conceiving *Bewusstsein* is consciousness' being-for-itself: "In thinking I *am free*, because I am not in another but remain simply with myself, and the object which for me is being is in an inseparable unity [with me], is my being-for-myself" (p. 152/243). I am conscious that my thought is mine and mine alone, "and my movement in concepts is a movement within my self" (p. 152/243). For the first time the object of consciousness is "an *immediate* unity of *being-in-itself* and *being-for-itself*" (p. 152/243). All this remains somewhat vague and general for consciousness, but it is a significant breakthrough for consciousness; it is self-determination, and it is consciousness thereof.

Here for the first time Hegel explicitly takes as his illustration for a manifestation of consciousness an historical phenomenon, an attitude of mind which is clearly identifiable, i.e., Stoicism. That the phenomenon is historical, however, should not delude us into thinking that Hegel is describing as an historical step the passage from the primitive relationship of slave to master to the sophisticated attitude of the Stoic. Nothing could be

---

[31] "In the master–slave situation, there is neither education, nor progress, nor history—only the repetitive fulfillment of the master's wants" (Kelly, "Hegel's 'Lordship and Bondage,'" in MacIntyre, *Hegel*, p. 213).

further from the truth.[32] Not only can there not be an immediate passage from one to the other, but Hegel himself recognizes in his *History of Philosophy* that the long, slow process of coming to consciousness of the individual's responsibility for his own thought-determinations begins with the Sophists, when men were first becoming conscious of being politically free, develops through Socrates, who faced individuals with the responsibility for their own thoughts, and then through all the refinements introduced by Plato and Aristotle. Stoicism, then, is simply an illustration of a principle, which neither begins nor ceases to be a stage in the development of self-consciousness with the historical Stoics. "Its principle is that consciousness (*Bewusstsein*) is thinking essence (*denkendes Wesen*) and that something has essentiality for it or is for it true and good only insofar as consciousness comports itself therein as thinking essence" (p. 152/244). It is the sort of consciousness which determines for itself what is true and good, does not accept it as coming from elsewhere, as imposed on it by the thinking of another. Consciousness is aware that all the distinctions it makes are its own doing, and nothing can violate this freedom.

The freedom of Stoicism, then, is the freedom of thought; it is just as free in a slave in chains (Epictetus) as in an emperor on the throne (Marcus Aurelius). It is a freedom which can sing to itself "stone walls do not a prison make nor iron bars a cage" and, in so doing, fail to be aware how "lifeless" such a freedom is. It is a step in the right direction, but it is not really an emergence from servile consciousness—or, at best, it is a very partial emergence. Servile consciousness, as we saw, denied its subjection to the master only to the extent of becoming a slave to its own stubbornness, "the freedom which latches on to one single thing" (p. 153/244). In so doing, however, it is able to recognize that, while the work forced upon it by the master is not free, the thought which goes into the work is. If this becomes more than the attitude of the isolated slave and is to take on the form of a consciousness common to an age, it will be "in an age of universal fear and slavery, but also in one of universal education," an age "which had raised education to the level of thinking" (p. 153/245). Slaves remain slaves, but their thinking is free, and thinking becomes that which is proper to them.

A freedom such as this is, obviously, a rather abstract freedom; it remains *indifferent* to the concrete facts of life: "freedom in thought has only *pure thought* as its truth, which lacks the fulfillment of life" (p. 153/245). This is the abstract *concept* of freedom, not its reality; it is secured by withdrawal, letting the reality of the world retain its independence of consciousness. It judges what is "true" and what is "good," satisfied that the only content which "true" and "good" have is what consciousness gives. Like all the other satisfactions which consciousness has had, however, this too must be destroyed, which it is with the realization that it has no content whatever. "But here, just as thought, being an abstraction, separates itself from the manifold of things, it has no content in itself, only a *given* content" (p. 154/245). Granted that thought is consciousness' own product, it is an empty

32 Cf. Hyppolite, *Phénoménologie*, I 176n19.

product, and its content is not its own. "Consciousness, it is true, cancels out the alien *being* of the content by thinking it, but the concept is a *determinate* concept, and this determination is the alien element in it" (p. 154/245–46).

The only criterion Stoicism has for the truth of its own thought is its *rationality*, a purely formal characteristic. To preserve itself from the contamination of an alien reality (it has done nothing to disalienate reality), it takes refuge in its own rationality—very edifying but very boring (p. 154/246). If consciousness is to be genuinely self-determined in its thinking, it must satisfactorily negate the otherness of its determinations, and mere withdrawal cannot accomplish this—the very determinateness of its own thought is not its own (p. 154/246). Having seen that its own thinking can withdraw it from the domination of the master, it neglects the activity which would have both kept it in touch with reality and brought reality under its domination, the transformative activity of work. The Stoic's consciousness will not be authentically self-determining if his work is not.

b) Skepticism

As we have seen before, and as we shall see again and again in what follows, the destruction of satisfaction in withdrawal does not immediately lead consciousness to take the steps which will lead to genuine satisfaction. Genuine freedom is too hard to take; it involves self-reliance and responsibility—for a world! What made the withdrawal into its own thoughts unsatisfactory was that the other-imposed determinateness of the thoughts followed it into its hiding place, leaving it not really master, even of its own thoughts. The immediate solution to this is along a purely negative route, that of Skepticism which secures freedom by simply denying the reality of any disturbing alien determinations of its thought. Instead of taking upon itself the role of determining, it *nullifies* what is determinate. "In Skepticism what comes *to consciousness* is the utter inessentiality and non-autonomy of this other" (p. 155/246). Unaware that it is taking the preparatory steps toward taking over the task of supplying the determinate contents of its own thought, consciousness simply cancels out any determinateness coming from elsewhere. It is an important step; for the first time consciousness relates itself negatively to external reality, thus liberating itself from subjection to what is outside itself. As we saw earlier, both appetition and work were negative in relation to the givenness of external reality, the one geared to consuming, the other to transforming it; but they could not carry out the negation in a manner adequate to self-consciousness. Skeptical negation, on the other hand, is successful because it confines itself to thought; whatever distinctions consciousness *finds* among things are the distinctions it *makes* (p. 155/247).

In its negative stance toward the given, then, Skepticism accomplishes two things. (1) It makes clear that the dialectical movement of sense certainty, perception, and understanding is a movement within consciousness. (2) It shows how what counts as the determinateness of reality is inessential (*a*) for the relation of domination and service, since it is the master who determines what is to count (even moral demands) and (*b*) for abstract thinking whose products are scientific concepts, related only externally to the independent being which constitutes their content, and yet are determinate no matter how abstract they are (p. 156/247). Only what consciousness produces from within itself counts; all else disappears: "What disappears is the determinate, or the distinction which, no matter how or whence it comes, presents itself as fixed and changeless" (p. 156/248). Skeptical consciousness permits no determinateness of reality to be imposed on it; its *thinking* simply negates all fixity, thus producing a true certainty of itself, because nothing else counts; "it is to itself the indifference (*Ataraxie*) of itself thinking itself" and becomes "absolute dialectical unrest" (p. 156/248); there is nothing to hold it down.

Skeptical consciousness, however, has paid a high price for its independence of reality as given; it is left with the purely contingent, dizzy chaos which it of itself produces. It is at once empirical—its objects are there—and non-empirical—its thoughts are its own—but it has no control; its objects are in no way guaranteed. As a result its life is not even one of genuine self-consciousness; it negates one object after another, singly, but that serves no positive purpose. It rises above the contingency of the confusing existent world which surrounds it and at the same time flounders in the very inessentiality it has created. It becomes hopelessly enmeshed in the contradiction between its thoughts and its actions. It *does* what it *claims* has no validity: "It pronounces the nullity of seeing, hearing, etc., and yet it itself *sees, hears,* etc.; it pronounces the nullity of moral entities and yet makes them the determinants of its actions" (p. 157/250). The picture of Skepticism is a good one; it is self-contradictory, not in the sense that it involves logical contradiction, to which it is indifferent, but in the sense that the way it thinks contradicts the way it lives; it is at once unalterably what it is and its opposite (pp. 157–58/250). Like a child, the Skeptic embraces contradiction for its own sake, contradicting whatever is said even if it agrees with what he himself has said—and he cannot live that way (p. 158/250). The "essentially self-contradictory consciousness" *has to* contradict itself, has to experience itself as self-affirming, the one source of its own thinking, and yet as producing hopeless confusion (p. 158/250).

What it comes down to is that the Skeptic cannot successfully be a Skeptic. He cannot have it both ways, cannot say "I'm right, and you're wrong," because a condition for being a Skeptic is that he also say the reverse. The servile consciousness was unsuccessful in attempting to liberate itself from domination by simply withdrawing into itself since that changed nothing. It has now proved unsuccessful in its attempt to liberate itself by changing everything into nothing. All it has succeeded in doing is doubling itself; in attempting simply to negate one side of the unsatisfactory relationship it has itself become both sides. What started out as two distinct types over against each other, the master and the slave, has now turned out to be one type who is both master and slave. Consciousness experiences itself as the master (in control) who is his own slave (controlled); its position is utterly arbitrary. Not all has been lost, however; in fact a gain has been made.

Servile consciousness, it is true, has purchased its freedom at too high a price, but it is on the way to the realization (which "we" observers have) that only in the reconciliation of two contradictory aspects of consciousness can genuine self-consciousness be achieved. Up to this point, however, all consciousness has achieved is the split: "and the *unhappy consciousness* is the consciousness of itself as the doubled, merely contradictory being" (p. 158/251). The reconciliation is yet to come.

This all might be summed up in terms of the contradictions which every self experiences in regard to itself: between the "true" self and the "false" self; the surface and the deeper self; the constant and the fickle self; the self which has found its identity and the self which has not. We might, in fact, say that consciousness has reached the stage of "self-consciousness" in that pejorative sense so predominant today of being conscious of "standing out like a sore thumb," conscious of being *exposed* but not of being *self-possessed*.

c) The Unhappy Consciousness
With the primitive life-and-death struggle wherein the master dominates and the slave capitulates, there is born the phenomenon of the servile consciousness which is conscious of itself only as fulfilling a role imposed upon it by another. In an attempt to liberate itself from this sort of determination by another consciousness, it then turns to what is unquestionably its own, its thought, seeking in it a liberty it is unwilling to struggle for, unaware that in its activity lies the key to self-determination. When this "Stoical" attitude proves unsatisfactory, consciousness goes even deeper into its own thought, not merely withdrawing from harsh alien reality but denying it, thus leaving itself with nothing but itself to contend with. Paradoxically enough, however, it eliminates an alien domination outside itself only to recreate the master within itself. The master it now serves is itself, but it continues to *do* the same old things. In this movement consciousness is not only doubled, but its two aspects contradict each other; it is at once the immutable source of its own determinations and changing with each determination. "We" can see both that the reconciliation of the two contradictory aspects must be effected within the unity of one consciousness and that the possibility of this reconciliation is revealed in "the concept of spirit come alive and entering into existence" (p. 159/251), but that is not to be realized at the stage where consciousness now is. Consciousness looks into itself, but what it sees is not itself but another: "It *is* itself a self-consciousness looking into another" (p. 159/251). The immutable aspect is, as it were, projected outside and looked upon as another.

That the consciousness Hegel is here talking about is a form of religious consciousness is clear both from the language he uses and from his references back to it in the section of the *Phenomenology* where he explicitly treats religion (Chapter 7). It is also clear that Hegel finds illustrations of this type of religious consciousness in certain aberrant forms of Judaic and Christian consciousness. It is not at all clear, however, that Hegel is here instituting, as a long tradition would have it, a critique of Judaism and

Christianity. Apart from the fact that the description applies too well to other attitudes also, e.g., Romanticism, even its specifically religious thrust concerns only religious consciousness pushed to the extreme of superstition.[33] The section on the Unhappy Consciousness is intended by Hegel to serve as a transition from inadequately rational forms of self-consciousness to that genuinely rational form which can take upon itself responsibility for its world of objectivity. In Loewenberg's words: "To attain the level of rationality, it is therefore incumbent upon self-consciousness to act, so to speak, as its own middle-man and middle term between the opposed aspects or strains of its nature." [34]

If consciousness is to effect this unity with itself, it must first experience a going outside itself, so to speak, in order to come to terms singly with the two poles which are to be reconciled. By so doing it relinquishes a part of itself, putting the responsibility for itself on another whom it projects. It is in this other that consciousness has its being. Immediately the unity of consciousness is one and indivisible, whether it be in the union of unity and multiplicity, universality and particularity, or stability and changeableness; but immediate unity is not the reconciliation of these opposites, nor has it been effected by consciousness' own activity. The activity, then, begins with a separation of united opposites, and here the emphasis is put on the opposition of the immutable and the changing. Both are aspects of consciousness, but *for* consciousness they are alien to each other as, once more, the essential and the inessential (like Plato's ideal form and sensible particular). Given the distinction, the opposition, the inessential must be sacrificed to the essential. If this division corresponds to that between the immutable and the changing, then the immutable is the essential and the changing the inessential. Seeing itself as changing, consciousness sees itself as inessential and, therefore, to be sacrificed; if it is to attain to the essential, it must free itself of itself. Thus, although it *is* itself both the immutable and the changing, it is not *conscious* of this and so *situates* the two as over against each other, related to each other in such a way that the changing, inessential *aufzuheben ist* (p. 159/252). This is the refusal of reconciliation.[35]

One might well ask why a consciousness such as this must be particularly "unhappy." It is, after all, simply the skeptical consciousness carried to its logical extreme, and skeptics are not notably unhappy. It is not, however,

---

[33] In recent years, Jean Wahl's study, *Le malheur de la conscience dans la philosophie de Hegel* (Paris: Rieder, 1939), pp. 21–50, has been largely responsible for the perpetuation of the above-mentioned interpretation. There is no question that Wahl's study is brilliant. Nor is there question that it traces accurately the troubled religious autobiography of Hegel's youth. There is question, however, whether Hegel's *Phenomenology*, a book written for the philosophical public and not merely for Hegel's own students, should be interpreted so much in the light of earlier writings which Hegel himself—presumably deliberately—did not publish. Granted that what Hegel *said* earlier can help us understand the torments he went through, may we not legitimately confine ourselves to what he actually *says* in the *Phenomenology*? Wahl's interpretation is further rendered suspect by its too great reliance on Karl Rosenkranz, who had his own axe to grind.

[34] *Hegel's Phenomenology*, p. 111.

[35] Where *aufheben* has only the meaning of "cancel," not that of "retain" or "lift up."

the unhappiness of the skeptic of which Hegel speaks; it is the unhappiness of that consciousness which has taken one step beyond skepticism in the realization that it has no one but itself to whom to turn, but does not find within itself the resources to heal the breach it has imposed on itself. The skeptic may well have taken refuge in absolute doubt, but in so doing he has deprived his own life of all meaning; if he is content to forgo meaning he may not be, existentially, terribly unhappy, but if the nagging desire for a meaning he cannot find ensues, he will be unhappy, and unhappier still if, having split himself into himself and another, he seeks meaning in that other. He is worse off than the slave who finds the whole meaning of his own life in the consciousness of the master. Consciousness is, in fact, a unity, but it is conscious of being a duality, and to find its unity on either side of the split is to find only a specious, unhappy unity. In this struggle, which has been transposed to within consciousness, to win at all is to lose; if either side emerges victorious, the other side which is equally the self is defeated—in either case life turns out to have no meaning: "The consciousness of life, of its existence, and its activity is simply the pain felt over this existence and activity, since it has consciousness only of its opposite as its essence and of its own nothingness" (p. 160/252).

For consciousness to look for itself in another, then, is to go nowhere, since the other is only a projection of itself. Worse still, by representing the other, the immutable, to itself it makes the other simply into another particularity, so that the other is pictured as both *outside* and *particular*, and what is achieved is a unity *"in which the difference of both is still dominant"* (p. 160/253). If, however, consciousness relates itself to this projected other as to a particular being, it can do so in three ways. (1) It can stand over against it, and since the other is the immutable, the essential, the relationship of domination and servitude is repeated—the divine despot is now the master. (2) It can transfer its whole being to the immutable, "and thus its whole manner of existence is surrendered to the other" (p. 160/253); selfhood has been relinquished completely—only God *is*. (3) It can see in the other the genuine reconciliation of particularity and universality, i.e., spirit, and thus find itself as "this particular" reconciled with its own universality in the immutable. "Since *the other* is an *image* of particularity, as it is itself, thirdly, then, it becomes spirit" (p. 160/253)—the true God of true religion. To relate in this last way, of course, is to cease to be the unhappy and to become the happy consciousness.

Still in the grip of its own unhappy split, however, consciousness is not yet ready for this third move; by representing the immutable to itself as a particular being, it has cut off this avenue and has for itself only another particular being who is all powerful or all encompassing. "What presented itself here as a mode of relationship proper to the immutable turned out to be the *experience* which the split self-consciousness has in its unhappiness" (p. 160/253). It is not this kind of God which makes for unhappiness; it is unhappiness which makes for this kind of God. Consciousness is aware neither of its own universality nor of the universality of the particular immutable being it has projected outside itself.

"We," of course, know that self-consciousness itself is the immutable to which it looks, and so the experience *of* the immutable is not a one-sided movement; it is a movement of the immutable too. But the consciousness which is conscious of itself only as *this particular* consciousness experiences its whole movement as going toward the immutable; there is no reciprocity. For this reason consciousness pictures to itself an immutable which is a particular being—"out there"—and keeps him out there. "In fact by virtue of the *picturing (Gestaltung)* of the immutable, the moment of out-thereness *(Jenseits)* not only remains but is indeed further intensified" (p. 161/254–55). The being which consciousness pictures to itself has all the trappings of a *sensible* being out there, and to be united with such a being is inconceivable (p. 162/255). There now arises a conflict between concept and imagination. The immutable as *conceived* is imageless *(ungestaltet)*; as imagined it is imaged *(gestaltet)*. But since the doubling of itself which consciousness has experienced and is unable to reconcile belongs to the conceptual, it makes an effort to get away from the conceptual and to find its satisfaction in an imaginative picture. Now it must try the impossible, to unite itself with this sort of immutable being: "What is initially an external connection *(Beziehung)* to the pictured immutable as an alien actuality, however, it must elevate to an absolute being-one-with" (p. 162/255–56).

Going back now to the way consciousness can relate to an objective reality over against itself, Hegel sees three ways in which it can seek to unite itself to its essential being pictured as out there: (1) being simply conscious of it as an object, a cognitive union; (2) relating in the way appetition and work related it to alien reality, a self-referential union; (3) being conscious of it as itself an independently conscious being, a spiritual union (p. 162/256). All this, obviously, needs spelling out, and the spelling-out is extraordinarily complex.

1) It should be remarked at the outset that without warning "the immutable," which had been designated up to this point as neuter *(das Unwandelbare)*, suddenly becomes masculine *(der Unwandelbare)*, designating some*one* not some*thing*, a good indication that Hegel is now talking about the personal God of a specifically religious consciousness—and that what went before need not have been specifically religious at all.[36] To be simply conscious of "the immutable" *(der Unwandelbare)* is to be somehow conscious of God as he is "in and for himself." But for God to be present to consciousness in this way cannot be the doing of consciousness itself, since only God himself could effect this sort of presence.[37] Nevertheless, this sort of presence cannot be adequate since, as *effected by God*, it is not the *presence of God*. Still, the kind of thinking consciousness does here has gone well beyond the merely abstract thinking of stoicism or the restless doubting of skepticism; it tries to come to terms with the particularity of consciousness in the

---

[36] Admittedly, this will require an explanation of the reversion to *das Unwandelbare* three pages further on (see n. 39).

[37] Hegel seems to be referring here to a Cartesian cognition of God.

face of the universality of the immutable.[38] But this thinking has not gone so far as to reconcile its own particularity with the universality of pure thought, in the sense that "pure thought" is not the thinking of anyone in particular. The reconciliation is achieved in the immutable, but consciousness is not aware that this reconciliation is its own. Strictly speaking, then, the relationship of consciousness at this stage to the immutable is not "thinking" in the full sense at all but only "devotion": "It only, so to speak, *approaches* thinking (*geht es . . . an das Denken hin*) and this is devotion" (*Andacht*) (p. 163/257). If thinking in the full sense is "grasping" (*Begreifen*), then this is a sort of *thoughtless* thinking, a vague, emotional thinking which does not get beyond "the discordant clang of ringing bells" (*Sausen des Glockengeläutes*), "the warmth of being filled with clouds [of incense?]" (*warme Nebelerfüllung*), a kind of "musical thinking" (*musikalisches Denken*), wherein God is not thought at all, as he is in the *concept* (*Begriff*) but only *felt*; to "think" of him in this way makes one "feel good." It is a consciousness of being known and recognized by a God who is a particular being out there (pp. 163–64/257–58). Such an immutable is unattainable; there is no union with it in its essential opposition to the consciousness which seeks to be related to it: [39] "Where it is sought it cannot be found, since it is supposed precisely to be *an out there*, to be such that it cannot be found" (p. 164/258).

What it comes down to is that the attempt to "picture" the immutable has to end in failure, because to picture God is to make God an it, which is to denature him. In seeking to *cognize* God as an object, consciousness has reduced him to a sensible particular in which there is no life, and in which it will not find its own life: "To consciousness, therefore, only the grave of its life can become present" (p. 164/258). This, however, is a step in the right direction; it is an experience of the vanity of looking for a particular being out there, since the particular separated from the universal is dead; "only through this experience is consciousness able to find particularity as true, i.e., as universal" (p. 164/259).

2) Precisely because the attempt to "picture" the immutable out there is a refusal to think, to grasp, to *conceive*, it trails off into sentimentality and becomes an emotional relationship. The "feeling" in question, as we saw, turns out to be a "feeling-good" which is the equivalent of a self-referential feeling (*Selbstgefühl*), and this works itself out in a relationship which parallels that of appetition and work, and the self which consciousness finds in this movement parallels the self of which it is immediately certain at the outset of this chapter. "The unhappy consciousness, however, *finds* itself only as *appetitive* and *working*; it is not obvious to it that at the basis of such a finding of itself lies the inner certainty of itself, and the feeling di-

---

38 Wahl sees this as an indication that "a phenomenological theory is the analogue of a theory of grace, in which one cannot separate what comes from God from what comes from free will" (*Malheur de la conscience*, p. 133).

39 Here Hegel reverts once more to the neuter, presumably because such a God is no personal God at all, not Spirit.

rected toward its essence is a feeling directed toward itself" (p. 165/259). Thus the alien essence which it thinks gives it enjoyment is really only itself; there is nothing out there corresponding to its projection.

In this case, of course, the relationships of appetition and work look neither to the destruction nor to the *Aufhebung* of the particular reality consciousness considers objective. As relationships to the immutable (once again neuter, *das Unwandelbare*) they cannot be. The object to which consciousness relates itself is as pictured, a particular; as simply "the immutable," it is universal, but this is no genuine reconciliation of the particular and the universal; it is simply that "its particularity has in a general sort of way (*überhaupt*) the significance of all reality" (p. 165/260). If there is to be any *Aufhebung*, then it must be the doing of the immutable itself, giving an image of itself for consciousness to enjoy. "As a result what essentially happens for consciousness is that the (*das*) immutable itself *surrenders* its image and hands it over to be enjoyed" (p. 166/260).[40] Because, however, the immutable surrenders only an image and not itself, the particular consciousness which is related only through the image continues to be a split consciousness of itself; what it is for itself is separated from what it is in itself, and the latter is lodged in the immutable out there. The very capacities consciousness recognizes in itself are no more than a gift from the almighty power: "They are the capacities and powers, a gift from another, which the immutable likewise hands over to consciousness for its use" (p. 166/260). Hence, even though consciousness is aware of acting on a passive reality facing it, it is also aware that both itself and this reality are swallowed up in the immutable. The result is that the relationship to the immutable, which should have been one of genuine thinking (*Denken*) and had managed to be only one of devotion (*Andacht*), now becomes one of thankfulness (*Danken*). Nevertheless, on the side of consciousness the activity is there, the activity of willing, of working, of enjoying—even the activity of *thanking*. In a very real sense it experiences these activities as its own. "In them consciousness feels itself as this particular and does not let itself be fooled by the semblance of divesting itself of itself, since the truth of this semblance is that it has not given itself up" (p. 167/262).

3) "With this there has entered on the scene the *third relationship* involved in the movement of this consciousness, a relationship which emerges as the kind it is from the second, which in truth by its willing and successful activity (*Vollbringen*) has become aware of its own autonomy" (p. 167/262). The struggle, however, is not yet over. Consciousness has returned into itself to find there its true reality, but in relation to the universal essence (out there) this reality is sheerly negative; it has no share in the reality of the immutable. "This third relationship in which this true reality is the *one* extreme is one in which the reality *in relation to* the universal essence is nullity. Now the movement proper to this relation is to be examined" (p.

---

[40] The Trinitarian and incarnational overtones in this language should not be missed. But it is a *burlesque*, not a critique, of Christian religion.

168/263). The awareness which consciousness has of its own autonomy in acting turns out to be an awareness of doing *nothing*, and its so-called enjoyment is a feeling of its own unhappiness because the content it gives itself has no universality. The kind of independent particularity it finds in itself is no better than that of an animal, and the functions which were so important in revealing it to itself, lacking the spiritual quality of universality, are simply animal functions. As a result we now "look only at a personality turned in on itself and its trivial activity, making itself brutish, as unhappy as it is impoverished" (pp. 168–69/264).

Unlike the skeptical consciousness which universally negated reality in order to affirm itself, the unhappy consciousness, faced with a universality in which it cannot see itself having any part, negates itself, affirming only its own nothingness and the insignificance of its own action. There is, however, a ray of light—and here again we see the religious motif asserting itself —a unity with the immutable, effected not immediately but mediately. In this way its own insignificant singularity can be salvaged by being united to the immutable through another. "*The mediate* relation constitutes the essence of the negative movement in which consciousness directs itself against its singularity, and this movement as *relation* is *in itself* positive and will for consciousness itself bring out its *unity*" (p. 169/264).[41] The two extremes of the relationship, the all-encompassing (universal) immutable and the changing singular, are too far apart to be united, but a mediator who partakes of both and can thus be the representative of each to the other can serve as a link between the two.[42] It is as though the mediator is the alter-ego of both, concretizing the universality of the one in an individual and lifting the mere particularity of the other to authentic individuality. "This middle is itself a conscious being for it is an activity mediating the consciousness as such; and the content of this activity is the elimination (*Vertilgung*) of its particularity which consciousness proposes" (p. 169/264–65).[43]

But since it was activity and enjoyment as its own which revealed to consciousness its autonomous particularity, its intention to get rid of its particularity turns into a separating itself from its activity and enjoyment, which is possible because the responsibility for it (and the fault connected with it) can be shifted to the middle-man. By the same token, the mediator becomes the one who *teaches* what is right action. "This mediator, as im-

41 Here the play on words involves "singularity" (*Einzelheit*), which might also be rendered "mere individuality," and "unity" (*Einheit*), which means "significant oneness."

42 In religious terms it seems fairly obvious that the paradigm of the mediator, the "middle man," is Christ, the divine-human mediator. In Hegel's own experience the notion of Christ as uniting in himself the finite and the infinite, the concretized universal, had tremendous philosophical significance. "Before being a method the dialectic is an experience wherein Hegel passes from one idea to another. . . . It is in part his reflection on Christian thought, on the idea of a God-made-man, which led Hegel to the conception of the concrete universal" (Wahl, *Malheur de la conscience*, p. v).

43 Rarely does Hegel employ the term "grace," but the inference should be obvious here: the activity of the mediator does not inhibit, it promotes, the initiative of the individual.

mediately joined to the immutable being, serves by giving *counsel* regarding the right" (p. 169/265). Consciousness, however, still has something on its conscience. Even though its work and its enjoyment have been made the responsibility of another, the fruit of the work in the form of possessions and of enjoyment in the form of pleasure remain. Thus, to make the self-renunciation complete, first it gets rid of any real autonomy it had by engaging in strange rituals and prayers which have no meaning for it; then it gets rid of external possessions by giving alms of what it has earned; [44] and it gets rid of enjoyment—or, at least, of the guilty feeling which goes with it —by fasting and penance, commonly called "self-denial." Having done all this, consciousness has eliminated whatever constituted its freedom, either exteriorly or interiorly, and self-consciousness becomes equivalent to a *thing*, since all that it is and all that it has has been turned into a gift from above. Still, one last satisfaction remains which tends to spoil the whole picture: its *giving up* everything is its own doing (p. 170/266).

It turns out that by giving up everything this consciousness has gained everything. (*a*) If its own consciousness is not its own doing, there is no reason to be unhappy; the very elimination of the unhappiness, however, is another's doing. (*b*) To have given up its own will is only from one point of view negative; from the other, in its concept, it is positive, because it has been replaced by the universal will of the other (p. 170/266). It "does God's will," a will which is expressed in the counsel of the mediator. (*c*) It gains a universality which is not its own doing, so that the nothingness of its own doing becomes everything in the other (p. 171/266–67).

There can be no question that the picture drawn here well describes a late medieval pietism (or quietism); not, however, medieval religious consciousness in general. What is more, the point is not to describe medieval religion at all; it is to draw a picture of a sort of complete emptying of individual consciousness preparatory to moving to a level where consciousness can be aware of itself as regaining everything, provided it make the transition to *reason*, which simply is not individual in the insignificant sense which Hegel has been caricaturing up to this point. The individual *has to* come to the realization that as merely individual it *is nothing*, if it is to become all that it is capable of becoming. "In this object, however, in which its activity and being, as belonging to this *particular* consciousness, is doing and being *in itself*, the notion (*Vorstellung*) of *reason* has come to it—the certainty which consciousness has of being in its particularity, *in itself*, all reality" (p. 171/267). Lifted to the universality of reason, its particularity will become the only genuine individuality.

---

[44] We can presume that Hegel has no objection to helping the poor with alms. The point here is the vanity of using alms as a means for consciousness to solve its own problems—a not uncommon practice with this kind of "religious" consciousness.

6

Reason

When we approach Chapter 5 of Hegel's *Phenomenology*, we run the risk of becoming engulfed in a confusion out of which we shall not subsequently be able to extricate ourselves. The plan of the work which initially seemed simple enough—despite the manifest difficulties we have already experienced in understanding the carrying out of that plan—now seems to explode, to get out of hand, not only for us but for Hegel himself. We have but to look at the table of contents as Hegel outlined it; there the confusion begins. There are three main sections, each designated by a letter of the alphabet. Section A (which contains three brief chapters and a total of 51 pages) is entitled "Consciousness" and deals with a series of attempts on the part of consciousness to come to terms with its object as something "out there." Section B (one chapter totaling 39 pages) is entitled "Self-Consciousness" and deals with the return of consciousness to itself following its failure to make sense of a world of reality "out there." Section C (containing four chapters and a total of 390 pages) bears no title at all.[1] This section is then divided into four subsections: (AA) "Reason" (Chapter 5); (BB) "Spirit" (Chapter 6); (CC) "Religion" (Chapter 7); and (DD) "Absolute Knowing" (Chapter 8).

There can be little doubt that while Hegel was in the course of writing Section C something happened. It is as though the plan of the *Phenomenology* initially conceived by Hegel took over its own structuring, once the inadequacy of mere objective consciousness and of mere self-consciousness had demanded a reconciliation of objectivity and subjectivity.[2] The reconciliation was not to be effected with one stroke; all that is implied in that reconciliation had to be worked out with infinite patience. But Hegel's teeming mind was not infinitely patient (nor was his editor). He wrote in great haste, and the result was a vast welter of implications, the disentangling of whose interrelationships demands infinite patience on the part of the reader. The reader who has that kind of patience will discover a logic which not only runs through the last two-thirds of the *Phenomenology* but

---

[1] In the Hoffmeister edition, Section C is entitled "Reason," but this does not make a great deal of sense, especially in light of the titles given to the subsections (cf. Otto Pöggeler, "Zur Deutung der Phänomenologie des Geistes," *Hegelstudien*, 1 [1961], 255–91).

[2] "If he wished to preserve at all costs the living concreteness of original direct experience, it must somehow be reconciled and united with a rational standard of objectivity. The establishment of this union eventually became the controlling concern of his *Phenomenology*" (Harris, *Hegel's Development*, p. 87).

also unites it with the first one-third.[3] Nor does the later, shorter form of "Phenomenology," which we find in the *Encyclopedia*, give any indication that Hegel repudiated the longer form we meet here.[4]

At the end of the dialectic of understanding, the last in a series of attempts to explain the consciousness of reality by an appeal to something outside consciousness, Hegel had pointed out that consciousness was forced to look within itself if any explanation was to be found at all. In returning to itself, however, consciousness ran the risk, which is manifested at every level of the dialectic of self-consciousness, of finding itself empty of all content, as in Stoicism and Skepticism, or possessed of a content for which another is responsible, as in the unhappy consciousness. To take upon itself the responsibility for its own content, then, means that the reality it previously sought to explain by going outside itself is to be found only within itself and that it will have achieved the autonomy of self-consciousness in being conscious of precisely this. Aristotle had said that in knowing the mind *becomes* that which it knows; Hegel will go further and say that in becoming that which it knows the mind does all the work; it is not acted upon by something alien to itself. The consciousness which does that, of course, is reason, whose autonomy had been celebrated since the days of Descartes and confidence in which had been fanned by every success of the new sciences.

What Hegel will seek to do, however, is to show that reason's confidence in itself cannot be based either on its own mere assertion of its universal competence or on the kind of "scientific" successes which in the long run touch only the surface of reality. Still, it will not even begin to move forward on the path to a realization of its own competence if it does not see, even in a vague sort of way, that it has only itself to rely on and if it does not make use of what scientific thinking has been able to accomplish in order to reveal itself to itself. The beginning, then, of the process which Hegel takes 390 pages to describe will be the result of the dialectic of self-consciousness, the realization "individual consciousness" had that it can find its own truth only within itself. It might be asked, of course, what assurance does it have that its own truth is to be found at all, but that is not a phenomenological question. What we are to do, Hegel tells us, is to watch it in operation to see if the steps it goes through do reveal to it its own

[3] "No one dreams of denying that 'something happened' during the writing of 'Reason Observing,' that Hegel, during that summer of 1806, so to speak, 'lost control of his work,' that he had willy-nilly to let himself be guided by his object's own dynamism. Still, paradoxically, far from constituting a break which would make the work contradictory by turning it against itself, this unforeseeable departure from the initial intention assures us of the very close connection between the 'two parts' which are distinguished in it—since it is the logic proper to the development itself which compelled Hegel to exceed the limits (if, in fact, that is the way it was) which he had perhaps set for himself at the beginning" (Labarrière, *Structures et mouvement dialectique*, p. 26). The expressions in quotes are from Pöggeler's refutation of Häring's thesis; cf. n. 1.

[4] In paragraph No. 417 of the *Encyclopedia* Hegel gives a very brief outline of phenomenology which fits equally well to the later abbreviated form and to the extended development of the present work. As we saw in Chapter 1, n. 35, Hegel repeatedly referred to the longer form as satisfactory.

truth. Hegel, of course, is confident that if consciousness consistently refuses to look anywhere but in itself for the universality which is the hallmark of knowledge it will find it, but he is also content simply to let us see this happening.

What it comes down to is that the consciousness which, even on the level of understanding, recognized that in thinking it universalized what initially appeared to it as particular can now come to the realization that there need be no cleft between the particularity of appearances and the universality of thought, because the universality of thought is not a form imposed by a subject thinking; it is the particular universalizing itself in thought. What is more, the singular consciousness has recognized that the universality on the side of consciousness requisite to the universality of knowledge is not outside itself, either as an abstraction or as "the immutable" guarantee (p. 175/272). When consciousness is "certain," however, *that* only within itself will it find all truth, it is still far from knowing *how* to find that truth or from *finding* it. The "certainty" involved here, Hegel tells us, is the principle of "idealism," and like every other (immediate) certainty it must be raised above itself in a movement which destroys it as mere certainty.

As a theory, of course, idealism is not new; but as Hegel presents it it is new. For him it is not a "theory" at all, not the "positing" of the ego as the only possible source of a knowledge of reality (Fichte), nor a "thesis" affirming the identity of subjectivity and objectivity (Schelling); nor is it the result of a "transcendental deduction" which discovers a "transcendental unity of apperception" as the basis of all knowledge (Kant). Rather, it is the result of a process wherein consciousness, having begun with an entirely different conviction (that of sense certainty), has step by step been brought to penetrate its own essence in the certainty that there and only there will it come to terms with reality. This is its "experience" of what reason is.[5] Thus, the "certainty" which consciousness has "of being itself all reality" (p. 175/272), even though as mere certainty it cannot give satisfaction, is a step in the right direction.

Idealism is a step in the right direction because it gets consciousness over the greatest hurdle it has encountered so far, the fear that a world of reality external to itself will be a threat to its own autonomy—the fear, we might put it, that in seeking "reason" it will find only "absurdity." Previously it had sought to assert its own autonomy "at the cost of the world" (Stoicism and Skepticism) "or of its own reality" (unhappy consciousness), "both of which appeared to it as the negative of its own essence" (p. 176/273). Now, as reason, consciousness can come to grips even with a reality external to itself, in the assurance that in getting to the heart of that reality it will find itself. "Its own thinking is immediately reality; it relates itself to reality as idealism" (p. 176/273). This is simply the conviction that reality is rational and that, therefore, in discovering reality consciousness will discover reason, itself as reason. That the reason it thus discovers will not be the naïve reason which begins the search will only gradually become mani-

5 Cf. Nicolai Hartmann, *Hegel* (Die Philosophie des deutschen Idealismus), 2 vols. (Berlin & Leipzig: Grünter, 1927) II 112–13.

fest. What is significant at this stage is that consciousness is not constrained to negate the reality of the world. What consciousness now has before itself is *"its* new real world, which is of interest to consciousness as remaining there, just as previously it was as disappearing, and this because the *continued existence (Bestehen)* of the world becomes for consciousness its own *truth* and *presence*: consciousness is certain of finding only itself therein" (p. 176/273). The world is no threat at all; it will enable consciousness to find itself—as reason.

Admittedly all this is very vague—*mere* idealism is—but gradually the awareness is growing that for consciousness *to be* the reality it knows is *to become* that reality; the rationality it discovers turns out to be its own rationality, but not merely its own. "Self-consciousness, however, is all reality not only *for itself* but also *in itself* only because it *becomes* this reality or, better, *proves* itself to be such" (p. 176/274). The "proving," of course, is the *process* of coming to grips (*Begreifen*) with both reality and itself. In one sense this process has already been going on in the movement from objective consciousness, for which reality is *in itself*, out there, through self-consciousness, for which the only reality there is is reality *for consciousness*, to reason, where the reality *for it* and the reality *in itself* are identified. In another sense, however, the process in question is only beginning with the "certainty" of the identity; the process of *identification (Begreifen)* is a long one. In this latter sense, reason is present "only as the *certainty* of that truth. . . . Thus it merely *assures itself (versichert)* that it is all reality, but does not itself come to grips (*begreift*) with this" (p. 177/274–75).

Precisely because the idealism Hegel is describing simply begins with such an assurance of being all reality, it is static. Immediate certainty is merely individual assurance, and as such everyone's certainty is as good as everyone else's (p. 177/275). "Reason appeals to the *self*-consciousness of any and every consciousness: *I am I*, my essential object is *I*; and no consciousness will deny it this truth" (p. 177/275). This, however, gives each and everyone an equal right to his own certainty; my certainty is all mine, but that is all it is, and as immediate certainty there is no way of saying that one's is true and the others' not true. If certainty is to be raised to the level of truth, it must be through a process of rational reflection which genuinely assures reason that its truth is the only truth. Certainties must be set over against each other, so that out of their opposition truth may emerge (the dialogue of dialectic). "Only when reason as a *reflection* out of this opposed certainty makes its appearance does its affirmation of itself emerge not merely as certainty and assurance but as truth; and not only *alongside* others but as the *only* truth" (pp. 177–78/275).

At this point Hegel inserts a remark which, although it is intelligible in the light of the whole of the *Phenomenology*, is not quite expected in view of the limited distance consciousness has traveled thus far. It is like an editorial comment made from the vantage point of the journey's end. As Hegel observes the journey, he knows that the inchoate reason of which he speaks here makes sense only as a manifestation of that larger reason which is the World-Spirit in the process of becoming conscious of itself. He also knows that the rationality of reality is not simply the mirror of merely individual reason, "certain" to itself that it is reason. What reason has discovered about itself and reality and what it will discover as it proceeds further is genuinely rational only when seen in the framework of the total process of reason's becoming all that it is to be, i.e., spirit. We, the readers, are to be made aware that what began as a "Science of the Experience of Consciousness" is now manifesting itself as a "Phenomenology of Spirit." Otherwise the gap between the assumed subjectivity of consciousness and the objectivity of reality will never be bridged; the self-development of consciousness will never be identified with the self-development of reality. This is but another way of saying that reason must become progressively assured that the way it *sees* reality is the way reality *is*. "Consciousness," Hegel tells us, "will determine its relatedness to otherness or to its object in different ways, according precisely as it stands on a level of the World-Spirit coming to consciousness of itself" (p. 178/275–76). Its immediate consciousness of itself at any point along the way will be a function of the path it has already traveled in determining both itself and its object. "The way spirit (*er*) at any point finds and determines itself and its object *immediately*, or the way consciousness (*es*) is *for itself*, depends upon what spirit (*er*) has already *become* or what it already is *in itself*" (p. 178/276). The process, in which consciousness is caught up, of spirit's coming to be all that it is is the process of its becoming identified with the reality of which it is conscious. An initial (immediate) in-itself is an abstracton; an in-itself which has become (developed) is reality, "this *in-itself* or this *reality*" (p. 178/276).

To get back, however, to the stage at which consciousness finds itself in the immediate certainty that reason has of being all reality: it is a certainty of a purely abstract reality. To know that in being conscious of anything one is being conscious of oneself is to know precious little; it is to know the I as "merely the *pure essentiality* of what is or the single (*einfache*) *category*" (p. 178/276), the one heading which embraces everything indiscriminately. To say that reality is as it is thought—whatever "is" may mean in the context—may be true enough, but it is at this stage not saying much. By the same token, to say that the being of which consciousness is conscious and the self of which self-consciousness is conscious are *essentially* the same (the *Sein* of *Selbstbewusst-sein* is the same as the *Sein* of reality) is to say very little; it is to be spelled out, as it has not been spelled out by idealism—be it of a Kant, a Fichte, or a Schelling.

This sort of idealism cannot spell it out because, having posited its one category, *the I*, it cannot justifiably posit the multiplicity of categories, without which reality remains radically indeterminate. For idealism to posit a multiplicity of categories is just as much a mere assertion as is its claim that "reason is all reality." "This assertion in general, as well as the assertion of any *determinate* number of kinds of categories, is a new assertion, which in itself implies that one can no longer be satisfied with it as an assertion" (p. 179/277). The immediacy involved in such expressions as "*asserting* and *finding*" has to be relinquished, and a genuine "coming to grips with" (*Begreifen*) must take its place (p. 179/277). This *Begreifen* is a process in which the categories of reality *emerge*; there is no other way of assuring their *scientific* validity.

There can be no question that, whether justified in so doing or not, thought classifies things on the basis of what they are essentially and in the same way distinguishes them from each other. To classify, however, is to impose unity on multiplicity, and to distinguish is to introduce multiplicity into unity. The determinations, then, whereby things are identified as essentially what they are and distinguished as essentially different from each other, are the products of thinking reason. The question is whether essentiality and distinction belong to things or are *only* the work of reason thinking. If there is a sense in which they do belong to reality, then there is a sense in which reality itself is rational. But if idealism simply rests on the unity of the "pure category" which embraces all reality under one heading, it cannot answer the question; it can only spin many categories out of one category without justifying the difference between the one category (genus) and the many categories (species): "For [to say that] the many categories are *species* of the pure category means that *the pure category* is still their *genus* or their *essence*, not opposed to them" (p. 179/277). The result is a situation in which the contradictoriness of the unity and multiplicity imposed by reason is not reconciled, and all that is left is the "singularity" of subjective reason (p. 179/277). Reason's mere certainty of being all reality must leave that reality indeterminate.

In the language of Hegel, the "pure category"—the unified I of which reason is certain—can give birth only to other pure categories, i.e., "pure essentiality" and "pure distinction" (p. 179/278), which are equally indeterminate. To know what one *means* by classifying and distinguishing is not to justify doing them if all one has to go on is the vague certainty that they are all there in the unity of the "I." Quite obviously Hegel is saying that neither Kant nor Fichte is justified, on the basis of reason alone, in affirming the manifold determinateness of reality. Both are caught up in a circle, out of which circle Kant gets by appealing to a sensibility which is not reason and in which circle Fichte stays. "The pure category implies (*verweist auf*) the *species* which turn into the negative category or singularity; this last, however, implies in reverse (*zurück*) the pure category" (p. 180/278). No exit; the I is itself, and that is all. "The pure category is itself pure consciousness which in each [of the above designations] remains to itself this clear unity with itself—a unity, however, which is likewise oriented to something else which, in turn, insofar as it is (*ist*) has disappeared and insofar as it has disappeared is once more produced" (p. 180/278).

The language is unquestionably obscure, but it highlights the futility of trying to *derive* a world of reality which is somehow other than consciousness from an affirmation of consciousness all by itself. If consciousness is nothing but pure consciousness, it is a contradiction in itself. It is a restless movement to and fro seeking to catch (*erfassen*) an alien reality which, in being caught (*im Erfassen*), ceases to be alien. At the same time pure consciousness is a calm unity certain of its own truth (p. 180/278). Everything is there, and nothing is there, since the everything is an indeterminate everything. This sort of reason looks for itself in its object and for its object in itself—and finds neither. It finds only inchoate reason and an object which *stands for* but *is not* reality. "Empty idealism expresses this first reason, which knows itself in its object. Such an idealism takes reason only as it is initially and, in pointing to this mere *mine* [6] of consciousness and expressing things as sensations or representations, it is of the opinion that it has pointed to being as complete reality" (p. 180/279).

It is thus that empty idealism turns out to be "absolute empiricism" (p. 180/279), since to give the mere "mine" a determinate and differentiated content reason has to go outside itself for a manifold of sensible representations. In doing this, idealism contradicts itself as much as did Skepticism in denying any reality outside itself and then using the very reality it had denied. The reason in question here is, of course, the purely regulative reason of Kant, which is dependent on a thing-in-itself which it does not know, if it is to have a content. "Such a knowing is at the same time asserted by the concept of this idealism to be not true knowing, since only the unity of apperception is the truth of knowing" (p. 181/280). Its truth, then, is an empty truth, and it is forced back to "intending" (*Meinen*) and "perception" (*Wahrnehmen*) for its content. This involves the contradiction of a knowing to which both the unity of apperception, sheer I, and the thing out there, sheer thingness, are essential. But there is no way of reconciling this sort of thingness with this sort of unity; the former, "whether it be called an *alien impulse, empirical* being, *sensibility*, or the *thing-in-itself*, remains in its concept alien to that unity" (p. 181/280).

The upshot of all this is that an idealism which is content merely to assert that "reason is all reality" has simply equated the true with an abstract concept of reason, and the totality of reality which such a reason is is not real. Worse still, idealism becomes a restless search for a reality it is convinced cannot be found. Nevertheless, abstract reason can become concrete; and its concreteness is the very process of concretization. This is but another way of saying that as soon as abstract reason recognizes that it is *not yet* reason it is in the process of concretization, of becoming authentic reason. The reason which is not yet reason in the fullest sense is a reason which is not yet all reality. The becoming of reason is its becoming reality: "It is driven to raise its certainty to truth and to fill out the empty *mine*" (p. 182/280). The movement will begin with a transformation of perception, consciousness' first contact with a full-blown reality outside itself, from a being-affected-by reality to a patient observation-of reality, wherein reason progressively recognizes its own contribution to the determinateness—and concreteness—of reality.

A. REASON OBSERVING

In this section Hegel turns to a consideration of the manner in which reason had in fact functioned in the sciences which had begun to assert their

---

[6] *Mein.* There is a reference back to the mere opinion (*Meinen*) of sense certainty.

intellectual hegemony with the Renaissance and which, particularly in his own day, were looked upon as models of rational thinking.[7] Characteristic of these sciences, of course, were patient observation of the data provided by experience, careful description of what was observed, controlled experiment, detailed classification of the data made available through experiment, and the formulation of "laws" governing phenomena. To some commentators this has meant that Hegel here takes a step backward rather than forward, returning to the sort of scientific thinking he had already criticized in the chapter on "Force and Understanding." According to these commentators, then, the "observing reason" of which Hegel speaks is not concrete reason at all but scientific understanding.[8] The point, however, is not well taken and tends to obscure what is going on here as abstract reason begins to concretize itself. For one thing, it ignores the very meaning of "concrete," which does not designate a *state* of reason but a *process* of concretization which begins when reason turns to observing the reality it is to become. For another, it fails to see that the concern here is not an explanation through abstract analysis of what is observed; reason is not trying to understand nature but to find itself, and in looking for itself it looks first at the objective reality it observes, in order to see the extent to which this latter manifests both the nature of reason and the part reason plays in the determination of reality. The dialectical movement is already familiar: reason engages in a connected series of attempts to achieve the veritable unity of itself and reality which has already been enunciated in its abstract concept; each attempt proves unsuccessful, but each is a step along the way to concrete identification of reason and reality.[9]

Historically speaking, then, the human spirit in the process of becoming aware of itself has with the upsurge of modern scientific investigation begun a rational conquest of the world. Reason's confidence in itself is un-

---

[7] Cf. Kant, *Kritik der reinen Vernunft*, B X–XIV.

[8] "That Hegel calls conceptless the understanding, which according to Kant is the proper faculty of concepts, cannot seem strange to anyone who is even to a slight degree familiar with the Hegelian theory of the concept. On the other hand, what is strange is that Hegel in the *Phenomenology of Spirit* under the title 'Reason Observing' treats that activity of the human spirit in which the latter makes inorganic and organic nature, the exterior, the interior, and the thinking of man the object of its observation. This, as Flugge already noted, can be no other than the activity of understanding, even though (*zumal*) it manifests all the characteristic traits of the cultivated attitude of consciousness. This must seem all the more strange, since in the *Phenomenology* he treats understanding at length in that context where, in accord with the logical development, it in fact ought to be treated. This obvious inconsistency which leads to misunderstandings, insofar as 'reason observing' in no way fulfills the presuppositions of concrete reason and threatens to erase the borderline between understanding and reason, might well be traced to the fact that Hegel, at the time he wrote the *Phenomenology*, had not yet achieved the clarity of logical distinction between understanding and reason which characterizes his later works" (Seeberger, *Hegel*, pp. 293–94).

[9] "It is by means of these successive failures that reason raises itself to its own truth. Starting from the most external relationship there is it discovers, beyond the investigation of psychological laws, beyond the dialectics of physiognomy and phrenology, the true identity of the self and the thing, an identity expressed in the *infinite judgment* posited as result" (Labarrière, *Structures et mouvement dialectique*, p. 104).

bounded, not because it has demonstrated its omnipotence but because, having eliminated all other contenders—myth, faith, authority, tradition, conjecture—it has had one astounding success after another and has come to rely solely on itself to dominate the world of reality. Philosophically speaking, however, this confidence in the power of scientific reason to master the totality of reality had in Hegel's day taken on two seemingly opposed forms. On the one hand, the popular and rather naïve rationalism of the Enlightenment had turned into the very sophisticated transcendental idealism of Kant and Fichte, which defined reason so narrowly that its scope was severely confined. On the other hand, the confidence in reason had issued in the mystical or intuitional romanticism of Jacobi, Schleiermacher, and Schelling, which vastly enlarged the scope of (intuitive) reason, at the cost of scientific rigor. Hegel sought to steer a course between the Scylla of narrow rationalism and the Charybdis of intuitive romanticism—or, better perhaps, to reconcile the two in a vaster synthesis of progressively expanding reason whose scope would be infinite without abandoning scientific rigor.[10]

Phenomenologically speaking, then, Hegel will let the two positions speak for themselves and thus manifest their inadequacies. To the extent that their positions are purely idealist Hegel has already come to grips with Kant and Fichte in the introductory section of this chapter. Now he will let the "observation" of scientific reason speak its piece.

Without abandoning its assurance that it will find only itself in the world it explores, then, reason returns to the objects of intending and of perception, i.e., to the world of sense. To observe, however, is more than to perceive; perceiving *happens to* consciousness, consciousness itself *institutes* observation. Reason, so to speak, employs the functions of sense and thus raises them to a higher level (*aufhebt*), thus *knowing* their truth, which means "to find as concept what for intending and perceiving is a thing, i.e., in thinghood to have only the consciousness of itself" (p. 183/281).[11] Reason's attitude is one of all-embracing interest in the world of things, because it is confident of being present there. This, however, is but an instinctive grasp of the rationality of reality, or of the "infinity" of reason, i.e., that no reality is recalcitrant to reason. It does not yet see how reason must be expanded, if this is to be true. At first it "merely surmises" (*nur ahnend*) that it is present in reality, knowing in a general sort of way that reality is "its own" (*das ihrige*) (p. 183/281). As it has been doing since the Renaissance, it moves forward with great confidence "to the universal ap-

10 "Now, it is precisely the epoch when, from the critical point of view, Hegel attacks: (1) rationalism or the philosophy of pure reflection such as he finds it in the systematic platitude of the popular *Enlightenment* and especially, on a much higher level, in Kant and in Fichte; (2) the romanticism of Jacobi, Schleiermacher, and Schelling, to his taste too sentimental or mystical. Break with a 'certain' rationalism and break with a 'certain' romanticism—it is all there. Hegel clears the ground to the right and to the left. He needs a synthesis of reason and the aesthetic emotion of romanticism" (Edmond Vermeil, "La Pensée politique de Hegel," *Revue de Métaphysique et de Morale*, 38 [1931], 483–84).

11 In the *Encyclopedia*, No. 439, Hegel defines reason as the consciousness that the determinations of consciousness are the determinations of things.

propriation of its assured property and plants on all the heights and in all
the depths the sign of its sovereignty" (p. 183/281).

This instinctive assurance of its sovereignty, however, does not get reason
very far; at this stage the sheer otherness of reality does prove recalcitrant
to it—reason is still abstract; it is overwhelmed by the multiplicity and distinctness of the determinations it finds in reality. It can only surmise (*ahnt*)
that it is deeper than the mere "I," the individual subject over against a
world of objects. It must, then, "demand that the distinction, the *many-
faceted being* itself, become to it as its own, that it look at itself as *reality*
(*Wirklichkeit*) [12] and find itself as outward form (*Gestalt*) and thing"
(p. 184/282). But this it cannot do by simply analyzing reality and making
it give up its secrets; it must first develop and perfect itself.

Here, it would seem, reason plays a little game with itself. Reason's purpose in observing reality is that it may find itself there, but it claims to be
concerned only with the things it observes, "*the essence of things as things*"
(p. 184/282)—the "objectivity" of the "scientist." What Hegel is saying,
however, is that, once again, "we" who look on can see that, if reason *is*
reason, it must be looking for itself, but because it is *not yet* object to itself,
it is not fully aware of the process. The irony of it is that, if reason were
already object to itself, it could simply plunge into itself without taking a
detour through things; and yet the detour is necessary, there is no direct
plunge into itself. Only in the recognition that the rationality of *consciousness* and the rationality of *things* are essentially the same will reason discover its own essence.

What reason does in observing things begins to reveal to it the difference
between observation and perception; observation "knows" things in a way
in which perception simply does not; "it transforms the sensibility of things
into *concepts*, i.e., precisely into a being which is at the same time I, thus
transforming thinking into a thinking which has being, or transforming
being to a being which is thought. In doing this, observation in fact affirms
that things have truth only as concepts" (pp. 184–85/283). What reason,
then, *discovers* in observing things are the concepts it itself *produces*. When
it gets to the heart of its own conceptualizing it will have discovered itself.
The task now before it is to examine its activities as it progressively discovers itself. The observation of things has already turned into the observation of the observation of things.

a) Observation of Nature

Although, in Hegel's view, rational observation is essentially higher than
perception, it is, nevertheless, concerned with what can be perceived, and
what the human subject can most obviously perceive is what surrounds him,
i.e., nature. To say that nature is susceptible of investigation by reason is to
say that reason can discover an explanation of why nature behaves the way
it is observed to behave. Of that every scientist, from Thales down to the
present day, has been convinced, although there may be some dispute as to

---

[12] Here too, *Wirklichkeit* could be translated as "actuality," but without all the implications that term later takes on.

the degree to which the order of nature is rational and as to whether reason discovers order *in* nature or imposes order *on* nature. Hegel is convinced both that nature is totally rational—even though we may not totally grasp that rationality—and that the distinction between "discovering-in" and "imposing-on" is a false distinction. The rationality of nature is not distinct from the rationality of the reason investigating it.[13]

In the dialectic of "understanding," it was already seen that in thinking "things" understanding universalizes them. What consciousness on the level of understanding, however, could not do was to give an account of the identity between the universality of thought and the particularity of things. It was left with abstract concepts of its own making which did not measure up to the reality of things. They "represented" the reality of things but did not render them "present" to consciousness. If reason is to do better than understanding, it must pass beyond "representing" to "presence"; but this it will be able to do only if reason itself is "present" in things, which it will be if its determinations are the determinations of things. At this point, however, reason has not yet recognized how this can be so.

The key to a recognition of how this can be so is the realization that the universalization of the singular is not some sort of abstraction which simply singles out the same characteristic over and over again, but a process, a movement, in which the dialectical relationship of reason and its object is such that the object is grasped in a more and more comprehensive totality, thus universalizing itself. "First this universal is thus merely *that which remains identical with itself*; its movement is merely the identical repetition of the same activity" (p. 185/284). This sort of abstract universalization is not even on the level of understanding; it is the superficial sort of thing which mere memory can accomplish, a descriptive analysis of what observation observes. "This superficial extraction out of singularity and the equally superficial form of universality into which the sensible is merely accepted, without in itself having become universal,[14] the description of things, does not yet have the movement in the object itself" (pp. 185–86/284). This is at best a universal word, certainly not a universal concept, one word which can be used to designate any number of things without being understood.

The kind of *knowledge* involved in this sort of description on the basis of external characteristics is a merely repetitious and boring classification.

13 ". . . to be noted that God made the world rational, but that this rational content does not yet have its rational thought-form in sensory intuition; rather, only through human reflection is this form produced (*erzeugt*). This means that the sciences which have to do with particular forms and manifestations of nature are sciences only because they determine by means of a universal characteristic these particularities scattered in the sensible appearing of non-rational externality, and because they reduce these particularities to genera, species, and laws, which genera, species, laws, universal characteristics, etc., are thought-forms" ("Über Philosophie überhaupt und Hegels Enzyklopädie der philosophischen Wissenschaften insbesondere" [1829], *Berliner Schriften*, ed. Johannes Hoffmeister [Hamburg: Meiner, 1956], p. 392).

14 We are reminded of the "conditioned universal" already met with on the level of perception, which had not made itself independent of the conditions of sensibility, the universal of the British empiricists, itself a sensible image *standing for* many, wherein the particular does not *universalize itself in being universalized*.

It can distinguish one "thing" or "kind" of thing from another—animals, plants, metals, mountains—by describing their external appearance, but it attains to no essential knowledge at all. "Observation can have no further knowledge as to whether what seems to be in itself is not accidental" (p. 186/285). Nor does the piling up of sensible characteristics constitute a knowledge of things. Here we might reflect that from a purely logical point of view any object we observe has as many attributes in common with any other given object as it has distinct attributes, and no mere enumeration of attributes will tell which count and which do not.

It would be a mistake, of course, to think that Hegel does not acknowledge the importance of just this sort of descriptive analysis to the natural sciences of his day and to the scientific endeavor in general. What he does deny is that "reason" can be satisfied with the kind of knowledge this analysis affords; it gets to the heart of neither reality nor reason. So long as analysis remains on the level of the sensible it cannot even make the distinction between what is essential or inessential, since as merely sensibly distinguishable it is meaningless to speak of any attribute as essential. The distinction, nevertheless, is made, and making it is the work of the concept raising itself out of the sensible order, i.e., not only is the concept *above* the sensible, it is a *transformation of* the sensible, i.e., the sensible *becoming* more than merely sensible. This means that in *knowing* the sensible consciousness is coming to grips with its own activity, a far more comprehensive grasp of reality than is afforded by the distinction and enumeration of superficial attributes. Thus, "knowing makes clear in this way that it has to do at least equally essentially *with itself* as with things" (p. 187/286). If it, in fact, does make the distinction between what is essential and inessential in things, it is consulting its own view of things, not merely the things themselves (if, indeed, they could even be consulted).

This raises the question, however, as to whether what is essential for the *knowledge* of things is also essential *in* things.[15] In classifying the things of nature science hits upon certain characteristics (*Merkmale*) which are the specific differences distinguishing one class from another. But how does it determine what attribute constitutes an essential difference and what does not? Is it a question of simply looking at things by themselves or of comparing them with each other? "Motionless being and being in relationship come into conflict with one another" (p. 187/287),[16] and mere observation cannot decide which counts; to it both are equal. It is the work of reason, then, to make comparisons, to grasp things in the context of their relationship to each other. "Reason, therefore, must rather advance beyond the static (*trägen*) determinateness, which seemed to be constant, to an observation of the same as it in truth is, i.e., must relate it to its opposite" (p. 189/288).

Once the intricate interrelationship of a multiplicity of factors comes in view, reason has moved beyond the mere description of constant characteristics to a network of variations which have, it is true, a higher constancy, but only in the framework of "laws" governing relationships. Once again, however, law bespeaks a rationality which makes sense only on the level of concept, "such that law emerges in the form (*Natur*) of the concept which has eliminated the indifferent constancy of sensible reality" (p. 189/288). But law, of course, is meaningless if there is no determinable connection among the varying factors it embraces. The naïve science of the Enlightenment had been content to conclude that the laws of nature are out there in nature, simply waiting to be discovered by observing reason. The more sophisticated position of Kant saw law as the work of reason in its purely regulative function. Hegel seeks to reconcile the two positions by going beyond them to a concept of law, which is clearly the work of thought, "without, for that reason, losing its nature and falling back into static constancy or indifferent succession" (p. 189/289)—order cannot be imposed where there is no order, or the order which reason effectuates *is* the order which reality manifests.

Law, then, is not simply reason's declaration of how things *ought* to behave if nature is to be rational; it is the affirmation that nature *is* rational, that it does behave in a definite way. "Ought" is not true if all it is is ought: "for reason is precisely this certainty of having reality, and what for consciousness does not have its own being, i.e., what does not appear, is for it nothing at all" (p. 190/289). Reason's "certainty," of course, has established little, but reason, says Hegel, at least cannot be satisfied with anything less than an interconnectedness of reality which manifests *necessity*, not mere probability. As was pointed out before, the "necessity" of which Hegel speaks, is not the logical necessity which both Hume and Kant had denied to any existential reality. Clearly, however, it is more than "probability," at least as Hegel understood probability. If it is said that even with these restrictions the necessity Hegel looks for in scientific laws is not to be found and that sophisticated scientists are content if they can achieve a very high degree of probability, this too is in a certain sense true. The point is, however, that Hegel quite clearly contends that the more-than-probability of which he speaks is not to be found in the empirical sciences at all, even though he can take as an illustration of the necessity and universality of which he speaks an empirical law, e.g., of the acceleration of falling bodies. To establish a law in this regard is to go beyond what is observed, since the universality of the law embraces all bodies, not merely those which have been observed. By the same token, to *know* that bodies fall at a definite rate of acceleration is to have something more than probability that they will so behave. Furthermore, that the law is susceptible of greater refinement in the light of further experiment is nowhere denied by Hegel. What he does contend is that laws of this kind, no matter how sophisticated their formulation, do not contain the kind of necessity he claims as reason's goal; they turn into formulated descriptions—not explanations—of what things do: "It counts, therefore, as a law because it manifests itself in the appearance and at the same time is in itself concept" (p. 191/291). Rational "explanation" must be more than mere "description."

It is here that the difference between mere empirical observation and experiment comes out. Experiment does more than observe; it manipulates the data of observation in such a way that it extricates them from the sensible material conditions in which they are first observed and thus relates them on a higher level of generalization. The example Hegel employs to illustrate this is instructive. The phenomenon, he tells us, which we call electricity was observed to act in one way when produced by the rubbing of glass and in another way when amber was rubbed. But to distinguish the two aspects of the electrical phenomenon by calling them "glass electricity" and "amber electricity" results only in a vague and not very fruitful concept of electricity (p. 191/291). To designate them as "positive" and "negative" electricity, on the other hand, not only raises the concept to a more fruitful level of generality, but also reveals that the intelligibility of electricity is vastly enhanced by the essential relatedness of its aspects: glass and amber are only contingently related; positive and negative are essentially related, each is constitutive of the other. From this he draws the conclusion that "things" are characterized essentially only in relation to other "things," i.e., all *essential* characteristics are *relationships* (p. 192/292). At this point the conclusion may seem rather trivial, but when it becomes the affirmation that relatedness (or interrelatedness) is constitutive of the very essence of reality and that relatedness is a manifestation of reason, the prospects are far reaching. What has been accomplished by the science of Hegel's day, however, in uncovering the constitutive interrelationships of reality has been obscured by the naïve assumption that they are in some sense "materials." [17] On the contrary, Hegel goes on to say, the "materials" which are not materials reveal the conceptual character of reality itself: "The *material*, on the contrary, is not a *something which is*, but being as universal or in the manner of the concept" (p. 192/292).

Because the reason which is thus far operative is instinctive, not self-conscious reason, it does what it does without being aware that it dematerializes its object. Still, when it turns to a particular kind of object, one whose interrelationships are internal rather than external, i.e., the organism, it is on the threshold of a better recognition of its own workings (p. 193/293). Among the objects of external nature which surround us, Hegel finds the best model for the rationality of interrelationship in the organism, whose reality, although not uninfluenced by its environment, is explainable from within.

Observing reason then turns to an observation of the organic. It is, of course, true that any and every organism, being also a material thing, is involved in any number of external relationships to its inorganic surroundings. But to multiply—and classify—the inorganic conditions for the existence (survival) of the organism in no way explains its inner reality. It

17 See *supra*, p. 59 and n. 16; p. 73. An assumption which scarcely stands in the way of contemporary science.

should be noted that Hegel in no way *denies* the influence of the environment on an organism—he does not even *deny* physical evolution, although
he apparently knew nothing of it—what he does deny is the adequacy of external conditions to *explain* either the inner working or the development
of the organism, precisely because such external relationships are not contained in the *concepts* of the relata (pp. 194–95/295)—as was, for example,
the relationship of "positive" and "negative." [18] What characterizes the
organism, then, any organism, is that within it is contained a "teleological"
relationship of self-development (p. 195/296). It contains within itself the
principles which explain not only its being what it is, as do even minerals,
but also its becoming what it becomes. [19]

Initially the teleology of organic development is seen as an external
teleology, i.e., a development with a purpose, but the purpose is coping
with the environment. [20] Characteristic of organic development is that it is
not produced by something external to the organism nor does the organism
as such produce something external to itself; it produces itself—and this is
also what rational thought does! "The organic does not produce anything
but simply *maintains itself*, or, what is produced is just as much already
present as it is produced" (p. 195/296). This is the model of teleological development; the end is already present in the beginning. If reason can really
come to terms with the teleological movement of organic development, it
will begin to come to terms with itself. "This determination [of the orga-
nism], as it is in itself and as it is for instinctive reason, should be worked
out more precisely in order to see how reason finds itself therein but in so
doing does not recognize itself in what it finds" (p. 195/296).

As Kant had made abundantly clear, however, to speak of purpose
(*Zweck*) as an external relationship not only is to explain nothing—what in
fact serves a purpose need not *be* for that purpose—but is to run the risk of
patent absurdities, like calling the purpose of bark on trees that we may
have corks for our bottles! For Hegel, however, purpose is more than internal; it is the very essence of that which has purpose (p. 195, 296–97). [21]
Of the organism, then, it can be said that it *becomes* what its *concept* is; it
brings itself into being: "The necessity in what happens is hidden and reveals itself only *at the end*, but in such a way that this end reveals that it

[18] "It is not possible to establish necessary relationships between the animal and the
element in which it lives; it is possible only to speak of a great influence or to establish
an arbitrary teleology. This is against Schelling who held for a sort of empirico-
metaphysical correspondence between the *organic* and the *inorganic*" (Hyppolite, *Phénoménologie*, 1 216n26). Later (p. 227n41), Hyppolite will say that Hegel's critique of a
quantitative philosophy of nature is also directed against Schelling. As regards Schelling,
the point is unimportant. It is clear, however, that Hegel is not so much criticizing the
natural science of his day as a philosophy of nature which does not get above such
"scientific" concepts.

[19] That Hegel's concept of "nature" corresponds to Aristotle's is, of course, unmistakable.

[20] It is interesting to note that even the theory of evolution was stymied until an
internal principle of development was discovered, gene mutation.

[21] This, of course, is but another way of identifying, as does Aristotle, the formal and
final cause of any organism. Its end is to be fully what it is, to become its "idea."

was also the first" (p. 196/297).[22] What an organism is finally to be it is to be from the beginning, and to know what an organism is to be is to know the concept which is *intrinsic to it*, just as to know the external purpose something serves is to know the concept which someone *has of it*.[23]

Hegel's purpose, however, in speaking this way of purpose is not to come up with a teleological science of the organic but to find in the organic world a model of the purposiveness of self-consciousness, whose concept is its becoming reason. In instinctively seeking the reason of things—why they are the way they are—reason instinctively seeks itself. "As the instinct of the beast seeks food and consumes it but in so doing produces nothing but the beast itself, so too the instinct of reason finds in its seeking only reason itself" (p. 196/297). So far, however, only we the onlookers grasp this; reason is its own end, its own concept, but it has not yet experienced this.

Although reason's instinctive activity is intrinsically purposeful, it thus far sees itself only as serving a purpose, not as being essentially directed toward that purpose (pp. 197–98/299–300). In this is revealed the difference between concept (*Begriff*) and being (*Sein*): in its concept is contained what it is to be, what it is in the process of becoming; in its being is contained only what it has become at any point along the way. It is only in its concept, then, that its purposive inner development is revealed. Admittedly, the activity of instinctive observing reason is external, in the sense that its analyses and descriptions are turned toward a reality external to it; the activity, however, is but the *expression* of a purpose which is *internal* (p. 199/300). In self-consciousness consciousness is to itself its own object; in the process of *becoming* object to itself it is reason, and in this process its external activity becomes revelatory of its interior concept. "Now we have to see what *form* (*Gestalt*) the internal–external has in its being. The internal as such must, just as much as the external as such, have an external being and a form"—the interior must express itself—"for it is an object or is itself posited as a being present for observation" (p. 199/301). As itself the object of which it is conscious reason *appears* to itself.[24]

What follows in Hegel's text can seem to us today some rather primitive biological explanation, seeking to come to grips with the life process in terms of "sensitivity, irritability, and reproduction" (pp. 200–207/302–11). Admittedly, the "science" in question is not very much to our more sophisticated contemporary taste. Its aim, however, is to highlight the teleological activity of organisms and to show both how the nature of reason itself is revealed in this sort of investigation and how the methods of observation remain inadequate in coming to terms with what is to be observed. Just as the observation of inorganic nature issued in "laws" of mechanics, so the observation of organic nature issues in "laws" of organic activity

---

22 The play on the word "end" is manifest: end can mean both *purpose* and *termination*.

23 The purpose (concept) of the natural object is internal to it; the purpose (concept) of the artifact is external to it, in the one who makes it, who intends that it perform a certain function.

24 Cf. *supra*, p. 9, where it was pointed out that the *appearing* of an object and the *consciousness* of a subject are one and the same movement.

(p. 202/306), which "laws" pertain to the concept of the organic, not to its mere being, i.e., the conceptualizing and the discovering of "laws" are identified (pp. 204–205/307–308). All of which serves to bring out that even the most refined anatomical *description* does not *explain* the process of life (pp. 206–207/310–11). What does emerge significantly from this, however, is the difference between consciousness at the level of scientific observation and consciousness at the level of perception and understanding. Both understanding and observing reason are concerned with the analysis of external reality; but reason has become explicitly conscious that in so doing it is dealing with *thoughts,* not with *things* (p. 208/311). Moreover, the reasoning here involved is an attempt to come up with a conceptual explanation more determinate than the vague, unsatisfactory concept of, for example, "force" (pp. 209–10/313–14).

Nevertheless, the overall results of the kind of scientific observation in question are still unsatisfactory. What it seeks to explain is life, an internal process, but the data available to it are only external appearances (p. 211/315). The problem, then, if reason is to come to grips with itself, is for it to get to the heart of organic reality, penetrating to the multiplicity of internal interrelationships which constitute its life process. This will mean, phenomenologically, determining how life *appears* to consciousness—without abandoning the results which the foregoing scientific analyses have made available. What is, after all, the *meaning* of life (pp. 211–12/315–17)? The answer to that question may be difficult to find; it is clear, however, that the answer will not be found at all in terms of relationships which are exclusively mechanical or chemical [25]—life is essentially an activity which is productive of itself (pp. 212–13/317–18). It remains to be seen just how much that is saying.

If, however, reason is to find out how much this is saying, it cannot rest content simply to stand on the outside, so to speak, looking in—any more than it can plumb its own depths by looking in from the outside. The best this sort of view can afford is a series of "representations" (*Vorstellungen*) in which life itself is not "present" (p. 216/321).[26] The point is that the scientific classifications of individual organisms under their species and genera are employing just such "representations" which give no knowledge of what life really is (p. 218/324), i.e., a process, in the sense of "self-systematizing development" (p. 220/326).

Very subtly at this point the tables are turned. What had begun as an investigation of organic life in order to find there the model for the life of reason will become an investigation of the life of reason in order to find

25 See *Logic,* "Mechanism, Chemism, Teleology." One is reminded of Socrates' dissatisfaction (*Phaedo*) with the rational explanation given by Anaxagoras.

26 Although it is true, lexicographically, that the terms *vorstellen, Vorstellung* could be translated "present," "presentation," it is clear from the present context that only "represent," "representation" will do. Hegel makes clear (p. 216/321) that the function of *Vorstellung* is *repräsentieren,* in the sense that something which is not the reality is made to "stand for" the reality in question. Added to this is the notion that *vorstellen* is the activity only of the subject thinking, not of the object thought. Cf. Wallace, *Prolegomena,* pp. 246, 251.

there the very essence of "self-systematizing development." In Hegel's view, organic development is merely repetitious and can, therefore, give no clue to the larger, overall system of development, which reason must embrace and which can only be historical. The "life" to be examined now is "a life of the spirit ordering itself into a whole—the system which is here considered and whose objective existence (*Dasein*) is world history" (p. 220/ 326). Consciousness has come to the realization that it can look into its life to find the answer it seeks, because in the life of consciousness, unlike organic life, the whole of that life is present in each individual consciousness (p. 220/326).[27]

This last remark can, of course, seem to be the sort of unjustified abstract generalization of the individual which Hegel had criticized Kant for perpetrating. It should be remembered, however, that Hegel has attempted to show the orderly process of development whereby consciousness has come to this realization, the realization that genuinely universal, all-embracing knowledge is possible only because individual reason and universal reason are not distinct but identical. Still, it is true that if all Hegel does is to make an assertion such as this he has not *achieved* the reconciliation of individual and universal reason. Only in spirit will this reconciliation be achieved, but consciousness now sees, however vaguely, the direction in which it is moving. As a result of examining organic life, consciousness has reached only "the intuition of itself as universal life in general . . . that its essence lies not in the organic as such but in the universal individual" (p. 220/326–27). Quite obviously, reason has not yet attained to science in the strictest sense of the term—it will do that only in the "absolute knowing" which terminates the *Phenomenology*—but it is at least clear to it both that the science it has so far achieved is not the science which can satisfy it and that it will move forward only by looking deeper into itself.[28]

b) *Observing Human Nature* [29]

It is simple enough to say that, having drawn a blank in its efforts to get at the truth of reality by observing nature—whether inorganic or organic—consciousness must now look into itself for an answer. The problem is to determine how the method of "observation," to which reason is at this stage still committed, can accomplish this. What can consciousness "observe" which will tell it anything about itself? The problem, however, is not that of gen-

27 Cf. Feuerbach, Marx, Engels, for whom man is a "species being" in the way no other living being is.

28 "It was made apparent, practically at least, that intelligence, with its hard and fast formulae, its logical principles, its keen analysis, was not deep enough or wide enough to justify its claim to the august title of reason. To be reasonable implies a more comprehensive, patient, many-sided observation than is necessary to prove the claim to mere intelligence" (Wallace, *Prolegomena*, p. 137).

29 Although in Hegel's text this section bears the long title "Observation of Self-Consciousness in its Purity and in its Relation to External Reality—Logical and Psychological Laws," the context of the dialectic, moving from the inanimate, to the living, to the self-conscious, justifies calling the last stage simply "the human." We know that for Hegel the human is essentially spiritual. The question, then, is how much the method of observation can tell us about the spiritual nature of man.

eralizing on the basis of an observation of what is necessarily singular, i.e., this or that consciousness; the conviction with which the last section ended, that to know any individual consciousness as such is to know universal consciousness, warrants this turn in the investigation. The problem, rather, is to determine what object of observation can possibly reveal the universal essence of consciousness. Since the investigation follows upon an examination of organic nature, whose key concept is *life*, and since the preceding investigation had resulted in the conviction that the universality of the concept of life demanded the move from an examination of merely organic life to the life of consciousness, it is inevitable that the dialectic should now turn to an examination of life as manifested in consciousness. The fundamental notion of life as "self-development" can, it is true, be gained from an observation of the teleological activity of even a single organism; but if the notion be limited to the self-development manifested in the interaction of spatially distinct parts of organic nature, it is a truncated notion indeed. Life can be comprehended only "in the concept existing as concept or in self-consciousness" (p. 221/329), the model of internal self-development.

If self-consciousness, then, is to be observed, two possible paths would seem to be open, the path of introspection, finding consciousness revealed in one's own activities, or extrospection, finding it revealed in the activities of others. If the activities are to be "observed," of course, they must be in some sense expressed externally. If, then, it is possible to observe logical and psychological processes which are peculiar to human consciousness, the investigation can get under way.[30]

For anyone even remotely acquainted with the methodology of experimental psychology, it should come as no surprise that Hegel should turn to this sort of investigation. It might, however, cause considerable surprise that he should begin by speaking of observing the "outer expression" of logical processes. Just what is there to be observed which is external to the processes themselves? In a manner which may or may not be convincing, Hegel assures us that the "laws" of logic are the external expression of the process of thought and as such can be "observed," presumably by introspection. The "laws" in question are, of course, those of formal logic and, leaving aside the question of their "observability," it can be asked to what extent they reveal the reality of thought as a function of consciousness. That Hegel should give formal logic such short shrift here is no indication that he did not appreciate its significance: he recognizes in it a useful tool in the regulation of the reasoning process. For his present investigation, however, its sheer abstractness makes it of little use. Thus, when he says of logical rules that "they have no truth," he does not mean that they are not correct but that, since they have no real content, they tell us nothing about reality: "They have no *reality* means simply nothing else than they are without truth" (p. 222/329). To know them is to know their formal truth, not to

---

30 "What could be more pertinent to human as distinguished from organic nature than logical and psychological processes? And observability of such processes in their outer expressions is precisely the basic issue before us" (Loewenberg, *Hegel's Phenomenology*, p. 136).

know the content to which they can be applied. In fact, the very universality of their applicability forbids them to have any determinate content; their only content is their own emptiness—the form itself (p. 222/329).

"Observation" simply "finds" the form-content of logic as "given," "merely there," static, a thought without movement, which is no thought at all, the paradox of a form of thought which as content is not informed by the dynamic character of thought. Formal logic manifests "a *motionless being* of relationships, a mass of separated necessities," which as "fixed content in and for itself . . . are in fact deprived of form" (p. 222/330). Taken by themselves, then, the rules of logic contradict the dynamic "unity of self-consciousness." "What is expressed as a fixed law constant in itself can be only a moment of the unity reflecting back on itself, can appear only as a disappearing magnitude" (p. 222/330). To "observe" logical rules is to *fix* them, turning them into "singular disappearing moments, whose truth is only the whole of the thinking movement, knowing itself" (p. 223/331). To separate the "laws" of thought from the "activity" of thinking is to empty them irremediably (p. 223/331). They do not reveal the reality of self-conscious reason at all.[31]

Fixed logical guidelines for thought, then, have quickly been eliminated as candidate for revealing to consciousness what self-consciousness is all about. They do not so much as reveal vaguely what the *activity* of thought is. With the disappearance of the first candidate, however, a new one comes on the scene, one which will manifest what "goes on" when consciousness engages in its characteristic activity. "There opens, then, for *observation* a *new field* in the operative actuality of consciousness" (p. 223/331). Psychology can observe human behavior (both introspectively and extrospectively) and infer from it to the self-conscious reality behind it. In doing so, it will discover "laws" of subjectivity, which like the logical laws of objectivity, are also "given" (p. 224/332). What immediately happens, however, at least in the kind of observational psychology Hegel is speaking about, is that observation finds all sorts of interior "faculties, inclinations, passions," etc., whose connectedness in the unity of the human spirit are like the unconnected connectedness of a lot of things tossed together in one "bag" (p. 224/332)—a congeries of unrelated yet "restless movements" (p. 224/333). Observation generalizes these various characteristics by making them vague and indeterminate, finding names for them which convey little meaning. But the universality conferred on each such characteristic by giving it a single name does not conceal the actual diversity of what is named when found in different individuals: "The unity of these diverse capacities is the opposed side of this universality, *actual* individuality" (p. 225/333).[32] The capacities, drives, passions, inclinations, emotions, etc. which psychology

31 "The method of observation and the laws of thought are equally grounded in the notion of fixity—the method is inoperative except in relation to arrested particulars, and the laws are applicable only in the shape of frozen universals. But static entities, whether things or thoughts, are abstractions from their dynamic contexts and organic relations, and it is in such abstractions that at this stage reason is shown to be constantly floundering" (*ibid.*, pp. 137–38).

32 Every empirical science, of course, needs a classificatory terminology if it is to raise

can enumerate do not pertain to the spirit and thus have neither the unity of interrelationship in one spirit nor the universality of being the same in each individual. "To take, on the contrary, conscious individuality without spirit as a *singular* empirical *(seiende)* appearance involves the contradiction that essential to it is the universality of spirit" (p. 225/333). The kind of universality which a "law" governing them demands is a universality to be found only in spirit, not in empirical being.

Observation, then, finds a host of factors not belonging to the organic makeup of the human individual, "circumstances, situations, habits, mores, religion, etc." (p. 225/333) and by accumulating them seeks to grasp the uniqueness of individuality. It has generalized names for the multiplicity of factors which influence each individual and make him different from each other individual—but only the spirit of each does that. It is not the sum total of influences which determines the individual to be this one and no other; it is the individual who by his response determines what influences him (p. 225/334). The influences are too general to have particular effects; it is the individual who particularizes their generality. "Religion," for example, has no effect on me; *my* religion does, and *I* make it mine.

Ultimately this sort of empirical psychology, which is limited to the observation of external phenomena, bodily manifestations like blushing, dilating of the pupils, gestures, etc., is pushed to the extreme of making the exterior into a mirror image in which the interior can be read. Of course, there are external factors which influence the interior, just as there are internal factors which influence the exterior; but there is no way of establishing "laws" which demonstrate any "necessary" connection. Whether psychology seeks to comprehend the individual by determining what his world is or seeks to determine what his world is by comprehending the individual, it is doomed to disappointment because it insists on remaining on the surface with what it can observe, measure, classify, and enumerate. What it takes to be a relationship of cause and effect *need* not be such at all. "As a result, however, *psychological necessity* becomes so empty a word that in regard to what is supposed to have had this influence the absolute possibility is there that it could have not had it" (pp. 226–27/335). If, like behaviorism, all it has to go on are physical phenomena, there are no laws (p. 227/336), certainly no laws regulating the spirit. But perhaps there are external phenomena whose connection with the interior reality of the human psyche are so intimate that one is justified in reading the interior in them. To this possibility observing reason now turns.

c) Observing the Immediate Expression of the Interior [33]
To us who today read the long treatment which Hegel accords to the patently absurd pseudo-sciences of physiognomy and phrenology, it can well

observation to the degree of generalization necessary to science. When, however, a "scientific" psychology employs such a terminology to classify what is essentially both dynamic and unique in each individual, it runs the risk of rendering the terminology itself practically meaningless.

[33] Again, the original is unwieldly: "Observing the Relation of Self-Consciousness to its Immediate Actuality: Physiognomy and Phrenology."

seem that he is either wasting his time or deliberately burlesquing what in his day these disciplines were supposed to reveal. There is, however, more to it than that. In the first place what is patently absurd to us—and to Hegel— was not patently absurd to the followers of Lavater (physiognomy) and Gall (phrenology) who had mustered what seemed to many to be scientific arguments supporting their position. Secondly, there is a certain plausibility, as even Hegel admits, in seeing the influence of interior states expressed exteriorly, especially in the face, and there is equal plausibility in seeing a certain effect of cerebral localization of mental functions on cranial formation.[34] What is questionable—and this is Hegel's point—is that anyone can construct an authentic "science" out of such plausibility, or that, if one does, it will afford much worthwhile knowledge. Thirdly, if these pseudo-sciences had not existed, Hegel would almost have had to invent them, since that is the direction in which the dialectic as he describes it is moving.[35] Finally, it is probably true that Hegel does a lot of burlesquing in order to get his point across.

Having failed to find in the "laws" of either logic or psychology an adequate key to the reality of consciousness on the level of reason, observation will not be satisfied until it has pushed its inquiries to the utmost absurdity in seeking to infer the very essence of self-consciousness from its outward manifestations, variable in the case of facial expressions, constant in the case of cranial structure. Because, however, it is still looking for "laws" relating self-consciousness to its external actualization, it is faced with the paradox of reading the *free* activity of consciousness in the *fixed* being of observable expression (p. 227/338). Attempts to do this on the basis of external influences on the individual have proved futile; it now turns to the individual's own body where his inner activities find expression (p. 227/338). His body, after all, is "the expression of his self *produced* by himself" (p. 228/338); it presents visible "signs" of what goes on in consciousness.

Stretching the meaning of the term a bit Hegel calls bodily patterns "organs" which render the inner "activity itself" visible (p. 229/340). This contention, however, is seen to claim at once too much and too little: too much, because it claims that *everything* is expressed exteriorly; too little, because in separating the expression from the soul it has to admit the possibility that the individual either is *unable* to express what he intends or can *intend* other than what is observed, i.e., can intend to deceive (p. 229/340–

---

34 In his article "Hegel on Faces and Skulls" (in MacIntyre, *Hegel*, pp. 216–36), Alasdair MacIntyre has contributed a discerning and enlightening study of the relevance of Hegel's examination of these pseudo-sciences to the overall plan of the *Phenomenology*. They are not merely positions to be refuted; they too are significant steppingstones in the movement of "observing reason" looking into itself. Nevertheless, MacIntyre observes perceptively, such "sciences" are doomed to ultimate failure because "the understanding of human beings is not predictive in the way natural science is" (p. 234).

35 "Detailed discussion of beliefs now dear only to the antiquarian must here of course be forgone. But they cannot be ignored entirely. For they are beliefs that seem as if made to order to illustrate the necessity of the course of the dialectic. Had there actually been no zealous advocates of them, Hegel would have been driven to invent hypotheses not unlike those of physiognomy and phrenology for the purpose of binding more closely the relation of mental life to its visible expression" (Loewenberg, *Hegel's Phenomenology*, p. 144).

41). At best the connection between the mental and the bodily is arbitrary, especially if the bodily has the non-fixity of facial expression (p. 230/341). From this sort of arbitrary connection no "law" is derivable. Because bodily expressions are merely external, "their relationship to each other is indifferent, and they do not have the necessity for each other which is supposed to be involved in the connection of an *exterior* and an *interior*" (p. 231/342).

Admittedly, speech as audible sound is closely connected with meaning, and so too is the hand with its gestures; neither, however, is the immediate *expression* of consciousness, both are *instruments* consciousness employs in acting (p. 231/343); nor is either adequate to express all that lies within, both by nature and as the result of development, i.e., the entire person (p. 232/344). The very variability of such expressions resists fixation by observation (p. 232/344); nor do they express what is most unique, the individual's reflection on his own activity (p. 233/344). There is no question that the internal is externalized, but it is not *definitively linked* to its externalization; if there is a connection, it is contingent (p. 233/345). Above all, the exterior cannot adequately express the interiority of the *will act* (p. 234/346). To think that it does is to confuse the *theoretical* and the *practical*, making what can be *observed* (the *Gestalt*) the essential and what can only be *done* (the *Handeln*) the inessential (p. 234/346–47). The whole thing becomes a matter of "opinion" (*Meinung*), and what the individual is thought to be *capable* of doing is taken to be what he *is*, independently of what he actually does (p. 235/347). To read an invariable connection between exterior expression and interior activity is as absurd as the sort of old wives' tale which links hanging out the wash with the advent of rain. There is no way of making a necessary connection between any "particular external configuration (*Gestalt*) and any particular self-consciousness" (p. 235/348).

As an indication that all this may not be as farfetched as it may seem, Hegel introduces one of his rare quotes from a contemporary, Lichtenberg, who in 1778 had published a critical account of physiognomy. "If someone were to say," says Lichtenberg, "you act, it is true, like an honorable man, but I see from your face that you are forcing yourself and are at heart a scoundrel, such an assertion would indeed, from now until the end of the world, be answered by any honest fellow with a box on the ear" (p. 236/349). Farfetched or not, however, reducing this position to absurdity permits Hegel to assert with confidence that the human individual's real *being* consists in his *doing*: "The *true being* of a man, rather, is *his deed*; in the latter, individuality is *actual* (*wirklich*), and it is this individuality which transcends (*aufhebt*) both sides of what was *opined*" (p. 236/349). If we are to find the true self of self-consciousness, we must look to its *activity*. Ultimately this will permit us to see the human individual as essentially spirit; here it brings us only to an acknowledgment of "the sort of being" the individual is (p. 237/350). Even investigating a man's actions, however, demands a caution: to break up the *act* into "intentions and that sort of detail" may help to analyze activity; it may also serve to obscure the issue (p. 237/350–51).

Although it has suffered one more defeat, the observational attitude is not yet dead. Even granted that action is what counts, there must be a way of getting at action through some fixed external effect which permits a determinate, incontrovertible reading. Suppose we invoke a *causal connection* between inner reality and outward expression; the activity of consciousness produces some *thing* which is its fixed expression (p. 238/351).[36] Since the result presumably produced is physical, of course, the activity of consciousness (mind) will need some physical instrument to produce this result, an instrument which works on the individual's own body, not on external reality (p. 238/352). This, then, brings up the question of what that internal physical instrument (organ) is going to be (pp. 238–39/352). Historically speaking, there have been a number of candidates: the liver, the heart, the nervous system, the brain, the ganglia (p. 239/353); it is not obvious which is the best candidate. Then there is the question of the result produced: the cranium, the spinal column, the breast; *locating* the spirit (mind) is quite a problem. In modern times other candidates seem to have been eliminated; the "organ" of "spiritual" activity would seem to be the brain, whose location is in the head—it is encased in the cranium (p. 240/354). In Hegel's day the brain was scarcely subject to direct examination—at least while it was functioning—so the obvious candidate for observation is the cranium. But the cranium is obviously not the "organ" of spiritual activity (p. 241/355); at best it is a "sign" (an "organ" in the sense of "observable expression") (p. 241/355). Pushing the burlesque as far as it will go, Hegel calls the brain "the living head" and the cranium the *caput mortuum* ("death's head") (p. 241/355). But what about causality? Do the activities of the brain produce the contours of the cranium, or do the contours of the cranium determine the activities of the brain? For this sort of pseudo-science, it really makes no difference; it is sufficient that they correspond—and with this, "causality" is out and "preestablished harmony" (hardly demonstrable) takes its place (p. 242/356).

All of this is unquestionably tedious (deliberately so?) and scarcely seems called for. It does, however, serve to get Hegel's point across, i.e., that it is an unwarranted contraction of the spiritual to confine it to any anatomical expression, especially since the sort of causality exercised in forming the cranium can in no wise be determined (p. 243/358).[37] Even if it were granted that self-conscious individuality can be somehow localized and, therefore, manifested in the brain, it is still important to recognize which has primacy (p. 243/358), that there is more to spiritual reality than its physical organ. If all we have to go on is "observation," however, the empirical being (*Dasein*) of the self-conscious individual has to be looked for in some *thing*—"a bone!" (p. 243/358). The inner, then, is no longer the spirit

---

36 "The attitude of observation supposes fixity in the being of that which is observed. Observation, we can say, cannot grasp *becoming itself*, the passage from one determinability to another; it seeks subsistent determinabilities" (Hyppolite, *Phénoménologie*, I 229n43; cf. I 222n33).

37 This last contention might today be disputed, but it is not likely that determining the causality of cranial formation would greatly advance the argument for phrenology—or for any anatomical reading of spiritual activity.

(mind), it is the physical brain; and the outer expression of that is the cranium: "This is the understanding of the relationship between the two sides of this connection which they have in the consciousness observing them" (p. 243/358).

The fact is that the cranium is not even a "sign" of mental life, i.e., indicating something other than itself; by itself it indicates only itself (p. 244/359). Like Hamlet we can *make* a skull remind us of the Yorick of bygone days, but that is not what a skull is for; nor is its function to tell us about the spirit. None of this means that Hegel denies either that feelings, spiritual activities, etc., can be "located" in certain parts of the brain or that the activities of these parts of the brain could have *some* influence on cranial formation (pp. 244-45/359-60).[38] He does deny that any very significant conclusions can be drawn therefrom, and he issues a warning against confusing symptom and cause (p. 245/360). Most of all he denies that a "mere thing," a "spiritless reality," can be adequate to reveal the reality of spirit (p. 245/360). The contention that it can becomes even worse when the attempt is made to locate every possible spiritual reality in some configuration of the cranium, which the *logic* of a thoroughgoing phrenology would be forced to do (p. 246/360-61). This, to carry the burlesque to the limit, would be like expecting the children of Israel, who were promised that they would be as numerous as the sands of the seashore, to find each his own corresponding grain of sand! Even if there is *some* correspondence, it *could* be coincidental. Observation can imagine (*vorstellen*) any number of connections; it is powerless to demonstrate that they belong to the *concept* of conscious individuality.

That it has been possible for observation to go to such extremes as it does here is due to an unwarranted generalization of a principle which in its own way has truth: "that the *exterior* is *the expression of the interior*" (p. 247/363).[39] Taken in this naïve way, the principle would justify looking for a complete correspondence between the external reality of body and internal life of mind—or it would do away with mind completely. It might, of course, be applied to animals who, Hegel is convinced, are mindless, but it cannot be applied to spirit whose unpredictable freedom cannot be mirrored in the fixed confines of any merely physical expression whatsoever. "The being of spirit cannot at least be taken as something so simply unvarying (*Unverrücktes*) or invariable (*Unverrückbares*)" (p. 247/363). Nor does it solve anything to say that, although the cranium need not reveal how

---

38 "This pseudo-science, having paved the way for the accredited doctrine of cerebral localization, may lay claim to some historical importance" (Loewenberg, *Hegel's Phenomenology*, p. 145).

"And between the anatomy of the brain and the anatomy of the cranium there must surely be some causal connection. It was the merit of phrenology, ludicrous though its tenets now appear, to have done pioneer work in cerebral localization of mental traits. Its basic error simply was, to seek access to the brain exclusively through the skull" (*ibid.*, p. 147).

39 In the *Logic*, "Doctrine of Essence," this will in other language become the extremely important principle that "essence must manifest itself exteriorly," the principle which permits the move from subjectivity of essence to objectivity of reality.

one is—thus safeguarding a kind of freedom—it does reveal how one "ought to be," the way, for example, paleontological remains reveal what an animal must have been. "If, however, the *actuality* is not there, then *empty possibility* counts for just so much" (p. 248/364)—i.e., as much as "it ought to rain when I hang out my clothes." The kind of "empty possibility" discovered in the physical exterior does not reveal even a spiritual tendency; freedom simply cannot be expressed in a bone! (p. 248/364).[40]

Now we can begin to understand what Hegel means when he says that "being" simply is not the truth of spirit. Quite obviously, it cannot mean that spirit *is not*; every word he has written cries out against that. Nor does it mean that what he said above about "the being of spirit" was illegitimate. What it does mean, however, is that the term "being" with its connotations of subsistence, constancy, fixed determinations, such that it lends itself to the formulation of empirical laws, cannot be used to designate spirit (p. 248/364).[41] "A being (*das Seiende*) without spiritual activity is a thing for consciousness, and so little is that the latter's essence that it is rather the opposite of the same, and consciousness is *actual* to itself only through the negation and elimination of this sort of being" (p. 249/364–65). It is the work of spirit to put its own dynamic mark on the dead being over against it. There can be no way of inferring the self as thinking or the self as thought from the dead exterior being of a bone. This is but another way of saying that no individual is the way he is *because* of the way his cranium— or any other externally observable part of his anatomy—is (p. 249/365); his spirit is his true reality, and no *thing* can express that (p. 250/366).

With this rather banal conclusion, reason has gone as far as mere "observation" will take it. It had to go the whole way, however, for two reasons: (1) its own logic forced it to exhaust every last possibility of finding a solution on the level of sensibly verifiable data; [42] (2) the logic of the dialectical movement demanded that it go as far as possible in the wrong direction in order to recognize the necessity of turning around, "for only the totally bad contains in itself the immediate necessity of altering its own course" (p. 250/366). This, of course, should not seem strange to us, now that we are familiar with the tendency of the Hegelian dialectic of going down every possible dead-end street. It is a tendency which from this point on will become more pronounced, and it will explain why forward movement seems to be accomplished by way of a series of attempts to go all the way in the wrong direction.

Reason, then, finds itself forced to "take its object back into itself . . . since spirit is all the greater in proportion as the contrast (*Gegensatz*) from

---

40 The "scientific" response to this, of course, might be that if freedom cannot be scientifically explained (on the basis of observation), so much the worse for freedom. To which Hegel's reply would be, "so much the worse for *your* science!" As Hegel sees it, freedom is not an *hypothesis* which requires scientific *verification*; freedom is itself a principle of verification—what contradicts its possibility has refuted itself.

41 "We see what meaning Hegel gives to the term 'Sein,' being, *natural being*. The spirit is not a being, or at least it transcends (*aufhebt*) being. Such is the result Hegel is going to draw from this study of phrenology" (Hyppolite, *Phénoménologie*, I 280n135).

42 A logic not unlike that employed by contemporary behaviorism which, since it cannot "observe" mind, is forced to deny it any reality.

which it returns to itself is greater" (p. 250/366). The more violent the contradiction, the more radical the turn which is demanded. Each previous dead-end street along the dialectical march had demanded only a slight change; now "observation" has to recognize that it is utterly incapable of coming to grips with reality. "Observing reason, then, turns to this [a wisdom conscious of itself], to the spirit, the concept existing as universality or to purpose existing as purpose; and from now on its own essence is its object" (p. 251/367). Previously, idealism had simply been sure of this from the beginning; consciousness as Hegel sees it had to have this move forced on it. The attempt to comprehend spirit in terms of mere "being" has resulted in treating it as a thing—like a "bone" (p. 252/369).[43] "Consciousness no longer wishes to find itself immediately, but rather to produce itself through its activity. *Its own self* is for it the purpose of its activity, just as in observation it had only to do with things" (p. 253/370).[44] It is true, of course, that right from the beginning reason was convinced that "it is to itself *all thingness*, even the *purely objective itself*," but what it had initially failed to recognize was that it is all "thingness" only "in *the concept* or that the concept alone is its truth" (p. 254/371). It will find itself by producing itself in its own proper activity of conceiving. The *movement* of rational *judgment*, as opposed to the *fixity* of the "scientific" *proposition* will reveal the essential *infinity* of reason, as opposed to the essential *finitude* of understanding. The identity of reason and reality will never be grasped if reason is looked upon as doing only what scientific understanding does, "if the self-transcending judgment is apprehended without consciousness of this, its infinity, but only as a static proposition; if its subject and predicate have validity each for itself; if the self is fixed as self, the thing as thing, and yet one is supposed to be the other" (p. 254/372). This is not to say that understanding is one "faculty" and reason another; it is to say that to identify consciousness functioning as reason with consciousness functioning as understanding is like identifying two totally different functions of one and the same bodily organ, the function of *generation* with the function of *urination* (p. 254/372).[45]

B. THE ACTUALIZATION OF RATIONAL SELF-CONSCIOUSNESS
THROUGH ITS OWN ACTIVITY

Even if we were to grant that the original insight into the unity of reason in both the rationality of nature and the rationality of self-consciousness is an accurate one, it has become evident that "reason" remains an empty abstraction if the only means of giving it a content is "observing" nature in

---

43 It is as though Hegel had here concentrated the entire dialectical movement of the *Logic*, going from *being* to *essence* to *concept*.

44 Once more the play on words (and on concepts) is unreproducible. The "activity" of consciousness is its *Tun*; "having to do," *zutun*, "with things" is not enough.

45 For a not totally comprehensible reason Hegel chooses to express this quite vulgarly— perhaps to shock the reader into a comprehension of the vast difference between the finitude of understanding (urination) and the infinity of reason (generation).

all the ways it is observable. The possibilities of basing the identity of rational thought and reality on an observation of the way things are, whether in the mechanics of nature, the biology of living organisms, or the bodily manifestation of mental states, have been exhausted. A new insight must supplement the initial one.[46] This means that attention must now be turned away from the merely physical to mental activity itself. Mental activity, however, first reveals itself not in the theoretical investigation of what is the case but in the practical work of guiding action. But it is individuals who act, and so the focus of attention becomes the practical activity of individual self-conscious reason. How does it reveal itself to itself in its activity?

The objective reality of self-consciousness which reason has been seeking to comprehend as it is in itself has now become the direct object of reason's investigation. The immediate assurance simply that "it is all reality" has been superseded "in such a way that the *objectivity* of self-consciousness now counts as merely superficial; the inmost essence of that objectivity is *self-consciousness* itself" (p. 255/374). It has found a way of looking at itself, thus becoming effectively at once both subject and object of the investigation. "We" know that it is the work of spirit to be both subject and object, but spirit itself in the form (*Gestalt*) of rational self-consciousness has only an initial "certainty" of this identification: "It is the *spirit* which has the certainty that it finds its unity with itself in the doubling of itself and in the autonomy of both aspects" (p. 255/374). Now, as on each previous level of the dialectical movement, mere certainty must be raised to truth; its vague abstractness must give itself a content—through its activity.

Hegel now seeks to tie the movement to be examined in with what has gone before; the steps in the actualization should somehow correspond with the path already traveled. If we look back at observing reason, he tells us, we shall see that its dialectic corresponded with the dialectic of objective consciousness: the observation of nature in general with sense certainty; the observation of organic nature with perception; and the establishment of laws—logical, psychological, physiognomical, phrenological—with understanding (p. 255/374). What is to be expected now, then, but a movement corresponding to the movement of self-consciousness from mere independence to the genuine liberty of self-determination (pp. 255–56/374–75)? But in turning to this sort of examination, reason cannot immediately make the transition to itself as universal; it must first look to itself as individual—among other individuals. "Initially this active reason is conscious of itself only as an individual, and it must as such demand and bring out its actuality in others" (p. 256/375); if it comprehends what it is for itself to be reason, it will grasp what reason is in others.[47] Where reason is truly present it is

[46] "That mind's objectivity is other than what mere observation is capable of affirming represents the new insight now definitely won" (Loewenberg, *Hegel's Phenomenology*, p. 150).

[47] "In the dialectical evolution of reason individualism serves as necessary transition to a collective life. Implicit in all subjective aspirations is an inevitable trend or nisus towards the community in which alone true individuality can find fulfillment and expression" (*ibid.*, p. 151).

the same for all; it must, however, be *recognized* in its universality. The individual must see in his own reason the universal "which in its own pure consciousness unites all self-consciousness" (p. 256/375). The dialectical movement, then, will consist in a series of attempts to universalize individual self-conscious reason.

Taking his cue from Kant and Fichte, Hegel sees as the area in which individual reason most clearly lays claim to universal validity the area of ethical judgment, *das Reich der Sittlichkeit*, where what is recognized as genuinely a "law" for the behavior of one is *eo ipso* a "law" for all. Granted that "law" in this sense is only abstractly universal until applied to a concrete instance, still, in it consciousness is actual to itself; its demand is an *actual* demand. "In the *abstraction of universality* this ethical *substance* [48] is only the law as *thought*; it is, however, just as much immediately actual self-consciousness, or it is ethical demand (*Sitte*)" (p. 256/376). What is for individual self-consciousness "law" *is* "universal ethical demand" (p. 256/376).

Hegel, however, does not derive such a universal "law" after the manner of the Kantian "categorical imperative," whose universality is bound to a logic of non-contradiction Hegel refuses to employ. The framework in which Hegel sees the universality of law actualized is the universe of human community, "in the life of a people" (p. 256/376), where universality consists in the conscious unity of its members, enabling each "to intuit in the autonomy of the *other* thoroughgoing *unity* with him" (pp. 256–57/376). In the other, who is the negative of myself, I find the same *objective* being as I find in myself (p. 257/376). Reason is the "universal substance" in all of us, not because I have abstractly universalized my own reason, but because in each there is the same self-consciousness, whose singularity has been subsumed in the community. The universalization of the individual is to be achieved neither by individual fiat nor by logical abstraction, but only by the concrete interrelationship of individuals in a community whose unity resembles that of an organism. "They are conscious to themselves of being these singular independent essences as a result of sacrificing their singularity and of the universal substance being their soul and essence; by the same token this universal is once again their *doing* as singulars, or it is the work they have produced" (p. 257/376). Concretely, then, the individual lives among other individuals, conscious that ethical demands apply to individuals, but to all alike. This sort of consciousness will, as we shall see, have to be refined as the true nature of reason is progressively revealed; but it serves here to tell more about the universality of the individual than either *logical* or *psychological* laws can, because it is a consciousness of laws regulating the spiritual–moral activity of real human beings.

If, however, we look at the activity of the individual only from the point of view of its singularity, we find an activity which is not truly spiritual at all, precisely because it ignores the relationship to others without which the individual is merely singular, isolated. "The *mere singular* impulsive activity of the individual is directed toward its needs as a being of nature, i.e., as

---

48 *Substanz*: Hegel's term for an objectively universal constant.

an isolated singularity" (p. 257/376). Nevertheless, even this activity, despite the singular individual, so to speak, takes place within the framework of a community uniting a multiplicity of individuals: "What the individual does *is* the universal orientation (*Geschick-lichkeit*) and the ethical demand (*Sitte*) of all" (p. 257/377).[49] Like the British economists with whom he was familiar, Hegel sees action which genuinely serves the self-interest of one as serving the interests of the community: "The *work* of the individual for his own needs is just as much a satisfaction of the needs of others as of his own, and he achieves the satisfaction of his own only through the work of others" (p. 257/377). This does not achieve, obviously, the universality even of the ethical norm; but it is aptly illustrative of an effort which on the face of it is purely individual but significant only in a universal framework. In economic *society*—scarcely the ideal of *community*—only if all are governed by the same rules can either the society or individuals survive. The universality of the work is unconsciously produced, but in producing it the individual becomes conscious of the universality of his object, which demands sacrifice of mere singular selfness for the sake of the whole.

At this stage of the dialectic, any notion of *obligation* in connection with the activity being discussed does, it is true, have to remain rather vague. That it touches all universally, however, makes sense, as does the contention that each understands his own "obligation" better in knowing it as the "obligation" of all; in the universal the individual is more comprehensively revealed. "In the universal spirit, therefore, each has only the certainty of himself, has no more to find in the existing actuality than himself; he is certain of others in the way he is of himself" (p. 258/378). The situation is one in which through experience, not through abstract generalization, each knows that what is true for each is true for all, and vice versa. This, of course, has to be fleshed out, or it will remain on a level of intolerable vagueness.

The fleshing out can *begin* with an initial example of subjective universality in *"the customs of a people"* (p. 258/378); they are subjective demands shared by all. The example, it is true, is not tremendously satisfactory, since the universality in question is only a sort of happy accident, not the genuinely unified self-consciousness of all, imposed, so to speak, on each individual self-consciousness, without too much reason behind it, because at this stage "the spirit is in the form of *being*" (p. 259/379), i.e., the universal obligation is *given* not *produced* by the activity of spirit. What it comes down to is that, in a situation where each consciousness is actually "isolated" from each other, each has, nevertheless, a "lofty trust" (*gediegenes Antrauen*) that his own universalizing of obligation is shared by the others. "Thus has the individual come face to face with laws and customs; they constitute a thought without absolute essentiality, an abstract theory without actuality; the individual, however, is as this I living truth to himself"

[49] We have to remind ourselves again that for Hegel the copula *ist* rarely denotes identification or even mere attribution of predicate to subject. It indicates a much more dynamic connection, like "implies," or "springs from," or "passes over into."

(p. 259/379). It is still all very individualistic, but it is on the move, and that is what counts.

Thus, even though a situation in which it just *happens* that each individual in seeking what is best for himself seeks what is best for the people is hardly satisfactory (pp. 259–60/380), still it is a step in the direction of concretizing the initial abstraction, to be followed by many more steps. "If, then, the truth of this rational self-consciousness is for us the ethical substance, so too for it the beginning of its ethical experience of the world is in this ethical substance" (p. 260/380). The individual's selfishness in looking only to his own self-interest will, if consistently pursued, issue in a more significant rational self-consciousness. This initial stage, then, can be seen as dividing itself into two stages. First, there are merely natural drives which have only the satisfaction of the individual as their goal. Their satisfaction turns out to benefit all,[50] and out of merely individual efforts there issues "the coming-to-be of the ethical substance" (p. 260/381). Second, individuals become gradually conscious of a higher goal, and their merely natural drives are transcended: "From this aspect, in the movement wherein is experienced what the truth of these drives is, their immediacy or crassness is lost, and their content goes over into a higher" (p. 260/381). But this still falls short of that aspect of self-conscious activity "according to which it proceeds from the substance itself" (p. 260/381), i.e., acting in a way *which* benefits all has not yet become acting in that way *because* it benefits all.

When the development of the "ethical substance" is looked at this way, it can be considered either in its original coming-to-be, in some primitive stage of society, or as being restored after having been lost. Since, however, Hegel's constant concern throughout his career is the moral regeneration of a Europe which had lost its soul,[51] it is more appropriate to see the development in terms of a movement from the impersonal "enlightened self-interest" of the British political economists to the authentic moral self-consciousness of the political order Hegel advocates. "But since more appropriate to our times is that form of ethical substance in which its moments appear after consciousness has lost its ethical life and in seeking it repeats those forms, the moments can be better presented as expressed in this latter way" (p. 261/381). In the three subsections which follow, the illustrative material will all be contemporary.

What Hegel seeks to portray is the movement wherein individual self-consciousness, which as individual has the universality proper to spirit only abstractly—"is initially only the concept of spirit" (p. 261/381)—actualizes itself. The process of actualization will be a process of overcoming isolation, but it will also be a process of discovering the inadequacy of intermediate forms of universality. That the individual self-consciousness affirms itself in terms of its activity and not in terms merely of its being is an indication

---

[50] This has been worked out in considerable detail in Marx's "dialectic of need and fulfillment."

[51] See Harris, *Hegel's Development*, pp. xxix–xxxi. Eric Voegelin says very perceptively ("On Hegel—A Study in Sorcery," *Studium Generale*, 24 [1971], 337): "As a philosopher Hegel had to be healthy enough to diagnose the spiritual state of society as diseased."

that it is moving in the right direction. It quickly learns, however, that self-affirmation at the expense of others is not enough (p. 261/382). Only in a collective framework where others are affirmed too does individuality make sense. In a series of attempts to achieve self-affirmation in a collective (social) framework, the first is entirely spurious. The only universality it recognizes is the universality of reference to the individual self: everything, and everyone, is there only for me; nothing counts except as existing for me, for my pleasure, an unmediated relationship to the universe of reality and of other individuals. To overcome this, the individual does an about-face, now engaging in a universal sentimental concern for the well-being of others, setting up its "law of the heart" (p. 261/382), which, again, turns out to be what the individual "feels" is good for all. Its "pleasure" is the well-being of others. The "good" to which sentiment is directed, however, turns out to be unattainable in the face of continued individual self-affirmation, and so this latter must be virtuously sacrificed for the sake of the universal "good." "In elaborating this *law* of its heart, however, it experiences that in it the *singular* being cannot hold out, that the good can be accomplished only through the sacrifice of singularity, and the individual turns to *virtue*" (p. 261/382). The movement, then, is from pure *selfishness* to pure *virtue*. It remains to be seen how this is spelled out and whether it is effectively a movement from singularity to universality.

a) *Pleasure and Necessity* [52]
The framework, to be sure, is a universe of multiple individuals, but the attitude of the singular individual in face of it is that of "doing what comes naturally." All is *there*, but the only thing which *counts* for this singular self-consciousness is itself; everything—even every other self-consciousness—is *for it* (p. 262/384). Morality, thought, knowledge, all are unimportant, so long as the individual can enjoy himself.[53] The model for this Hegel finds not in history but in imaginative literature, in Goethe's first *Faust*,[54] and Hegel's description of the model takes on a highly imaginative character: "Replacing the spirit shining from heaven, the spirit of the universality of knowledge and action, wherein sensation and the enjoyment of singularity keep silent, there has entered the spirit of the earth, for whom all that counts as true reality is the being which is the reality of the singular consciousness" (p. 262/385).

With this sort of attitude the individual does not even produce its own

---

[52] It should be noted that a not so subtle change has been introduced into the dialectic, even into the descriptive titles of its stages. Each attempt at universalization is now introduced *along with* its opposite number which cancels it out. The unmitigated quest for "pleasure" comes a cropper in the "necessity" of fate; the irrational "law of the heart" turns into "conceited folly"; and contentless "virtue" folds when applied to the reality of "the world's course" (the course of events).

[53] One is reminded of the unmitigated pleasure Plato describes in the *Philebus*.

[54] "It is characteristic of Hegel to discern in imaginative dress typical examples of human comportment possessing greater authenticity than those present in the episodes of history or in the disquisitions of the learned" (Loewenberg, *Hegel's Phenomenology*, p. 155).

enjoyment; he simply takes the pleasures life has to offer. Science, laws, principles constitute obstacles which must disappear. Life is like a ripe fruit to be plucked; nothing must come between it and the self-realization of the individual. This has gone far beyond the "appetition" which was the initial impulse toward self-consciousness; it does not crave this or that object; it craves only pleasure. What subjective attitude could be more universal? Is the picture farfetched? It does seem to describe one of the perennial ways of "seeking an identity," where experiencing self and experiencing pleasure are synonymous.

In any event, even as a *possible* form of self-consciousness, this sort of pleasure-seeking turns out to be self-defeating rather than self-revealing. Pleasure in isolation is not even pleasure; to seek only one's own pleasure is to find none. It does not work as a universal principle unless it works for everyone. Unconsciously the selfish consciousness has affirmed the universal legitimacy of selfishness, "for self-consciousness does not become object to itself as *this one alone* (*dieses einzelne*) but rather as *unity* of itself and the other self-consciousness, thus as superseded singular or as *universal*" (p. 263/ 385–86). Its own individuality turns out to be the merest of abstract concepts. Thoroughly impoverished, it is "the poorest form of self-realizing spirit, since it is to itself only the *abstraction* of reason, the *immediacy* of the unity of *being in itself* and *for itself*" (p. 264/386). In attempting to find itself too rapidly, self-consciousness comes up empty-handed.

Pleasure-seeking turns out to be the harshest form of necessity. The complete absence of self-determination, utter slavery. Unlike subjection to the *rational* necessity of *law*, which in Hegel's eyes is freedom, this is subjection to the *blind* necessity of *fate*, which is the diametric opposite of freedom. "Sheer singular individuality, which initially has as its content only the pure (abstract) concept of reason, instead of propelling itself out of dead theory into life, has rather propelled itself into a consciousness of its own lifelessness, and it has as its portion itself only as empty and alien necessity, as *dead* reality" (p. 265/387). The universality of pleasure has turned to ashes in the mouth of the one who sought it. "Everything is for me" turns into "there is nothing for me"; the attempt to grab the whole of life immediately finds nothing there (p. 265/388).

The individualist, then, has learned something: the "turn" (*Verkehrung*) from "vital being to lifeless necessity" (p. 265/388) is as lacking in mediation as was the craving for pleasure, and sheer pleasure has turned out to be no pleasure at all, only slavery. Not that pleasure is without purpose or significance, only that "feeling" cannot get at them. Pleasure makes sense only in relation to a "pure self, which is a universal, i.e., thinking" (p. 265/ 388). The pleasure of the spirit is something else again; in the "feeling" of pleasure, consciousness does not get to know itself at all; it is a riddle to itself—caught up in a universal necessity it cannot comprehend: "*Abstract necessity*, then, amounts to the merely negative uncomprehended *power of universality* against which individuality is shattered" (p. 266/388). The attempt to affirm only one's own individuality results in the complete loss of individuality. All that is now available is the opposite extreme, sheer universality. The individualist becomes universalist, but in his heart, not in his head.

b) *The Law of the Heart and the Insanity of Self-Conceit*

That the move which individual self-consciousness now makes in its attempt to achieve universality will prove futile is already indicated in the title of the subsection. For Hegel, "law" is always the work of reason—one of the reasons why understanding was inadequate to its own object—and to speak of a "law of the heart" is equivalent to speaking of a square circle. But since Hegel's concept of reason is a far cry from that of the rationalist, it would be a mistake to think that in reason he finds no place for the heart or that the kind of universal law the heart seeks to establish has no significance as a moment along the path to adequate rationality. The inadequacy, then, of a "law of the heart" is not that the heart is involved in it but that the consciousness which is recoiling from individualism should seek a remedy in a sentimental universalism of ethical demand, which, because it is sentimental, is ineluctably individualistic. Sentiment is not a framework which can contain the universality proper to reason. The heart, in fact, is a false guide precisely because "it knows *immediately* that it has the *universal* or the *law* within itself" (p. 266/391).

The sentimental "law," like the Kantian "maxim," is a guide purely for individual behavior, but without the intervention of even a categorical imperative, it is set up as law governing everyone's behavior. "Like the previous form of consciousness, this one is essentially isolated (*für sich*) as a *singularity*; but it is richer in having the determination that it takes this *being for itself* as necessary or universal" (p. 267/391). From what it sees—in its "heart"—to be good for itself, individual self-consciousness immediately concludes that the same is good for all. This is the romanticism of the sentimental visionary, who would make the world over in his own image—not for his own good but for the good of the world—"a violent ordering of the world" (p. 267/391). It is the reforming zeal of a Karl Moor in Schiller's *Brigands*. The reform is needed, because everyone else in the world is under the law of necessity (p. 267/391), and so the world must be cured of the necessity under which it labors. "This individuality, then, is directed toward eliminating both the necessity which contradicts the law of the heart and the suffering therein entailed" (p. 267/392). The pleasure principle has not been abandoned but refined; the pleasure of this sort of philanthropist is to bring about the welfare of mankind. His well-wishing, however, has not had the benefit of discipline and so proves to be an unreliable guide. "The actualization of the immediate [abstract], *undisciplined* notion (*Wesen*) [55] counts as presenting something outstanding (*eine Vortrefflichkeit*) and as producing the welfare of mankind" (pp. 267–68/392).

Mankind, however, does not necessarily share the reformer's enthusiasm, either because *its* heart is not in *his* law, or because in following the law it does not enjoy itself, while lacking any awareness of its own excellence if

---

[55] There is simply no way in this context that *Wesen* can be translated either "essence" or "being." It is too abstract to be either.

it does not enjoy itself. It would seem, after all, that the law of anyone's
heart is as good as that of anyone else's, and any agreement between them
would be purely accidental, not having reason to guarantee the agreement
(p. 268/392-93). "The individual, then, establishes the law of his heart; it
becomes *universal order*, and his pleasure becomes a lawful reality in and
for itself" (p. 268/393). Not only is such a law arbitrary; it is also self-
defeating. By establishing it, the individual loses control of it; because it is
not a demand of reason but only of individual sentiment it gets out of
hand, becomes a universal *power*, inimical even to the heart which produced
it. Like Kant's "maxim" it has no genuine universality, only a universality
imposed on a content essentially individual (p. 269/394).

That other hearts should find themselves in this same law is nothing but
an assumption. "It is not some one determinate law whose establishment
was in question; rather, the immediate unity of a single heart with universality is a mere thought raised to the level of what is to count as a law, i.e.,
the law that in what is law *each heart* must recognize *itself*" (p. 269/394).
The only semblance of obligation left in this law is the obligation on others
to find that it is the law of their hearts, too, and they do not; in fact, the
very intransigence of it turns them against it.

Once again, we ought not to see too much implausibility or burlesque in
this. The newspapers are full of stories of reformers who want no rational
questioning or discussion of their vision of the good life; the law of the
heart demands unquestioning obedience, the only kind of universality it
can enjoy. The heart which is only heart cannot even recognize the kind of
universality proper to genuine law. The law is necessary by fiat, and that
is all there is to it. But this sort of necessity is actually an impediment to
the recognition of genuine rational necessity (p. 270/394), the necessity
proper to the unified consciousness of a community, not to the idiosyncratic
consciousness of any individual in the community (p. 270/395).

The experience of contradiction between the universality *in* the consciousness of the community and the universality *imposed on* his own
heart's product drives the sentimental reformer insane. Universality is essential to law, but one universality conflicts with another, and "the beating
of his heart for the welfare of mankind turns into the tumult (*Toben*) of
insane self-conceit" (p. 271/397). This turns into fury against any authority
representing another order (p. 272/397).

What has been wrong from the beginning is exclusive reliance on the
heart as the seat of universal order. What was supposed to be a true law has
turned out to be a mere opinion, "which, unlike the existing order, has not
lasted out the day" (p. 272/397). This last, incidentally, does not mean that
Hegel is canonizing the *status quo*; he is, however, issuing a warning against
irrational rebellion; and mere heart is the very essence of irrationality
(p. 272/398). Existing laws, as much in need of reform as they may be, have
more rationality in them, and under them individuals are more genuinely
individuals, because if they are *laws* at all, they have roots in reason. Abol-
ish them in the name of unreason, and all order is gone; it has become perverse order (p. 273/399).

Because there are as many laws of the heart as there are hearts, the only universality achievable on the level of heart is universal opposition of each law to each other (p. 273/399). By the same token, since reason has been eliminated the only order left is that provided by "the course of events" (*der Weltlauf*), i.e., by what *de facto* happens, without asking whether it *ought* to happen. But this is no more than "the illusion of a constant process, whose *universality* is only *opined* and whose content is rather the aimless (*wesenlose*) play of singular happenings (*Einzelheiten*) coming on and off the scene" (p. 273/399).

Once more consciousness has wandered down a dead-end street, one which, of course, was necessary in order to indicate the direction it must now take. That direction is away from the idiosyncratic individual with his arbitrary opinions to a dedication to "the true and good in itself" (p. 274/400). It is individuality which has now become perverse (*das Verkehrte und Verkehrende*). Consciousness relinquishes its singularity to become "virtue," and another universality has made its appearance (p. 274/400).

c) Virtue and the Course of Events

Once more, in the very title of this subsection, Hegel announces the two poles of a dialectical movement which will eliminate both by lifting them to a higher level of consciousness. More than that, however, the two poles of the dialectic are operative not merely in the title but in the very beginning of the movement described. The reason for this is that the transcending of individuality necessitated by the frustration of both pleasure-seeking and sentimental reform zeal immediately points in two directions: toward the abstract ideal of "goodness" and toward the hard fact of a course of events uncontrolled and uncontrollable by any individual. "To the consciousness of virtue, *law* is the *essential* and individuality is what is to be superseded, and that just as much in its consciousness as in the course of events" (p. 274/402). There would seem, of course, to be a significant difference in the implications of the two directions. In subjecting itself to the universal under the heading of whatever is "truly good," individuality at the same time preserves itself, whereas in surrendering itself to an impersonal order of events it relinquishes whatever might have characterized it as individual. The difference, however, only *seems* to be great. It is true that conscious activity on the part of the individual brings "virtue" into being, but it does so under the extremely vague aegis of the "true and good in itself" (p. 275/402), which is not of its own doing. What it has in fact surrendered to, then, is *the way things are.*

Because the only content which consciousness discerns at either of the two poles is the rather negative universality of the "reverse" of individuality, there is little to distinguish the two. If we put together "both previous movements of self-consciousness" (p. 275/403), i.e., the sheer individuality of pleasure-seeking which trails off into the universal "necessity" of fate, and the empty universality of a "law of the heart" which continues to be hopelessly individualistic, we find them both swallowed up in an ineluctable "course of events." If, on the other hand, we try to solve the dilemma of individuality by an appeal to the vague universality provided by "the heart," we run up against the dispersed individuality of each and every heart; the only egress is a "law" which is not of the "heart," the abstract law to which "virtue" submits.

This last would seem to be an escape both from the sheer necessity of fate and the insanity attendant upon the hopeless individualism of sentimental zeal, since it is an approach to the benign necessity of genuine rationality, but individual consciousness is not out of the woods yet. "The universal law, it is true, maintains itself in opposition to this self-conceit and no longer makes its appearance as an empty something opposed to consciousness, no longer as a dead necessity but as a *necessity belonging to consciousness itself*" (p. 275/403–404). Still, as related to a stubborn reality which resists its ideal of truth and goodness, it does not escape insanity; as objectively real, it says no more than "whatever is the reverse" (*die Verkehrtheit überhaupt*) of the way things are (p. 276/404). "Thus, granted the universal presents itself in the two poles as the power of their movement; but the existence of this power is simply universal reversal" (p. 276/404). Individualism has been eliminated by simply asserting whatever is its opposite, reversing what individuality had reversed in its insane self-conceit. "Now the universal is supposed to get its true actuality from virtue by the transcending of individuality, the principle of reversal" (p. 276/404).

What it comes down to is that "virtue" takes up the battle where the "law of the heart" had unsuccessfully left off. Faced with a "perverted" (*verkehrten*) world, it will "reverse" (*verkehren*) its course and thus *convert* it: "to reverse again the perverted course of events and to bring out its true being" (p. 276/404). Virtue, then, struggles with the worldliness of the world in an attempt to bring about the good. Whether or not virtue will win depends on the weapons it employs, and its weapons are what it is essentially: "For the weapons are nothing else but the *essence* of the warriors themselves; only this goes forth for both of them" (p. 276/404). Only if virtue is the true essence of rational self-consciousness will it stand a chance.

From the outset the battle between virtue and the worldliness of the world would seem to be uneven; how to fight reality with an abstraction.[56] There is question of an *end* to be brought about. For "virtue" this end is an abstract goodness in which it "believes"; for the "course of events" the end is an orientation actually contained within what comes about (p. 276/404–405). Virtue, however, will not give up the struggle. If it can find in individuals a universality corresponding to the universality of "the good," victory is possible, perhaps even assured. The uniqueness—nonuniversality—of each individual notwithstanding, there are "talents" (*Gaben*), "capacities" (*Fähigkeiten*), and "forces" (*Kräfte*), common to all individuals even in their uniqueness, and these constitute a "spiritual" reality capable of overcoming the world; they can be put to work for that purpose. They "exist," it is true, only in individuals, but they are universal—they are the universality of the individual! "There is a way in which the spiritual is such that it is represented as a universal which needs for its vitalization

---

[56] Cf. Marx, "Against the Critical Critics": "The task is not to criticize the world but to change it."

and movement the principle of individuality" (p. 277/405). Yet since talents, capacities, forces, etc. are such that they can either be used or misused, and "virtue" contains no guarantee that they will not be misused,[57] to act at all involves the risk of acting wrongly. If virtue is to remain virtue, therefore, it must abstain from action. "Since this universal stands at the service of the course of events just as much as of virtuous consciousness, there is no way of foreseeing whether thus armed virtue will triumph over vice" (p. 277/405–406). The very same capacities, after all, are both good and bad, depending on how they are used; mere virtue has no way of determining them to good use, and the course of events is indifferent (p. 277/406).

Once again, Hegel turns to an illustration from imaginative literature, this time not so contemporary but certainly familiar to educated German readers. The "Knight of Virtue" (Don Quixote) is stuck; all he has to go on is his faith that the good will prevail, a faith which precludes any great significance to his own activity. His own contribution, in fact, becomes "a shadow-boxing (*Spiegelfechterei*) [58] which he *must* not even allow to become serious" (p. 277/406) because the weapons employed in the fight are indifferent to good and evil. A virtue not rooted in reason, which is what Hegel is talking about, is condemned to be as ineffective as a faith not rooted in reason.

The dilemma of the virtuous consciousness goes even deeper. It cannot effectuate the abstract good,[59] and whatever good it does effectuate becomes integral to the course of events against which it is struggling. It is forced to struggle against the "existence" of the good because only in the course of events is any "existence" possible. "Precisely such existences of the good, which become thereby ineradicable relationships, are all moments in reality which ought to have been opposed and sacrificed by virtue itself" (p. 278/407). In its zeal for changing the world virtue must refrain from changing the world; a changed world is still the world. It cannot employ its own weapons, good as they may be; it cannot destroy the weapons of the enemy, since they are the same weapons; "for all are noble parts of the good for which it entered the battle" (p. 278/407).

The fight is indeed an uneven one. There is no defeating the course of events, precisely because for it nothing which happens is a defeat; whatever happens is simply absorbed in the course of events: "Its power, then, is the negative principle to which there is nothing constant and absolutely holy, which can rather risk and withstand the loss of anything and everything" (pp. 278–79/407). It can accept everything, including the Knight of Virtue, whereas the Knight is pledged to the abstract good for which he fights, and this good is truly good only as long as it is unreal. "Virtue, then, is conquered by the course of events because in fact its own end is the abstract,

---

57 It becomes more and more clear that the "virtue" of which Hegel speaks is a far cry from the ἀρετή of Plato and Aristotle or the *virtus* of Thomas Aquinas. Rather, it is a vague sort of "goodness," the "virtue" against which Nietzsche inveighs, whose rules are *given*.

58 Literally, "dueling before a mirror."

59 Cf. Aristotle's critique of Plato's "Idea of the Good," *Nicomachean Ethics* 1.

unreal idea (*Wesen*), and because in regard to actuality its activity rests on *distinctions* which are merely verbal" (p. 279/408). Thus, the consciousness which has relinquished individuality in order to *actualize* the good fails because *actuality* is always individual (p. 279/408).

The "good in itself" is only an *idea* for consciousness, an idea which cannot be actualized without ceasing to be what it is. If individuals do not effectuate the good, there is no real good; if they do, the good they effectuate becomes part of the course of events (p. 280/409). The victory of the course of events over virtue is a victory over the abstractions which virtue is forced to rely on, such as "what is best for mankind," "sacrifice for the good," "misuse of talents," etc., which both say nothing and accomplish nothing. "Such ideals and purposes sink together as empty words which edify the heart and leave the reason empty. They edify, but construct nothing" (p. 280/409).[60] Here there is a great difference between the "virtue" Hegel is pillorying and the virtue of the ancients, not merely because the ancient virtue was more susceptible of rational explanation, which could also be abstract (e.g., doing the *right* things for the *right* reasons), but, more significantly, because it was rooted in the communal life of the people and from that drew concrete meaning. "It had its definite and secure significance because in the *substance* of the people it had its *content-full foundation*, and for its purpose it had a *real already existing* good" (p. 280/409–10). To such a virtue, actuality and the course of events were no threat (p. 280/410). When the ancient wise man was asked what is good for the people, he could say; when the Knight of Virtue is asked what is good for mankind he can answer only with rhetoric because, having withdrawn from the reality of life, he has no concrete good to talk about. The "virtue" for which he stands has universal significance only by *prescinding* from real individuals in a real world.

At the beginning of this subsection, it was noted that not only "virtue" but also "the course of events" were somehow opposed to individuality; in both, individuality is sacrificed for the sake of the universal. The dialectic has now moved far enough along to enable consciousness to see that universality is not to be achieved by the sacrifice of individuality and that "the movement of individuality is the reality (*Realität*) of the universal" (p. 281/411). Thus the impersonal, indifferent course of events is also conquered; it cannot be separated from the "being-for-itself of individuality." If there is to be universality at all, it will be the result of activity, and only individuals act. If individuals can act in such a way that the source of their activity is a universal principle, the task will have been accomplished. The individual can very well seem to be acting only for his own benefit, but if in so doing he makes of himself a genuine individual (we might say a "real person"), he is in fact actualizing the universal (pp. 281–82/411). "The *activity and impulse of the individuality*, then, is its own end. It is *the use of its powers, the play of its outward activities (Äusserungen)* which gives life to what otherwise would be dead abstraction (*das tote Ansich*). The

60 The play on *erbauen* ("edify") and *aufbauen* ("construct") does not come through in English.

in-itself (*Ansich*) is not an unfulfilled, non-existent, abstract universal, but is itself immediately the presence and actuality of the process of individuality" (p. 282/411–12). The individual who *comes to be* all that it is to be an *individual* is universal—truly spirit—but not by looking only for individually subjective satisfaction.

C. INDIVIDUALITY WHICH IS REAL IN AND FOR ITSELF

Although the individual in search of an identity has come a long way—a way of sophistication—from the unhappy stage of the consciousness which was content to forgo an identity and leave its fate in the hands of the absolute master, the paths he has taken have been tortuous. Sometimes they seem to have landed him back where he started; always they prove unsatisfactory and drive him on to further attempts, each dictated by the precise failure which preceded it. Beginning with an attempt to discover the substance of his own rationality in the simple idealistic assertion that his own rationality and the rationality of the world are identical, the emptiness of such a claim leads him to look into the reality whose rationality he takes to be a given. On the level of nature, however, he does not find rationality given; not in physical laws, not in biological laws, not in any laws, derivable from observation, which would presumably reveal the essence of his own rationality. He turns, then, to action; certainly a more sophisticated approach, one in which the individual will remain in control of affairs. But whether as "sophisticated hedonist," "utopian dreamer," or "preacher of the selfless life," [61] he finds the nature of things too untractable to allow him to remain in control, even of his own individuality. When he tries to assert the universal validity of his own individual position, it turns out to be hopelessly singular; when he insists on his own singularity, he finds himself caught up willy-nilly in a universality he did not intend. Now, for one last try he will turn to his own thinking, first theoretical then practical. Surely of that he is as an individual in control, and surely it has a universal validity which the world of reality cannot take from it—so long as he does not run afoul of "things" out there. He will find the very substance of his rationality by looking into himself.

At the beginning of the overall dialectic of reason, Hegel tells us, it was only "we" philosophical observers who had the concept of reason as "being all reality." We saw consciousness "planting its standard" of reason everywhere, but consciousness itself did not yet know where to look for the essence of this "standard." Now the individual has at least a vague awareness of something universal about himself, in the "faculties" he shares with all mankind. What he has been looking for, his "goal," the very "essence" of his own rational activity, will reveal itself in "the self-moving interpenetration of the universal—those talents and capacities—and his individuality" (p. 283/414). It is precisely in what he shares with others that his own individuality will achieve fruition.

[61] Loewenberg, *Hegel's Phenomenology*, p. 167.

He has to be "objective," of course, but the secret of that objectivity is to "have as the object of rational consciousness the category as such" (p. 283/414), i.e., his self as the heading under which all reality comes. The vague "certainty" he had initially is about to become "truth" because rational activity itself, not some alien object, is the truth of reason. "The activity is in itself its own truth and reality, and the *presentation* or the *proclamation of individuality* is the essential goal of its activity" (p. 284/415). The previous forms of rational self-consciousness noted above are, of course, not simply abandoned; they are recognized as "moments" in a union which is dynamic, not static: "In *all* of them consciousness holds fast to the simple unity of being and the self, which is their *genus*" (p. 284/415). Attention, then, is turned to the immanent activity which engages only consciousness as opposed to any activity expressed outwardly; it is in immanent activity that the individual is realized as himself: "The *material* worked with and the *goal* of the activity are in the activity itself" (p. 284/415). This sort of activity has no relation to anything outside itself; it is the passage from one immanent state to another. "The activity transforms nothing and is directed to nothing; it is pure form of going from *not-being-seen (dem Nichtgesehen-werden)* to *being-seen (das Gesehenwerden)*" (p. 284/416).[62] It is *activity* in this sense which constitutes the *actuality* of the individual—his *doing* is his *being*; there he can find his true reality (p. 285/416). The ideal of "self-systematizing development," which was but vaguely glimpsed in the observation of organic nature and more explicitly focused on in the attempt to "observe" the inner functioning of self-consciousness,[63] now seems on the threshold of being realized in a rational activity which is at once individual and universal. It will not be, until every attempt to achieve universality by abstract means has been found wanting.

a) *The Realm of Spiritual Animals—Deception—What Really Matters* [64]
What is being treated in this subsection is a first attempt on the part of the individual to give universal significance to the immanent activity of his own consciousness. Can the identification of reality and the self, "the category," be achieved in purely individual mental activity? The answer would

---

62 Why Hegel here used what seems to be rather crude visual metaphor is not clear. What he is saying, however, is clear enough: the activity and the awareness of the activity are identical.

63 Cf. *supra*, pp. 142–45.

64 *Die Sache selbst.* Perhaps no expression of Hegel's has caused translators—into any language—so much embarrassment as this. Apart from the fact that there is no precise English equivalent for *Sache*, there is no one *meaning* of it in the various contexts in which Hegel uses it. Baillie, who seeks consistency, renders *die Sache selbst* as "the real fact." Royce, much more imaginatively, says, "the cause." It could also mean "the thing itself," as it does when Husserl in his battle-cry says *zu den Sachen selbst!* The meaning has to be gathered from the context. The "activity" (*Tun*) of which Hegel has been speaking translates the Latin *agere*, and the *Sache* comes close to translating the Latin *res* in the expression *res de qua agitur*. Hegel is talking about the kind of objectivity connected with sticking to *die Sache selbst*—the cause, the task, the inquiry, art for art's sake, knowledge for knowledge's sake, etc., what really matters, what it is all about, an objectivity with no intermingling of subjectivity—which turns out to be a "deception."

seem to have to be no, since the individual has gone back to the empty assertion of the identity of his "I" and the whole of reality with which the
dialectic of reason had begun: "The absolute reality which individuality
knows itself to be is, therefore, as individuality becomes conscious of it, *abstract universal* reality, without the fulfillment of a content, merely the
empty thought of this category" (p. 285/419). There is, however, a difference. Where the initial concept is the *result* of the individual's conscious
activity, the concept is empty; where the concept is the activity itself, it progressively gives itself a content. Thus, to look at the concept as the *product*
of mental activity is to cut it off from the process which seems to confine it;
but, in fact, the very cutting off makes the concept abstract. To see the activity precisely as activity which produces no *result* other than itself is to do
just the opposite, "for this latter is in this case a complete relating of *itself
to itself*" (p. 285/419). To grasp this, consciousness must see its own activity
as simply not the activity of a *nature* which is, in fact, oriented to producing
some *result*: it is not the individual's *nature* which constitutes his individuality; his nature is merely the "element" in which his individuality unfolds (like the water in which the fish swims) (p. 285/419).

Little by little the individual is coming to realize that it is his *spirit*
which makes him to be an individual in the authentic sense, the sense in
which only the human is individual, i.e., has meaning in himself, not
merely in the generality of the species, as does the animal.[65] The pathos,
of course, comes when the human individual seeks his universality in the
natural unity of the species rather than in the *spiritual* unity of the community—but that is jumping ahead. What counts here is a clarification of
the distinction Hegel is making between "being," the framework of *natural*
process, and "acting," the framework of individual (spiritual) process (p.
286/420). It is by "acting" that the individual *negates* his merely natural
being, thus determining himself to be more than natural. "The *acting*,
however, is itself nothing other than *negativity*; in individuality acting,
then, the determinateness (*Bestimmtheit*) [of nature] is loosed in simple
negativity" (p. 286/420). Mental activity is not the product of nature; it is a
negation of the limitations of nature. "It is the concept containing (*Inbegriff*) all determinateness" (p. 286/420). To negate the confining determinateness of nature is to affirm the ever-widening determinateness of the
individual, whose self-determination is his activity—he becomes a self
through his activity.

Lest we think, as apparently did Marx, that Hegel is plumping for some
sort of disembodied self-consciousness, it should be noted that he quite
clearly affirms that the human individual is the development of an "original
nature." The activity whereby that "original nature" develops into an in-

---

[65] There are as many interpretations of Hegel's *das geistige Tierreich* as there are
interpreters. It seems clear enough, however, that the principal point Hegel is making is
that to seek the distinctive feature of the human individual in the order of *nature* rather
than of *spirit* is to treat human individuals as *animals*. Loewenberg, I am afraid, has
contributed not a little to the confusion here by interpreting the whole section on the
basis of a few side remarks Hegel makes.

dividual, however, is not merely natural activity, because consciousness is over and above mere "nature." Initially, in fact, the individual's "nature" is present to his consciousness as an object, as that which is to be developed (p. 286/420). In this sense, then, the goal (*Zweck*) of natural development is the individual, and the activity of consciousness which is more than merely natural brings into being individuality as developed nature (pp. 286–87/ 421). If, of course, one insists on imputing to Hegel a concept of "body–mind" duality, for which he had no use, then a distinction of what is from "nature" and what is from "spirit" could seem to imply a disembodied spirit. The distinction which Hegel is making, however, is between *activities*—"spiritual" and "natural"—which distinction does not require distinct *substantial* sources of the activities.

This could, of course, seem quite inconsistent, but only if we forget that for Hegel human nature, even as "original," is not merely animal; spirit is present in it. The "particular potentiality, talent, character, etc.," with which a human nature is originally endowed, constitute a "special touch of spirit" (p. 287/421). The activity of spirit which is, so to speak, embedded in nature is at the same time the negation of mere nature; it goes beyond nature as "*a nothing (ein nichts)* working toward *nothingness (das nichts)*" (p. 287/421).[66] Nature continues to be the foundation of individual activity, but the activity, which is the work of consciousness, reveals to consciousness that it is itself spiritual; "only that consciousness may be *for itself* what it is *in itself* must it act, or its action is precisely the coming-to-be of spirit *as* consciousness" (p. 287/422). Consciousness (*Bewusst-sein*) is more than merely natural being (*Sein*).

If, then, the goal of the dialectic of rational self-consciousness is the discovery by the individual of just what it is to be a rational individual, said individual must through his activity become what he is in order to know what he is. "The individual, therefore, cannot know what *it is* before it has through activity brought itself to actuality" (p. 287/422). Thus, a new problem arises: the activity of the not-yet-individual is goal oriented in the sense that it is directed toward realizing authentic individuality, but at the same time the individual cannot be conscious of what the goal to be achieved is prior to achieving it through activity (p. 287/422). In what sense is a goal a goal if one is not conscious of the goal precisely as goal? The circle seems inescapable: the individual "comes to know *only as a result of its act* the original essence which must be its goal, and yet, in order to act it must *previously* have *that goal*" (p. 288/422).

The whole issue has been somewhat confused—deliberately perhaps—by Hegel's seemingly indiscriminate use of a number of terms denoting *activity*. The verb *tun* means "to do" or "to act"; and what such activity produces is *die Tat*, "the deed," a purely immanent product, not really distinct from the doing. On the other hand, the activity which is characteristically human is "productive activity," *Handeln*, and it is in this characteristically human

---

66 If we remember that "nothing" also means "no thing," and that Hegel quite clearly wants to say that the spiritual does not belong to the order of "things," the strangeness of Hegel's expression need not prove an obstacle.

activity that the human individual must rise above his mere nature and achieve individuality. What the "productive activity" of *Handeln* produces is not the "deed" but the "product," *das Werk*—which, of course, can in English be given the same ambiguity it has in German by translating it as "the work." We have, then, two kinds of activity: productive, which terminates in a "work"; immanent, which terminates in a "deed" and is ultimately a determination of the doer. In one sense, then, every "doing" has its productive side, and every "producing" has its doing side. But in human activity, there is danger of confusing all this by concentrating on the productive aspect of *Handeln* in such a way that the distinction of "deed" and "work" is obscured.[67]

In this context the "goal" (*Zweck*) of human activity can also have two meanings. The goal of productive activity (*Handeln*) is the "work" to be produced, and of this the individual acting should be conscious if the activity is to make sense. On the other hand, the goal of the activity as immanent (*Tun*) is the individual in the process of coming-to-be, a goal which is known as goal only when it is already actual. If, then, we look at the process of productive activity, we can find the beginning, middle, and end of the process already contained in the human "nature" which has not yet achieved individuality. There are, to begin with, a host of "circumstances" (*Umstände*) calling for activity (*Handeln*), and there is the "interest" (*Interesse*) of the agent specifying what is to be produced. The "means" of producing will be determinate activities on the part of the agent conditioned by his capacities (talents, etc.). Finally, there will be the "thing" produced, the "work" (pp. 288–89, 423–24).

Although this description of the process is rather glaringly schematic, it serves the very important purpose of tying the "work" produced to the activity of producing it, which is both transitive, related to the "work," and immanent, related to the developing consciousness of the individual. To look, then, for an adequate expression of the individual in the "work" divorced from the individualizing activity of the individual's self-consciousness is to miss the "spiritual" (as opposed to "natural") character of individuality (p. 289/423–24). "Over against the work, however, consciousness characterizes itself as that which has in itself the determination of sheer *negativity*, immanent activity (*Tun*). Consciousness, then, is the universal in contrast to the determinacy proper to the work" (p. 289/424). If, in fact, productive activity were no more than natural, the work produced would adequately designate the agent, and individuality would be no more than a determination of nature. That, in turn, would mean that the distinction of one individual from another would be only numerical, and the comparison of one individual with another would not make sense; each would have an equal share of the "original nature," and comparing one human being with another would be like comparing one dog with another (pp. 289–90/424–25).

---

[67] It is perhaps this distinction, rather superficially interpreted, which leads Ernst Bloch, in an otherwise illuminating study (*Subjekt–Objekt*, p. 67), to conclude, at best arbitrarily, that the whole section on *Das geistige Tierreich* is Hegel's description of the world of capitalism!

It seems rather obvious that individuals do not look upon themselves as distinguished from each other merely in the way in which one horse is distinguished from another: "This is the concept which the consciousness which is certain of itself as absolute interpenetration of individuality and being forms regarding itself" (p. 290/425–26). The question now is whether experience justifies this certainty. "Let us see whether the concept which consciousness has is confirmed by experience and whether its reality corresponds with the concept" (p. 290/426). To do this, consciousness has to step back from the "work" produced and look rather at the activity which is proper to it precisely as consciousness. Unlike the productive activity which terminates in the particular "work," the proper activity of consciousness universalizes, and it is universality which characterizes consciousness even as individual. "The consciousness which steps back from its work is in fact universal consciousness—because it becomes *absolute negativity* or the activity in opposition to its work which is the *determinate*" (p. 291/426). The "work" is simply out there for others to see and judge; it is not what characterizes the individual; in fact, it misrepresents the individual. "Thus, the work is as such something transitory which in conflict with other forces and interests is canceled and represents the reality of individuality more as disappearing than as perfected" (p. 292/427). The individual comes to consciousness of self as individual not through the *thing* he produces but through the conscious activity which characterizes him.

If the self-conscious individual is to get at this true reality, he cannot be satisfied with what is but a contingent expression of his individuality. Thus, since producing this or that result or acting in this or that way to produce it are merely contingent matters, they cannot express his essential reality. His immanent activity, on the other hand, has a necessary connection with his genuine individuality, makes him to be the one he really is. "The *necessity* of immanent activity consists in the fact that goal is directly oriented to *actuality,* and this unity is the concept of that activity. Productive activity is engaged in, because immanent activity is in and for itself the essence of actuality" (p. 293/429). That the product turns out to be what the individual wanted to produce is contingent; that the activity makes the individual is not.

In this context, then, "what really matters" (*die Sache selbst*) is not the *thing* produced but the activity wherein the individual develops. "In this way, then, consciousness reflects on itself and away from its transitory work and affirms its own concept and certainty to be *what is constant* as opposed to the experience of the *contingency* of action. It experiences, in fact, its concept, in which actuality [68] is only a moment, something *for consciousness,* not the in-and-for-itself" (p. 294/430) (not the essential reality). "What really matters" is the activity, precisely *as* the activity of this individual (p. 294/430). The distinction here is between the mere "actuality" characteristic of a "thing" (*Ding*) and the "reality" which characterizes "what matters" (*die Sache*). "With this, *what really matters* expresses *spiritual* essentiality, wherein all these moments are superseded as counting of them-

---

[68] "Actuality" (*Wirklichkeit*) here is the contingent existence of the "work" (*Werk*) which "activity" produces.

selves and wherein to consciousness its certainty of itself is something objective, *something which matters"* (pp. 294–95/431). Here the individual has an objective grasp of what really constitutes his individuality. "In *what really matters*, then, i.e., in the interpenetration of individuality and objectivity which has become objective, consciousness has attained to its true concept of itself or has become conscious of its own substantial reality" (p. 295/431).

When the individual by turning his attention to "what really matters" has gained an objective view of himself, he has not yet grasped himself as *subject* in the full sense, as universal subjectivity, only as universal substance (p. 295/431–32). What this means is that the individual is aware of the predicate, "substance," under which all subjects come—to be subject is to be substantial subject—but is not yet aware of precisely what it is to be subject. "It is the *genus* which finds itself in all these moments as being its *species* and is, by the same token, free from them" (pp. 295–96/432). This is objectivity without a trace of subjectivity, disinterested, an "honesty" which will not inject subjective prejudice into the realm of objectivity: "The consciousness is called *honest*. . . . whose concern is only objectivity" (p. 296/432). "What really matters" is objectivity, and the "honest" consciousness has only this in mind, whatever it does. "It may go in whatever way it wants to, it still has brought about and achieved *what really matters,* for the latter as this *universal* genus of those moments is the predicate of all" (p. 296/432).

In this context it makes no difference whether this or that goal is achieved; "what really matters" is *willing* a goal; *something* always gets done, and there is no subjective interest to dictate more than that (p. 296/432). "What really matters," then, is doing—for its own sake. Strangely enough, however, this turns out to be more subjective than objective, a sort of interest in being disinterested. What counts for the individual is not so much that something gets done but that the doing be his own. "What really matters is to him precisely the *unity* of his *decision* and *reality*; he affirms that *actuality* would be nothing more than his *liking*" (p. 296/433). "What really matters" has lost all significance because it has become a predicate to which any subject whatever can correspond (p. 297/433).

The activity which was supposed to be "pure activity," i.e., for its own sake—like art for art's sake, or knowledge for its own sake—turns out to be "the activity of this individual," and "what really matters" becomes an "abstract actuality—*his* affair" (p. 297/434).[69] This is where "deception" enters in. What the individual gives out as purely disinterested objectivity turns out to be pure self-interest. The scholar, for example, whose only interest is "that the truth may appear" turns out to be concerned only that *his* truth may appear. But he also deceives himself; his emphasis on the *his* of "his affair" cannot cancel out the universality of "what really matters": "Because he seems ultimately to will only *his* affair and *his* activity, there

[69] *Sache.* As noted before the term not only can but must be translated in a variety of ways. When preceded by the personal pronoun it has a particular meaning. *Meine Sache,* for example, can mean "my business."

is question once more of the *matter as such* or of constant, independent, essential actuality" (p. 297/434). The "what really matters" which had initially seemed significant as an objective content of consciousness becomes equally significant as a form of consciousness and as such has another kind of universality: that proper to the process of consciousness as such (pp. 297–98/434). The individual presents it as his own, but in being presented it becomes common property; the interpenetration of individuality and universality has gone beyond the narrow confines of the individual who wanted it all for himself. He deceived others by pretending to be concerned only for what is universal; he deceived himself by failing to realize that he could not keep it for himself (p. 298/435).

There ensues a mutual deception, not unknown in the world of savants. An individual seeks "to bring out" (*auszuführen*) something which is a contribution not to his own glory but to "what matters" (*zur Sache*). In doing this he "acts" not for himself but for the common interest; his concern is with reality (p. 298/435). Others are attracted to the same activity, convinced that they too are disinterested, that what counts is that *die Sache* make its appearance, no matter who does it. But the actual interest of each is that *die Sache* be his own doing (pp. 298–99/435–36). There is deception all around, because pure objectivity is not really the motive on any side, and yet something has been brought forth *for all* (p. 299/436).[70] To make things worse, if something is praised, ostensibly its author is being praised, but very subtly the *praising* becomes the point; each is concerned with *his own* doing in praising. But even this welter of self-referential activity turns out to be deceptive. Each in doing anything at all reveals himself, and the whole thing becomes everyone's "affair" (pp. 299–300/437).

What it all comes down to in the context—and the context seems to be that of the "intellectual" community—is that anyone who *does* anything significant will soon find others flocking to do the same, not because of "objective" interest but because each wants it to be his own doing. Still, no one can be satisfied merely with the consciousness of doing it; each wants others to be aware of his doing. Slowly but surely there is surfacing in the self-conscious individual a realization that any attempt to be nothing but individual is doomed to failure; neither genuine objectivity nor genuine subjectivity is possible at this level. Witness the subjective hurt of the scholar whose "objective" findings are disputed but who cannot admit, even to himself, how subjective his objectivity is. An objectivity separated from the subjective activity of the individual—each individual—is a chimaera; and a subjectivity whose activity is only its own is cut off from the possibility of realizing itself as objectively real. To look for a realization of the individual on a level of merely individual activity is to look for what cannot be found, because only on the level of an activity which is "spiritual," not merely individual, does authentic individuality make sense. What is in

---

[70] "The scholar's deception lies in the arrogant substitution, hidden or overt, of the particular for the universal, as if his contribution to learning, precisely because it is *his*, were co-equal with the ideal cause of truth" (Loewenberg, *Hegel's Phenomenology*, p. 171).

question is an "activity of *each* and *all,* the essence which is the essence of all essences, *spiritual essence*" (p. 300/438).

The result of all this is the recognition that, just as substance which is only substance, i.e., universal (predicate), is not subject, so too the individual who is merely individual is not (yet) subject. The series of attempts on the part of the individual to qualify as subject in relation to "what really matters" prove to be but "moments" of an individuality becoming universal, i.e., a subject whose activity is not simply that of one individual (p. 300/438). The "what really matters" now becomes "substance shot through with individuality" (p. 300/438), an individuality which recognizes itself as not confined to one individual (pp. 300–301/438).

We are brought back, then, to the original certainty with which the dialectic of reason began, the certainty the individual has that to know all reality is to know the self or that objective consciousness and self-consciousness are one and the same. "The *pure what really matters* is what was earlier designated as the *category,* the being which is I or the I which is being; but still as a *thinking* which distinguishes itself from *actual self-consciousness*" (p. 301/438). What consciousness knows in knowing itself is a universal content; and the knowing is a universal knowing. The "category" is at once the form and the content of all consciousness. The universality which belongs on the side of knowing equals the universality which belongs on the side of the known (p. 301/438). Where, then, do we find the model of a universality which is as subjective as it is objective? In the concept of the *moral law,* an objective law whose source is universal subjective reason and whose binding force extends to all rational beings.

b) Legislative Reason

In his quest for a reason which is universal, Hegel now turns to that reason which regulates human activity insofar as that activity can be designated good or evil. This is an activity which, if we follow the Kantian concept of morality, reason and reason alone has the capacity both to dictate and to evaluate—in regard to *all* men. What follows is a rather truncated, certainly not adequate, presentation of the Kantian position. That it should be so truncated—and so unsubtle—may well seem strange, but we should remember that in a "phenomenology" of consciousness Hegel is concerned with the Kantian position from one point of view only, from that of the alleged "immediacy" with which reason knows law as universal.

The activity, then, which practical reason claims either to regulate or to evaluate is purely spiritual activity, an activity which clearly remains within self-consciousness and which pertains to any and every individual self-consciousness. Hegel is convinced that it is no longer necessary to consider even the possibility that consciousness might be a function of *nature* (p. 301/440). By the same token, even though the moral judgment is one which an individual makes regarding his own behavior, he does not in making the judgment regard himself as this or that individual but under the rubric of universality of applicability; a moral law is not a *law* if it binds only one individual as such. What is more, when moral reason speaks, the individual is *conscious* of the universality of his own reasoning (p. 301/ 440). Thus, that of which the individual is here conscious is absolutely true, always and everywhere true; independently of contingent facts, this is the "absolute fact" (*die absolute Sache*) (p. 301/440).[71] The ethical consciousness of an individual is a genuinely universal consciousness: "This fact is, therefore, the *ethical substance*, and the consciousness of this is *ethical consciousness*" (p. 302/440). Moral laws are, of course, multiple, but they are all united under the one heading "of the absolute essence" (p. 302/ 441), the ethical.

Since the laws in question are absolutely *a priori*, saying what *ought to be done*, without any appeal to the experience of *what is done*, their truth is immediately recognized. "Healthy reason" need not look outside itself; it "knows immediately what is *right* and *good*" (p. 302/441). Examples of the kind of rule in question will show that this is true. As a first example Hegel states the seemingly simple proposition, "Everyone should speak the truth" (p. 303/442). Clearly the proposition contains the required generality, no exceptions, and it contains its own justification for being enunciated—if "everyone should speak the truth," then this truth should be capable of being put into a proposition. The difficulty is that putting it into a proposition not only falsifies it but violates the proposed rule, since it has to be modified by a condition, "*each time in accord with his knowledge and conviction of the truth*" (p. 303/442). It might seem, of course, that the more complex proposition has solved the problem, but, says Hegel, the added condition has changed the universally necessary proposition into a contingent one. Its universality is "only in the *form of a proposition* in which it is expressed" (p. 303/442); it is contingent that one should know the truth supposed to be expressed.

Hegel might well seem to be quibbling here, but the point he makes is important: how to speak of an obligation to speak the truth, when the obligation cannot be put into a proposition—its truth cannot be spoken. Speaking the truth becomes contingent on knowing the truth; and if the contingency of that is removed, we have "the truth ought to be known" (p. 304/443), but an "ought to know" which has no content says nothing; and one which does have a content is not "immediately recognized" (p. 304/443).

Try another example: "Love your neighbor as yourself" (p. 304/443). Apart from the fact that the truth of the "as yourself" is scarcely immediately evident, says Hegel, "love" would seem to have to have a meaning if the proposition is to be true. "Love," then, will mean, even minimally, act in such a way as "to keep harm from someone and do him good" (p. 304/ 443). That, however, demands "knowing" what is good or bad for him and that cannot be known *a priori*. In anticipation of a position he will present only later Hegel then states: "Doing good in an essentially intelligent way, however, is in its richest and most significant form the intelligent

71 "There is but one absolute cause (*die absolute Sache*) to which the individual owes allegiance, this being the moral law, and this alone, since it is definable by a homogeneous reason, unites him with all other individuals" (*ibid.*, p. 175).

universal function of the state" (p. 304/444). The point he wants to make is that on the individual level the rule would turn into mere "do-gooding" which, when put into practice, could well do just the opposite (p. 305/ 444). The proposition is too vague to be a law at all; without a content it says nothing, with a content it is not *a priori* (p. 305/445). The conclusion is that reason cannot legislate behavior *a priori*; at best it can set up a criterion whereby to judge whether a particular content can be raised to the level of a binding law. "Legislating reason has been demoted to a merely *testing* reason" (p. 306/445). The renowned Kantian "categorical imperative" will now be subjected—very briefly—to critical examination.

c) *Reason as Judge of Laws*

The question at issue here is that formulation of the categorical imperative which enables Kant to take a "maxim," which does have an empirical content, and to determine in the light of pure reason alone whether it can become a universal law of moral behavior. If reason can do this without any appeal to experience, asking only whether the law in question would contradict itself, it would seem to have overcome both the difficulty of calling on experience and that of formulating its laws in those empty general terms which plagued reason's attempts to legislate. To avoid a "universality" which is as vague as was "what really matters," then, reason considers the universal law in relation to the determinate instance in order to see whether or not they are compatible (p. 306/446). There is, however, a difference. Formerly the law was formulated *a priori* and then applied; now the content of the law is given, and it is examined—not applied—to see whether it contradicts itself or not. If it contradicts itself, it cannot be a law; if it does not, it is tautological and, therefore, capable of being a law (p. 306/ 446–47).

Once again Hegel turns to examples, not of laws but of what might form the subject matter of laws. The first of these is: "Should there be a law that there be private property?" (p. 307/447), i.e., apart from any extrinsic usefulness it might serve? Is there any contradiction in there being private property? The answer has to be no. Neither is it contradictory, however, that there be no private property, i.e., common ownership. Whether or not there be property, then, is indifferent in itself. It can cease to be indifferent if the question of survival is introduced, but that is to introduce an existing fact, a need. We begin to face the same problem of generalization as before. There is no "property"; there are only "things" which are owned. To call things which are owned for a purpose, i.e., to be used, to be consumed, "property" is to confer on them a nominal universality, fixity, constancy, which would contradict their essential transitoriness (p. 308/448). On the other hand, to consider any "thing" as earmarked for ownership by any individual would contradict the universality of "thingness."

The language seems a bit farfetched, but again the point is clear. How can we talk about "contradiction" as a criterion of law when what we are talking about can be considered either contradictory or non-contradictory? "The criterion of law which reason has in itself fits everything equally well and is thus, in fact, no criterion" (p. 308/449). Whatever is in itself non-contradictory can in certain circumstances become contradictory. It may, of course, be argued that this is an unfair treatment of Kant's elaborate justification of the categorical imperative. The point Hegel is making is clear: if the only available *a priori* test of a law is its contradictoriness or non-contradictoriness, there is no way of concretizing this in action. "The result, then, seems to be this: that neither determinate laws nor a knowledge of them can come about" (p. 309/449).

Even granted that individual reason does have both legislative and testing functions in regard to universal moral laws, these functions turn out to be meaningless except in the framework of a movement away from the mere singularity of individual consciousness. "They are but instable *moments* of ethical consciousness, and the movement in which they emerge has the formal sense that by means of them the ethical substance presents itself as consciousness" (p. 309/449–50). A moral law is *much more* than the consciousness one has of it. Still, presented as it has been presented, the empty universality of law requires a content which is contingent (p. 309/450). As the subjective "law of a singular consciousness," its content is "arbitrary" (p. 309/450). The universality of ethical substance simply cannot reside in the singularity of individual consciousness whose legislative and judicial functions do not justify the universality of its "laws." "The unity in which they are merely moments is the self of consciousness, which now placed in the spiritual essence makes the latter actual, fulfilled, and self-conscious" (p. 310/451). All the unsatisfactory forms of rational consciousness which have been paraded before our eyes are turning out to be *moments* of the process wherein consciousness becomes aware that only as spirit is it going to make sense at all, and this is the process of spirit becoming aware of itself as spirit. What is necessary, then, is not that self-consciousness universalize its moral demands, which it does in the categorical imperative, but that it itself become universal (p. 310/451). If law is to be truly law, eternally valid, it is to be rooted in the *will* of all. It cannot be a "maxim" which *ought* to be a "law"; "it simply *is* and *is valid*" (p. 310/451). "Laws are the thoughts of the absolute being's absolute consciousness" (p. 310/451), and to follow them is not to obey the will of someone else; nor does the following of them rest on *belief* but on knowledge (p. 310/451). Ethical consciousness is valid not because it finds validating grounds in itself but because it is one with the absolute; "it has superseded itself as singular . . . it is the immediate self-consciousness of the ethical substance" (p. 311/452).

The question, then, as to what makes a law to be a law, what makes it universally obligatory to follow it, is not to be answered by looking into the logical reasoning which supports it. Laws, in fact, are not to be rationally *derived* from some *a priori* principle at all. They are constituted as laws by the inherent rightness of what they command, and only universal spirit can be the source of that rightness. Thus, they descend from heaven, so to speak, and their rightness is in themselves, not in the correctness of someone's reasoning (p. 311/452). It is the law which makes following it the right thing to do, not the fact that *I* find no contradiction in following my

own subjective principle. "Thus, not because I find something non-contradictory is it right; rather, because it is the right thing to do is it right"
(p. 312/453).

The whole inquiry has been turned around. No longer is there question
of finding what my reason demands or sanctions and then raising that to
the status of law. Now there is question of finding out what the universal
moral spirit commands and seeing to it that reason corresponds with that.
"Because the right thing to do is manifest to me in its essence (*mir an und
für sich ist*), I am taken up in the ethical substance; this, then, is the *essence*
of self-consciousness. The latter, however, is the *existing actuality* of that
substance" (p. 312/453). To determine, then, what reason truly is, individual
consciousness must turn from its own self-examination to an examination
of spirit, precisely as universal.

Just as it would be asserting too much to claim that in these last two subsections Hegel has effectively refuted Kant's moral reasoning—that is not
his intention—so, too, it would be futile to seek in the entire dialectic of
reason the logical inevitability of each step's necessarily following upon
another.[72] What Hegel has been seeking to do is not to *prove*—or to *refute*
—something at all, but to *describe* the process wherein individual rational
self-consciousness, after making every possible attempt to find itself by looking only into itself, comes to the realization that this is not enough. The
universal dimension of human spirit is not to be attained by simply gen-
eralizing what is essentially individual; rather, the individual is to be recognized for what it essentially is by turning to the subjective universal which
is spirit.

[72] "It would be vain to pretend that the dialectical pattern of this section on Reason
has anything of the inevitability commonly associated with the rational, or that it could
not have been *otherwise* developed at practically every point. It is vain to pretend, further,
that many of Hegel's transitions are not highly arbitrary, in some cases scandalously so.
On the other hand, it would be vain to deny that Hegel's methods generally strike tinder,
that in his least justifiable transitions there is not also a queer aesthetic appropriateness,
an extraordinary breaking of light. There is as much hidden logic in Hegel's apparent
arbitrariness as in T. S. Eliot's *Waste Land*. One only longs for the terminal glosses that
would have saved the reader much blood and sweat" (Findlay, *Philosophy of Hegel*,
p. 113).

7

Spirit

As has been observed more than once already, the moving force of the Hegelian dialectic of consciousness in its passage from mere consciousness of a world of things, through a reflection on itself precisely as being consciousness and not a thing, to the realization that the self of which it is consciousness is reason, and, therefore, contains in itself all that of which there is to be consciousness, has been the dissatisfaction experienced in the inadequacy of the successive forms consciousness has assumed in the process. It should come as no surprise, then, that rational consciousness, at the term of its minute examination of itself in its individual instantiation, should once more experience a dissatisfaction which drives it forward to an examination of a more-than-individual consciousness. Nor should it come as a surprise that in moving forward to this new vantage point reason should be merely "certain" that it will find itself only as more-than-individual.[1] "Certainty" is, so to speak, the assurance that there is nowhere else to look. Just as the failure of the objective stance to provide satisfaction had made consciousness "certain" that it had nowhere to look but into itself, and the failure of the self-conscious stance to resolve satisfactorily the split between mere self-assurance and a recalcitrant reality over against it had revealed that there was nowhere else to look but in itself for reality, so now the failure of individual reason to find within itself the reality it seeks shows it that there is nowhere else to look but into a more-than-individual consciousness. "We" observers know that the only more-than-individual consciousness there is is "spirit," but consciousness has not yet *experienced* this. The experience with which it begins to move forward, then, is the certainty of the direction in which it must move; the movement will gradually reveal itself as a movement toward becoming "spirit"; and it will become evident that the movement toward becoming spirit will be the movement whereby spirit becomes conscious of itself. Now it is that the "Science of the Experience of Consciousness" has to be the "Phenomenology of Spirit."[2]

[1] At the level of the initial dialectic of self-consciousness, ushered in by the opposition of two extreme forms of self-image, that of the master and that of the slave, the issue was the self's need of other selves in its process of self-realization. The issue now has changed; it is no longer question of the individual's need of others in order to realize self; it is the need for the individual himself to be more than individual if self is to be thoroughly meaningful.

[2] Up to this point the Hegelian term *Geist* could conceivably be translated as "mind." Hereafter that is impossible. There is no more-than-individual, no communal "mind"; there is a communal "spirit," and the progressive "spiritualization" of consciousness is the progressive "communalization" of its activities.

Before plunging into the extremely complex overall dialectic of spirit, Hegel pauses, so to speak, in order to formulate a rather elaborate—and yet concise—introduction to what is to follow. The introduction begins with an indication that we shall be able to comprehend the subsequent movement only if we recall the preceding movement wherein reason, beginning with the simple assurance that "I" is the "category" which is to unite the totality of the known, gradually comes to the realization that the principle of unification is constituted by the rational "laws" which it *finds* in nature, *imposes* on human activities, or *justifies* by its attitude of strict objectivity. In this movement "the object of consciousness, the pure category, raised itself to rational concept" (p. 313/457). In the process individual reason came a long way, to the point of recognizing that it indeed functions universally when it deals with laws of moral behavior, which are universally binding on all men, not merely on the one who thinks them out. The mistake that the individual thus makes, however, is to think that the laws in question derive from his own reasoning, not from the universal moral nature of man.[3] By thus separating himself from the "universal substance," i.e., ground of morality, the individual, so to speak, leaves the ground where it is, universal *in itself* but without consciousness thereof—universal ground but only individual consciousness. Only in spirit will this universal consciousness of universality be achieved: "The essence which is both *in* and *for itself* and at the same time actual to itself as consciousness, representing itself to itself, is *the spirit*" (p. 314/458).

What spirit is essentially, then, is to be found in the ultimate ground of moral behavior, which is what it is, whether we are conscious of it or not—what is right is right; what is wrong is wrong. Spirit "actually exists," however, only where there is consciousness of this "substance" of morality, the moral nature of man, where men act the way they do because they are conscious of a moral demand which is not their own doing.[4] The abstract morality of a course of action is antecedent to the action, but only the action itself is concretely moral or immoral. The "essence," then, "of spirit" (*das Wesen des Geistes*) is the "moral substance" (*die sittliche Substanz*), whereas "spirit" itself is "moral actuality" (*die sittliche Wirklichkeit*), that which makes morality effective: "It is the *self* of actual [moral] consciousness" (p. 314/458). Spirit is the self of which consciousness is conscious, which is to say that the self of which the individual is conscious, when the individual is

---

[3] Cf. "Über die englische Reformbill," *Schriften zur Politik und Rechtsphilosophie*, pp. 288–89. Hegel's opposition to the mere positivity of law highlights his insistence that law, rights, etc., must spring from the moral nature of man, not from man merely as individual.

[4] Throughout this introduction and the first major section of the chapter, we shall be confronting the term *sittlich* and its derivatives. The word, as Hegel uses it, is not only untranslatable, it changes its meaning with the context. Since it is derived from *Sitte* it can mean "based on custom," but since the German derivation corresponds to both the Greek and the Latin, it can also mean "ethical" or "moral." The important thing to remember in each context where it occurs is that it refers to an obligation based not on individual reasoning but on a universal rightness or wrongness of a mode of action whose source is somehow communal, spiritual (see "Introduction," n. 28).

moral, is more than individual.[5] By the same token, the moral universe, "the world," in which the individual lives is the world of the more-than-individual self. Spirit, then, is "the unshaken and untrammeled *ground* and *point of departure* for the activity of all" (p. 314/458). Its "substance" is "the universal work" produced by a universal "activity" (p. 314/458).

Spirit is truly spirit when it is the spirit of a community, and all the forms of consciousness previously examined have been but abstractions of this. That these abstract forms are possible is due to spirit's "analyzing itself, distinguishing its moments, and lingering in some of them" (p. 314/459). Spirit is the presupposition for the very possibility of considering these moments in isolation, and it is the foundation for the movement in which these moments are dissolved (pp. 314–15/459). Whether we knew it or not, the consciousness we have been examining all along has been spirit (p. 315/459).[6]

As a starting point for the consideration of spirit, "insofar as it is *immediate truth*," then, Hegel proposes "the *life* of a *people regulated by immemorial custom*" (p. 315/460).[7] This "beautiful *sittliche* life" has to be transcended, and it will be as spirit goes through a series of forms, which "are the real spirits, proper actualities, which, rather than forms of consciousness alone, are forms of a world" (p. 315/460). A series of "worlds" (ways of life) will pass in review, because "the *living moral* world is the spirit in its truth" (p. 315/460). The movement will take spirit from "an abstract *knowledge* (*Wissen*) of its own essence" (p. 315/460) to "the spirit which as *conscience* (*Gewissen*) is *certain* (*gewisse*) of itself" (p. 316/461)—from "immemorial custom" to "conscience" as the guide of human action.[8]

A. TRUE SPIRIT—THE NORM OF IMMEMORIAL CUSTOM [9]

The introduction to the dialectic of spirit has been wrapped up in abstractions, and there the consideration will remain unless "action" (*Handlung*)

---

[5] "The distinction made here by Hegel is very important for all that is to follow. Spirit is 'substance,' and, as spirit, is opposed to individual consciousness which it transcends infinitely. But this substance surrenders itself to individuals and, conversely, becomes their work. The movement of self-consciousness is precisely that which constitutes the life of the substance" (Hyppolite, *Phénoménologie*, II 10–11n4).

[6] It has been argued, of course, by Kojève, Findlay, Kaufmann, et al., that because for Hegel the supreme principle is *Geist*, not God, he is an atheist. It would be difficult, on the basis of the *Phenomenology* alone, to refute this contention. But since *Geist* is clearly not reducible either to individual "mind" or to some abstract generalization thereof, his conception of *Geist* would be just as unacceptable to an atheist as would God—which both Feuerbach and Marx saw so well. See Quentin Lauer, s.j., "Hegel on Proofs for God's Existence," *Kantstudien*, 55, No. 4 (1964), 444, 446.

[7] *Das sittliche Leben eines Volkes*. The context clearly shows that *sittlich* here designates a code of behavior whose origin is unknown and which is neither thought out nor questioned. It is the most immediate—and inadequate—form in which spirit presents itself.

[8] "Man is essentially spirit, and spirit is essentially this: to be for himself, to be free, to place the natural in contrast to himself, to withdraw himself from immersion in nature, to separate himself from nature and only through and on the basis of this separation to reconcile himself with nature" (*Vorlesungen über die Philosophie der Religion*, ed. Georg Lasson [Hamburg: Meiner, 1925], 2. Teil, 1. Kapitel, p. 29).

[9] In the original, simply *die Sittlichkeit*.

intervenes. Only when human beings do something is morality a concrete issue. It is, in fact, action which divides spirit into "substance" (foundational reality) and "consciousness of the same," and thus action becomes ethical (or unethical) since in it is a consciousness of the rule of behavior. In this sense *sittlich* can mean "ethical" and *Sittlichkeit* "ethical behavior," not in the sense that the rule is consciously rational but that there is a rule of which those who act are conscious. What distinguishes "the ethical" in this context, then, is that it involves sacrificing the *particularity* of individual reason to the generality of communal consciousness.[10] In action the individual raises "his isolated actuality" to the level of the "universal essence" and gives to the "universal essence" an "actuality" it does not have in its sheer generality. If the individual acts ethically he realizes in his action the universal: "He brings forth the unity of his self and the substance as *his work* and thereby as actuality" (p. 317/463).[11]

The ambiguity of *Sittlichkeit* and *Moralität* in the *Phenomenology* and in the properly ethical works of Hegel (e.g., *Philosophie des Rechts*) can be cleared up. *Sittlichkeit* is a general term covering any behavior based on norms provided by the general consciousness of the community. Initially the rule of behavior is simply "given"—not questioned, disputed, rationally examined—whether as "divine law," whose origins no one can trace, or as "human law," which the community, so to speak, gives itself without reflection on its rational grounds, which are present only incognito. *Moralität*, on the other hand, is a more sophisticated attitude of rational reflection either on traditional norms or on the demands of reason as such. The community through its members—and the members through the community—act with a consciousness of the rational grounds for acting. *Sittlichkeit* on a higher level, treated in the *Philosophie des Rechts* but not in the *Phenomenology*, is a synthesis of the two, found in the rational laws of the truly rational community, the state.

The "ethical activity" of which Hegel speaks in this early section is that which takes place in a "world" which is at once culturally complex and ethically very simple (Loewenberg calls it an "ingenuous world," the "world" of Sophoclean tragedy [12]). This world is split into two, according to whether its members follow the "divine" or the "human" law in their actions. Both laws are universal foundations of behavior; but because they turn out to be mutually opposed, they are mutually destructive—in their irreconcilable opposition "*Sittlichkeit* has collapsed" (p. 318/463). Out of this collapse there will arise an "effectual self-consciousness," which is not regulated by an ambiguous "given," but is fully conscious of *its own* universality.

a) The World Regulated by Custom [13]—Human Law and Divine Law— Man and Woman

The unity of spirit, then, first manifests itself in a world where all "ethical"

10 See *Philosophie des Rechts*, No. 157.

11 His "work" (*Werk*), which is also a "deed," is the "actuality" (*Wirklichkeit*) of the "ethical substance."

12 *Hegel's Phenomenology*, pp. 189–91.

13 To translate *die sittliche Welt* here by "the ethical world" cannot but lead to

behavior is regulated by custom, which is an overall rule of life covering each case which arises (p. 318/466). The multiplicity of human activities comes under a common self-consciousness which Hegel calls a "common essence" (*Gemeinwesen*) (p. 318/466). It is the kind of unity—or *community* —manifested in "a people": "as *actual substance* spirit is *a people*; as *actual consciousness* it is the *citizens*" (p. 319/467). Here it is that the conscious-ness of the individual citizen is identified with the consciousness of the people as a guide to action. In this sense the spirit of the people as a whole finds expression in "human law" regulating the life of all—no exceptions—as a community (p. 319/467). Over against this is another, a "divine law," which is equally universal since it is observed by all the people, but which regulates another form of behavior and is, thus, oriented to a different "common essence" (*Gemeinwesen*)—"a *natural ethical* common essence—the family" (p. 320/468). Although the family is a constituent of the larger whole, it has its own spirit—the "Penates" of Greek myth (*sic!*). Where cus-tom rules there are, so to speak, two "spirits," both common to *all* the peo-ple, but in conflict with each other.

Although it is true that the family is a "natural" unit, bound together by ties of blood, sentiment, and love (in whatever sense the latter two can be looked on as merely "natural"), the family relationship Hegel wishes to consider is not "natural" but "moral" (*sittlich*) (p. 320/468), i.e., a rela-tionship of *duties*, whether of the individual member to the whole family or of the family to the individual. If we look upon the family as a community with its own purpose, then the primary orientation is that of the family to the individual member: "The *positive* end proper to the family is the individual as such" (p. 320/469). The required familial "moral action" (*sittliche Handlung*) is universal, however, in the sense that it devolves on *all* members of the family.

Because the individual is at one and the same time a member of the larger community, "the people," and of the family, the duties of the family toward the individual turn out to be those which devolve upon it when the indi-vidual is no longer a member of the larger community, i.e., when he is dead (p. 321/470). In this sort of society, then, duties toward the dead belong uniquely to the family; care of the dead, an extremely important duty in ancient society, is a *familial* (or, at most, *tribal*) responsibility. It is up to the family to see to it that death be not the complete surrender of the indi-vidual back to *nature* (p. 321/470). Since it is no longer the *consciousness* (*Fürsichsein*) of the individual which raises him above nature, it must be the consciousness of the family which does (p. 322/471), thus retaining him as a member of the family (p. 323/472). Simply as an individual he must live on in the consciousness of the family. This "moral" duty (love is "natu-ral" not "moral") is regulated by "divine law"; all other duties come under "human law" (p. 323/472). All of this may seem unnecessarily narrow, but it must be remembered that Hegel is not *explaining* either how things *ought* to be or how things *must* be; he is *describing* a form of society which he con-

---

ambiguities. The point is that it is a world wherein human behavior is universally regu-lated by traditional "laws" which are simply not questioned.

siders to be representative of a stage in the development of communal consciousness, where a *religious* consciousness of relationship to the dead is familial, a prime example of ties which are not "natural" but "spiritual."

In the spiritual world of moral relationships, then, there are two forms of "common essence," each universal, each with its own mode of self-consciousness; and the individual identifies both with the self of the family and with the self of the people, and these modes overlap. To distinguish the *levels* at which this identification takes place is to indicate "the mode of *activity* (*Betätigung*) and of *self-consciousness* belonging to both *universal* essences in the world regulated by custom as well as their *connection with* and *transition into* each other" (p. 323/473). In a very significant sense the larger (political) community is the superior; there the "spirit" resides primarily, located in the government (*Regierung*); and of this community families are only the "components." Life in its fullness pertains only to the larger whole (p. 324/473) (a reason, perhaps, why Hegel sees war, where life is put on the line, as performing an important function in preserving consciousness of the primary community spirit—*at this level*). If individuals were members only of the family, they would be merely beings of "nature"; to be genuinely "spiritual," they must be members of the more thoroughly spiritual community, whose concern is the whole of life on earth, as opposed to "the nether world" where it is "the divine law" which is "essential" (p. 324/474).

Once again, it may well seem that Hegel's employment of the mythical is farfetched or that it obscures the issue. Still, as a means of introducing a distinction between two sets of relationships in which each individual human being is involved and of showing the inadequacy of immemorial custom to regulate *all* relationships, it serves a significant purpose. In detailing family relationships under the rubrics of husband–wife, parent–child, and brother–sister,[14] for example, Hegel is able to clarify to a great extent what he means by a "moral" (*sittlich*)—real "spiritual"—relationship as opposed to a merely "natural" one. On the merely family level, i.e., where "human law" does not intervene to change things, he tells us, the relationship of husband and wife, one of mutual "recognition," but rooted in mutual "feeling" and "love," is regulated by "nature," not by "custom," and is, therefore, not *sittlich*—nor is it a "blood" relationship. Whatever moral-spiritual character the relationship has is realized in the generation of children who unite mother and father. The relationship of parents to children, even though the child is but the "natural" product of the union of husband and wife, is a moral-spiritual one, because the "feeling" and "love" toward children have their rational ground in the ties of blood. On the side of the children, on the other hand, the relationship takes on a peculiarly dialectical character, since children become aware that their own growth involves the decline of their parents and that their becoming what they are to be is conditioned by a separation from their origin. Thus far, then, we have relationships which are partly natural and partly moral-spiritual, therefore "mixed." "The unmixed relationship, however, takes place be-

---

[14] Neither brother–brother nor sister–sister is mentioned.

tween *brother* and *sister*" (p. 325/475). This is not a relationship of mutual attraction (*Begierde*); nor is it one of mutual recognition grounded in "feeling" and "love," or one of product to source—it is one in which "free individuals freely relate to each other" (p. 325/475–76).

If we do not recognize that the entire foregoing description is Hegel's build-up to a consideration of what he sees as the model of the "immediate" moral world of which he has been speaking, the world of Sophocles' *Antigone*, we may well miss, first, that Hegel is using metaphors to describe very real types of relationships, and second, that he is describing a stage in the evolution of "the spiritual." [15]

Looking at the brother–sister relationship first on the side of the sister, Hegel finds that she has "the highest instinct for (*Ahnung*) the essence of the moral" (p. 325/476), whose demands are rooted in a "spirit" of which she is not "conscious" in the full sense of the term, since she has not thought it out; she has, so to speak, a feeling for the truth of spirit (p. 326/476). She shares with all human beings that relationship to her parents whereby she comes to maturity as an autonomous being in their disappearance. As a woman she can share the relationship of wife to husband or mother to children, both of which are partly natural and partly spiritual, with the added note that both a lost husband and lost children can be replaced. As a sister, however, she has no merely natural relationship to her brother at all, and, since he is simply not replaceable, "her duty toward him is the highest" (p. 327/477).

The brother, about whom Hegel has much less to say than about the sister, is the classic representative of the dialectical relationship of separation. It is in his leaving the family to be on his own, where he belongs, that the immediate, elementary, self-enclosed, and, therefore, merely negative, ethic of the family is dissolved. He moves toward a self-conscious *Sittlichkeit* which, when it is fully self-conscious, will be *Moralität* (p. 327/477). Because it is the brother who moves more and more in the direction of involvement uniquely with the "human law," the sister must become the unique guardian of the "divine law," of family ties (both within the framework of an accepted ethic). Thus comes about a division of roles between the sexes, which characterizes the world of Sophocles and which, it would seem, Hegel finds quite appropriate in his own day. The place of man is in the public forum; of woman, in the family circle. What is important for the dialectic as it unfolds here, however, is the description of a movement out of the realm of the

15 "When Hegel asserts the ethical primacy for woman of the relationship to her brother, or when he speaks of the burial of another as the highest duty one can have toward him he is not making these claims on his own behalf, as if he considered them timeless truths: he is trying to perform a marvel of empathy, not just reading *Antigone* and being effusive about its beauty or profundity but trying to see the world through Antigone's eyes. And he supposes that Antigone is not merely one figure in one old tragedy which he himself happens to like especially: he takes her to represent an ancient ethic—laws of which she says, in words that Hegel quotes before he commences his discussion of *Sittlichkeit*,

    Not now, nor yesterday's, they always live,
    and no one knows their origin in time. (pp. 456–457)"
(Kaufmann, *Hegel*, p. 147).

divine and into the human, exemplified in the man, and a movement of return to the divine, exemplified in the woman. The balance of the two is
like the complementarity of the two sexes—as equals (p. 328/478).

Because both man and woman have "acted" in behalf of the one law and
the other, the overall ethic which was initially simply *given* becomes "the
deed and the work of the one who finds it" (p. 328/479). Gone is the series
of abstract attempts to universalize what is irrevocably individual—the
hedonist's "pleasure-seeking," the utopian's "law of the heart," the reformer's "virtue," the idealist's "what really matters," and the rationalist's
"laws of reason"—all are, as it were, telescoped in actual doing (pp. 328–
29/479–80). The "rightness" of what is done takes on new significance (p.
329/480). Because the conscious effort to substitute for the merely natural
in man an activity which is rationally *willed* calls forth a "balancing"
(*Gleichgewicht*) of the values represented by the two sexes, there results a
movement from the instinctual grasp (feminine) of what spirit dictates to
the conscious willing (masculine) of the values inherent in a way of acting
(p. 330/481–82). Although it would be a mistake to conclude from all this
to any one-sided views as to what is masculine and what feminine in the
realm of human values, it is clear that until the values which have historically been assigned to the masculine are reconciled with those which have
been assigned to the feminine, in an action which is neither—and both—
because it is truly human, the human spirit will not expand to its true
dimensions.

b) Behavior Regulated by Custom—Human and Divine Knowing—Fault and Destiny

When Hegel turns from a general discussion of duty in a world regulated
by immemorial custom to a more concrete investigation of a case in point—
eine Tat (p. 330–31/484)—we are not by this time surprised that he takes
his illustration from Greek tragedy and not from verifiable history. The unstable equilibrium between "divine law" and "human law," which characterizes society regulated by custom, remains nonetheless an equilibrium,
as long as nothing is actually done—or is to be done—which disturbs the
harmony. The consciousness of duty, however, which simply accepts duty as
given, is bound to produce in action a conflict between the "divine" and
the "human." Nor is the conflict to be resolved on this level of consciousness; destiny simply swallows up the tragic consciousness of the Greeks.

Hegel points out very carefully that the conflict here is not the conflict of
passion and duty, which is tragic enough. Nor is it the conflict of two duties
within one consciousness, which Hegel somewhat implausibly calls "comic,"
because one duty cancels another, and what was taken to be absolute duty
turns out to be no duty at all. Rather, it is the conflict of two consciousnesses of duty, each adhering (consciously) to one duty, with the result that
each comes into irreconcilable conflict with the other (pp. 331–32/484–85).
That the conflict should present itself under the rubric of the contrasting
roles of the two sexes is due to Hegel's choice of an illustrative example,
the *Antigone* of Sophocles. The point, however, is not the supposed opposi-

tion of the male consciousness to the female, but, rather, the inevitable conflict of two attitudes, both equally decisive, each seeing its own law as
essential, each caught up in the tension between abstract duty and actual
fact. The consciousness to which the "divine law" is essential (Antigone)
sees the inexorable carrying out of the "human law" as nothing more than
"contingent human *violence*" (p. 332/486). To the consciousness which sees
as its duty the safeguarding of the "human law" (Creon), adherence to the
"divine" command seems sheer "stubbornness and disobedience," merely
individual will opposing the inviolable will of authority (p. 332/486). It is
a case of conflict between the self-conscious male convinced that the law of
his society is absolute and the instinctual female who is convinced that the
"divine law" is to be followed at all costs. "The absolute right of the
ethical *self-consciousness* comes into conflict with the *essentially* divine
right" (pp. 332–33/486).

Both sides are confronted with harsh facts which simply cannot be
wished away: Creon with the fact that Antigone's brother Polyneices has
borne arms against his native city and, therefore, according to its laws
must be left unburied; Antigone with the fact that her brother's body remains unburied, and the inviolable law of the family demands that he be
buried. For both, the law must prevail over mere facts. There is, however, a
difference. Creon not only is conscious of the law, he also has the absolute
power to enforce it; therefore he simply cannot let Antigone (or any individual) violate the law with impunity. If he had right without power, he
could do nothing; if he had power without right, he *should* do nothing. As
things stand, Creon's duty is clear: the situation *must* be as his "ethical
consciousness" *knows* things must be (p. 333/487).

It would seem to be clear enough that Creon is right and Antigone
wrong. It was not Antigone, however, who split immemorial "custom" up
into two laws—the split is simply inevitable, and no one consciousness can
split itself up into absolute adherence to both (p. 334/487–88). It is not
that Creon is right and Antigone wrong but that both are wrong, since to
act at all is to violate one law or the other (p. 334/488). Nor is it merely
Creon and Antigone who are involved in fault, because of the peculiar
situation in which they find themselves; given the kind of law which
prescribes their duty, whether adherence to it be self-conscious, as with
Creon, or instinctual, as with Antigone, to act at all in accord with one or
the other is to incur fault, because the laws themselves are fundamentally
in conflict (p. 335/489).[16] "Now the self-consciousness regulated by custom
experiences [*sic!*] in its own deed the involved nature of *actual* behavior,
just as much when it followed the divine as when it followed the human
law" (p. 335/489). Both laws are essential, in the sense that they apply

---

16 Hegel might well seem to be contradicting himself here, saying that the two laws both
conflict and do not conflict (cf. *supra*, p. 16). The point, however, is that simply as laws
prescribing completely different kinds of duties they do not conflict; whereas when,
existentially, one duty is actualized (by Antigone), it calls forth a conflicting actualization
of the other (by Creon). Precisely because integrated reason is not operative, existential
conflict is inevitable.

whether or not one is conscious of them or conscious of having violated them. Thus, the fulfilling of one calls forth the operation of the other in opposition to the act. Hegel is not saying, of course, that this is the way it should be but that this is the way it is in the tragic Greek situation where "destiny" in fact rules. In this situation fault is not a matter of consciousness at all, just as it was not in the case of Oedipus; it attaches to *action* not to *consciousness* (p. 335/490). Consciousness of duty calls for action, but action violates duty, because the two aspects of one life, as a citizen and as a member of a family, have not been integrated, and in a society regulated by such laws they will not be.

In a very peculiar sense Hegel speaks of inevitable fault being "purer" when, as in the case of Antigone, one is conscious of violating the law in question—unlike Oedipus, who has in fact violated two laws without being aware that he has done so (p. 336/491). At the same time, however, it is *Sittlichkeit* which demands that she do what she does and that she acknowledge her crime in so doing. "Because we suffer"—from having done what duty demands—"we acknowledge that we have been at fault" (p. 336/491). The situation is intolerable, but it is inevitable where human beings have nothing to say as to what the law is, where only an impersonal, alien "substance" dictates what is to be done. Antigone, in fact, adheres to this "substance" in obeying its dictates and, in acknowledging her fault in violating the opposite, she denies adherence to her "substance." It is the "pathos" of the individual in a world in which laws are simply *given*— there is no escape (p. 337/491). In one sense both Creon and Antigone are right, in another they are both wrong—and *destiny* swallows up both of them (p. 337/492).

It is as though any attempt on the part of the individual to be him- or herself, to control his or her destiny, is doomed, because unconscious destiny sucks them back in as soon as they have emerged from it. Thus, Hegel tells us, turning to Antigone's two brothers, Polyneices and Eteocles, they emerge as individuals from the "unconscious essence," the "spirit of the family." By a peculiar trick of fate they fight against each other, and both are killed. Because one fought *for* the city, the larger "common essence," he is in the right, and the other who fought *against* the city is in the wrong. Therefore, the honors due to the dead from the family are accorded to one, not to the other (pp. 338–39/494). The only one left to take the part of the one who is dishonored is she who has not emerged from the common family spirit, the sister, the female. But, in taking her brother's part, she has committed a fault against the larger community, which she *knows*, and thus she too emerges from the protective spirit of the family (p. 340/496).

Here Hegel indulges in what can only be a remarkable *tour de force* which, nevertheless, has something very familiar about it. Having found subjection to two opposing impersonal forces, the spirit of the family and the spirit of the community, impossible, Antigone simply negates the larger community entirely, making only the family count. Given the world of custom in which she lives, the individual has been effectively suppressed, but in her consciousness what takes the place of the individual is not the authentic community but the singular cohesion of the family as a unit (p. 340/496). But if the human individual is to achieve genuine selfhood, this kind of singularity must also be suppressed. "The common essence, however, can maintain itself only by suppressing this spirit of singularity" (p. 341/497). Still, in suppressing both the autonomy of individuals and the singularity of family pretensions, the community must use individuals as its instruments. When it does, a reversal takes place. The strength and good fortune of young manhood which the tradition-bound community had to use for its own ends takes over, the *sittliche Substanz* collapses, and individualism runs rampant—to the strongest go the spoils (p. 341/497–98).

This result is as inevitable as were the tragic conflict and the destiny of Antigone. What the bond of custom could not do, another force, another form (*Gestalt*) of the spirit, will take in hand. "The decline of the ethical substance" is at the same time "its transition to another form" (p. 342/498).[17] Because the "substance" was simply *given*, the relation of consciousness to it merely "immediate," it had no staying power. "Immediacy contains the contradictory meaning of being at once the unconscious repose of nature and the self-conscious restless repose of the spirit" (p. 342/498). Rampant individualism will have to be contained in another way.

c) Legal Status

It can scarcely be claimed that Hegel has, in the foregoing subsections, given an adequate exposition of the ethos of the ancient Greek world, the world of Oedipus and Antigone. Nor is that what he was trying to do. It cannot be insisted often enough or emphatically enough that Hegel is out to give a dialectical not an historical account of the stages of consciousness and of their relationship to each other. There is, obviously, no conceivable historical connection between the sophisticated ethos of Kant's categorical imperative and the relatively naïve ethos of the Greek social structure which immediately follows it in the text of the *Phenomenology*. There is, however, a very definitive dialectical connection between the last attempt of rational consciousness on the individual level to give itself universal significance in terms of the rational "laws," the justification of which it looks for in itself, and the turn to already universal "laws" which bespeak a kind of universality which individual consciousness does not impose but in which it partakes. The account of this turn need not be complete, only sufficient to show that its outcome is quite contrary to the universalism to which it pretends, is in fact an unmitigated individualism without any ties of spirit to bind individuals together.

By the same token, when Hegel now turns from the ethos of Greek tragedy to that of Roman law, his treatment is neither strictly historical nor complete—in fact, it is painfully incomplete. But, once again, what he is trying to do is clear: not to give an historical account of the status of the individual "person" before the law in the Roman system, but to describe a stage of consciousness wherein the individual is not immediately related to

17 "Decline" = *Untergang*; "transition" = *Übergang*.

an ethical universal which swallows him up nor mediately related to a law whose universality is merely his own doing, but finds his own formal universality in a set of rationally formulated laws which define all individuals universally. As we shall see, the individualism in which the previous stage issued is not here overcome, but it is set in the framework of an elaborately universal social context. As Loewenberg says, Hegel gives us the "portrait of a society drawn chiefly if not exclusively in terms of its jurisprudence." [18] Gone is the ethical cohesion secured by immemorial custom, and in its place is the enforced cohesion secured by a set of man-made laws which society will not permit any individual to contravene, thus *giving* equality to all, precisely as individuals.[19]

The result, then, of the previous movement has been that the immediate unity of the individual with his "ethical substance" has retreated into a "common essence" from which spirit, genuine common self-determination, is absent, and each individual is "for himself"—*only* (p. 342/501). The universality which could be maintained only by the suppression of individuality has broken up into the multiplicity of atomic individuals whose only claim to an identity is the "sameness" of all as "persons" (pp. 342–43/501). Such individuals are no longer just "members" of a family, nor is individuality accorded to them only when they are dead; individuality characterizes the living, and it characterizes all indiscriminately (p. 343/501). With the retreat of the "absolute powers" into the facelessness of "destiny," there emerges "the *I* of self-consciousness" (p. 343/501), which demands recognition as this individual *I*.

Inevitably we are reminded here of the negative independence of the stoic who is content with simply recognizing his own identity in the seclusion of his "thought." Here the recognition demanded is positive rather than negative but it is scarcely less abstract than that of stoicism, since its consciousness of independence is a consciousness merely of being as independent as everyone else is (p. 343/502). What characterizes such an individual is that he has "rights," and all have the same rights: no individual is distinguishable from another on this count (p. 344/502). What the individual is depends entirely on what the law defines him to be—the "person" is *impersonally* defined. Just as the insistence upon recognition of the individual *I*, then, recalled the empty independence of the stoic, so the movement of stoicism into the self-contradictory independence of skepticism foreshadows the present movement into "the *empty one* of the person," whose "content" (meaning) is not of his own doing, is but "a contingent existence, a movement and activity without essence" (p. 344/503), because the mere "person" is not self-defining, and the "rights" which characterize the person turn out to be no more than the right to say that something is "my own" (p. 344/503). In fact, equality before the law turns out to be no more than an ability to say that the "right" accorded by the

18 *Hegel's Phenomenology*, p. 206.
19 It is indeed questionable whether "equality before the law" is genuine equality if it is not antecedent to the law. If men are "equal," only because and in the way the law says they are, equality has little meaning.

law, and existing only as so accorded, is "my right" (p. 344/504). A "right" which has no more ontological status than its recognition by the law is no right at all; it is a legal fiction, on whose basis the individual "person" enjoys no personal dignity at all.[20] It is the indiscriminate and arbitrary subordination of all individuals to the only real power there is.[21] To be a "person" in this sense is to *receive* independence at the cost of *selfhood*— and "rights" serve but to camouflage the absence of *real* self-determination. "The consciousness of right, therefore, experiences in the very affirmation of its actuality rather the loss of its reality and its utter inessentiality. Thus, to designate an individual as a *person* is an expression of scorn" (p. 345/504).[22]

The logic of this atomization of individuals into "persons" results in the gathering of the scattered many into "*one* point alien to them and equally without spirit" (p. 345/504). This is the "universal power and absolute actuality" (p. 345/504), the master who is as faceless as his subjects. All power is concentrated in the hands of *one*, but that one, too, is merely a "person," alone and isolated, uniting in his person a multiplicity of indistinguishable ones, "for the singular as such is true only as universal multiplicity of singularity" (p. 345/504). The Roman emperor, "the master of the world," is the one power which exists, the external guarantee that all men under him are equally "persons"—and no more.[23] The point Hegel is making is that where the only distinguishing mark of "persons" is equality of all before the law, an equality which the law itself defines, the emergence of the "all powerful person" is inevitable. What is more, the concentration of all power in the person of the emperor leads with equal inevitability to his apotheosis: "Knowing himself then as the sum total (*Inbegriff*) of all actual powers, this lord of the world is the grotesque (*ungeheure*) self-consciousness which knows itself as actually God" (p. 345/505). His is an alien power which does not really unite; the *destructive* force concentrated in him does not promote but prevents the emergence of authentic self-consciousness in the mass of individuals subject to him. The unity of self-consciousness which is a *conditio sine qua non* of authentic individuality is in the Roman Empire a merely *formal* unity whose *content* is imposed from without, more rational than the Greek subjection to im-

20 Hegel, it would seem, was anticipating the absurdities not only of "legal positivists" but also of those who think that ethics should be determined by law, rather than vice versa.

21 "In Rome, consequently, we find this free generality, this abstract freedom, which on the one hand sets the abstract state, political power, above concrete individuality, subordinating the latter entirely. On the other hand, over against this generality, it creates the personality—the liberty of the ego in itself, which it is necessary to distinguish clearly from individuality" (G. W. F. Hegel, *Vorlesungen über die Philosophie der Geschichte*, ed. Hermann Glockner, Sämtliche Werke XI [Stuttgart: Frommann, 1928], p. 362).

22 To get the flavor of this we might recall that those who play *assigned* roles in a play are called "persons" (*dramatis personae*).

23 "Political institutions were concentrated in his person; there was no longer any moral cohesion. The will of the emperor was superior to all; under him equality was absolute" (Hyppolite, *Phénoménologie*, II 47n83).

personal forces, but equally alien. Where the rights which "persons" enjoy are defined by one all-powerful person, the individual *subject* is cut off from his own true *substance* and thus from anything like authentic self-hood. "The right-full personality, then, because the content which makes itself valid in him is alien to him, experiences . . . rather his own depriva-tion of substance" (p. 346/506–507). The emperor himself lacks authentic self-consciousness, because as the concentrated expression of all unreal in-dividualities he himself is not really an individual either.

Despite the inadequacy of a self-consciousness, however, whose only claim to distinction is the possession of "rights" determined by a central-ized authority, the movement it represents away from blind subjection to the forces of tradition is a forward movement. The "legal status" of the Roman citizen is nearer to "actual *self*-consciousness" than is the custom-bound status of the Sophoclean tragic figure. Despite the fact that the "un-happy consciousness," in which the movement of the slave through stoi-cism and skepticism terminated, has now been transferred to an "absolute essence," resulting in a consciousness which is equally "unhappy," the way is open to further development—not along the lines of subordination to an alien force, but through a process of "self-development." The achievement of "personhood" will turn out to be not a complete loss. "The actuality of the self which was not present in the world regulated by custom has been won by retreat into the *person*. What was unified in the former stage now emerges as developed, but self-alienated" (p. 346/507). The human spirit can come to terms with itself only by getting outside itself in a process of cultural development (*Bildung*). The progressive experience of an outer self estranged from an inner self which we have observed in the dominance of mere custom or mere legality now becomes a conscious separation of the inner and the outer—and at the same time a cultivation of the outer in such a way that the inner will be transformed from a merely natural to a spiritual self.

B. SELF-ALIENATED SPIRIT—CULTURE [24]

Ever since the transition from a mere consciousness of self—which termi-nated in a split (unhappy) consciousness finding in itself only its inessential self and the essential outside itself—to consciousness of being as reason all the reality there is to know, the movement of consciousness has consisted in a series of attempts to reconcile the universality of reason with the singu-larity of one (my) rational consciousness. Each attempt has proved inade-quate, but no attempt has proved fruitless; each has contributed to the ineluctable overall movement away from a consciousness which is merely a function of "nature" toward a consciousness which is truly a function of

[24] It should be pointed out that the Hegelian notion of "alienation"—whether the term in question be *Entfremdung* or *Entäusserung*—has little in common with various contem-porary, including the Marxist, uses of the term. If nature is to *become* spirit, it must become other than it is (alien to itself); if spirit is to *become* at all it must change, and this means changing itself—through "culture."

"spirit." What has happened has been a gradual realization—so far only negative—that the "self" which consciousness seeks is not simply to be "found"; it must be brought into being, and its coming into being must be its own doing. It is to this doing, this "making" of spirit, to which Hegel now turns, and he does so under the heading of "culture" (*Bildung*), which, however vague the term may be, is clearly a lifting of the individual out of what he is merely by nature into what he can become by conscious "cultivation" of his natural propensities. Historically, even though somewhat narrowly so, the movement Hegel will now describe for us takes him from the impersonal jurisprudence of imperial Rome, through the complex personal loyalties of feudal civilization, to the supremely cultured personalities of the court of Versailles, all concentrated around the "absolute" personality of the monarch, Louis XIV.

That Hegel should have chosen a very particularized historical development to serve as a model for a universal movement of spirit may well seem highly arbitrary. The absolute monarchy in France, after all, was not the only result attendant upon the breakup of the Roman Empire into the multiple feudal principalities of the Middle Ages. Nevertheless, if we take "culture" in the broadest sense of that term as designating the development of a whole civilization, not merely of isolated individuals, along political, social, economic, artistic, and intellectual lines, the development which culminated in the reign of Louis XIV in France can be looked upon as typical of a development which is "cultural" and only that, i.e., not authentically "spiritual." At the same time we can see it as calling for a development which is "cultural" in a far more profound sense of that term. What had concerned Hegel even from his youth was the fragmentation of European society which followed in the wake of the cultural unity it had enjoyed under the hegemony (intellectual, political, social) of France in the seventeenth century. That the *de facto* cultural development he chooses to depict should culminate as it did can well be acknowledged to be inevitable. That the cultural development which actually *did* take place was typical of a development in self-consciousness which *had to* take place might be disputed. That one should look, however, for a model of the logical culmination of a collective development which was merely cultural in seventeenth-century France, the most "cultured" nation of its era, need not be arbitrary. Add to this a conviction—not, perhaps, philosophical— that the spiritual leadership of France was destined to pass to Germany,[25] and the consistency of the development Hegel depicts is at least intelligible.

Let us recall that for Hegel man is not by nature an "individual," in the profoundest sense of that term; he is at best a "singular" being, like any animal in the "spiritual animal kingdom" or any "person" in the "legal situation." If genuine individuality is to be achieved, then, the "natural" (given) individual must be sacrificed to the artificial (culturally developed) individual, which means that he must *become a stranger* (alienate himself) from his mere nature in order to become what he truly is—spirit. As an

25 See *infra*, p. 193: "Spirit . . . abandons this land of culture and emigrates to another land, the land of *moral consciousness*."

attempt to do this, Hegel takes the collective effort to "cultivate" what is at best only latent in nature. That the result of a cultivation such as this should be an individual who is actual as such only to the extent that he *conforms* to a culture which he himself has not *formed* should not come as a surprise.

As an introduction to this all-important section on culture, Hegel takes as his point of departure the split which has manifested itself between the self which consciousness seeks and the foundation which gives consistency to that self (its substance). That there was a unity in the ancient world which bound together the individual members of society is not to be denied, but it was a unity imposed from outside and as such was bound to culminate in a serious fragmentation. The same sort of fragmentation Hegel detects in the world in which he lives, and just as the fragmented world which followed the breakup of the Roman Empire needed a new, more internal principle of unification, so his own world now needs the same. The world which succeeded the Roman Empire Hegel characterizes as "something external, the negative of self-consciousness" (p. 347/509). It was a world, it is true, in which the self had more to say regarding its structuring, but what it had to say was primarily negative, in the sense that it was emerging from the merely "natural" state which both the city-state and the imperial state had taken for granted. The emerging self is alien to the merely natural self, but has not yet replaced the latter; it remains in a state of subjection (p. 348/510).

In this context, "spirit," which is the "self-conscious identity of the self and its true being (*Wesens*)," is in a state where the self is alienated from its true being, because consciousness in its purity is opposed to consciousness in its "actuality" (p. 348/510). What is to follow, then, can be summarized as a movement toward universalization of the self precisely through an estrangement of the self from what it merely naturally is in order to become what it truly is. The world which spirit inhabits is no longer a given one. Spirit must make its own world, but even this world is initially twofold: a world which belongs purely to consciousness (a world which it has made its own), and a world for whose actuality consciousness is not responsible. "This spirit constructs (*bildet aus*) for itself, therefore, not merely *one* world but one which is doubled, divided, and opposed" (p. 348/510). In the "world regulated by custom" (city-state), it is true, there was opposition to the merely natural self, but this lacked the negativity of conscious opposition. In the imperial world, to the extent that the impersonal "will" of the regime stood over against the consciousness of the individual "person," the only "actuality" the person had was received from outside; personhood involved no "indwelling spirit" (pp. 348–49/511). The result was that self-consciousness inhabited two realms; the one, "wherein *self-consciousness* is *actual* and at the same time is its own object"; the other, "the realm of *pure* consciousness"—each man inhabited both a public and a private world (p. 349/511). The first of these corresponds on its level to what will later be a world of "belief," of affirmation without the possibility of establishing grounds for the affirmation; and the second corresponds to a later world of pure insight, of affirmation on grounds which are purely internal to rational consciousness (p. 349/511). It is "pure insight," which, "as the self which comprehends itself, puts the crown of completion on culture" (p. 349/512); its intellectual vision is guaranteed by the culture which has formed it. "Pure insight embraces nothing but the self, i.e., it conceptualizes (*begreift*) everything, cancels all objectivity, and transforms all *being-in-itself* into a *being-for-itself*" (p. 349/512). This is "enlightened" reason which, in opposition to "belief," refuses to go beyond the world in which it lives and finds in its own rationality all the explanation it needs of this world.

When, in "pure insight," the work of conceptualization is complete, there is no more room either for a "real world" which is in any way recalcitrant to intellect or for a "realm of belief" which is impenetrable to mere rational insight; "actuality has lost all substantiality" (p. 350/512); there is no "given," there is only what reason conceives. To achieve this, however, the self-alienated spirit must reintegrate itself, which it cannot do on the level of a culture which perpetuates the dichotomy between the individual spirit and the cultural norms to which it must conform despite itself. The result is revolt against the tyranny of culture; "this revolution produces *absolute freedom*, wherein the previously alienated spirit has completely returned into itself" (p. 350/512). In doing this it not only forsakes the hypothetical realm of culture but also the land (France) where culture had been put on a pedestal. Arbitrarily enough, it would seem, Hegel sees the spirit now moving to Germany, where alone its reintegration will be possible. "Spirit . . . abandons this land of culture and emigrates to another land, the land of *moral consciousness*" (p. 350/512). All chauvinism aside, these words betoken a realization that without the seriousness of moral consciousness, "culture" turns out to be an empty game and the cultivated man an empty shell. The world dominated by custom had disintegrated; it failed to be reintegrated into a world dominated by culture; it must become a world dominated by law which finds its foundation in authentic moral reason [26] —the "indwelling spirit."

1. The World of the Self-Alienated Spirit

Having painted in broad strokes a picture of the overall movement from disintegration to reintegration, Hegel now turns to a more detailed account of the process through which the human spirit goes in becoming whole. That the beginning of this movement be situated in spirit's own self-alienation is inevitable. In seeking to resist domination by an alien force, it immediately finds itself living in a double world: a world of fact for which it is not responsible and from which it cannot escape, and a world of its own which it constructs for itself (p. 350/513). Initially this second world is de-

[26] "A world dominated by law, in distinction from one ruled by custom, depends for its genesis and development on man's deliberate spiritual effort. Law is spiritual not merely in the sense of owing its creation to mind, it is spiritual in the deeper sense of having been explicitly designed for the purpose of serving as a rational basis of a social order" (Loewenberg, *Hegel's Phenomenology*, p. 207).

fined by its very *opposition* to the first. But since to be defined by opposition-to is to be dependent-on, the second world is not *free* from the first and thus constitutes but another form of alienation of spirit. The second is a world in which spirit *believes*. Still, the world in which it believes is a world which belongs to the *conceptual* order, over against the world of brute fact (p. 350/513). Spirit has at least the awareness that it can "build" a world of its own—its world cannot be forced upon it—but if it is to do that, it must, so to speak, get outside itself, loose the bonds which tie it to its merely natural self. "Culture" opens the way for its doing just that.

a) Culture and Its Realm of Actuality

What now needs to be determined is just what "culture" does effectively bring into being. How far can spirit go along these lines? That Hegel chooses but one historical example of the development in question becomes more intelligible if we look upon the development which culminated in the reign of Louis XIV as simply paradigmatic of this sort of culture's running its course. In any event, it is not difficult to see in the breakup of the Roman Empire the demise of a system in which the law *confers* on each individual the title of "person," whose whole dignity is that of being "equal" to every other person, but who is left interiorly just as much a *being of nature* as he was without the law. With the breakup of the system, then, there devolves upon each individual the task of *giving to himself* a form of universality which is more than that of mere "equality" (*Gleichheit*) with everyone else (p. 351/514). An individuality which genuinely distinguishes will never be the work of a "law" from without. In a very broad sense what is open to each individual is the path of "culture" (*Bildung*) as an "*estrangement* of *natural* being" (p. 351/515). Getting outside this merely natural being becomes a conscious goal, requiring a conscious effort to actualize what individuality essentially is: in overcoming the merely natural "this individuality makes itself (*bildet sich*) into what it is *in itself*" (p. 351/515). On the level of nature there are no individuals, because all are simply alike; strictly speaking, they do not even interact constructively.

Culture enters in to change all this. Obviously culture is not the work of individuals as individuals, nor does it create individuals. It is the work of many individuals acting unconsciously in concert and creating "types" which serve as *models* for individuals to aim at (p. 352/515). Aiming at the type, of course, is a matter of individual effort, and individuals can be adjudged "good" or "bad" on the basis of their approach to the type aimed at. Thus, in one sense the self-conscious individual sets his own goal, prescribes his own "common essence" (*Gemeinwesen*); but in another sense this is but a contrived unity of individual independence (*Fürsichsein*) and ideal (*Ansichsein*), since success ("good") and failure ("bad") are no more than conformity to type and failure to measure up (p. 354/518). What actually happens is that two superpowers arise, "the power of the state" and "wealth," fealty to which determines conformity and non-conformity (pp. 354–55/519). Individual behavior becomes a matter of relationship to one or the other or both (p. 355/519–20).

From the spiritual point of view, "state power" would seem to have the edge in this confrontation; its ends are more universal than are those of wealth and can, therefore, more legitimately enlist the loyalty of individuals.[27] On the other hand, "wealth" involves another kind of universality—inasmuch as its source is the *work* of all, and its purpose is to be *enjoyed* by all—and thus enables individuals to avoid being swallowed up in the state: it is "the constantly *increasing result* of the *work* and *activity of all,* and it produces *enjoyment* by all" (p. 355/520).[28] Previously (cf. *supra,* pp. 170–72) Hegel had spoken in rather abstract terms of an individual activity, seemingly self-centered, which actually benefited all. Now he indicates how that actually works out in a liberal economy of "enlightened self-interest," where working to increase one's own wealth inevitably increases the wealth of all. It should be noted that Hegel puts only a very qualified stamp of approval on this theory.

The point is that the very existence of two opposed universal powers permits the individual a certain liberty between them; neither can claim his total allegiance (p. 356/521). What counts is whether what he does is *good* or *bad,* and he can make his own judgment regarding the claims of the two universal forces—even though the existence of only two cuts down the field of choice. In any event, "to self-consciousness that object is now *good* and *as it should be (ansich),* wherein it finds itself; whereas that one is bad, wherein it finds the contrary of itself" (p. 356/522). "Finding self" has become a significant criterion of good and bad—far more significant than conformity to type.

What is more, precisely in relation to "state power" and "wealth," the notions of "good" and "bad" are given a discernible content. From one point of view, the relation to "state power" demands an *obedience* which oppresses the individual self, and this is *bad.* "Wealth," therefore, is *good: "In itself* it is universal benefit" (p. 357/523). From another point of view, "state power expresses to him what his true being *(Wesen)* is" (p. 357/523). The state gives unity to a multiplicity of individuals and organizes their collective activity. "Thus, the individual finds his basis and true being there expressed, organized, and activated" (p. 358/523). From this point of view enjoyment of wealth becomes divisive and, therefore, *bad.* Depending on the point of view, therefore, each can be *good* or *bad,* and the individual can revert to the criterion of which better permits him to find his self-identity (p. 358/524).

As the attitudes toward the "power of the state" and "wealth" crystallize in the historical process Hegel has chosen to trace, we find that in the transition from feudalism to monarchy one kind of consciousness, the "noble," finds its self-identity in service to the state, which is therefore

27 "By serving the state the self serves a power concerned with universal ends, ends cognate with his superior but alien to his inferior nature" *(ibid.,* p. 218).

28 The accents of Adam Smith are unmistakable. According to Hyppolite, Hegel had read *An Inquiry into the Causes of the Wealth of Nations* as early as 1803–04. He manifests a sophisticated grasp of the principles of political economy (see *Genèse et structure,* p. 382nn1&3).

good, and at the same time he finds in "wealth" a guarantee of independence (pp. 358–59/525). There is, however, another type of consciousness which finds in "state power" only an impediment to the flowering of the independent self; in which context "wealth" becomes something which separates it from the state. This consciousness—presumably bourgeois— Hegel calls "base" (*niederträchtig*), one which places neither itself nor its wealth at the service of the state.

Although in both cases what is *good* and what is *bad* continue to be what promotes or impedes self-identity, the judgment as to what does either becomes the conclusion of a reasoning process, a syllogism. The noble becomes the vassal whose service of the state is heroic, because he judges service to be a virtue "which sacrifices what is singular to the universal" and makes himself into "the person who forgoes possession and enjoyment, finding his own actuality in working for the established power" (p. 360/527). In doing so he finds his own value precisely in this service, and "*state power* is what for him *truly counts*" (p. 360/527). Such service, however, entails sacrificing also his own will, becoming "the *proud* vassal" (p. 361/528), for whom the "honor" accorded him is sufficient reward. If he speaks at all, it is to give "counsel" (*Rat*) which proceeds not from inner conviction but from an attachment to a problematic "what-is-best-for-all" (p. 361/528). What is "best for all," however, becomes all too readily what is best for the class (*Stand*) to which the individual belongs.[29] The noble self-sacrifice of the vassal is authentic only when it turns into a sacrifice of life; otherwise it becomes a subtle form of self-seeking, and thus *base* (p. 361/529).

Once the monarchical power has become firmly established, the service which helped to establish it is no longer needed, and the vehicle of service becomes *language*. The formulating of "laws," the giving of "commands," the contribution of "counsel"—all are functions of those who surround the monarch and who thus serve the state. Gradually language, which is but a *form* of expression, takes on a value of its own; what it expresses is not so much an objective meaning as the subjectivity of the one who employs it; what language conveys is the "I" of the speaker (writer). "The *I* which expresses itself is comprehended (*vernommen*)" (p. 362/530). In this way the "I" achieves a kind of universality, that of being out there to be comprehended by all (p. 363/531).

With this a further step has been taken toward the identification of substance and subject, which is, as Hegel tells us in the Preface, the coming-to-be of spirit. The self which is being sought for is substantially present in the universal intelligibility of language. The spirit, then, whose will has been surrendered to the will of the state and whose language has been turned into service of the state is that which expresses in its own individuality the very being of the state; the state as substantial power has been individualized. The individual whose whole reality is absorbed in the state is substantialized. It is spirit which emerges as the existential link between

---

[29] One is forcibly reminded of Marx's penetrating remarks on the predominance of "class interests" in the conduct of government.

the universal power of the state and the universal expression of that power in language. "The spirit, then, is the mean which presupposes those extremes and which is brought into being (*erzeugt*) by their existence (*Dasein*)" (p. 363/531). Abstractly speaking, "state power" is the authority which is obeyed, and "noble consciousness" is the obedience rendered; both are given actuality in *language*. In the process, however, language becomes degraded. What was a service *expressed* in language becomes a language which *is* service, the lip-service of "flattery": "The heroism of silent service turns into the *heroism* of *flattery*" (p. 364/533). Where the monarch has become all powerful, the only service left to be performed is that of flattery, which is a language which conditions both the monarch's consciousness of himself and the courtier's consciousness of himself and, in so doing, alienates both, since each has to find in the other and not in himself the reality of his own self-consciousness. The movement from abstract authority to the concrete person of the monarch and from abstract obedience to the person of the courtier (one and the same movement) has been accomplished, and the moving force has been the denatured language of flattery. The monarch, who has been given complete, unique individuality through the proper name, "Louis," whereby he is addressed, can say *L'état, c'est moi*, and he *depends* on flattery for the consciousness which permits him to say that. A long step has been taken from the unself-conscious unity of the city-state or the imperial state; the fragmented consciousness of feudal particularism has been reintegrated in the all-embracing self-consciousness of the absolute monarch (p. 365/534).

For this unified monarchical self-consciousness, however, a high price has been paid. Little by little the unity of state power which has been established in the person of the monarch through the medium of flattery is transferred to the "noble consciousness" upon which the monarch's self-consciousness depends. The "wealth" which previously stood over against "state power," and which could command only the "base" allegiance of the bourgeoisie, turns wealthy courtiers into "powers behind the throne." And this is but a first step in the degradation of not only monarchical power but also the power of the state itself. Wealth becomes the impersonal force which rules; men have created a monster in whom all are alienated (p. 367/536). The quest for self-identity has culminated in the complete loss of self-identity.[30] Wealth, which we might now conveniently call "capital," has become the all-embracing impersonal force which controls the whole of life, economic, social, political, religious. "Personality" has reached its nadir, alienated in a totally impersonal power (p. 368/537). The relative "fragmentation" (*Zerrissenheit*) of self-consciousness which followed upon the disintegration of the Roman Empire has become a more catastrophic "absolute fragmentation" where wealth which was once for the benefit and enjoyment of all has become "the universal power" (p. 369/539). The "spirit" which the power of wealth ushers on the scene is no spirit at all; it

---

[30] Hegel's analysis of this sort of self-alienation, although perhaps less vivid than that of Marx, is no less devastating.

is "totally essenceless opinion, superficiality devoid of all spirit" (p. 370, 539–40).

Where "culture" is all that counts, "wealth" is bound to take over, and even the witty language of French "esprit," which previously served to flatter the monarch's self-esteem, is now put to work in the service of wealth. The "noble" self-consciousness established the self-consciousness of the monarch through flattery; now all that is left is "base" self-consciousness to flatter the glories of wealth. Once more "equality" reigns, the equality of the identical judgment, "wherein one and the same personality is both subject and predicate" (p. 370/541), which is to say that judgment has disappeared completely. The "universal power" with which all this began was an abstraction which became concrete in a variety of ways, all pushing toward the same culmination, the "personality" which is no personality at all, but only impersonal wealth. Judgment has lost all meaning, because "good" and "bad," "noble" and "base," have lost all meaning; the "reversal" already seen in the dialectic of "understanding" has once more set in: "By the same token, everything, considered formally, is *outwardly* the reverse of what it is *in consciousness (für sich)*" (p. 371/542). The only *spiritual* thing which survives the collapse is *cultivated speech* (p. 372/543).

Spirit, which had started out to come to terms with itself in action, now finds that it can express itself only in language. It is not easy to explain why at this point Hegel steps out of character and gives what is, for him, an unusually large number of quotes from Diderot's dialogue-satire, *Rameau's Nephew*.[31] Whatever the reason may have been, the dialogue does serve admirably to point up the degree to which in France in the seventeenth century (and into the eighteenth) the *form* of language far outweighed in importance its *content*.[32] What language *means* had become indifferent, as long as one spoke with "esprit"—whether *what* was said was true or false, good or bad, made no difference (p. 372/543). "Culture" (*Bildung*) had become such a burlesque that it ignored "nature" entirely, thus leaving nothing to "build" on (p. 373/544–45); "culture" and "artificiality" had become synonymous. Hegel's reaction to French "esprit" was violent[33]—but it provided him with a transition to a new, more significant manifestation of spirit's progress.[34]

The danger of mere cleverness in the use of language goes even further. Putting one's thoughts into the mouths of fictitious characters—like "Rameau's nephew"—runs the risk not only of retreating from reality (the writer of fiction can abdicate responsibility for what his characters say), but

---

[31] The dialogue, which at the time was not yet available to French readers, had been translated by Goethe in 1805.

[32] For a succinct statement on the importance of language in the seventeenth century, particularly in France, see Niel, *De la Médiation*, pp. 152–53. It helps us to understand the "noble consciousness."

[33] "This is in harmony with his distaste for artful and contrived (*nachdrückliche*) formulation; his judgment of the 'spirited language' of the self-alienated spirit, of mere culture, was unsympathetic. Thus had the Germans constantly reacted to Voltaire and Diderot" (Adorno, *Drei Studien*, p. 135).

[34] Cf. Loewenberg, *Hegel's Phenomenology*, pp. 210, 216.

also of creating mere "types" (*espèces*) which studiously avoid life in the concrete (p. 374/545). The solution is not to be found either on the individual level or on the level of an artificially "universalized individuality" (p. 374/545). Nor is it to be found in a return to the *natural*—dialectical development permits no return. The cultivated spirit must find a solution in itself—which it might well begin doing by laughing at itself (p. 374/546). Genuine laughter, however, is not sarcastic criticism; standing off from what has come to be the case and judging it critically is no solution either. Spirit must "come to grips with" (*fassen*) its own situation (p. 375/547). It must honestly recognize its own "disintegration" (*Zerrissenheit*) and then return to itself in a movement of reintegration (p. 376/548). Once more consciousness is "unhappy," but that it must find the solution to its unhappiness in itself is clear—it must regain itself, its own *inner life*.[35]

b) Belief and Pure Insight [36]
The world of "culture," as historically "actual" as it may have been (at the beginning of the eighteenth century), has crumbled. Spirit has been forced to seek refuge in a non-actual world "of *pure consciousness* or of *thinking*" (p. 376/549). The *public* world of artificiality has been replaced by the *private* world of autonomous thought, where alone, it would seem, the *content* of thought really counts. The turn, however, is too abrupt to get consciousness completely out of the "actuality" in which it is enmeshed. It has sought asylum in its own thoughts, which are truly its own, but has not shaken off the imagery (*Vorstellung*) which clings to thoughts and still binds them to "the sphere of actuality" (p. 376/549). The form this takes, it is true, is that of an "*actuality common to all*" (*eines Gemeinwirklichen*), but this is not yet the universality of pure thought—divested of imagery (p. 376/549). In its previous stages of development, consciousness had not gone beyond the "formal" universality of thought, whose content, tied to a world "out there," was still particular. Now it is a question of discovering universality in the *content* of thought, but as yet only in one's own thought, not in thought as such (p. 377/550).

Hegel points to *religion* as an example of what he is talking about. In one sense, it resides in the interior of each individual religious consciousness; in another, it unites many consciousnesses in relation to a common content. At this stage, however, the framework in which religious consciousness is real is the world of "culture"—even as a retreat from it into "belief"

35 "The bearing of our conclusions is evident. For Hegel it is only modern consciousness —that which has its roots in the end of the Roman Empire and which finds itself completely only in the eighteenth century—which lives in this world, while thinking its essence in another world alien to the former" (Boey, *L'Aliénation*, p. 87).

36 It would seem arbitrary to translate *Einsicht* by any term other than "insight," even though the English term does not carry the full impact of the German. Hyppolite translates the term by *intellection*, but in English this will not do. If we recall the medieval distinction between *intellectus* and *ratio*, however, we may come close to Hegel's meaning. *Ratio* (discursive reasoning) comes close to Hegel's *Räsonnieren*, characteristic of "rationalism." *Intellectus* (intellectual penetration) comes close to Hegel's *Einsicht*, a function of "reason" (*Vernunft*) in its profoundest sense—denoting spirit's plunge into its own depths.

(p. 377/550). As we know, this sort of thing has appeared before, on the level of "unhappy consciousness," but there the attitude was not properly one of "belief" (p. 377/550–51). Here there is question of "belief" properly speaking, a characteristic of "pure consciousness" in its retreat from the "actuality" of the world of mere "culture" (p. 377/551), but it is only belief, not genuinely autonomous thought (p. 378/551).

Precisely as *flight from* the "actual" world, the religious attitude carries within itself its own alienation; it is at once individual (private) and universal (common), but it has not reconciled these two aspects (p. 378/551–52). It is at once movement (away from an alien world) and rest (in the interiority of its own thought), which means that it combines the interiority of "insight" and the exteriority of "belief," without realizing adequately that "its own object, however, is simply the *pure I*" (p. 379/552). Because at this stage "pure insight" has no content ("pure I" is not a content, only a "category" of contents), its content is supplied by "belief." [37] Both "belief" and "insight," it should be noted, are modes of thought, but each has its inadequacies. "Belief" is thinking as a function of objective consciousness, not yet of self-consciousness—its object is "*outside* consciousness of the self" (p. 379/553). The form in which what is believed is expressed, therefore, is essentially "representation" (*Vorstellung*) of a "suprasensible world" which is *other* than the world of self-consciousness (p. 379/553). For "pure insight," on the contrary, "only the self is its own proper object" (p. 379/553). Quite obviously, to bring the two together will be to go beyond both.

In any event, since both "belief" and "pure insight" constitute a retreat from the "actual world of culture" (p. 380/554), both reside in "pure consciousness." Each, then, can be looked at from three points of view: (1) simply as what each is in itself (*an sich*) and how each sees itself (*für sich*); (2) in the relation of each to a world "over against it" (*entgegengesetzt*); and (3) as related to each other. If we look at "belief" from these three points of view, we find that (*a*) it is not dependent on outside confirmation of its object, which is "absolute being" (*absolutes Wesen*); (*b*) believing in this "absolute being" is synonymous with its making itself known; (*c*) "belief" thus gives to the return to self in "insight" a content. The movement "outward" to the object of faith is inseparable from the movement "inward" to an increased knowledge of self (p. 380/555). In one sense, of course, "belief" is directed toward the "actual" world in which it lives; it interprets the latter in the light of the "absolute" object. In another sense, it eradicates the "actuality" of that world as mere "vanity" (p. 381/555). The "service" and "flattery" which characterize the world of culture are replaced by "obedience" to God and "worship." This replacement is the work of the concept within the believer; but in a "belief" which is only that, the concept does not reveal itself as concept—the believer is not aware that in "believing" he is "conceiving" (p. 381/556).

If we turn now to an examination of "pure insight," we find that its "actuality" is entirely in the conceptual order; there is no movement "out-

---

37 One might profitably paraphrase Kant: "Insight without belief is empty; belief without insight is blind"—remembering, of course, that Hegel's *Einsicht* is intellectual, whereas Kant's *Anschauung* is sensible.

ward" at all. To the extent that it has any object which is not the product of its own conceiving, that object is supplied by belief (p. 381/556).[38] In examining it we can, once again, see it from three points of view: as it is and sees itself (*an und für sich*); in relation to the "vanity" of the actual world; and in relation to belief (p. 382/556). (*a*) In itself this sort of insight is essentially a knowledge which spirit has of itself, making no appeal to anything outside itself for consciousness of itself. *Ein-sicht* is simply a "looking-into" itself. (*b*) Still, even this is not without its relation to an external actuality; it is, after all, situated in a world which is not of its own making. The problem is that in relation to this world from which "looking-into" itself is a retreat, it would seem to be "looking-into" just *one* consciousness; it gets away from the vanity of it all by conceptualizing all objectivity. Its "intention" (*Absicht*) [39] is to accept only a world which it itself has conceived. The "purity" of this "intention" may be admirable, but it does not succeed in emerging from "the spiritual animal kingdom" to a realm of true spirit, where "pure insight becomes the property of all self-consciousnesses" (p. 382/557). Unless intellectual competitiveness is abandoned, only spiritual isolation can be the issue (p. 382/557). This means that genuine clarity of insight will reveal that the whole congeries of efforts to come to terms with reality on the level of merely individual reason has to be jettisoned. Otherness does not have to be abandoned—that would be unrealistic—but the only otherness which counts is the otherness of other "I's": "What is other in this for the I is simply the I itself" (p. 383/558). The individual will never be rational by himself; only a shared rationality is authentically rational.

No longer can individual consciousness be satisfied to seek its own identity in being rational; its purpose now is, so to speak, to campaign for rationality; reason must be concretely universalized in the rationality of all.[40] "Pure insight," then, is not in itself rationality, but it is a call to the only rationality worthy of the name, universal rationality. "This pure insight, then, is the spirit which calls to *every* consciousness: *be for yourselves* [be aware of] what all of you are *in yourselves* [what you really are]—*rational*" (p. 383/558). It is the battle-cry of the Enlightenment which proclaims to all men, "do not rely on anything but reason." The battle begins when the Enlightenment turns its guns on any and every form of superstition, any and every *outside* source of truth, under which heading it includes the "belief" which up to this point seemed to harmonize so well with "insight." As we shall see in a later chapter, reason will be truly reason, and not merely faith in reason, only on the condition that it be reconciled with faith—in the spirit—but here the struggle must go on.

ii. Enlightenment

At first glance a faith which is only faith ("pure belief") and an intellectual insight which is only insight ("pure insight") would seem to be poles apart.

---

38 *Fides quaerens intellectum*? (cf. Lauer, "Hegel on Proofs for God's Existence," 445).
39 *Einsicht* becomes *Absicht*, an obviously untranslatable play on words.
40 Cf. *supra*, "The Law of the Heart."

Each, it is true, constitutes a withdrawal from the sophisticated but superficial values of a world of mere culture, and each is a return to a world affirmed in the innermost depths of consciousness ("pure consciousness"). Belief, however, relies on a source outside itself for the affirmation it makes, whereas insight relies only on itself. It is for this reason that insight looks upon belief as an obstacle to intellectual purity and, hence, to the autonomy of the human spirit. The "intentions" (*Absichten*) of belief are "uninformed," and its "insights" (*Einsichten*) are "perverted," because they have been imposed from without, not conceived from within (p. 383/559). It should be remembered, however, that the "belief" of which Hegel here speaks is not that which characterizes authentic religious faith but only a pietistic attitude toward the world which culture has constructed. Nor is the "insight" of which he speaks the intellectual profundity characteristic of informed reason, but only that faith in reason which was the "Enlightenment's" reaction to a world of values imposed by culture, tradition, or authority of any kind. What both belief and insight have in common, then, is that each bypasses the inner struggle of coming to consciousness of what it is to be thoroughly rational.[41]

Thus, the "pure insight" of enlightened thinkers like Voltaire and Diderot had all the attractiveness of an "undisturbed consciousness" over against the tumultuous disintegration which "culture" brought in its wake (p. 383/559). As a consciousness simply "looking into" itself, however, "enlightened" thinking contains no "special insight" into the vapidity of the world of culture. The latter, Hegel tells us, looks into itself, finds there a state of spiritual fragmentation, and then covers up its own lack of spiritual resources with a "critique in spirited language touching all aspects of its own situation" (p. 384/559)—enlightened thinkers produce sad little satires like *Rameau's Nephew*. "Pure insight," then, is but a confirmation of the cultured world's judgment of itself. In Hegel's view, the Voltaires and the Diderots are products of the very world they criticize, who fail to get above it; their function as satirists is to make others conscious of the situation, not to change anything (p. 384/560).[42] The individual critic, aware of the vanity of the world in which he lives, engages in an equally vain critique of his world; preferring the vanity of "clever" formulation to constructive criticism, he gets bogged down in negative ideas. Put them all together and they come up not with genuine universality but with a "collection" (*Encyclopedia?*) of witticisms. "The collection (*Sammlung*) reveals to most of them a better, to all an at least more complex, witticism than their own . . . with this the interest of only one, which was still present, cancels itself out, and the insight of only one is resolved into the general insight" (pp. 384–85/560).

---

41 "Here Hegel had a correct view, historically as well as systematically, when he looked upon Enlightenment and Pietism not so much as contraries but rather merely as different manifestations of one and the same mental attitude of ignoring concrete historical contents of thought. Reliance on an inner light, the *lumen internum*, is their common root" (Erwin Metzke, *Hegels Vorreden* [Heidelberg: Kerle, 1949], pp. 245–46).

42 Marx, as we know, takes up precisely this point in his contention that the rational task is to change the world, not simply to criticize it.

Hegel's scathing judgment may be unfair—to Voltaire at least—but it does point up the decadence of mere cleverness.[43]

It would be a mistake, however, either to construe the Enlightenment as a merely negative outgrowth of the world of culture or to think that Hegel so construes it. On the long journey toward rational autonomy of spirit, it is a "necessary" stage, and even though it misconstrues the essence of religious faith, it is at least a preliminary antidote to the superstition which constantly threatens to infect religion (p. 385/560).

a) Enlightenment's Struggle against Superstition [44]
"Pure insight," as we have seen, is primarily an individual function. It can be generalized in either of two ways: the individual can generalize his insight formally by way of abstraction, or he can "spread" the insight by enabling others (all) to come by themselves to the same view. The question, of course, is just how authentically universal the insight would be in either case. In any event, Hegel characterizes "Enlightenment" as "the *spread of pure insight*" (p. 385/561). Like belief, insight resides in consciousness and in consciousness alone. But belief is in consciousness simply as "thinking," i.e., without self-consciousness; while insight takes the form of "concept," i.e., with self-consciousness. One, we might say, is the "inner light" directed outward, away from the self; the other is the same directed inward, into the self. From this point of view, belief has a world of content, the absolute content, whereas insight has no content at all, merely an empty self. Insight must *give* itself a content, and this it does by negating whatever belief affirms: "By its negative movement against what is negative to it, however, it will realize itself and give itself a content" (p. 385/561). Insight is in the rather precarious position of living off belief, which it universally labels "superstition." With superb disdain it sees belief as such simply opposed to "reason and truth," a "tissue of superstitions, prejudices, and errors" (p. 385/561), which it rejects wholesale. Thus, not only is believing a "false insight" (*Einsicht*) on the part of "the masses," but what is believed is the result of an "evil intention" (*Absicht*) on the part of a deceitful "priesthood" (p. 385/562). The Enlightenment, then, finds itself called to fight a war on three fronts: against the stupidity of the masses who believe; against the deceit of the priests who seek their own advantage; against the despotism of the state which seeks a false synthesis of the real and the ideal by promoting religion (p. 386/562).

The focus of the Enlightenment's attack is not the believing (subjective) of the believer, which is honest enough, but what the believer believes (objective)—that is where the deceit lies (p. 386/562–63).[45] The task is to "enlighten" the masses, and this "Enlightenment" will do by attacking the

---

43 Seeberger notes (*Hegel*, p. 440) that "enlightened" thinkers, like Locke and Voltaire, seem to have experienced no difficulty seeing black men as slaves of white men.

44 The German term for "superstition" (*Aberglauben*) indicates that it is a degraded form of "belief" (*Glauben*). We might call it "unwarranted belief."

45 Like the English terms "belief" or "faith," the German *Glauben* or *Glaube* can mean both "holding on faith" or the sum total of "beliefs" common to a religious body.

sum total of "beliefs" and thus cleansing "pure believing consciousness" of its impurities (p. 386/563). Since as "pure consciousness" the latter is receptive to "concept," the spread of "insight" will be calm and gentle, like the spread of "a penetrating contagion" (*Ansteckung*) (p. 387/563). "Enlightenment" is the imperceptible transformation of the spirit of an age. In accomplishing this transformation, of course, Enlightenment has unshakable confidence in the validity of its own insights and in the invalidity of what is opposed to them. The metaphor of "contagion" for this sort of rationalism is a good one; if belief tries to justify itself by giving reasons, it has already been infected and has lost the battle (p. 387/564). For "Enlightenment" the battle has been an easy one: it has toppled the idols of Christian faith before believers knew it, and the only weapons left to them are "Enlightenment's" own (p. 388/565). What has happened, however, is that a new object of worship has been substituted for the old; the "cult" of reason is in full swing.

Actually this sort of rationalism does not get off quite so easy. It wants to be nothing but quiet refutation, but it is forced into a strident campaign against the opposition which, for lack of positive content of its own, rationalism *needs* as an ever-present whipping-boy (p. 388/565). This need of being negative, in fact, is so essential to Enlightenment that it becomes negative in regard to itself. The insights it seeks to spread turn out not to be universal at all, and one insight struggles with another, with the result that in seeking to fight its opposite, Enlightenment ends up fighting itself (p. 389/566). Reason, which presumably is one, is pitted against *another* reason. Because it *must* fight religion rather than find its own truth in religion's content (it itself has no content), it becomes the negation of any affirmation whatsoever. Nor can it recognize what it is doing; only "we" can. "This nature of Enlightenment's war on errors, that in warring on them it wars on itself and condemns in them what it itself affirms, is *for us*, or it is what Enlightenment and its war are *in themselves*" (pp. 389–90/566–67). In the end it is no more than a "belief" in the product of its own consciousness, which it is no better able to justify than is religious belief (p. 390/567).

What all this comes down to is that discrediting belief accomplishes nothing positive; it in no way establishes the opposite of what is believed, which itself is only an opposite belief (p. 390/567); faith in reason does not guarantee that it is in fact reason which is believed in—rationalism cannot justify itself. Furthermore the belief which enlightened insight has discredited is not even belief in the full sense of the term; it is lacking in what Hegel calls *Vertrauen* (*fiducia*), which itself is a kind of insight uniting the believer with the object of belief. "*Vertrauen* is, however, belief, because its consciousness is *directed immediately* to its object, and thus intuits this, that it is one with the object, is in it" (p. 390/568). Unlike the essentially individual, merely subjective insight which Enlightenment seeks to *spread*, the insightfulness of belief is itself a community affair, both subjectively, i.e., believing, and objectively, i.e., what is believed (p. 391/568).

The object of insight, "looking-in," after all is self. If self is not a community of selves, however, then the other selves to whom insight must be spread are simply *other*, and "spreading" makes no sense, except as itself a matter of belief (p. 391/569). Enlightenment wants to have things both ways: a belief which is *common* to the community is the product of deceit and priestly trickery; an insight which is *spread* and thus made common is a matter of autonomous insight on the part of each member of the community. "But here the Enlightenment is thoroughly nonsensical; belief experiences it as a talking which does not know what it is saying, which does not understand the matter when it speaks of priestly betrayal and deceiving the people" (p. 391/569). Apart from not understanding its own emptiness, Enlightenment tries to claim at one and the same time that consciousness cannot have anything imposed on it from without and that it does have belief imposed on it by trickery (p. 392/569).

The fact is, Hegel says, that you cannot fool the consciousness of a whole people; in the faith-consciousness it has of its absolute object, it is conscious of its universal self, and there is no deceiving the universal self—"regarding the being in which consciousness has immediate *certainty of itself*, the thought of deception disappears completely" (p. 392/570). What is more, in this, Enlightenment digs its own grave by contradicting itself when talking about deceiving everyone. Belief is not going to be disturbed by a self-contradictory Enlightenment, although it can learn more about its own essential nature by a critical examination of Enlightenment (p. 392/570). How, then, does belief experience Enlightenment?

To begin with, like the physiognomist who knows a dishonest face when he sees it, no matter what a person's actions are, Enlightenment tells the believer what it is he really believes. In attacking superstition, which it defines as any and every sensibly imagined object of belief, it is Enlightenment, not belief, which *makes* the object into a *thing*, "with a view which simply is not present in worshipful belief, such that it simply lies when it foists this view on belief" (p. 393/571). It is the enlightened thinker not the believer who cannot distinguish between the object of belief and its sensible representation. In fact, Enlightenment is incapable of comprehending the *ground* of belief, i.e., absolute spirit giving testimony to itself, which it foolishly takes to be alien to "pure consciousness" (p. 394/572). In saying, correctly, that consciousness should not rely on external grounds for its affirmations, Enlightenment fails to see what the genuine ground is. It is very astute in criticizing the Bible, a book which human beings *happened* to write, as though the written word were the ground of *inner* belief. "In fact, however, it does not occur to belief to attach its certainty to such contingent testimonies" (p. 394/573). It is not the Bible, but God, who guarantees the validity of religious belief (p. 395/573). "It is the Spirit himself who is witness to himself, just as much in the *interior* of *each* consciousness as through the *general presence* of the belief all have in him" (p. 395/573). It is not the dead letter but the presence of the living spirit which grounds belief. It is for this reason that if belief seeks to validate its own claims by verifying what the Enlightenment has discredited, it gives proof that it has been infected by the latter (p. 395/573). By what right does this sort of rationalism set the terms on which religious faith is allowed to justify itself?

As for the religious activities which flow from faith, Enlightenment declares it silly to forgo pleasure for the sake of what one believes—failing to see that for the sake of having anything, including "insight," one must forgo something else (p. 396/574–75). More seriously, Enlightenment is saying that one should rise above the grasping attitude of merely "natural existence" and then finds it "foolish" to *do* anything to accomplish this. Once more it contradicts itself: "Thus, it disclaims itself both as pure insight, since it disclaims immediate purposeful activity, and as pure intention, since it disclaims the intention to prove itself liberated from the purposes of singularity" (p. 396/575). In effect, Enlightenment is saying simultaneously that it is foolish for the individual not to seek the higher things and foolish to give up the lower.

In short, Enlightenment presents itself to belief as a purely negative attitude which the latter need not take too seriously (p. 396/575). "We," however, can look more closely to see if it has a positive side. *"Just what is the truth which Enlightenment has spread in place of prejudice and superstition?"* (p. 397/576). (*a*) To begin with, by denying *whatever* content belief has given to its "absolute being," Enlightenment comes up with a vacuum with no attributes, no predicates (p. 397/576). Its "insight" is certainly "pure"—purely finite. (*b*) Secondly, with its insistence on the finite, it is back where "sensible certainty" was, but this time not as a consciousness which can develop; it has gone as far as it can go: "Now brought back to its first form through pure insight, consciousness has *experienced* this form as *result*" (p. 397/577). Effectively, in utterly rejecting belief it has rejected all the forms of consciousness which necessarily culminate in belief and, in so doing, has raised sense certainty to "absolute truth" (p. 398/577). (*c*) Thirdly, with the *development* of consciousness reduced to insignificance, the world of consciousness becomes completely arbitrary; everything is the way uninhibited consciousness sees it, and that is all there is to it (pp. 398–99/577–78). Man is back in the state of nature, where he is naturally good, and whatever else is is *for* him. The "platitude" of utilitarianism is the logical outcome of enlightened insight, and reason becomes no more than a *useful* means of seeing to it that everything is useful, not harmful to man—reason's function is to *moderate* pleasure (p. 399/579). This, of course, is given a specious sort of universality by making *everyone* seek what is most useful to himself, which will guarantee that each seeks what is most useful to everyone else—every*thing* and every*one* are useful to *everyone* (p. 400/579–80).[46] In this context, however, religion returns to the scene; it is most useful for everyone!

Faith is useful; religion is useful; God is useful—provided he be construed as *l'être suprême*—Hegel finds this "abominable" (*abscheulich*) (p. 400/580). "To faith, this *wisdom*, which is Enlightenment's very own, necessarily appears as at the same time vacuity (*Plattheit*) itself and the admission of vacuity" (p. 400/580). All enlightened religion (Deism) knows about the "absolute being" is *that* it is the "absolute being"—and, thus, the only real *knowledge* left is knowledge of the finite (p. 400/580).

In an apparently oblique reference to the *Antigone* of Sophocles, which

---

46 Since the *Phenomenology* considerably antedates the utilitarianism of both Bentham and Mill, the analysis is indeed surprising.

he had discussed earlier, Hegel speaks of the "divine right" of the absolute, infinite object of belief as pitted against the "human right" of the essentially finite object of enlightened intelligence (p. 400/581). Like the "divine law" represented by Antigone and the "human law" represented by Creon, the two clash, and neither can satisfy the other; each asserts itself as "absolute right," and each simply negates the other. On this view, represented, on the one hand, by pietistic (fideistic) theologians and, on the other, by rationalistic philosophers,[47] there is no reconciling faith and reason, the infinite and the finite (p. 401/581).[48]

The opposition, however, is not such that Enlightenment can simply replace the faith it negates. Rather it enables faith to become conscious of its genuine orientation: "It simply brings together for faith faith's *own proper thought* which had unconsciously become separated" (p. 401/581). Although by inverting each of the moments of faith Enlightenment seems to faith simply to be lying, as a matter of fact it is making faith conscious of its own truth, contained in the dynamic *concept*, which is more than mere *thought* (p. 401/581–82). Thus, "Enlightenment" (*Aufklärung*), which is not "enlightened" (*aufgeklärt*) regarding itself, helps faith to clarity regarding itself. Enlightenment ought to find its own truth in the *content* (absolute) of faith,[49] but its purely negative attitude toward faith prevents it from doing so (p. 401/582). The truth of Enlightenment too is in the concept, but it cannot see this because it refuses to see that the concept is really in "believing consciousness"—with the result that the reality of the concept, "dynamic movement," is lost on it, and it remains chained to a static "pure insight" (p. 402/583).

After this scathing critique of an Enlightenment with which he is obviously impatient, Hegel would seem to want nothing to do with it. We have seen, however, that the enlightened "cult of reason" has helped push faith toward a recognition of its own true role. More than that, the Enlightenment, as Hegel saw it, was necessary in order to effect the transition from the Reformation idea of religious freedom to the modern concept of rational freedom.[50] Finally, even though Enlightenment recognized neither the dynamic nature of reason nor the reality of reason's objective content, it had helped to elevate rational thinking to its rightful place in the universe. It remains to be seen how the Enlightenment's own inner logic prevented it from reconciling faith and reason.[51] (a) First, Hegel tells us, Enlightenment asserts that the conceptual object of consciousness is consciousness' own

[47] With Kant, Fichte, and Jacobi caught somewhere between the two (see G. W. F. Hegel, *Glauben und Wissen*, ed. Georg Lasson [Hamburg: Himmelheber, 1962]).

[48] "Neither of the opposed theories satisfies Hegel; the *Aufklärung* despises man because of his superstitions; positive, supra-naturalist theology despises him because of his weakness. The former remains immersed in an experience without beauty; the latter thinks that the most exalted needs of humanity demand the affirmation of transcendence. Each separates man and the universe itself into two parts contrary to each other; the human is entirely on one side, the divine entirely on the other" (Wahl, *Malheur de la conscience*, p. 87).

[49] As "absolute knowing" will do after the dialectical movement of "religion."

[50] Cf. Pannenberg, *Idea of God*, p. 151.

[51] To the very end of his life Hegel insisted that the opposition between faith and reason—two complementary positions of spirit—should be overcome, but not at the

product, the "absolute being" of believing consciousness is not simply *there*; it is *conceived* (p. 402/583). Faith, therefore, is an activity of consciousness which *produces* its own object (pp. 402–403/583). So far so good. (*b*) The *conceiving*, however, Enlightenment sees as a contingent event which produces only "fictions," "representations" (*Vorstellungen*). At the same time Enlightenment says the exact opposite: that the object of faith is *alien* to consciousness, "its way impenetrable, its being unattainable" (p. 403/584). (*c*) This last opens the door to Enlightenment's claim to tell faith what faith's object *really* is, i.e., some *sensible thing* (p. 403/584). In claiming this, Enlightenment is but revealing its own incapacity to reconcile a sensible image with a suprasensible object and is thus itself left with the only being it can stomach, one "abandoned by spirit" (p. 404/585), "an unshaken finitude which would not even be a *moment* in the spiritual movement of the [absolute] being (*Wesens*), not a nothing, nor yet a something *which is* in and for itself but something which disappears" (p. 404/585). For Enlightenment the finite is "absolutely" finite; there is no infinite movement of which it can be a "moment." (*d*) Enlightenment is so intent on reminding faith that faith's "knowing" is contingent and its object "imaged," that it itself fails to do what it thus enables faith to do: to recognize that the contingent image is "inessential" and must be transcended. By concentrating on the inessential, Enlightenment fails to see the passage, within consciousness itself, from the *inessential* to the *essential* (p. 404/585). The "idols" it topples are not idols. (*e*) Finally, Enlightenment completely misses the point of asceticism dictated by faith, seeing in it only an unjustified and purposeless abdication (rejection) of possessions and pleasure. The fact is that faith too recognizes that mere "giving up" is by itself insignificant, but overcoming the merely "natural" orientation toward *things* is not (p. 404/585–86). For faith, "not only is the activity of its absolute being as its object something universal; the single consciousness too must show itself completely and universally free of its sensible being" (p. 405/586)—which it does not do by simply giving up this or that *thing*.

What Enlightenment has done, in the last analysis, is to isolate the interiority of consciousness from the exteriority of actuality, making reconciliation impossible. Small wonder that it fails to see the union of the interior (concept) and exterior (image) in faith (p. 405/587). In doing this, however, Enlightenment has helped faith to come to terms with itself, to recognize its own double character, living a finite existence but oriented to infinite being. In this orientation there is contained a reconciliation of the finite and the infinite, but as yet the reconciliation is not actual; it is only a "longing" (*Sehnen*) (p. 406/588). In a sense, faith now finds itself in the same situation as is Enlightenment: its infinite object is beyond it. The difference is that

<hr />

expense of the infinite content of both (see "Vorrede zu Hinrichs' Religionphilosophie" [1822], *Berliner Schriften*, pp. 59–60). "What is theology without a knowledge of God? Just what a philosophy is without the same, sounding brass and tinkling cymbal" (*ibid.*, p. 81; cf. "Aphorismen über Nichtwissen und absolutes Wissen im Verhältnis zur christlichen Glaubenserkenntnis" [1829], *ibid.*, p. 298; and "Der Idealrealismus" [1831], *ibid.*, p. 408).

faith can get out of this situation; Enlightenment cannot. "In fact, with this, faith has become the same as Enlightenment, namely consciousness of an orientation of what is in itself finite toward an absolute without predicates, unknown and unknowable; but *Enlightenment* is a *satisfied*, and faith a *dissatisfied*, enlightenment" (p. 407/588–89). Faith, then, has the dialectical advantage; dissatisfaction is the key to dialectical advance. Enlightenment cannot attain to its own truth (content), because that is contained in the faith which Enlightenment has unceremoniously rejected.

b) The Truth of Enlightenment
After what can well seem an unnecessarily long and negative treatment of the "Enlightenment"—not nearly so unnecessary in his "enlightened" day—it may come as a surprise that Hegel still does not let the topic drop. Loewenberg, in fact, in his treatment of this section,[52] indicates some puzzlement as to why Hegel should have included this section at all and as to what "truth" means in the context. Is it what is true *in* the Enlightenment or the truth *about* the Enlightenment? The former would seem to be precluded by the negative attitude Hegel has already adopted; the latter would seem to be unnecessary in view of all he has previously said. The puzzlement, however, would seem to be unjustified on both counts. To take the second count first, Hegel is treating neither the true *in* nor the truth *about* the Enlightenment, but, as in "Perception," "the truth of sense certainty," he is to bring out the "truth" of which Enlightenment is merely the "certainty." As to the first count, since the vehicle of dialectical advance is now faith, and since the truth toward which it is oriented (with hope of attainment) is the same truth to which Enlightenment is oriented (without hope of attainment), it is not otiose to focus on one in terms of the other.

If the "pure insight" which Enlightenment seeks to spread is as intellectual as it is claimed to be, it "is *in itself* concept" (p. 407/590), which is to say it is authentic only if it is the genuine product of conceptual thinking. Since, however, from the Enlightenment point of view this insight is essentially *negative*, it negates its own conceptual character, and all that is left to it as object is a "pure thing" (p. 407/590). As a result, an insight which is only insight is not properly conceptual at all but only "pure feeling," corresponding as it does to "pure thingness," thus preventing Enlightenment from seeing the essential identity of objective reality and self-consciousness. In trying to "look-into" consciousness, insight finds only emptiness and therefore posits a "thing" *out there* as its real object, an object not *conceived* but *felt*, i.e., which impresses itself on consciousness: "Thus the essential counts for consciousness only in the form of objective out-thereness (*Jenseits*), whereas the consciousness which makes distinctions and which in this way holds what is outside itself to be the in-itself counts as finite consciousness" (p. 408/591). The long journey of consciousness has turned out to be a circling back to where it started from.

A *result* such as this, then, splits the Enlightenment into two, correspond-

52 *Hegel's Phenomenology*, pp. 242–48.

ing to the previous split between itself and belief. On the one hand, there is a looking-into itself; on the other, a looking outward. What each sees is different from what the other sees, and what each sees is "pure," in the sense of being unmixed with the other, and in the sense that each is unmixed with any of the other forms of consciousness. The result is two Enlightenments, one of which has as its object the same as had "sense certainty" and "perception"—except that now the object is only "thought" (p. 409/591–92), a thought, however, which is not movement but only abstraction from "sense" and "perception." The other has as its object all that is left, i.e., "pure matter," which turns out to be a "pure abstraction," a "predicateless absolute," which owes its whole being to thought, and to finite thought at that (p. 409/592). For both, then, the only absolute object of thought is without discernible attributes, whether it be a "predicateless supreme being" or an equally "predicateless matter," and both are "outside of" consciousness, in a sort of disembodied thought. "One Enlightenment calls the absolute being that absolute without predicates which is beyond actual consciousness in the thought which is its point of departure—the other calls it matter" (p. 409/592). As conceived in thought both are the same; whatever differences there are are differences in subjective point of view (p. 409/593). The result is a "thinking" identified with "thingness" or a "thingness" identified with "thinking" (p. 410/593–94)—and the side of thinking which has *self* as its object is eliminated; pure objectivity has been achieved, and it is empty.

Neither form of "Enlightenment," then, reaches even the level of Cartesian metaphysics, which recognizes that what is clearly the object of the concept really is (p. 410/594). The essential negativity of enlightened thought turns being into nothing more than the *not-self* (p. 410/594), a static being over against the activity of self thinking (p. 411/594). Since the being which this thinking thinks is simply out there, the only qualification which consciousness contributes to it is in consciousness' judgment as to its "usefulness." "Actuality as object for the actual consciousness of pure insight is—*usefulness*" (p. 411/594). Usefulness does not reside in the object "out there"; it is consciousness which relates reality to itself as useful, and in so doing it has found itself. In stamping on reality the character of being simply "for another," it has "expressed the concept of pure insight" (p. 412/595). A self-consciousness of this sort, however, is sheer "vanity": "It contemplates the attained object as related to this whole sphere, and thus the actual world of culture had gathered itself into the vanity of self-consciousness" (p. 412/596). Consciousness has separated reality from itself and has then related it back to itself as "useful": "The *useful* is the *truth* which is likewise the *certainty* of itself" (p. 413/597). Self-consciousness has become *selfishness*—and more singular than ever. Even the suprasensible world is significant only as useful: "Both worlds have been reconciled, and heaven has been transplanted to earth" (p. 413/598). Man is free, not because he determines himself interiorly, but because he has determined everything else to be for himself. The "truth" which the Enlightenment ("enlightened self-interest") will bring to self-consciousness is a freedom little better than that which skepticism achieved—with this difference: reality need no longer be negated; it can be *used*.

III. Absolute Freedom—and the Terror

Why Hegel should have passed from the "Enlightenment" to the "Terror" succeeding the French Revolution, without, properly speaking, passing through the Revolution itself is not thoroughly clear. We do know that, not only as a young man was Hegel highly enthusiastic about the principles of the Revolution but also in later years he said of it, "Never before in history did man seek, as he did here, to model a society on the rational concept of man." [53] In 1806–07, however, he had become disillusioned with abstract "liberty, equality, and fraternity," issuing as they did in the "Terror"; likewise, in tracing the development of consciousness to spirit he was more concerned with showing the outcome of the ambivalent universality of Rousseau's "general will" than he was with the historical events of the French Revolution.

Without speculating, then, on what Hegel might have said about the French Revolution itself, we can get back to the topic of usefulness, the dead-end street of Enlightenment. The attribute "useful" is taken as the paradigm of a qualification of objective reality which is meaningful only in relation to subjects. What better way for consciousness to return to itself than by making all reality relative to itself, even though the self in question is not yet "immediately the self of consciousness," a self which would be, so to speak, its own possession (p. 414/599)? To make everything relative to even such a self is to make that self supreme and thus to introduce "the new form of consciousness, *absolute freedom*" (p. 414/599). Such a "form of consciousness," of course, would be scarcely distinguishable from the hedonism long since overcome in the dialectic of individual reason if "usefulness" were predicated of reality only in relation to one particular individual. Either utilitarianism looks to the good of all, or it looks to the good of none (pp. 414–15/600). What is more, the consciousness of self growing out of the relationship of universal utility must be a universal consciousness proper to a universal self. This it cannot be if all it is is cognitive consciousness. "Pure thought," it is true, can have all "being" as its *object*, but only "will" can *relate* all being to the self. It is as "willing," then, that consciousness can universalize not only being but itself (p. 415/600–601). If each individual wills what is good (useful) for all, there is but one will which is the will of all—"the general will" (p. 415/601). It dictates an activity which is consciously the activity of all for all, and this is "the undivided substance of absolute freedom" (p. 415/601).

Universalism is now triumphant; the spurious "equality" of all before the law of the Roman Empire has become the subjective equality of all in the "general will" (p. 416/601–602). Even "utility," a step along the way to

---

[53] *Philosophie der Geschichte*, pp. 557–58.

universalized consciousness but still a predicate of "alien being," is gone because the opposition between consciousness and being is gone; what is "willed" is not "being" but the universal self.[54] The only "opposition" left is that which "consists solely in the distinction between the *singular* and the *general* consciousness" (p. 416/602), and the merely "singular" is eliminated in a willing which has as its object the "freedom" of all (p. 417/603). "Freedom," however, is an attribute of consciousness alone which, when universalized, brings into being "the universal *self*" (p. 417/604). Nor is this self universal merely as "represented"—whether mentally (*vorgestellt*), legally (*repräsentiert*), or morally (*vertreten*) [55]—"it is effectually . . . in this universal work (*Werke*) [56] of absolute freedom" (p. 417/604).

The problem with all this, however, is that in theory it is fine, but in practice it does not *work* that way. The notion of universal "freedom" is necessarily an abstraction; when it is concretized in actual practice, the universality of the "general will" becomes crystallized in the will of one: "For the universal to go into action it must gather itself together into the one of individuality and set a single self-consciousness on the pinnacle" (p. 418/604). Universal freedom as such simply gets nothing done; it is indistinguishable chaos, "the *fury* of disappearing" (p. 418/604). Freedom is meaningful only when concretely each single individual is free, but that too has its own problems. If universality is not concretely distributed among individuals, it is cold and unbending.[57] If freedom is only individual, no matter how widely distributed, it is merely an abstraction (p. 418/605)—"none is free until all are free." Coldly universal, doctrinaire freedom, when it goes into action produces only one thing, death—and meaningless death at that. "The sole work, the deed, of universal freedom, therefore, is *death*, and indeed a *death* which has no inner comprehensiveness and fulfillment, for what is negated is the dimensionless point of the absolutely free self. It is, thus, the coldest, flattest of deaths with no more meaning than cutting through a head of cabbage or taking a drink of water" (pp. 418–19/605).

Freedom, of course, is also meaningless if it is not freedom in a concrete political order. In the political order, however, doctrinaire "universal freedom" means the freedom of a "faction" to take over the government. The community is a merely political entity, not a moral entity at all, and in it the only "effective" (*wirklicher*) will is the will of this faction. What is opposed to this is not even actual will, only "intention" (*Absicht*), and it is not actually willing something on the part of the individual which becomes a fault in these circumstances, but merely being "suspected" of "intending" something (p. 419/606). The result: any form of authentic self-consciousness, individual or universal, is eliminated (p. 420/606–607). The accuracy of this

---

[54] A far cry from the initial "appetition" of "self-consciousness," which wills only the recognition of the individual self.

[55] Nowhere, to my knowledge, does Hegel more clearly link the three meanings (even in English) of "representation": "notion" (*Vorstellung*), "acting for" (*Repräsentation*), and "substituting for" (*Vertretung*).

[56] The link between "work" (*Werke*) and "actuality" (*Wirklichkeit*) is unmistakable.

[57] One is reminded of the unconditional freedom to which the Sartrean individual is "condemned."

not only as a description of what *did* take place but also as a prediction of what *will* take place wherever "universal freedom" becomes a shibboleth is frightening. As an introduction to the need of a genuinely *moral* order if the universally self-conscious freedom is to be realized, it is masterful.

The movement thus far described culminates where we should expect it to; along with the "unhappy consciousness" of the slave and the "cultured" consciousness of the obsequious courtier, it culminates in fear of the "absolute master," but not one who is truly, concretely universal (p. 420/607).[58] This is brought about through the empty negation of "absolute freedom," which is but "meaningless death, the pure terror of the negative, which has nothing positive nothing fulfilling in it" (p. 421/608). The result is inevitable, it is "the general will—in this its ultimate abstraction" (p. 421/609). Rousseau's "general will" has been pushed as far as it can go, and it has culminated in the pure abstraction of contentless knowing and willing (p. 422/609). The self-determination which is freedom has turned out to be determination without a self. "By the same token, for the self *objective* reality (*Wirklichkeit*), *being*, is form from which self is simply absent, since reality would be something not known; to know this, however, is to know knowing as its essence" (p. 422/609–10). Both knowing and willing have been separated from what is known and willed.[59]

The upshot of all this is the recognition that the universalization of self-consciousness, "a consummation devoutly to be wished," is not to be accomplished on the level of a willing which does not reconcile the individual and the universal, because it is a willing still kept distinct from the consciousness doing the willing—willing is seen as an *activity* not a *form* of consciousness, as though consciousness were an agent which wills. It is for this reason that the "general will," which cannot be effective unless concentrated in *one* will, affords no solution, since there is no way of saying how it can be at once "one" and "general." Admittedly there is a formal sense in which it is general, since it is the only effective will in the community, but this solves nothing. There is, in fact, only one solution: to move forward to another "form" of consciousness, to another manifestation of spirit, to the authentically "moral" spirit, which enjoys at once the individuality and the universality of moral reason, i.e., an individual reason whose grounds are universal (p. 422/610).

C. SPIRIT CERTAIN OF ITSELF—MORALITY

The importance of culture in the spiritual development of man should in no sense be minimized. It marks an effort on the part of the human spirit to emerge from its immersion in nature and to realize in itself an activity

---

[58] Prior to 1806 Hegel had thought of Napoleon as the genuinely concrete universal self-consciousness, "the World-Soul . . . riding a white horse." Like other "world-historical figures" (Alexander, Caesar), however, Napoleon, too, turned out to have clay feet.

[59] This will ultimately be Hegel's critique of Kant's philosophy, in both its theoretical and practical aspects. Here the critique is more general.

which is in no way a being acted upon from without. When man "culti-vates" himself he does just that; he becomes more and more spiritual through an activity whose source is spirit and only spirit. That the succes-sive manifestations of this spiritual effort should prove inadequate to the task of authentic spiritual development is not unexpected—not only in terms of the dialectical movement which has become somewhat predictable, but also from the necessity that spirit reconcile itself with the self from which it has been estranged. It is all very well to negate nature in order to affirm spirit, but if the *whole man* is to develop, there must be a place for his "na-ture" in the end result of the development. As a matter of fact, that "na-ture" has been asserting itself all along the line: mere culture has not been able to overcome it, nor has either belief or insight, however "pure" they may be; in its struggle with "superstition" the Enlightenment was unable to do it, because it had to empty insight of all content in order to keep it pure; and the final effort to affirm spirit as the one and only source of its own activity in a claim to the "absolute freedom" of total self-determination culminated in anarchy, because it simply pitted a multiplicity of absolute freedoms against each other, with only the "absolute master" emerging victorious.

There is no question that freedom, self-determination, is a spiritual de-sideratum—in fact, *the* desideratum—but if a freedom which knows no limits, "absolute freedom," is no freedom at all, we must look elsewhere for man's realization of spiritual selfhood. In what human activity is man's spirit authentically the unique source of that activity, not merely as an isolated individual but in union with all others, who as equally human are equally free? The answer, not surprisingly in a world still dominated by the powerful thought of Kant, is that men are authentically free when they act *morally*, which is to say when they act in the way they are *obliged* to act. This answer is only seemingly paradoxical—that men are most free when obligated—since it is also true, in the Kantian framework, that man is authentically obligated when he obligates himself, i.e., to do what he *sees* is to be done. Moreover, this has been hinted at ever since the first at-tempt to situate the reality of spirit in "lawful" activity, whether according to Greek "custom" (*Sitte*) or Roman "law" (*Recht*). There too, Hegel tells us, we had a hint of what was missing: what ultimately determined the hu-man individual, in both the city-state and the empire, came from outside himself. Nor did spirit's effort to be self-determining by getting outside itself solve the problem, since this effort culminated in a mere "general will," which was "general" only on condition that each individual *not* be the determining agent in the "willing." The generality achieved in this is a generality of *knowing*, whose object is the knowing itself, but in which knowing and willing are still somehow separate (p. 423/613).

In this sort of "knowing," however, a solution is to be found. The moral movement proves to be one from acting "ethically" (*sittlich*) without know-*ing why* to acting "morally," which involved *knowing why* (p. 423/613). For spirit to do this is "to transcend (*aufzuheben*) the abstraction of im-*mediate existence* (*Daseins*) and become a universal to itself" (p. 424/614).

It is this knowing which opens the door to a morality of self-determination, because it eliminates any obligation imposed from without; only that obligates which one "knows" to be obligating (p. 424/614), and obligation is obligation only when it is universal, not particular.

a) The Moral World-View
What follows is a critique of the Kantian moral position. As a presentation of that position it may be superficial; as a critique it may be unfair—it is certainly vigorous—but there is no need to go into that. What Hegel is trying to do is to trace a development, which here begins with a knowledge (universal) of obligation which determines action (individual), and the Kantian notion of "duty" (*Pflicht*) is supposed to accomplish just that. Duty is universal because it obliges each and every one without exception; it is known because it consists in the knowledge one has of it; it is self-determination because consciousness of it is consciousness determining itself (p. 424/615). Thus, for Kant, knowledge of duty is knowledge in the most rigorous sense of that term. At the same time the knowledge which as knowledge is necessary does not necessitate consciousness to an action which will fulfill duty, give it a "being" which is "other" (*Anderssein*) (pp. 424-25/615). When an action has been performed, something has been brought into being which belongs to the world of nature, not to that of consciousness. There is, then, a return to the "nature" which had previously been ignored; not to nature in general, however, but to the nature of the agent in question, "my nature," which as such functions without concern for moral self-consciousness. The moral and the natural, then, are "in and for themselves" unrelated to each other, but the "moral world-view" relates them (p. 425/616). The activity of nature is indifferent, it just happens; the activity of moral consciousness is purposeful, it is rooted in "duty" to be done. In this context duty is essential, whereas nature is inessential; but the moral world-view reconciles the two by enabling morality to determine how nature should act (p. 425/616).

That there is moral consciousness is presupposed in the present context. We might call it the experiencing of what ought or ought not to be done, which, again in Kantian terms, is the relationship of action to duty. At the same time moral consciousness is an experiencing of mere nature's unconcern with any ought, any duty. For this reason there can be a conflict, a consciousness of duty, "pure duty," accompanied by a failure to carry it out, a failure of consciousness to guide nature, and this is "immoral consciousness" (p. 426/616). The point is that the motive for acting, if one is to be moral, must be duty and duty only. Thus happiness cannot be a motive for moral action. Still, humanly speaking, happiness cannot be simply disregarded; if it is foreseen that happiness will in fact result from doing one's duty—at least the happiness of having done one's duty—it will be part and parcel of the full purpose of acting (p. 426/617). This, however, means that morality has to be more than a mind-set (*Gesinnung*); if happiness plays any part in it at all, morality must look to action (*Handeln*). By the same token, the disharmony between moral consciousness which is purpose-oriented and nature which is indifferent to those purposes can be harmonized only in a morality which looks to actualization in the moral activity of individuals. This in turn means that moral activity has to be *thought of* as related to happiness—but as *necessarily* thought of, the relationship is simply *postulated*, i.e., inseparable from the very *concept* of morality (p. 426/617). Nor is the demand (*Forderung*) that this should be so merely a wish; it is a demand of reason (p. 427/618).

Gradually Hegel is moving into the position of characterizing the Kantian morality as postulatory, precisely because, even though it points to moral action, its moral force remains in the realm of thought. More than that, a morality whose only motivation is fidelity to "pure duty" brings in its wake a number of postulates, all of which tend to remove morality from the individual acts it presumably has in view. The first of these postulates, expectedly enough, concerns the relationship of moral consciousness and the "nature" of the individual who is to act, i.e., one characterized by "drives" and "inclinations" which are rooted in sensibility and have their own goals independent of moral purpose (p. 427/618). Because these drives and inclinations are responses to stimuli from without, they offer opposition to "pure will" which is wholly from within. What is more, the morality of moral consciousness depends on the opposition of *reason* and *sensibility*, since without this opposition reason would be otiose.[60] That there should be a harmony (unity), then, of moral reason is a "postulate," something which *has* to be *thought of* (p. 428/619). At the same time, the harmony can be made *actual* only by an "acting self," whose action has to be "indefinitely delayed" if moral consciousness is to remain "moral." The opposition of moral reason and sensibility is essential: without it there would no longer be "moral consciousness," and effective action would eliminate the opposition, thus eliminating what is essential. Complete harmony, therefore, is not to be achieved, only thought of, postulated, as an "absolute task" (p. 428/620); one might say it is not even desirable. The result is a peculiar contradiction: the task must remain a task, or morality is gone; moral consciousness must be oriented to the carrying out of the task, or it is immoral. "Absolute duty" loses its force, since a condition for its being at all is that it be unreal (p. 429/620).

Upon this follows a second postulate. Since "pure duty," if it is to be meaningful, must apply to the many "cases" which *fall* under it,[61] it must be broken up into a number of "laws," a number of "duties." Since, however, a multiplicity of duties would necessarily be determinate, they would forgo the "purity" of "pure duty" and thus for moral consciousness not be "holy" (p. 429/621). Still, if acting morally is not simply to be eliminated, "duties" ordered to such action must "be" in some consistent and determinate way (*an und für sich seiend*) (p. 429/621). This, however, they cannot be independently of any moral consciousness—if not in the conscious-

---

[60] In this rather crude form this might be looked on as a parody of the Kantian position. Still, it is well known that, for Kant, acting in accordance with one's "inclination"—even *love* as an inclination—runs the risk of sullying the "purity" of one's morality.
[61] The German for "case" is *Fall*.

ness of the individual who is to act for motives of "pure duty," then in another moral consciousness (pp. 429–30/621). The resulting postulate is that the relationship of duty to action with a determinate content must belong to another consciousness, one in which the particular and the universal are united, whose "concept, then, is the same as the concept of harmony between morality and happiness" (p. 430/622), a harmony which can be achieved only by one who has the power to bring it about, the "Lord of the world" (p. 430/622).[62]

Still, there will be action only if individuals act, in which context an individual consciousness of "pure duty" could turn out to be a hindrance rather than a help to action. "Pure duty," then, resides not so much in the consciousness of the individual as in that of the "holy legislator" (pp. 430–31/623). What had begun as an attempt to correct the excesses of a consciousness of "freedom without limitation" (absolute Freiheit) and still retain the autonomy of the individual in following "duty" has turned out to involve another sort of heteronomy, precisely because the determining (finiteness) of individual consciousness makes it unable to guarantee the validity of duty. The knowledge the individual has is incomplete and contingent; his willing is affected by his "sensible nature" (Sinnlichkeit). This means, among other things, that the "happiness" which the individual sees as connected with being morally good is not seen as rationally necessary; it is looked for as a favor (Gnade) [63] (p. 431/623).

None of this means that Kantian moral consciousness has to give up the thought of "pure duty," no matter how ineffective it may prove in practice. "Even if its actuality is admittedly imperfect (unvollkommen), still in relation to its pure willing and knowing duty counts as essential; it is in concept, insofar as that is opposed to reality, i.e., in thought, then, that it is perfect (vollkommen)" (p. 431/623). Thus, "pure duty" is also a postulate, which means that the only reality finite consciousness can give it is thought reality. "The absolute essence, however, is this essence which is thought, postulated as outside actuality" (p. 431/623). It is only by conforming to the will of this postulated "absolute essence" that human purposes take on moral value, and any human happiness connected with moral action becomes a matter of merit imputed to moral consciousness from without. "The absolute essence, therefore, is the thought in which morally imperfect knowing and willing counts as perfect. By the same token, since the absolute essence takes moral knowing and willing to be of the utmost importance, it distributes happiness on the basis of worthiness, i.e., on the basis of merit imputed to it" (p. 431/623–24).[64]

The result of all this, in Hegel's view, is that "pure duty" and its "actualization" become "moments" of a being which consciousness "represents" to itself, a being which, as perfect, is in fact not a "moral" being, since the

---

[62] For Kant, as we know, the God who can be an "object" only for faith and not for "speculative reason" is a postulate of "practical reason."

[63] The religious overtones of Gnade, which also means "grace," are unmistakable.

[64] Here we find a critique not only of Kantian moral philosophy but also of the Lutheran theology of grace and merit.

conflict essential to morality is not present in it (pp. 431–32/624). The "moral world-view," then, does not in fact get beyond the concept of a self-consciousness in which morality resides, since the object of this moral consciousness is not an "actual reality," only a *thought*, its *being* only "represented" (*vorgestellt*) (p. 432/625). There is no question that moral consciousness is really moral, but there is question as to its effectiveness; it sets up the harmony of morality and actuality as a goal, as an *object* of thought, which it is unable to effectuate (pp. 432–33/625). Such a moral consciousness, moreover, is not a moral *self*-consciousness, since the essential "non-harmony of duty-consciousness (*Pflichtbewusstsein*) and actuality" makes it impossible that the "moral" be also "actual." Duty is the "object" of consciousness, but consciousness cannot get duty done; if it does, what is done is not "pure duty"—like the "ought" (*Sollen*) which when actualized no longer *ought to be* but *is* (p. 433/626). Only as what "ought" to be accomplished, but "is" not, is duty still duty. "Since, however, this consciousness is . . . *one* self, then it is *in itself* [implicitly] the unity of duty and actuality. This unity, then, becomes its object, as perfected morality—but as *outside* its own actuality—and yet ought to be actual" (p. 433/626). The contradiction of moral duty and its actualization would seem to be inescapable—and irreconcilable.

In the Hegelian dialectic, where contradiction is inescapable, the contradictory terms become "moments" essentially related to each other and to be synthesized at a higher level. Thus, in the dialectical movement of moral consciousness, "duty" (*Pflicht*) and "actuality" (*Wirklichkeit*) are "moments," indissolubly linked to each other, dependent on each other, engendering contradictions whose resolution will be meaningful only in a higher form of consciousness embracing both duty and its accomplishment. "As a result there is enunciated (*hergestellt*) the first proposition that there *is* a moral self-consciousness. This, however, is linked to the second that there *is* none, i.e., there *is* one but only in a representation (*Vorstellung*); or in fact there is none, but it is still allowed by another to count as one" (p. 434/626–27).

b) *Dissimulation* [66]

Despite his criticism of it, the moral world-view Hegel has been describing does constitute for him an important step forward in the march of consciousness toward becoming truly spirit, since herein consciousness does *consciously produce* its own object (p. 434/629). In doing this it demonstrates its own autonomy. At the same time, however, this moral consciousness posits its object as both *out there* and dependent on self-consciousness

[65] There is an enormous play on words here, which is impossible to render but which helps us to get at the meaning of what Hegel is saying. *Verstellung* (from *verstellen*) is related to the terms *hergestellt* ("enunciated") and *vorgestellt* ("represented") in the previous sentence, and to the term *aufgestellt* ("put forth") in the second paragraph of this subsection. *Verstellung* also means "displacement," "subterfuge," "tergiversation," "pretending," but these latter terms must be understood in a context of "placing" (*stellen*), thus carrying the connotation of "placing in reverse" (cf. *die verkehrte Welt* of "Force and Understanding"—also involving a critique of Kant).

(p. 434/629). As a result, the Kantian moral world-view becomes involved in a "whole network of contradictions": whatever it is it also is not; every position it "puts forth" (*aufstellt*) it also "puts in reverse" (*verstellt*) (p. 434/629); "it confesses thereby that in fact it is not serious in regard to any of them" (p. 435/630). As an example of this Hegel takes the "presupposition that there is an actual moral consciousness" (p. 435/630). Let us, he says, turn from that to the first postulate regarding the harmony of morality and human "nature." Abstractly (*an sich*) this harmony of the two is supposed to obtain, even though when activity does take place they contradict each other; morality being taken as given and actuality posited in such a way as not to be in harmony—else the opposition which is essential to morality would be absent and, with nothing to overcome, morality too would vanish (p. 435/630). On the other hand, it makes no sense to speak of an actual moral consciousness which is not to culminate in action, which means that its actuality is "reversed" (*verstellt*) and said to be in harmony with it. But the postulate of harmony was supposed to remain a postulate, and by acting consciousness "pretends" that there is actual harmony, thus showing that the postulate was not serious, "since the sense of the action is rather this, to make present what should not have been present" (p. 435/631). Thus the contradiction: harmony is postulated with a view to action, and at the same time with a view to action "this harmony is posited as *not actual*, as *outside*" (p. 436/631).

As so often happens, one wonders why Hegel had to make all this so complex. If morality is to be taken seriously, it must be presumed to be concerned with morally acceptable activity. If, however, the only motivation which can be considered authentically moral is "pure duty," then a harmony between one's motive, which dictates what one's consciousness should be and not what one actually does, does not make sense. Only inaction is consistent with such a moral consciousness, with the result that neither moral consciousness nor moral action is to be taken seriously. Hegel goes on to say that if one acts at all, then the lack of correspondence between moral *purpose* and *actuality*, which can be effected only by an activity which calls upon *nature*, cannot be taken seriously (p. 436/631). Action would seem to be serious, but since all action is this or that contingent "doing" (*Tun*), and what is to be realized is the universal goal of reason, the latter is out of reach. If the one acting is not motivated by the universal goal of reason, he does not act morally, and "because the universal best is supposed to be brought forth, nothing good gets done" (p. 436/631)—assuredly a self-defeating morality.[66] More than that, in actual practice the "nullity" of effective action and the "reality" (*Realität*) only of the universal moral purpose is again "reversed" (*verstellt*), because if duty really is the essential, then the bringing about of what it is a duty to bring about

---

[66] It is, of course, a moot question whether this is a fair criticism of Kantian morality; it does, however, point up the dilemma of any morality which is too "pure" to be real. Herder had criticized Kant on the same grounds. "It is easy to formulate a law which is not followed, which without motives even cannot be followed" (Johann Gottfried Herder, *Schriften*, ed. Walter Flemmer [Munich: Goldmann, 1960], p. 143).

cannot be serious either, because the bringing about could not have as its goal "pure duty," which has to remain "non-actual" if it is to remain "pure" (p. 436/631–32). That there is no question of "*actuality*" here, however, is also "dissimulated" (*verstellt*), since duty is made to mean that one has a duty to act, which would make of the moral law a "natural law" (pp. 436–37/632), i.e., action which is possible only if nature acts would be seen to be necessary, and the "drives" and "inclinations" of nature, which have no moral value, would be in the service of morality.[67] If nature does, in fact, dictate what is in accord with morality, morality is superfluous. On the other hand, if the goal of moral action is the realization of a harmony of morality and nature in action, then its goal is the cessation of morality: "with the result that the absolute goal is that moral actions do not at all take place" (p. 437/632). Either "pure duty" dictates that nothing be done or it dictates that something be done whose motive is not "pure duty"— and the whole thing cannot be taken seriously (p. 437/633).

As Hegel sees it, Kantian morality *needs* a nature which is recalcitrant to it and yet *wants* nature to be in harmony with it. The latter would mean not the suppression of inclinations but bringing them under the control of reason. If it is claimed, however, that reason and inclinations are so distinct as to be opposed, it would seem that bringing inclinations under the control of reason would make them cease to be what they are; their "mainspring" (*Triebfeder*) would not be in *nature* but in a *reason* separate from nature (p. 438/634). For this reason the harmony in question has to be *only* a postulate; the actual disharmony of rational morality and sensible nature (*Sinnlichkeit*) has to continue (p. 439/634). This is but another way of saying that the demand that "pure duty" be the only motive for moral action is self-defeating; it rules out "action" (p. 439/634–35).

In addition, Hegel looks upon such a morality as inevitably static, since progress or regress would be meaningless, where "pure duty" is not susceptible of *more* or *less*; one can be moral or immoral, not more or less so. In relation to such a morality, then, happiness would not even be "earned"; it could only be a "favor" (*Gnade*) granted, without regard to morality (p. 440/635). This would mean, too, from the side of those who judge the actions of others, that there could be no saying who should or should not be happy, except out of an "envy," "which covers itself with the cloak of morality" (p. 440/636).

The conclusion is that in Kantian "moral consciousness morality is incomplete" (p. 440/636). If morality is incomplete in one's consciousness, "then morality itself is in a being other than actual consciousness, and that other being is a holy moral lawgiver" (p. 441/637). If one "pure duty" is ineffective, then there must be many duties, whose "truth" is not contained in a consciousness of "pure duty" but in another being outside moral consciousness. Once again, however, "this is a displacement (*Verstellung*) of the matter (*Sache*)" (p. 441/637), because, in fact, moral self-consciousness considers itself to be "absolute" (the final arbiter); for it only *duty* and what it

---

[67] One is, in fact, tempted to ask whether, when Kant insists that acting in accord with inclination, e.g., love, and not from pure duty is not moral (N.B. not *im*moral), he is being serious.

knows to be duty counts, and placing duty elsewhere cannot be taken seriously (p. 441/637).

In one sense, then, a morality of "pure duty" would demand that God himself be judged against the light of "pure duty." In another, even "pure duty" would have to reside elsewhere than in actual moral consciousness, since as *actual* the moral consciousness would be "natural" consciousness and, therefore, not "pure" (p. 441/638); it would be "a contingency of the free will" (p. 442/638). To speak of "morality" residing in "another" who would be God, however, makes no sense, since by definition God, who has no negative relationship to nature and sensibility and therefore no "struggle," cannot be moral (p. 442/638).

The ultimate contradiction which Hegel sees issuing from all this is that morality *cannot* be actual (put in practice) and at the same time *must* be actual: "Its truth is supposed to consist in being opposed to actuality, free of it and empty, and again to be in it, to be actuality" (p. 443/640). How, then, is moral consciousness to get back into itself, to become moral *self*-consciousness, and at the same time to make an advance over its previous position? As a start it should retreat from the "hypocrisy" of *pretending* that its truth, which it knew to be "pre-given," is its own product (p. 444/641).[68] The move is back to a consciousness which is "conscience" (*Gewissen*), which takes upon itself complete responsibility and "immediately acts conscientiously" (p. 444/641).[69]

c) Conscience—Beautiful Soul—Evil and Forgiveness

There can be little question that the appeal to "conscience," in any moral system—and in any language—is an appeal to personal autonomy in judging either what is to be done or what has been done; it is related to concrete action. For conscience "duty" is not some ideal, abstract "law"; it directly relates to the concrete instance. This in opposition to the previous "moral consciousness" which constantly found itself separating "pure duty" and concrete "action" (p. 445/644).[70] In this context Hegel calls conscience a "third self"; not the "person" whose only claim to dignity is being "recognized" as such by the law (p. 445/644-45), nor the self returned to itself out of the world of empty "culture" with a claim of "absolute freedom" (p. 446/645), but a self which recognizes that the limitations which morality places on its freedom are limitations it imposes on itself.[71] Conscience is a

---

[68] A quick perusal of Kant's *Metaphysics of Morals* would indicate that it comes up with no conclusions which are not already considered morally acceptable.

[69] It might well seem purely accidental that the German for "conscience" (*Gewissen*) and "conscientious" (*gewissenhaft*) should have the same root as "certain" (*gewiss*) and "certainty" (*Gewissheit*). The note of "immediacy," however, is clearly present in both.

[70] "*Gewissen* is concrete moral consciousness, certain of its concrete duty at the very moment it acts. On the contrary, the previous moral consciousness was in fact incapable of passing to action; it constantly separated the in-itself (pure duty) from the concrete case" (Hyppolite, *Phénoménologie*, II 171n61).

[71] "Morality is a late chapter in the life of mind, and depends for its emergence on the dialectic of the preceding stages of experience. As Hegel considers it, the moral consciousness grows out of the demand for absolute freedom" (Loewenberg, *Hegel's Phenomenology*, p. 275).

claim to total responsibility for conduct, which requires both a *knowledge* of what is to be done (*duty*) and a capacity to *will* the doing (*actuality*). "Only as conscience does moral self-consciousness have in its own *certainty content* for the previously empty duty as well as for empty right (*Recht*) and empty general will; and because this self-certainty is also the *immediate*, it has actual existence" (p. 446/645). Because this is "concrete moral spirit" it has eliminated the need both of "subterfuge" (*Verstellung*) and of "duty" as an empty criterion opposed to "actual consciousness" (p. 446/646). By the same token, the continuing opposition of "duty" and "nature" has been eliminated in the recognized complementarity of the two. "Pure duty as well as the nature opposed to it are transcended moments" (p. 446/646). For the first time "moral essence" and "action" are *concretely* brought together (pp. 446–47/646).

Put it this way: "There is present a situation (*Fall*) calling for action" (p. 447/646). The action-situation is an *object* of *knowledge*. Conscience *knows* this immediately and concretely—somewhat as "sense certainty" knows its object. The *actual* object is the *action* in question, and, as in "sense certainty," in knowing it consciousness does not alter it; nor does it break the action up, thus "separating the circumstances of the case into different duties" (p. 447/647).[72] Within the one action, then, there is only one duty to be considered, not a conflict of duties—only one question, "is it to be done, or not?" (perhaps, "should it have been done, or not?"). The point is that conscience finds in itself all it needs to answer the question; there is no duty "out there" to conflict with the actuality of decision (p. 448/648). "Conscience has *for its own self* its truth in the *immediate certainty* of itself" (p. 449/648). It has its own "personal *conviction*" that it is right (p. 449/649).

Conscience, then, is a consciousness of being conscious of a present obligation: "a single (*einfaches*) self which is at once *pure* knowing and a knowing of itself as this *unique* consciousness" (p. 449/649). Because this is a "knowledge" of duty, it has "universal" force (p. 449/649), i.e., it is a "law" governing the self in its action, which is to say, consciousness does not merely *take it* to be its law; it *is* its law (duty) (p. 449/649). What is more, it is a law whose being is to be *in* consciousness; any separate being it might have is but a "moment" in its coming-to-be (p. 450/650). That this last not seem unduly complicated, we might simply note that in obligating itself conscience may well be imposing on itself a duty which is generally accepted as such without relinquishing its own total responsibility for imposing the obligation. The point is that what impels it to act is its *own* conviction: "For the *essence* of the action, duty, consists in conscience's *conviction* of it" (p. 450/651). Conscience in this sense is not merely individual whim; it is universal by virtue of being universally "recognized" (p. 450/651); and this recognition gives it a concreteness which the formal universality of the "categorical imperative" cannot attain (p. 451/651).

---

[72] One is reminded of Aristotle's contention that the "moral essence" of an act include both what is done and the circumstances in which it is done (see *Nichomachean Ethics*, 1105A30).

What has happened is that "what really counts" (*die Sache selbst*), which for the "honorable consciousness" of fragmented individuality was merely a *predicate* of what it *wanted* for itself, has become *subject*, i.e., "what really counts" is that the subject act on its own. The movement, which in the Preface Hegel characterizes as "substance" becoming "subject," is not only progressing rapidly but also becoming more intelligible. "*What really counts* has substantiality as such in behavior regulated by custom (*Sittlichkeit*), externalized existence in culture, the self-knowing essentiality of thinking in morality; in conscience it is the *subject* which knows that these moments are its own" (p. 451/651–52). In grasping the "moments" of this process conscience becomes *knowledge* of what in the concrete is to be done; its *knowledge* is "what really counts": "At first, then, it relates itself as knowing to the *actuality* of the *case* where action is called for" (p. 451/652). Since the "case" includes the circumstances, this "knowing" includes the circumstances too (p. 451/652). The difficulty is that the very "immediacy" of this knowing makes it incomplete, and mere conscience is not aware of this. "Its incomplete knowing, because it is *its own* knowing, counts for it as adequate, perfect knowing" (p. 452/653).

Conscience too, then, is not quite adequate to the moral demand; it has, it is true, reduced the complexity of the "case" to one simple "duty," but it does this by way of a "conviction"—"its duty lies in its pure *conviction* of duty" (p. 452/653)—and a "pure conviction" is ultimately as empty as "pure duty." It says no more than "action is necessary." The individual must determine *what* action is necessary (p. 452/653), and in doing this he calls upon his "natural consciousness," his "drives and inclinations" (p. 453/653); as "immediate," conscience has not eliminated the force of outside influences; its *content* is not genuinely "absolute"; it has not escaped "the arbitrariness of the singular and the contingency of its unconscious natural being" (p. 453/654). What it comes down to is that, even though individual *conviction* is aware of the emptiness of "pure duty," it has not eliminated the influence of the unconscious on its convictions, which it only *takes* to be thoroughly rational—the "immediate" never is. The individual can, after all, *rationalize* whatever he does. He can, for example, see it as his duty to increase his own wealth—for a number of good *reasons*—and ignore the fact that for others this can involve violence and injustice (pp. 453–54/655). The list, of course, could be lengthened.

"Conviction," in fact, is scarcely a good argument for truth. Thus, to argue on the basis of conviction that something else ought to be done (or to have been done) does no more than substitute another "determinate content"—determined by individual preference—of "pure duty" (pp. 454–55/656). It is true, of course, that the vague "what is best for all" has to be judged by the one acting; he must also judge that to fulfill his duty toward himself is to be useful to all (p. 455/656), but that scarcely relieves his "conviction" of arbitrariness. It does not solve the problem of just how much "knowledge" (*Wissen*) there really is in "conscience" (*Ge-wissen*). It depends, in fact, on just how much genuine self-knowledge is in it. "Conscience is the spirit certain of itself, which has its truth in itself, in its knowing, and in this as a knowing of duty" (pp. 455–56/657). Even granted that it brings out a determinate content which is only implicit in universal duty, it is a content "which it takes from its natural individuality" (p. 456/657). If, however, the general law of duty and the determinate content supplied by the individual are seen as complementary "moments," then the very knowing of what to do becomes effectively synonymous with duty, which can be generalized in another way, i.e., in the recognition by all that it is valid for each to follow the self-certainty of conscience, for "everyone to act according to conscience" (p. 456/658). But even if this is universally recognized as a principle, this does not mean that the action which issues from it will necessarily be "recognized" by all as acceptable (p. 457/659). Conscience, therefore, and the action which flows from it can be judged differently—and in society they are. We may admire someone for always following his conscience; we need not always admire what he does.

Once it becomes possible for others to judge separately one's actions and the conscience which dictates those actions, it becomes either unnecessary or impossible to judge whether conscience is good or bad. As freed from any duty determined other than by conscience itself each one's conscience is just his over against another's. The result is that each is either indifferent to the conscience of another or assumes that it is *bad* because it expresses the self of another and not one's own; ultimately moral goodness or badness is not what is judged at all, only what each likes or dislikes (p. 457/659–60). By the same token, actions are not judged to be moral or immoral; they are simply what each individual *wants* to do to satisfy himself, and thus each is "recognized" as a *self* who acts, but his actions are not acknowledged as moral (p. 458/660).

Once conscience and action have been separated, conscience cannot be judged directly at all, and all that is out there for another to judge is what one *says* (p. 458/660–61). Language, then, is the expression of the self, and what language says, its content, is the only self available. This self is, of course, not the fragmented and inverted self of "culture" and its language; it is the self certain of itself, but all it can express is its "conviction," i.e., neither the word of command or complaint characteristic of those who live in the world of *Sittlichkeit*, nor the silent assurance of moral consciousness (p. 458/661). What now counts is the language in which one expresses one's convictions. Each can say, "I *assure* you, I am convinced that I am doing what is right" (p. 459/662). There is no way of gainsaying that, of determining whether the "assurance" of the "conviction" is true; each one's "intention" is a right intention, simply because it is his own (p. 459/662).

Because there is no disputing convictions, everyone is right, and because there can be no universally valid judgment regarding either conscience or action, the only universality involved is the universal intelligibility of the language one uses in assuring others that he acts according to the conviction of his conscience (p. 460/663). This, however, lands us back where we were with "pure duty." Just as "pure duty" was susceptible of any content, which only individuals could determine, so conscience makes anything right; it cannot be questioned; its prerogatives are "divine" (p. 460/663). Gradually conscience becomes God, not merely for the one who acts according to it but also for the community; it is the only force which has any right to dictate conduct at all; it is all that counts; ultimately it is objective simply by the fact that it is (p. 460/663).

"Conscience" has turned into a travesty of "moral consciousness"; "good intention" has been substituted for moral goodness. "The spirit [of the community] and the substance which unite its members are, then, the mutual assurance of their conscientiousness, their good intentions" (p. 461/664). Everyone is good, because everyone is presumed to have good intentions; what they actually do is no criterion at all. Objective consciousness ceases to have any significance; all that counts is each one's consciousness of himself (p. 461/664). The result is a complete abdication of moral consciousness—on all sides—in any significant sense of the term. "Elevated to this purity consciousness is its own most impoverished form, and the poverty which constitutes its only possession is itself a disappearance. This absolute *certainty* in which the substance has dissolved itself is absolute *untruth*, which collapses into itself; it is absolute *self-consciousness* in which *consciousness* comes to grief" (p. 462/665).

This virulent, even vicious, attack on "conscience" as a guide to moral action may appear unwarranted, especially since conscience started out as a corrective of a morality of pure duty. Two things, however, should be borne in mind: first, that the whole of the *Phenomenology* is, so to speak, a campaign against "immediate certainty," at whatever level it is found; and second, that the sentimentalism which accords to conscience unquestioned validity, even though it be a morally uninformed conscience, has to be rooted out from time to time. It is all very well to say, "let conscience be your guide"; sometimes conscience is a very bad guide, as history abundantly testifies, particularly when conscience itself has no genuine moral guidelines—"moral blindness" cannot simply be rendered a meaningless expression.

[*The Beautiful Soul*]

Hegel has also been accused of making a travesty of this image with which the literature of his day was replete and which characterizes so many of the "Romantics" whom Hegel vigorously opposed. As for the literature of his day, one wonders with what eyes the critics of Hegel read it if they do not see, for example, in the "Confessions of a Beautiful Soul" in the second part of *Wilhelm Meister*, the irony with which Goethe treats what is fairly obviously a *sick* soul. As for Hegel's attitude toward the Romantics—in particular his rather cruel reference to Novalis and the latter's mental derangement—it is, perhaps, less easy to justify. Still, Hegel may be excused for seeing in Romanticism an irrational intuitionism, the opposite extreme of the rationalism he condemns with equal vigor—each the antithesis of authentic *reason*.

In any event, out of the sentimental universal acceptance of a conscience which is valid simply because it is conscience, comes in Hegel's view a complete reversal of the "unhappy consciousness" in the dialectic of self-consciousness. Whereas for the former "unhappy consciousness" all responsibility was abdicated and transferred to the "absolute master," here all responsibility is nullified by being placed completely within the individual. Even the "talking" (*Rede*) in which conscience expresses its "conviction" becomes a talking to itself; no negative dialectical moment is left which might possibly contradict it (p. 462/666). Conscience has so completely turned in on itself that "it lives in fear of sullying the magnificence of its interior by action and external manifestation (*Dasein*)" (pp. 462–63/666). To act would be to put itself out where others might judge it; better to remain silent and do nothing, write itself a diary! The obvious trouble is that the negative satisfaction of an *un*-sullied conscience is an empty satisfaction—one, perhaps, does no *wrong* if one does not act, but one does no *right* either. "In this transparent purity of its moments an unhappy, so-called *beautiful soul* extinguishes the light of these moments in itself and evaporates as a formless mist which dissolves in the air" (p. 463/667). The ultimate "purity" of conscience is its ultimate absurdity.

Since *doing* anything runs the risk of sullying its purity, for the "beautiful soul" *saying* the right thing becomes all important (p. 463/667). It is uniquely responsible for its own content, but that is zero: "Its pure self, as empty knowing, is without content and determination" (p. 464/668). "Duty" as a universal affecting all is gone, and all that is left is duty's "reflected light" (*Reflektiertseins aus ihr*) (p. 464/668). In fact, the only duty the "beautiful soul" has is to itself, and any regard for universality becomes an obstacle, "inessential" (p. 464/668). The reverse of this, of course, is just as bad; the moral consciousness which looks only to "universality" sees the dictates of individual conscience as "evil." "Because conscience is the incommensurability (*Ungleichheit*) of its *being within* with the universal, and because at the same time conscience expresses its own doing as commensurability with itself, as duty and conscientiousness," the attitude of moral universality calls it "hypocrisy" (p. 464/668–69).

Actual conscience is neither the one nor the other; it reconciles universality and individuality. It is not bogged down in a private sort of knowledge and volition, nor is it caught up in a universal duty which is universal only by its own *fiat*: "It is not this clinging to a knowing and willing which is opposed to the universal; rather, the universal is the element of its *existence*, and its language expresses its doing as recognized duty" (p. 465/670). Its universality is not the formal universality of abstract generalization; it is the concrete universality of actual recognition by an entire community (p. 465/670). The abstract universality of duty, which prides itself on opposing the particularity of conscience, does not, in fact, resolve the presumed "hypocrisy" of individual conscience; it simply sets up a situation in which each conscience is free to appeal to its own "law" (*Gesetz*) (p. 465/670). Practically speaking, consciousness of universal duty defeats itself; it says of this duty that it *should* be universally *acknowledged,* and at the same time, by finding fault with non-recognition, it admits that it is *not* recognized (p. 466/670). It has not established any right to say that disagreement with its contentions is not justified (p. 466/671).

How is all this to be resolved? To begin with, both consciousness of duty as universally obligatory and conscience as determinative of individual behavior must be recognized as equally empty, equally inoperative. Consciousness of duty as a universal, however, can *judge* the adequacy of individual "conscience," and out of this judgment comes the "introduction to a resolution" of the conflict (p. 466/671). By judging conscience, moral consciousness avoids the contamination of "actuality" while preserving the universality of its thought, thus asserting that its action is its judgment. This, however, is an action which is not action, which in fact contradicts a "will" to actualize duty, and is hypocritical in looking upon judgment as an actual doing; "instead of acting it proves its righteousness by the expression of excellent attitudes" (p. 466/671). Moral consciousness finds itself in the same boat with the individual conscience which does nothing but *talk.* In both, actuality is different from talk: the one has a selfish purpose in acting but talks a good game of morality; the other does not act at all but talks a good game about the necessity of action (p. 466/671).

Once the relationship of moral judgment to action has become that of *passing judgment* on the actions of others, *what* others do can be quite readily ignored and attention focused on the *intention* of the doer. By itself, however, intention is no more open to direct objective scrutiny than is *conscience* or *conviction,* and so the basis of judgment becomes the *circumstances* surrounding an action. Whatever accompanies an action *can be* —and *is*—judged to be the intention in acting. Thus, if an action brings with it pleasure, good reputation, gain, or whatever, these can be looked on as what was *intended* (p. 467/672-73). Hegel's remark that a hero is not a hero to his valet, not because the former is not a hero but because the latter is a valet, is quite apropos; one who sees all the trifling things his master does—and the trifling motives for doing them—tends to lose the capacity to discriminate between the significant and the trivial. Nor is moral judgment exempt from this lack of discrimination: "For critical judgment, then, there is no action in which it could not oppose to the universal side of the action the side of individual singularity, thus playing the part, in regard to the one who acts, of morality's valet" (p. 468/673).

The consciousness which is critical in this sense is "base," because it breaks action up into its trivial circumstances, thus making it less than it really is; and it is hypocritical, because it prefers itself and its glib talk (*Rede*) to action (p. 468/673). More than that, the moral critic wants to impose upon the man of action the obligation of justifying himself in words, with the result that everything is leveled off, and the very distinction between good and evil becomes a matter of words. Worse still, even when the one criticized admits that he has done something wrong ("evil"), the critic does not admit the same in regard to himself; as critic he is not subject to criticism, not even the criticism of the spirit itself (p. 469/674). The critic's self-certainty has no criterion; it is all within himself, and its form of expression is words (p. 469/674).

[*Evil and Its Forgiveness*]

This self-certain "spirit," this "beautiful soul," has no sympathy with others —it is the most self-centered of all the "forms" (*Gestalten*) of spirit yet seen. Incapable of going into action itself, it despises action (p. 469/674). It makes itself everyone's equal—if not superior—because it can find something wrong with what anyone *does*. In fact, it puts so much negative weight on deeds, that it fails to see that even the "wounds" (evil deeds) of spirit can be healed, that "the deed is not the irreparable" (*Unvergängliche*) (p. 470/676). Its pride is such that it is unable to comprehend that self-realization in action, critical judgment, and the establishing of a distinction between the universal and the individual aspects of action, are all but "moments" in the whole process whereby spirit emerges to selfhood (p. 470/676). The critic serves a purpose, it is true, but only in that overall process where there is (*a*) recognition that an evil deed has been done, (*b*) confession of guilt on the part of the one doing it, (*c*) forgiveness on the part of the one passing judgment, and (*d*) reconciliation in the emergence of spirit. Given all these steps, there is genuinely concrete mutual recognition; there is a spirit which is ultimately "absolute" (p. 471/677), because it is not isolated in its own singularity.

This spirit is truly moral, because it neither merely acts without moral judgment, nor merely judges without sympathy. It knows its duty, and the source of that knowledge and that duty is itself; not, however, an isolated individual self, but one whose horizons have been broadened to take in a multiplicity of selves, all mutually recognizing each other as selves and thus constituting the only authentic concretely universal self, the community. This spirit, "knowing that its *pure knowledge* is the abstract *essence*, is this knowledge of duty in absolute opposition to the knowing which knows itself to be the essence as absolute *isolatedness* (*Einzelheit*) of the self" (p. 471/678). The expression is intolerably tortured; the thought, it would seem, is clear.

There are, then, two spirits, each certain of itself; one sunk in the contemplation of its own individuality; the other broadening its horizons to take in the complex ramifications of the concept. "Both spirits certain of themselves have no purpose other than their own pure selves, and no other reality and existence than this pure self. They are, however, still different; and the difference is absolute, because it is set in this element of the pure concept" (p. 472/678). In both there is pure self-knowledge, but the difference is enormous. The genuinely rational concept cannot be the private preserve of individual moral consciousness, even when that consciousness universalizes and thus establishes a "law" (duty) for all rational beings. The formal universality arrived at by abstraction in individual consciousness must give way to a concrete universality rooted in the rational cooperation of all; and the model for this, at the present level, is moral thinking, the moral concept.

The question remains, what do "evil" (sin) and its "forgiveness" have to do with all this? Very simply, we might say that since sin is a human and forgiveness a divine prerogative, the forgiveness of sin is a model for the reconciliation of the human and the divine, the finite and the infinite. On a more complex level, however, it is necessary to say that, in Hegel's view, the forgiveness in question here, and the reconciliation, are both human and divine, the divine dimension of the human. What is to be reconciled here is not simply, so to speak, a human debtor with a divine creditor, but individuality and universality on a number of levels: individual consciousness and self-consciousness with universal consciousness and self-consciousness; individual action with universal thought and will; individual obligation with universal duty. The reconciliation, as we shall see in the next chapter, will not be accomplished short of a religious consciousness which has the absolute (reconciling) being as its object; nor, as we shall see in the final chapter, will an ultimate reconciliation be accomplished short of an "absolute knowing" which is the function of "absolute Spirit," both the subject and the object of that knowing. At the point where we are, however, i.e., on the level of moral spirit, consciousness has come to the realization that action, which is always individual, is when isolated from the universal spirit less than human. By the same token, evil brings with it the realization that reconciliation is the as yet most concrete manifestation of universal spirit, in which human individuality is lifted to its divine, universal dimension. If men can forgive each other they are on the road to union with each other in the divine. "The reconciling *yes* in which both I's relinquish their opposed *existences*, is the *existence* of the *I* extended to duality. The I which therein remains the same as itself and which both in its complete outgoing (*Entäusserung*) and in its opposite number (*Gegenteil*) has certainty of itself—it is the God who appears as pure knowing in the midst of those who know themselves" (p. 472/679).

8

Religion

NOWHERE IS IT MORE IMPORTANT than when speaking of religious consciousness to stress that Hegel's work, which began as a "Science of the Experience of Consciousness" and ended as a "Phenomenology of Spirit," is from beginning to end an investigation of the growth of the human spirit. With the failure of individual reason to come to terms with the reality over against it, it became clear that the human spirit had to rise to the level of a communal subjectivity if it was to do justice to the universality of objectivity, if consciousness was to find in itself a universality corresponding to the universality of its object. With concrete universalization on the subjective side of the consciousness relationship, however, arises the discrepancy of a concretely universal subject whose object is only formally universal. Only a concretely universal object could meet the requirement, and for Hegel that meant an absolute object, a divine object, God, the Absolute Being.

But since consciousness of an absolute being makes sense only if the consciousness itself is absolute, and since an absolute consciousness does not make sense unless conscious of itself as absolute, i.e., absolute self-consciousness, the suspicion has been created in the minds of some that Hegel is no longer concerned with the growth of human self-consciousness but rather with the divine. Loewenberg, for example, considers the entry at this point of "a superhuman spirit" to be "intrusive" into the biography of "human spirit."[1] It should be emphasized, therefore, that religious experience is an essentially human experience, albeit on a higher level than that of self-legislating consciousness of moral obligation, no matter how concretely universal that may be. What Hegel is saying is that the human spirit adequately conscious of itself is conscious of an object which is divine, which is not to say that "human" and "divine" have become synonymous.

To borrow, for the moment, from the *Science of Logic*, we might say that the universal object of consciousness is being. But being makes sense only if it is ultimately absolute being, i.e., in no way infected with nonbeing. "In itself," therefore, the object of consciousness is absolute being. Furthermore, to speak of a being which is absolute makes sense only if that being is conscious of itself, i.e., spirit. To be conscious, however, that the ultimate object of consciousness is an absolutely self-conscious being involves a long process. An even longer process is required to recognize that the absolutely self-conscious object of consciousness is also the object of self-consciousness, since that means that to be fully conscious of self is to be

[1] *Hegel's Phenomenology*, p. 298.

conscious of the divine. For Hegel, then, religious consciousness is indispensable in the march toward adequate self-consciousness; it is at once consciousness of the divine and consciousness that to be adequately conscious of self is to be conscious of the divine—without the self-consciousness' ceasing to be human.

Religious consciousness, of course, did not have to wait until this point in the *Phenomenology* to make its appearance. As Hegel points out in the introductory paragraph to this chapter, "consciousness of the *absolute being* as such" has cropped up more than once along the way; not, however, as "spirit's own self-consciousness" (p. 473/685). The vague awareness that the object of consciousness is ultimately consciousness itself made itself felt at an early stage in the development; the implications of this now demand a thoroughgoing investigation of the ultimate object of consciousness, the absolute, divine being.

Turning back, then, to the level of objective consciousness, Hegel reminds us that as "understanding" consciousness was an awareness of a "suprasensible" reality transcending what is immediately perceived. This, however, was no more than "the universal" as object, without any hint of selfhood, a far cry from "spirit." On the level of "self-consciousness," the unattainable absolute "out there" is that toward which the "unhappy consciousness" futilely turned, unaware that in so doing it was inhibiting its grasp of itself as spirit (p. 478/685). On the level of individual "reason" (rationalism), religious consciousness did not appear at all, "because on that level self-consciousness knows or seeks itself in *immediate* presence" (p. 473/685), where spirit is not to be found. It is only in "the world governed by custom" (*der sittlichen Welt*) that consciousness first becomes consciously religious as "belief" in the universal sway of "fate" or the particular patronage of the "Eumenides," both in relation to the dead (pp. 473–74/685–86). This "belief in the netherworld" then became a "belief in heaven" which collapsed before the onslaughts of the "Enlightenment," the latter, in its turn, becoming a peculiarly "empty" religion of the understanding (p. 474/686). Finally, moral consciousness had unmistakable religious overtones and gave to "absolute being" a "positive content," an object *for* the self, but still distinct *from* the self of consciousness (p. 474/686–87).

Thus, we can now see that two parallel developments have been taking place in the course of the *Phenomenology*. Right up to "the moral spirit certain of itself" as "conscience" (*Gewissen*), the human spirit has been only vaguely aware of what it is to be spirit, of what the spirituality of its activity implies. Along the way, however, it has been developing as religious consciousness too, whose object progressively reveals itself as spirit, thus revealing what spirit truly is. As Hegel now explicitly calls our attention to the progressive development of religious consciousness, he recapitulates, so to speak, all that has gone before in an explicit phenomenology of religious consciousness wherein the human spirit comes to the realization that to be fully human (fully spiritual) it must be the way the absolute (divine) Spirit is. Without ceasing to be human, the spiritual activity in question must become divine. The object of religious consciousness is "in itself" constantly the same; the consciousness of it constantly progresses—and this is progress in *self*-consciousness, essentially a community consciousness.

The recapitulation which Hegel institutes, however, would not have taken place had it not been ushered in by the ultimate in moral consciousness, the "conscience," which finds its certainty in itself alone and yet is impotent to reconcile the good and the evil which dwell within it.[2] It is religion, we might say, which gets conscience out of the vacuum in which it floats into a real world where alone spiritual activity and the consciousness of it have meaning. Only as religious can consciousness see that there is no conflict between the world of reality and the world of spirit, because they are one and the same world.

When the human spirit, then, is explicitly religious, its consciousness of spirit and its consciousness of itself can become identified. Initially, as we have learned to expect, this identification is simply immediate: "The spirit knowing itself is in religion immediately its own pure self-consciousness" (p. 474/687). It is a synthesis of the "true" spirit, the "self-alienated" spirit, and the spirit "certain of itself," but it is as yet unaware that it needs the mediation of a world of reality in order truly to know itself (p. 475/687). Conscience, it is true, "represents" to itself a world in which action takes place, but in such a world spirit is only "thought of" as universal, not realized. The difficulty, of course, is that religion tends to be but one facet of a life which is for the most part non-religious; nor is this to be resolved by simply giving a religious coloring to all the activities of life (p. 475/688). Only where the human spirit is conscious of itself as religious in all that it does can a reconciliation be effected. Incidentally, only in the latter situation can it be conscious of acting as spirit in all that it does. Ultimately, says Hegel, even religion—in any of the forms it has taken up to the present—will be inadequate to the task, because in religion consciousness "represents" to itself "absolute spirit" in one or another "*determinate* form"; it is not "present" to itself as absolute (p. 476/688). At any stage in its progress, religious consciousness is "the present actuality of the whole spirit" (p. 476/689), but only at a final stage of "absolute knowing" which transcends representational religion will the whole spirit be wholly present to the human spirit, as its consciousness of its whole self (p. 476/689). One could, of course, interpret this last, as does Feuerbach, as meaning that the only "absolute" of which the human spirit is ultimately conscious is itself. But one can also interpret it as meaning that consciousness of self short of consciousness of the "absolute" is not consciousness of the whole self. The latter interpretation would seem to be implied in what follows.

Although neither interpretation imposes itself conclusively at this point, one thing is clear: the human spirit cannot be adequately conscious of itself as spirit until it is conscious of spirit as a whole—"only the whole has actuality in the proper sense" (p. 476/689). The whole movement of spirit, through objective consciousness, self-consciousness, reason, and the immedi-

---

[2] "And conscience it is, representing the strange union of the self's certainty and the self's impotence, the source of sin and the longing for forgiveness, which ushers in religion proper" (*ibid.*, p. 294).

Religion 233

ate spirit which still lacks full consciousness of what spirit is, is an essential presupposition for religious consciousness proper, and religious consciousness is "the absolute self of them all" (p. 476/689), i.e., it is the recognition of the self they all imply. At this point Hegel inserts a remark which makes it clear that, however "historical" the *Phenomenology* may seem to be in terms of the development it depicts, it in no sense presents a series of forms which succeed each other in time. Even though spirit can manifest itself only in time, the stages (or states) described in the book are not intended to be distinguished temporally (p. 476/689). They are, nevertheless, distinct levels of spiritualization in the activity of spirit (p. 477/689–90). In this context, then, the fundamental development throughout is religious, in the sense of a progressive awareness of the absolute, and the "forms" this takes are religion's "externalized actualization" (*daseiende Wirklichkeit*). "The becoming *of religion as such* is contained in the movement of its general moments" (p. 477/690). Thus, each of the "forms" contains a determination proper to developing religious consciousness. "The whole spirit, the spirit of religion, is again in the movement whereby, beginning in immediacy, it attains to a *knowing* of what it is in itself or immediately. The goal to be achieved is that the *form* in which it appears for its own consciousness will completely correspond to its essence and that it should see itself as it is" (p. 477/690). It is, in fact, the one spirit, the "substance" of all the forms which prevents any one of them from isolating itself and taking itself to be the whole. They all are but moments in the total process and have significance only in the framework of the total process (p. 478/691). Spirit, then, is a dynamic totality; each of the forms is a form of spirit, but it makes a difference that spirit is conscious of itself now in one now in another, and that in their succession spirit *progressively* manifests itself (p. 479/692). This can be said only of the progressive development of the *human spirit*.[3]

Where the human spirit truly knows itself, then, the distinction between spirit as the object of consciousness and as the object of self-consciousness is erased; "its consciousness and its self-consciousness are equated" (p. 479/692). Initially, however, religion is no more than an immediate awareness of a vague absolute being. To some degree this corresponds to the concept of religion; in it there is a consciousness of being conscious of the absolute, but not a consciousness that the absolute itself is spirit and not merely an *object* (p. 479/693), a being who is more than a vague "creator of a nature,"

[3] For an understanding of all that Hegel has to say of religious consciousness, all that went before it must be stressed. "Religion *presupposes*—but in the logical not the temporal sense—the *entirety* of the constitutive elements (moments) described in the six preceding chapters. Which can mean only this: it is real *concrete* man who is religious and who does theology; it is not a 'pure' consciousness, not a 'pure' desire, not a 'pure' action, etc.; it is man-conscious-of-himself-in-his-active-life-in-the-world. And Hegel says that religion *logically* presupposes the *entirety* of this life in the world, which is to say *history*" (Alexandre Kojève, *Introduction à la lecture de Hegel: Leçons sur la Phénoménologie de l'Esprit, professées de 1933 à 1939*, ed. Raymond Queneau, 2nd ed. [Paris: Gallimard, 1947], p. 217; this passage is not contained in the English edition, *Introduction to the Reading of Hegel*, trans. James Nichols, Jr. [New York & London: Basic Books, 1969]).

who is a spirit and whose "manifestations" (*Gestalten*) are "spirits," "which together constitute the completeness of its appearing" (p. 480/694). Thus, what we are to look for are not merely the forms of consciousness we have already seen, which are the presuppositions of religious consciousness, but the successive forms of explicit religious consciousness itself.

The first form of religion is thoroughly "immediate," in the sense that the human spirit in no way intervenes to make God known; he is revealed in the workings of *nature*—what Hegel calls the "religion of nature," where God is a felt need in man's response to nature; what characterizes Oriental religion in general. A second, higher level of religion's appearance is in the form "of transcended naturalness or of the self" (p. 480/694), where God is revealed in the product of the self-conscious artist. This is the Greek religion where the human spirit fulfills the need which men feel, but where the only divine presence in the work of art is what the human artist puts there. On the third and highest level, which for Hegel is that of Christian religion, the divine spirit is truly present, makes himself known to the human spirit. Here spirit speaks to spirit, not through nature, not in the work of men's hands, not in audible or legible words, but in man's own spirit. "If in the first the spirit as such is in the form of consciousness, and in the second in the form of self-consciousness, then in the third spirit is present in the form of the unity of both; . . . and because the spirit is here represented the way it is in and for itself, this then is the *religion of revelation*" (p. 480/694).[4] Even a divine revelation, however, is a revelation made through the medium of human instruments who speak a language of "representation." In the "religion of revelation," then, God is "represented" in the self-conscious human spirit. If God is to be adequately present to the human spirit, the "form of objectivity" proper to "representation" must be transcended, and God must be grasped in the concept. But only a divine concept is adequate to a divine being, i.e., only the infinite can grasp the infinite. In some sense, then, the human spirit must be infinitized if it is to be *capax Dei*. This is religion raised to the level of "absolute knowing," which is adumbrated in the final chapter of the *Phenomenology* and spelled out in the *Science of Logic*. At this point we are still on the level of religious consciousness, where the "absolute being" makes its presence known in a series of forms to the human spirit.

A. RELIGION OF NATURE

What Hegel attempts to do in his detailed and sometimes overly complicated description of forms of religious consciousness is neither to present a study in the history of religions, for which he was not equipped, nor to work

---

[4] The expression which Hegel uses, *die offenbare Religion*, causes some difficulty to the translator. It cannot be translated as "revealed religion," which would be *die geoffenbarte Religion*, and it has been frequently rendered as "manifest religion" which simply shelves the issue of revelation—a work of spirit. If, however, *die natürliche Religion* can justifiably be translated "religion of nature," and *Kunstreligion* as "religion of art," "religion of revelation" would seem to be a justifiable translation of *die offenbare Religion*.

out a philosophy of religion, which he leaves to a later date. He is engaged in tracing phenomenologically the development of human consciousness to which, he is convinced, the development of religious consciousness integrally belongs. That human consciousness of a superhuman (divine) presence in the world is as ancient as human society itself need not be questioned. The question is whether that consciousness manifests a progression —not necessarily rectilinear—from the vaguest attribution of divine power to natural phenomena to the recognition of a God who is personal, related personally to human beings. For Hegel there is the additional question whether such a progression in human consciousness constitutes also a progression in human self-consciousness, such that the progressive spiritualization of the God of whom man is conscious is concomitant with a progressive recognition of the spirituality of human consciousness. That Hegel should say of such a progress in human consciousness that it is a development in the presence of the divine spirit in human spirit should come as no surprise to those who are familiar with what has already taken place in the *Phenomenology*. Nor should the contention that in this development the human spirit gradually finds itself, gradually comes to the realization of what it is to be spirit, the responsible agent of its own activity.

Unlike the phenomenology of human consciousness in general, the phenomenology of religious consciousness does not begin with an individual experience which only gradually becomes aware of its social implications. As Hegel sees it, religious experience is from the beginning a corporate experience, whether of human society as a whole at a given stage or of a segment of that society which is taken as paradigmatic of a stage in the overall development.[5] The issue throughout is how spirit (not the divine) is present to itself in consciousness, but this, for Hegel, is inseparable from the question of how the divine Spirit is present to human consciousness and thus, ultimately, to itself. Simply stated: if all consciousness has already been seen to be self-consciousness, then, consciousness of the divine is also self-consciousness; and if consciousness of the divine is to be adequate, it must be divine self-consciousness. Whether this will ultimately mean a divinization of the human spirit or a humanization of the divine spirit remains to be seen.

In any event, the various religions which have made their appearance in history, from the most primitive to the most sophisticated, are the various forms in which the human spirit has experienced the divine, and one form of religious experience differs from another according to the "representation" each has of spirit, i.e., "according to the *determinateness* of the form in which the spirit knows itself" (p. 481/696). Phenomenologically speaking, moreover, the process of religious experience manifests a direction: "Thus, the movement is oriented toward (*hat . . . das Ziel*) transcending this principal difference [between consciousness and self-consciousness] and toward giving to the manifestation (*Gestalt*) which is the object of consciousness the form (*Form*) of self-consciousness" (p. 482/697). So long, however, as

---

[5] Obviously different from the Jamesian "religious experience."

God is merely "represented" as a self-conscious being, religious experience will not be adequate; "the self which is *represented* is not the *real* self" (p. 482/697). God must be "actually" present in religious experience; the religious subject's "representation" of God is not enough. The question, then, comes down to: how can the divine Spirit be "present" in the self-consciousness of human spirit?

A hint as to the outcome of this process is given in Hegel's contention that in each successive stage *what* is "represented" (not the "representation") in one stage is "appropriated" (*angeeignet*) in the following stage through the "activity" (*Tun*) of "self-consciousness" (p. 482/697), i.e., that which in one stage is the object of consciousness is in the other the object of self-consciousness.[6] If nothing else, this means that *what* is believed at any stage in the process is in itself more than the believers are aware of but *actually* conforms only to the representation at the given stage: "So, for example, the incarnation of God which appears in Oriental religion has no truth, because its actual spirit lacks this reconciliation [of the divine and the human]" (p. 482/698). Thus, the various ways in which the divine appears along the line have significance only as leading up to the religious consciousness in which they culminate (p. 483/698).

a) God as Light
It could, of course, be argued that Hegel's knowledge of Oriental religion, and in particular of Zoroastrianism, the "religion of light," [7] is at best very primitive and unreliable; but such an argument misses the point. Hegel is talking about the vague deification of any one cosmic force, such as "light," not about the nuances which may have attached historically to this phenomenon in Zoroastrianism. It is simply presented as a *type* of religious consciousness for which the "really real" has the "formless substantiality" of light (p. 484/700), i.e., the kind of "determination . . . which belongs to *immediate consciousness* or *sensory* certitude" (p. 483/699). Even at this primitive stage the vague divine "being" is *active* in human affairs and is, thus, "filled with spirit," but the only "form" it has is that of "formlessness" (p. 484/700). Over against "light" there is only the equally formless "darkness." Light, epitomized in the sun, rises and sets, but it does not return into itself and is, thus, not a subject (p. 484/700). What light stands for is, in fact, the divine Spirit, but an utterly indeterminate spirit, whose "only determinations are attributes" (p. 484/700), what men *attribute* to it.

b) Plant and Animal
"Life," too, is a cosmic force, as mysterious as light, but more determinate, particularly when imaged in the totemistic plant or animal. What comes under this heading Hegel calls "the religion of spiritual *perception* (*Wahrnehmung*)" (p. 485/702). To the vague, formless sense of the divine, reflec-

---

[6] The futility of translating *Bewusstsein* and *Selbstbewusstsein* as "consciousness" and "self-consciousness" becomes more and more clear. The meaning is clear enough: what at one stage has the *being* of an *object* at another has the *being* of a *self*.

[7] See *Philosophie der Religion*, 2. Teil, 1. Kapitel, p. 195.

tion attributes determinate forms of life. In one sense the determinations are still only *attributed* to the divine being by men, but as *vital* determinations they are seen as *belonging to* the divinity. Where the totem in question is a plant the life it symbolizes is "calm"; where it is an animal the life is "turbulent." The point may seem trivial, but it marks a passage in the "animation *(Beseelung)* of the spirit realm" (p. 485/702) "from the calm powerlessness of contemplating individuality to destructive independence *(Fürsichsein)*" (p. 485/702). The distinction says little about the divine spirits in question; it says a great deal about human spirits at this stage in their evolution. In particular it says a great deal about human activity which manifests itself as *destructive* before it is channeled and becomes *constructive* (p. 485/703). From the point of view of religious consciousness, it is significant that the activity attributed to the divine is projected-out-there (p. 486/703).

c) The Artisan
The scene changes once more when man begins to do more than find—or project—divine being in the forces of nature, and by instinctively mimicking natural forms *makes* the things which the gods inhabit. It may be unfortunate that Hegel attributes this form of religious consciousness to the Egyptians or, worse still, finds in Egyptian religion examples only of *artisanry* and not of *art*, but once again the faulty historical illustration should not obscure the valid distinction in primitive religious consciousness. What is important is that Hegel is trying to draw out the parallel between primitive religion and primitive (objective) consciousness, which began with seeing the "religion of light" as related to "sensory certitude," moved to a "religion of life" related to "perception," and now turns to a religion of constructed natural forms related to understanding. Furthermore, the constructive activity in question, guided as it is by understanding, not only *gives* the gods a habitation, it puts the artisan himself in what he constructs, thus bringing the divine and human closer together, however vaguely (p. 486/704).

Without a word about the glories of Egyptian sculpture, Hegel speaks only of the mathematical form of Egyptian artisanry (pyramids and obelisks) and the conceptualized plant and animal forms which were employed primarily as decoration. Since the mathematical form is the object of "understanding," it is for Hegel "without spirit" (p. 486/704); the material which the artisan molds does not come alive (pp. 486–87/704). Nevertheless, since it is the product of at least partially self-conscious work, the activity of spirit does appear in it, even though only as the "abstract side of spirit's activity" (p. 487/705). Because the artisan himself is anonymous in this sort of work, his spirit although present in it is not made manifest in it; the work is more "thing" than living reality (p. 487/705). When, on the other hand, the artisan makes use of the decorative motifs of plant and animal, he introduces his own conceptualization into the work (p. 487/705), thus making it more truly his, making himself live in it (p. 488/706). Even then, however, that life within the product is a formless life, an interior which does not speak (p. 488/706–707). Only when the work of the artisan becomes the work of the artist does it begin to have an inner life of its own (p. 489/708).

B. RELIGION OF ART

It would certainly be stretching a point to say that Hegel's treatment either of Egyptian religion or of Egyptian art is satisfactory. That it is not satisfactory is due in part to his lifelong fascination with Greek culture, in particular with its classic art and its totally politically integrated religion; in part to his primary concern in treating Egyptian religion at all: to find a transition from a vague sense of the divine in the contemplation of nature to the self-conscious religion of a people who brought their well-articulated gods to earth and there gave them a dwelling place; in part, too, by his desire to find in the phenomenology of religious consciousness parallels not only to the three major stages in the dialectic of spiritual development, consciousness (religion of nature), self-consciousness (religion of art), and reason (religion of revelation), but also to the three stages in the dialectic of consciousness, sensory certainty, perception, and understanding.[8] It should be noted, too, that Hegel is not engaging in a full-scale aesthetics here; his interest is not primarily classical art but the religious consciousness which expresses itself in art. Having traced the movement of the divine presence from a formless cosmic force, through differentiated forms of life, to the work of men's hands, he now turns to that creative work which is most clearly infused with man's creative spirit, the works through which both the divine and the human spirit speak—more authentically than in the works of nature alone.[9]

The self-conscious artisan, whose consciousness of himself is in himself and not in his work, has now become the "spiritual worker" (p. 490/709). The spirit which works through him is "the *ethical* (*sittliche*) or the *true* spirit" (p. 490/709). In religious form it is the spirit which unites an entire people, giving spiritual force to their political cohesion. Here we have "the free people, wherein custom (*Sitte*) constitutes the substance of all, the substance whose actuality and outward expression (*Dasein*) each and every one knows as his own will and deed" (p. 490/709). In a religion such as this, the people "entrust" themselves to the customs and laws which bind them; but this trust lacks the profundity of trust in self, because "in it the self does not know itself as free in its singularity" (p. 491/711). Such a religion goes to pieces when trust in the customs and laws which constitute the substantial unity of the people is lost, and it turns, in the age of tragedy, into sadness over a lost world (p. 492/711).[10] The artistic activity which

---

[8] That the intricate parallelism is not further traceable in the divisions of the religion of art and the religion of revelation is understandable. The chapters on self-consciousness and reason had become too unwieldy to make such parallels feasible, and the chapter on spirit had made them unnecessary.

[9] See G. W. F. Hegel, *Aesthetik*, ed. Friedrich Bassenge, 2 vols. (Frankfurt: Europäische Verlagsanstalt, 1955), I 14.

[10] It is significant that the age which the great Greek tragedies depict is not the age which gave them birth.

gives to the ethical substance a dwelling place within the authentic self-consciousness has already been conceptualized so that in it "the spirit produces itself as object" (p. 492/712). The movement, then, is from a taken-for-granted "substance" which the self of the people projects, through a more authentic self which emerges in conceptual thought, to a religious consciousness wherein spirit "has its own concept as its form, such that its concept and the created work of art mutually know each other as one and the same" (p. 492/712). The language is confusing: the Greek art work does not know its creator; the god, however, whom it represents is one who knows the human spirit, and the work which the human spirit produces is one in which "the universal spirit" is "individualized and represented" (p. 492/712). The gods are more determinate figures than they have ever been before.

a) The Abstract Work of Art

Whether or not it is historically true to say that the manifestation of the spirit in plastic art (sculpture, painting) precedes other artistic manifestations, the movement which Hegel is trying to describe phenomenologically is that from the lifeless presence of the spirit in a marble statue to the living presence in what Hegel considers to be the most spiritual of all the Greek art forms, dramatic poetry. Once again it should be noted that he is undertaking neither a history of art nor an aesthetic judgment of the relative superiority of works of art. From the religious point of view, it is true to say that the original statue in which the god is thought to be present and which constitutes the cultic object is an inanimate "thing," which is animated only in the activity of "cult" (p. 493/712). It is the individual "embodiment" (Behausung) of the universal object it "depicts" (darstellt) (p. 493/713).

What is important is that the form in which the spirit is depicted is not simply an imitation of a form found in nature which understanding can grasp; it is a creation in which human consciousness can grasp itself in a way in which merely objective understanding cannot (p. 493/713). The god who dwells in the statue "is suffused with the light of consciousness" (p. 493/714). Religion has passed from the vitalistic to the anthropomorphic stage—with the help of sculpture (p. 493/714). "The essence of the god, however, is the union of the universal existence (Daseins) of nature and the self-conscious spirit, which in its actualization appears over against the former" (p. 494/714). The gods have become "clear ethical spirits of peoples conscious of themselves" (p. 494/715). The people know what they are honoring when they honor abstract qualities such as their gods represent.

The god who is depicted in the statue, then, is a "universal being" with all the necessity proper to the abstract quality represented; the image of the god, on the other hand, is a contingent event (p. 494/715). The god of the statue, however, has no self-consciousness; the only self-consciousness involved is that of the artist who created the work, and that self-consciousness he cannot infuse into the work (p. 494/715). The artist succeeds in capturing in his work what is proper to the god as "universal substance"; he does not succeed "in giving actuality in it to himself as a determinate individuality" (pp. 494–95/715). He expresses himself in the self-conscious activity of creating the work, but once it is out there it is dead; only the human spirit which looks on it can give it life (p. 495/715–16). In it there is a *reminder* not the *presence* of the god. "As a result the artist experiences in his own work that he has *not* produced a being *like himself*" (p. 495/716); the statue is not a spiritual being. Even when the reverence of the crowd animates the statue, the artist still knows that all that is there is what he made; *he* is the master of his own god (p. 495/716).

Marble, then, or any material element, proves to be inadequate to the presence of a god. A higher element of artistic expression is required if the work of art is to be more than a *thing* which forever remains simply what it is. This higher element is "language," a human product, which is at the same time "an expression (*Dasein*) which is immediately self-conscious existence," at once *individual*, as expression, and *universal*, as meaning (p. 496/716). Initially, says Hegel, this language takes form in a "hymn" which is the "spiritual outpouring" in which "devotion" is expressed as one and the same activity of a whole community (p. 496/717). When the language is expressed as "oracle," it takes on a divine aura, although the words are still human, the universal significance of which is due only to the vague, ambiguous terms in which the oracle is couched, a significance which is ultimately trivial (p. 497/718). Oracular speech, which is taken to be "the language proper to the god who is the spirit of an ethical people" (p. 497/718), is calculated to determine the contingent actions of individuals, but it is only the decision of the human individual, who can interpret its ambiguities as he will, which gives it meaning (p. 498/719). Unlike the statue of the god, which remains forever the same, the words of the god are passing, but they too are without life, just as they are without permanence, except in the deliberation and decision of the human being who hears them (p. 498/720).

Just as it is the devotees of the god who give life to the inanimate statue and meaning to the animated oracular words, so it is these same devotees in unison who synthesize both life and meaning in the temple ceremony where the god is rendered present in the collective consciousness of the people. "*Abstract* cult, therefore, raises the self to the point where it is this pure *divine element*"—it is a means of achieving blessedness, which is a dwelling with the god" (p. 499/720). The temple ceremony, then, is a means of reconciling human consciousness of the divine with human consciousness of self (p. 499/721); it gives "actuality" to what was merely "abstract" (p. 500/722). The initial act of this ceremony is the sacrifice of some possession as a sign of both a gift of self and a raising of the self to the god (p. 500/722). Once again, then, the self is the center of attraction, and as the sacrifice culminates in a "meal" for those who offer it, it comes back to them as a kind of self-affirmation (p. 501/723). Even the temple itself, built with human hands, is man's way of designating where the god is to dwell. In the long run everything in the temple ceremony is referred back to the people who honor the gods (p. 501/724) and thus seek their "favor" (p. 502/724). This is what the inner, religious "life" of the people means.

b) *The Living Work of Art*

Once the temple ceremony has been stylized as an expression of collective life, it proves to be a transition to more creative forms of worship in which the substantial unity of the people is artistically expressed. Abstract stylization comes alive, so to speak, and "ceremony is the vitalized actuality of all." [11] Gradually the people becomes more conscious of a common expression of its religious and political life. "The people which approaches its god in artistic religious ceremony is the ethical (*sittliche*) people which knows its state and the activities of the state as its own will and self-completion" (p. 502/725). With more spontaneity—but less profundity—the people recognizes its own selfhood in the divine "substance" which is its spirit; the spirit of the people has become the people's god (p. 502/725). Individuals come to identify with this god in the "mysteries" wherein they are consecrated and in which they experience oneness with the god (p. 503/726–27).

The people's joy of life, expressed in "enthusiasm" directed to the god, must now "produce a work which, it is true, like the statue of the earlier artist, stands over against this enthusiasm as an equally perfect work, but not as a self which in relation to the people is lifeless but as a living self" (p. 504/728). In this sort of art work, human beings come alive as they act out their worship, and in it the god is present not merely as a reminder but as living. The "work" takes a number of forms: (*a*) the feast, where in eating *with* the god the people share his divinity; (*b*) the mysteries, where individuals are more intimately united with the god, either in secret (Ceres) or openly (Bacchus); (*c*) the dance, where the movements of the human body express the presence of the god; and finally (*d*) ecstasy, where words become necessary to express the divine–human feeling (p. 505/728–29). In all of this the living human being takes the place of the dead statue; the god is present in him, in his movements, even if he is no more than a "torchbearer" (p. 505/728). As worship becomes an art, with its special times, special places, special actions, and special words, the human performer becomes important, conscious of himself as god-bearer. As he does, once more the need of language as a vehicle of expression makes itself felt; now, however, the vehicle is the disciplined, artistic language of poetry (p. 506/730). By infusing life into his work the human artist has effected the transition from a religious consciousness to which the divine is present only as an abstraction to one in which the divine spirit *acts*, albeit not yet as spirit speaking to—and in—spirit.

c) *The Spiritual Work of Art*

In Hegel's view the most significant form of human expression is language, and the most significant form of artistic expression is poetry. In the language of poetry, the spirit of man shines through with unmistakable clarity. By the same token, if man is to express his union with the divine, a union in which he is at his most spiritual, he will do it in language, the language of poetry. This, too, however, has its stages. It can begin, Hegel tells us, only when the cult of this or that individual god (individualization had

[11] Hartmann, *Hegel*, p. 138.

been a necessary step in personalization) gives way to a gathering of all the gods under one roof, "whose element and embodiment (*Behausung*) is language" (p. 506/731). Such a gathering is possible only as the work of a whole people gathered together as a multiplicity of individuals with a unity of purpose. It is through the *Sittlichkeit* common to all that each individual shares in the common enterprise. "This initial communality (*Gemeinschaftlichkeit*), therefore, is rather a gathering together of individualities than the domination of an abstract thought which would rob individuals (*die Einzelnen*) of their self-conscious participation in the will and the activity of the whole" (p. 507/731). Moving away from the unquestioning acceptance of immemorial custom, religious consciousness is becoming the consciousness of a community made up of distinct, self-conscious individuals. There are still many gods, but they are in the process of being cut down to size as substantified projections of the overall self-consciousness of a people (p. 507/731–32). There is a universality to these gods, but it has the form accorded to them by the consciousness in which they appear. The form now is no longer that of activity (temple worship) but of representational language—and self-conscious expression in such a language is poetry (p. 502/732).[12]

The first poetic language to make manifest this universality of the gods—in the sense both of gathering them all together in a common life and of identifying them with universal attributes—is the epic, "at least as the *completeness* of their world, even though not, it is true, as the *universality* proper to *thought*" (p. 507/732). The minstrel is the flesh-and-blood individual who fleshes out this universality in "memory" (*Erinnerung*).[13] The gods of the epic, however, are not individuals in the strict sense, not persons; they are "organs" of the muse (p. 507/732), vehicles of epic action. In his epic tale the minstrel relates the people, in the person of its "heroes," to the "world of the gods," thus creating a "representation" (*Vorstellung*) of the spiritual, divine–human relationship. "The epic individualizes in heroes and divine figures the whole spirit of a people."[14] Both gods and heroes are individualized figures whose actions are given universal significance, and thus the responsibility for human affairs is both divine and human. "What the gods do, consequently, appears as an activity in which they are just as free and for which they are just as fully responsible as are men in their activity" (p. 508/734). Significantly, the actions of both are individual, it is men—the minstrels and their hearers—who do the universalizing (pp. 508–509/734).

In this context the gods are characterized as "the eternal beautiful individuals who, at rest in their own peculiar kind of existence (*Dasein*), are lifted above transitoriness and alien violence" (p. 509/734). They are, however, equivocal characters, not very godlike: they struggle with each other—in a very disedifying manner—but they can neither win nor lose (p. 509/

---

[12] Although he does not say so expressly, Hegel does seem to contend that all poetry is originally religious, i.e., the self-conscious expression of a people's religious consciousness.

[13] Here as elsewhere Hegel plays on the etymology of *Er-innerung*, meaning "a rendering-interior."

[14] Hartmann, *Hegel*, p. 139.

735). Worse still, they are, despite their superhuman power, caught one and all in the grip of necessary fate, which empties them of their divinity—no one can escape fate, not minstrel, not heroes, not gods (p. 510/735-36). The epic turns out to be the saga of submission to fate.

Inevitably, then, the Greek religious consciousness must move on to tragedy, where the hero no longer simply submits to fate but works it out and in so doing images the fate of all. Where previously the story of the divine–human relationship was merely *narrated*, now self-conscious individuals on the stage *act it out*. These individuals are "men who *know* the right and the purpose they have, who *know* the power and the will of their own determinateness, and who know how to *say* it" (p. 511/737). Without taking away from the artistic genius of an Aeschylus, a Sophocles, or a Euripides, what this is saying is that the tragic actors themselves are artists who bring the religious relationship to the stage (p. 511/737). What is more, the accumulated wisdom of the people is put into words by the chorus (p. 511/737), which thus echoes the helplessness of gods and heroes in the face of fate (p. 512/738). Ultimately, in tragedy the religious consciousness of the community is brought to the surface in the actions and sufferings of the hero, the reflections of the chorus, and the emotions of the spectators (p. 512/738-39). What we saw of the "ethical substance" of the people in the dialectic of Spirit is here given content in such a way that the previously abstract relationship of the divine and the human, the family and the state, the female and the male, is concretized, and the confusing multiformity of divine beings shrinks to a small number of divine powers more nearly individualized and thus recognizable as personal (p. 513/739).

This last, of course, is not without its disadvantages, but even those divine powers represent a step forward in religious consciousness. The individual hero who *acts* (and thus represents every man) finds himself in an ambivalent situation. Because the gods speak in equivocal language (riddles), man both knows and does not know what he is doing; he becomes the plaything of the gods (p. 513/739-40). At this point Hegel takes something of a flyer which is with difficulty reconcilable with an analysis of Greek religious consciousness, but which does point the direction which religious consciousness will have to take out of the tragic situation. Oedipus, he tells us, was led to destruction by his perfectly sincere interpretation of the ambivalent words of the oracle; Macbeth suffered the same fate because his evil intentions led him to interpret the voices of the witches in his own favor; while Hamlet, the most authentically self-conscious of heroes, recognizes that the voice of his father's ghost could be the voice of the devil and so does nothing (p. 514/740). What begins as complete trust in a vague divine governance of the cosmos becomes a tragic confrontation with individualized powers, and ends as a mistrust in the kind of gods who play with man's destiny (p. 514/741). The Greek religious consciousness was caught in a trap of ambiguity; its gods were the personified attributes of the ethical substance, but it could not please one without offending another. The voices of the gods were found to be not the appearing of truth but warnings of deception (p. 515/742), and the human spirit was damned if it did and

READING HEGEL's *Phenomenology*

damned if it did not. The only resolution of the contradiction in which consciousness found itself was "forgetfulness," either "the forgetfulness of the *netherworld* in death or the *forgetfulness* of the *world above* in the remission, not of guilt, since because it has acted consciousness cannot deny its guilt, but of crime"—all of which resolved nothing (p. 516/743).

In the last stages of tragedy—with Euripides—heaven has already begun to be depopulated; only Zeus really counts as a god, and human beings begin to count as individuals: "The hero who walks on stage before the audience has been reduced to his mask and to the actor, to the role and to the real self" (p. 517/745). The depopulation is completed in comedy; the gods have been cut down to human size and are thus revealed to have been "moments" in a process, not *persons* (p. 517/745). Their true character as abstract projections of human qualities becomes manifest, such that the human actor "wearing this mask expresses the irony of a mask which wants to be something for itself" (p. 518/745). Man has become conscious that it is he who has put the gods on their throne, which means that it is he, too, who can dethrone them. It all ends in ridicule; such gods are but the ridiculous individuals into which the universal substance had been split (p. 518/746)—and in laughing at them man knows that he is laughing at himself, not at his spirit but at the absence thereof (p. 519/746–47).

The path is now clear for a "rational thinking" of the divine (Socrates-Plato); to the "conceptless" wisdom of the chorus it opposes the simple moral ideas of "the *beautiful* and the *good*" (p. 519/747). Dialectical thinking, however, does away with the merely *given* and gives to these abstract ideas a rational content, a meaning, which comedy could not do (p. 519/747); all comedy could portray was "the play of opinion and the arbitrariness of the contingent individual" (p. 520/748). The culmination of the religion of art is the triumph of the "singular self": "The *singular self* is the negative force, through and in which the gods, as well as their moments, existing nature, and their thought-determinations, disappear" (p. 520/748). But this negation, this disappearance, has positive significance; the singular self is present to itself as the only reality which counts (p. 520/748). Man is now the actor on life's stage; "the actor's proper self and his role coincide" (p. 520/748). He is also the spectator who finds himself in the role he sees portrayed (p. 520/748). Religious consciousness has become consciousness of self; man must now find his true self within himself.

C. THE RELIGION OF REVELATION

Up to this point it has not been too easy to see why, for Hegel, religious consciousness should be essential to the onward march of human consciousness toward full consciousness of itself or why religious consciousness should constitute the penultimate step in that onward march. Why, after all, should the ways in which the human spirit is conscious of the divine be so many ways in which that same spirit becomes progressively more adequately conscious of itself? If, however, we now look back at the various forms of religion which have passed in review before us as a series of attempts to substitute divine beings for the most intimate and adequate object of spirit's consciousness, namely itself, we can understand both that comedy which depopulated the ancient pantheon put an end to all gods "out there" and that only a God who is himself totally spirit could satisfy the demands of a human consciousness gradually becoming more fully aware of its own spirituality. Not only does the departure of the gods usher in "a new conception of man," it calls for a new conception of God which will be to man a revelation of what man himself is.

Thus, although it may seem strange historically to link Greek comedy and Christian religion, or phenomenologically to substitute "the problem of Christology, a problem belonging to a special historical religion," [15] "for the general problem of incarnation, which the dialectic demands," [16] it is not strange that Hegel should see in the Christian revelation of the God-man a revelation just as much of what man is as of what God is. Just as "the religion of art," which Hegel presents as exclusively Greek, culminates in a revelation of man to himself, so too "the religion of revelation," which he presents as exclusively Christian, is seen as a more thoroughgoing revelation of man to himself. Whether this is to mean ultimately a humanization of God or a divinization of man is a question which a study of the *Phenomenology of Spirit* alone is not likely to answer. One thing is clear: what Hegel has to say in this section is not likely to be clear to those who are not familiar with Christian theology.[17] He seeks to interpret "spiritually" five of its major themes—Incarnation, Trinity, Creation, Original Sin ("The Fall"), and Redemption—in such a way that they reveal to man his own self-conscious spirit.

Central to all of this, for rather obvious reasons, is the Incarnation. The inadequacy of all previous forms of religious consciousness was that they represented to themselves either a god (gods) not recognizable as spirit, i.e., in nature, or gods who had indeed some of the attributes of spirit but were not present in their man-made representations. In none was the abstract divine–human relationship concretized into a relationship of God and man. In Christian theology, on the other hand, the Incarnation—however it be interpreted—presents to religious consciousness a uniquely concrete union of the divine and the human in the God-man, thus revealing to human consciousness that to be totally human is to be divine. Jesus Christ is for Hegel the unique self, who is at once "absolute" and human, who reveals to man the utmost in human potentialities and makes of Christianity the religion which manifests "the infinite value of the individual." [18]

---

15 Loewenberg, *Hegel's Phenomenology*, p. 337.

16 *Ibid.*, p. 336.

17 "Is Emmanuel Hirsch correct when he writes: 'Hegel's error is not that he is too little Christian but rather the reverse; that he founded the philosophic–scientific view of reality too strongly on notions which are available only to Christians'?" (Carl Günther Schweitzer, "Die Glaubensgrundlagen des hegelschen Denkens," *Hegelstudien* I [Beiheft, 1964], 238). One is reminded of Goethe's complaint (Conversation with Eckermann, February 4, 1829) that Hegel drags the Christian religion into philosophy where it does not belong.

18 Franz Grégoire, *Études Hégéliennes: Les Points capitaux du système* (Louvain: Presses Universitaires de Louvain; Paris: Beatrice-Nauwelaerts, 1958), p. 243.

In Jesus Christ he finds a God who is self-conscious spirit and a man who is conscious of himself as divine. This is the ultimate in religious consciousness; its implications will carry human consciousness to the ultimate in self-consciousness. Whether, when it reaches the ultimate in self-consciousness, human consciousness will cease to be religious remains to be seen.

Phenomenologically speaking, Hegel sees the Christian religion as the necessary sequel to the Greek religion of art not merely because the latter culminates in a depopulation of the pantheon but, more significantly, because the Greek spirit had thus ceased to be religious at all. The divine "substance," which the Greek consciousness had fragmented into many gods, was, nevertheless, the unifying spirit of a people. In turning to the human subject, however, the Greeks had simply eliminated the unifying "substance." The "incarnation of the divine being" in the self-sufficiency of the human subject meant that "all essentiality was buried in the spirit which is certain of itself in the isolatedness (*Einzelheit*) of consciousness," and the isolated self has become the only "absolute being" there is (p. 521/750). This self is not the empty "person" of the "situation of right" (p. 522/751), which is only "the thought of itself" and ultimately an "unhappy consciousness" (p. 523/752).[19] The consciousness in which comedy culminates is "happy," but its happiness is "the complete emptying (*Entäusserung*) of the substance," a rejoicing because "God is dead" (p. 523/752–53). The happiness, however, cannot last; "in the situation of right"—the Roman world in which Christianity came into being—"the ethical world and its religion are engulfed in comic consciousness, and the unhappy consciousness is the knowledge of this total loss" (p. 523/753). The whole "religion of art" has collapsed, because there is no "living spirit" in it (p. 523/753). All that is left is a "benign destiny" which, like a beautiful maiden, proffers the glories of Greek art as fruits to be consumed (p. 524/753). "Thus in giving us the works of that art destiny does not give their world, not the spring and summer of the ethical life, where they bloomed and ripened, but only the enshrined (*eingehüllte*) memory of this reality" (p. 524/753). The pantheon in which the gods are gathered is "the spirit conscious of itself as spirit," minus the substance (p. 524/754). Thus, "the all-pervading pain and longing of the unhappy self-consciousness are their point of convergence, and the communal birth pains of its emergence are the simplicity of the pure concept, which contains those forms as its moments" (p. 525/755).[20]

[19] One wonders whether those who simply identify the "unhappy consciousness" with Judaism and medieval Christianity have read this far in the *Phenomenology*.

[20] "These are the two moments of which a dialectic synthesis is to be made. The unhappy consciousness seeks to attain its absolute, *immutable* certainty of itself and pushes it out into the beyond; it is the alienation of the self. Comic consciousness, on the contrary, showed us all substantiality returning to the self. But *in itself* and for us the unhappy consciousness is the happy consciousness which does not yet know itself, and comic consciousness is a consciousness which does not know its unhappiness, which does not know that *God is dead*. Hegel is going to develop this last part, the consciousness of the *disappearance of the divine* in the following paragraph" (Hyppolite, *Phénoménologie*, II 260n6).

The stage is now set for the advent of the incarnate God; in emptying itself the "substance" has become a "self-consciousness." The incarnate God reveals at once (a) an absolute being which is *an sich* self-conscious: "The emptying out of substance, its becoming self-consciousness, expresses the transition to its opposite, the unconscious, *necessary* transition, or that it is *in itself* self-consciousness" (p. 525/755); and (b) an externalized self-consciousness which is *in itself* "the universal being" (p. 525/755). For religious consciousness the divine "substance is self-consciousness and, thus, spirit" (p. 525/756). Through Jesus Christ who is at once God and an individual man, the divine Being is self-conscious and, therefore, spirit. For this reason Hegel says of him "that he has an *actual mother* but a *virtual* (*ansichseienden*) father" (p. 526/756); as divine his relationship of son is metaphorical, as human it is real. The divine and the human are "his two moments, through the mutual emptying of which, as each becomes the other, he enters existence as their union" (p. 526/756).

Prior to this, religious consciousness had been "consciousness of" a "spiritual being" who did not have this consciousness "in himself." Which is to say, there was consciousness *that* the god who appears in all forms of religion is a "spiritual being," "but this meaning is borrowed, a cloak which does not cover the nakedness of the appearance and deserves no belief and reverence; it remains only the murky night which swallows up (*die Verzückung*) consciousness" (p. 526/756). Still, the *object* of this consciousness *is* "the self-knowing spirit" (p. 526/757). By the same token, however, even the incarnate God, merely present sensibly in flesh, is present only immediately, not as all that he really is, not as *who* he is. Immediately he is but "the contentless object of sensory consciousness"; only when he ceases to be merely that "does he become an I for consciousness" (p. 527/757), an I in which "the actual World-Spirit has attained to this knowledge of himself" (p. 527/757). For Hegel, the consciousness which God has of himself is the self-consciousness of Jesus Christ.

Faith in Jesus Christ, which Hegel somewhat unaccountably calls "*the world's faith*," is belief "that the Spirit . . . *is present* as an actual man, that he is present to immediate certainty, that believing consciousness *sees* and *feels* and *hears* this divinity" (p. 527/757); God is incarnate, not merely symbolized. The God in Jesus is not a construct of the believer's thought. In being conscious of Jesus the believer is directly conscious of God (p. 527/758); and in being conscious of himself Jesus is conscious of God (p. 528/758). The Incarnation, then, is "the simple content of the absolute religion. In it the [divine] Essence is known as Spirit, or this religion is the divine consciousness of being Spirit" (p. 528/758). Thus is the divine "substance" subject; thus too does the divine Being *reveal* itself as what it is; it is "object of consciousness as Spirit," and all the "attributes" of God—good, holy, just, creator, etc.—are "predicates" of a subject, a self, a source of activity (p. 528/759). In the self-consciousness of Jesus, "God is known as self-consciousness and is to self-consciousness immediately manifest (*offenbar*), for he is this self; the divine nature is the same as what the human nature is, and it is this unity which is contemplated" (p. 529/759–60). Strange as this language may seem to the Christian theologian, the point Hegel is making is that the form in which God is here present to consciousness corresponds to God's self-consciousness as no previous form had (p. 529/760).

From one point of view, Hegel goes on to say, this could *seem* to be a "lowering" of the divine to the human; in fact, it is a *concretization* of the abstract "supreme being" (p. 529/760). "That the supreme being is to be seen, heard, etc., as a manifest (*seiendes*) self-consciousness is in fact, then, the completion of its concept; and through this completion the Being is just as immediately *present* as it is Being" (p. 529/760). The consciousness to which God is present is, of course, "religious consciousness"; "here, then, God is *manifest* as *he is*; he is *present* as he is in himself; he is present as spirit" (p. 530/761). Divine Spirit is present in human spirit; but spirit can be "present" only to "speculative knowing," not to "understanding," where it can only be "represented" (p. 530/761). Christian religious consciousness, then, knows God as knowing himself, and this is "to see what absolute Being is and to find oneself therein" (p. 530/761). Ultimately the self-consciousness of the Christian *is* the self-consciousness of Christ.

As long, however, as the self-consciousness which knows God is only the self-consciousness of the individual God-man, God is there, it is true, in concept, but the implications of the concept have not been worked out; "this concept of the Spirit's knowing itself as Spirit is itself the immediate concept, not yet developed" (p. 530/761). The identity of Christian God-consciousness and Christian self-consciousness is not yet explicit (p. 530/761–62) because it is still particularized in the sensibly perceptible man Jesus Christ (p. 531/762). The one who *was* seen and heard must become the object of a spiritual not a sensible grasp; the self of which the individual Jesus is conscious must come to life in the Christian community [21] —*death* of the individual and *resurrection* of the universal. "As the immediate existence (*Daseins*) of the one known as the absolute Being disappears, the immediate takes on its negative moment: the Spirit continues to be an immediate actual self, but as *the universal self-consciousness* of the community (*Gemeine*), a self-consciousness residing in its own proper substance, such that the substance present in that self-consciousness is universal subject" (p. 531/763). Incarnation is not limited to one individual. "It is not the singular individual for himself but together with the consciousness of the community (*Gemeine*), and what he is for the community is the complete totality of that same consciousness" (p. 531/763). God himself is fully present as Spirit—both "substance" and "subject"—only in the spirit of the "community" (*Gemeine*).

With the disappearance of the individual Jesus from the scene, however, the divine Spirit is not yet universalized in the community. So long as God

---

[21] A certain amount of confusion is introduced into the text by Hegel's use of two terms for "community," seemingly but not really interchangeably. The terms are *die Gemeine* (rather unusual) and *die Gemeinde* (the usual term for "community"). The difference seems to be that *Gemeine* is more general, referring to the ongoing "community of the faithful," without limitation in time; whereas *Gemeinde* is more particular, designating the "community" as it is constituted at a given point in time. Since the distinction is rather conjectural, the term being translated will be indicated each time.

is still "represented" in the form of the one individual God-man, God himself is not yet the object of "pure thought" (pp. 531–32/763) and, therefore, not totally Spirit. The form in which God as Spirit "is conscious of himself in this, his community (*Gemeine*), is one in which his transcendence (*Jenseits*) and his immanence (*Diesseits*) have not yet been reconciled, because the "moments" of his self-revelation are "represented" as separate. "The content is the true one, but all its moments, posited in the framework (*Elemente*) of representation, do not have the character of being comprehended in unity (*begriffen*); rather they appear as completely independent aspects, externally related to each other" (p. 532/764). The Christian community's consciousness of God in Jesus Christ must raise itself to self-consciousness which ultimately it will do only as "absolute knowing," pure "speculative knowing." [22]

It is not enough, then, that the divine Spirit be "the substance of the community (*Gemeinde*)," i.e., that which consolidates this particular community; the Spirit must become a "real self," "must reflect on itself within itself and be subject" (p. 532/764). This is a "movement which the Spirit brings to fruition in its community (*Gemeinde*); in other words this is the Spirit's life" (p. 532/764). This will entail getting beyond simply remembering the one individual God-man, since "spirit" is to be found only in "concept," which is to say in the "consciousness of the community (*Gemeine*)" which is "self-consciousness" (p. 533/765). Just as the "unhappy consciousness" was consciousness of a self which was not its own substance, so initially "believing consciousness" is consciousness of "the self-less *Essence* of the world or essentially the *objective* content of representation" (p. 533/766). The community is not yet aware that its consciousness of God as self-conscious in Jesus Christ is its own self-consciousness; the "Spirit" of Jesus Christ is not yet the "spirit" of the community; the community has not yet found its identity in that Spirit (p. 534/766). The movement from the empty *word* which calls absolute Spirit "the eternal Being" to the presence of that Spirit in concept, a presence which is not simply that of an "object," has not been completed.

In order, now, to come to terms with this whole "movement," which neither begins nor ends with the Incarnation in the one man Jesus Christ,

---

22 "Consequently the Incarnation repeats and completes the total movement of religion. In expressing the presence of God in the immediate the Incarnation confronts a consciousness which it determines as the exact antithesis (and complement) of the unhappy consciousness. What has happened is that the self of the Spirit is no longer a reality 'thought or represented' (religion of nature), nor a reality 'produced' (religion of art): 'But this God is immediately contemplated as a self, as an objective singular man; it is only thus that he *is* self-consciousness' (p. 528). Still, the very immediacy of his appearing imposes the necessity of a transcending of the singular figure in which he expresses himself: the death of Christ is the condition for his resurrection in what is ultimately the universal being of the community of believers. This result is itself partial, because this 'universality,' as a 'totality of selves' who remain effectively distinct and separated from each other, exists only in the element of representation: 'To take a determinate example: the superseded *sensible this* is at first only the thing of *perception*, not yet the *universal* of understanding' (p. 531). Only absolute knowing will permit us to go beyond the as yet imperfect form of this true result" (Labarrière, *Structures et mouvement dialectique*, pp. 181–82).

Hegel will seek to fathom conceptually the mystery of the Trinity. There is no question, of course, that the theology of the Trinity has been couched in metaphorical terms, the language of "representation," and that the theology itself has been traditionally an attempt to "understand" the relationships which constitute the divine Being. For Hegel, as we already know, neither "representation" nor "understanding" is adequate to "speculative truth," precisely because speculative truth is essentially dynamic. What Hegel will seek to do, then, is to come to grips with (*begreifen*) the *dynamics* of Trinitarian doctrine and, ultimately, of the whole divine–human relationship. That this "coming-to-grips" should take the form of what some consider fitting the doctrine to the Procrustean bed of Hegel's own system should really cause no great surprise. It is just as plausible, however, to say that he fitted his own system to his interpretation of Trinitarian and divine–human relationships.

In any event, he begins his dynamic *Begreifen* traditionally enough. That God as Father "generates" a Son Hegel sees as a "representational" way of saying that in knowing himself God has "othered" himself and thus knows himself in another, and that this knowing himself in another is a return to himself. "The Essence contemplates only himself in his being-for-himself," and "this is the Word" (p. 534/767). The distinctions which are made in an effort to come to grips with the Trinity are seen to be meaningful only if they are at the same time not distinctions—again a not unexpected "speculative" insight—"such that the distinctions which have been made are equally immediately made as dissolved; and what is true and actual is precisely this self-revolving movement" (p. 535/767). What is more, it is this self-movement which expresses "absolute Being as *Spirit*"—to say of a God who is not self-moving that he is "Spirit" is to utter an empty word (p. 535/767). Because the "community" (*Gemeine*) "represents" this, i.e., does not grasp it in "comprehensive (*begreifende*) thinking," it sees the relationship in the static terms of "Father and Son," and sees the revelation itself as coming from the "Spirit" who is "another" (p. 535/767-68). The community's "belief," then, does not penetrate to what is the innermost truth of the mystery: "In this the pure externality of belief is clung to, an externality that is without knowledge, dead. The *internality* of this exterior has disappeared, because this would be its concept which knows itself as concept" (p. 535/768).

As religious consciousness grows, then, it becomes aware not only that "absolute Being" is a most inadequate designation of God but also that it designates but a "moment of spirit," incomplete without the further moments of knowledge and love (p. 536/769). The movement embracing all these moments is comprehensible as a movement which both distinguishes and dissolves the distinction only in the "concept," which is only muddied by representations, be they mathematical (the number three), or biological (the distinction of substantified persons) (p. 536/769).

The inadequacy of "representation" or of the language proper to it to capture the dynamic reality to which only the "concept" is adequate allows Hegel now to introduce a whole series of Christian representational terms which need conceptual clarification. In keeping with what we have already

seen, in clarifying the divine he will be clarifying the human spiritual reality. God is said, for example, to have "created" the world. But "*create* is the
representational word for concept according to its absolute movement"
(p. 536/769). If religious consciousness represents God as "making" something, it has missed God's spiritual activity of knowing the world in knowing
himself and knowing himself in knowing the world (pp. 536–37/770). At the
same time it has failed to recognize that this, too, is the way the human
spirit knows itself; it is "the *existing (daseiende) spirit*, that is, the individual
self which has the consciousness and which distinguishes itself from itself as
other or as world" (p. 537/770). To know the world of reality adequately is
to know the self; to know the self adequately is to know the world of reality,
and any attempt to know one without the other is to lose both. To know
that this is the case, however, is not yet to know one's spirit as spirit; the
movement of becoming other must precede the return to self, i.e., it is all
one movement. "That the individual self be in fact self and spirit it must
first become to itself another, just as the eternal Being presents itself as the
movement wherein in its being other it is the same as itself" (p. 537/770).
The other which spirit knows in knowing the world is not another out there
to be discovered; the knowing is the work of consciousness, and to know the
world is to reconstruct it in concept, the unique work of spirit (p. 537/770).
For God to "create" a world is to "know" that world in knowing himself; for
the human spirit to "know" the world is to re-create that world in conceiving it.

After "creation" comes "the fall," and Hegel submits both it and the
images used in narrating it—"the tree of the knowledge of good and evil,"
the "fruit," "the angel of light" (Lucifer)—to the same conceptual scrutiny.
He finds that, like the notion of "Son," they are all "representations," whose
inner content is the movement of man's taking upon himself responsibility
for his world (p. 538/771). Even terms like "good" and "evil" Hegel interprets not in a moral but in a dialectical framework. "On the basis of these
moments, then, it happens that, just as the evil is nothing but the entry into
self of the spirit's natural existence (*Daseins*), conversely the good enters into
actuality and appears as an existing self-consciousness" (p. 539/773).

All of this leads once more to a consideration of the Incarnation, since for
Christian theology creation, fall, incarnation, and redemption are part and
parcel of one and the same movement. The Incarnation Hegel now calls "the
alienation of the divine Being." [23] "The self of the Spirit and the simple
thought of that are the two moments, whose absolute unity the Spirit itself
is" (p. 539/773). Religious consciousness in one way sees the divine Being as
essential and the becoming human as inessential, in the sense that it is a free
choice. In another, however, the abstraction of "divine Being" is seen as inessential, and the personality expressed in the self-consciousness of the incarnate God is seen as essential (pp. 539–40/773–74). When, however, incarnation is comprehended as a movement, all of whose moments are inseparable,
the opposition between essential and inessential ceases. In the concept which

23 Echoes of St. Paul's κένωσις.

comprehends the whole movement incarnation is seen not as a free choice but as a necessary externalization of a God who would otherwise remain abstract (p. 540/774). Furthermore, even the death of Christ, seen as a moment in the overall movement, is necessary (in the concept): "This death is his rising as Spirit" (p. 540/775). The Spirit is not all that it is as Spirit until the immediate presence of the self-conscious Christ is "superseded" and has come to life again in constituting the "community" (*Gemeinde*) (p. 541/775).

[RECAPITULATION]

Having said this much, Hegel now recapitulates, translating, so to speak, the language of "representation" into that of concept (pp. 541–43/775–78).

a) The divine Being takes on human nature, not as something separate; the union of the divine and the human is so intimate that God literally "becomes man."

b) By the same token God's "creation" is not "evil"—not even dialectically—because it is not over against the divine Being who is "good." "The moment of *being within himself*"—which representation sees only in the Incarnation—"constitutes rather the essential moment of the Spirit's *self*" (p. 541/775). In terms of the "concept," creation and incarnation are two moments of one and the same outpouring.

c) Still, only when the incarnate God sacrifices himself "is the [divine] Being *reflected into himself* and thus Spirit" (p. 541/776), because only in this redeeming act are good and evil, God and man, fully reconciled.

d) "Not one or the other [moment] has truth but rather precisely their movement. This means that simple sameness is an abstraction and, hence, is absolute difference; but absolute difference as difference in itself is differentiated from itself and, thus, is sameness with itself" (p. 542/777). The language, admittedly, is tortured, but it enunciates a most basic dialectical principle: where reality is dynamic, a distinction of "moments" is necessary, and yet these moments must coalesce in the unity of the total movement.

e) This means that where the truth to be enunciated is "spiritual" (*speculative*) the simple copula "is" cannot express it; [24] concepts do not lend themselves to expression in the language proper to "understanding." "The difficulty which occurs in these concepts is simply clinging to the *is* and forgetting thought, wherein the moments just as much *are* as *are not*—are only the movement, which is spirit" (p. 543/777).

f) To comprehend the "becoming of Spirit," then, which Christian theology seeks to *analyze*, the concept which unifies the whole movement from "absolute Being" to the vitalizing Spirit of the "community" is necessary. "The Spirit, then, is in the third element, in the *universal self-consciousness*; it is its *community* (*Gemeinde*)" (p. 543/778). The goal of the whole is summed up in the meaning of the sacrificial death of Christ: "The dead

---

[24] We have already seen that Hegel does not employ the copula the way it functions in the formal proposition. He is well aware, of course, that the language of Scripture, particularly of the Gospels, is replete with such "speculative" propositions—paradoxes.

God-man—or man-God—is *in himself* universal Self-consciousness; he has to become this *for this self-consciousness*" (p. 543/778).

g) The story of God, then—Trinity, creation, sin, redemption—is the story of man; the self-consciousness of Christ is to become the self-consciousness of man as he passes from the merely "natural" ("evil") to the "spiritual" ("good") (p. 543/778).

The "is" of the language of "representation" is replaced on the level of "concept" by *movement, passage*. Spirit, *is*, then, its own *becoming*. Since *passage*, however, is from one opposite to another, spirit "is" both. If, for example, as "natural" spirit is "good," to pass from that to its opposite is "evil." If, on the other hand, to be *merely (an sich)* natural is "evil," to pass from that to its opposite is "good." This is what "reconciliation" (redemption) is all about (p. 543/778). "Because, that is, the [divine] Being (*Wesen*) is *in itself* already reconciled with itself and is a spiritual unity wherein the parts proper to representation are *superseded parts* or *moments*, then what takes place is that each part belonging to representation takes on a meaning *opposite* to the one it previously had" (p. 544/778–79). Where the "content," then, is spiritual, no "meaning" is complete, save in relation to its opposite. "The spiritual," Hegel tells us, "is unity in being-other"; it is "the identity of identity and non-identity," i.e., to *be* spirit is to *become* what spirit is not yet (p. 544/779).

As examples of giving "spiritual" meaning to what the language of "representation" expresses metaphorically, Hegel now takes "the fall" (original sin) and "the death of God." That "natural consciousness" should have entered into itself was the entrance of "evil" into the world; man came to "know" evil. "This knowing, it is true, is a becoming evil, but only the becoming of the *thought* of the evil, which is, therefore, recognized as the first moment of reconciliation" (p. 544/779). With the advent of sin, the process of redemption (getting away from the merely natural) is already underway. The process culminates in the death of the God-man, his reconciliation with himself. "The full comprehension (*Ergreifen*) of this representation now expresses more determinately what was previously called in its language the spiritual resurrection, i.e., his singular self-consciousness becoming the universal or becoming the community (*Gemeinde*)" (p. 545/780). Death, which previously signified an end, now signifies a beginning. "From what it immediately signifies, the non-being of this individual, death is transfigured into the *universality* of the Spirit, which lives in its community (*Gemeine*) [25] and in it daily dies and rises" (p. 545/780). What dies is the particularity of the singular individual: "His particularity dies totally (*erstirbt*) in his universality, i.e., in his *knowing*, which is the Essence (*Wesen*) reconciling itself with itself" (p. 545/781). The story of this "knowing" contains all the "moments" of spirit coming to consciousness of itself, of spirit "returned into its concept" (p. 545/781); the implications of what was there all along have been explicitated. When we comprehend the death of "the mediator," we see that he ceases to be an isolated "object" of contemplation; "his particular inde-

[25] The implication of dynamic presence and ongoing life is clear here.

pendent being has become universal self-consciousness" (p. 545–46/781).

The death of the God-man, however, the mediator between God and man, is also the death of God—as no more than an abstract being, of the "substance" who is not yet "subject." "The death of this representation, then, contains at the same time the death of *the divine Being as an abstraction*, which is not posited as a self" (p. 546/781–82). To know God this way is to know man; not that the *propositions* "God *is* man" or "man *is* God" are true, but that the *process* of God's becoming "Spirit" and of man's becoming "spirit" is the same process. "This knowing, then, is the en-spiriting (*Begeistung*) whereby substance has become subject, its abstraction and lifelessness have died, and it has become *actual*, and is simple, universal self-consciousness" (p. 546/782).

The movement, whether of divine Spirit or of human spirit, is complete when spirit is both *object* and *subject*, i.e., when spirit recognizes its "knowing" of itself as its own "doing" (p. 546/782). "What moves itself is spirit; it is the subject of the moving and at the same time *the moving* itself, i.e., it is the substance which the subject penetrates" (pp. 546–47/782). In religious consciousness of the movement of the divine Spirit, then, man "transcends the differentiation of his own *self* from the *self he contemplates*; the former, like the latter, is subject and likewise substance. Man himself is the spirit, precisely because and insofar as he is this movement" (p. 547/783). God and man are *not* one and the same *being*; they *are* one and the same process.

The process, however, is not yet complete. The self-consciousness of Christ has, it is true, become the self-consciousness of the "community" (*Gemeinde*), but because the community still "represents" Christ to itself, it is not yet totally conscious of its own reality: "It is spiritual self-consciousness, which is not as such object to itself, i.e., has not opened itself to consciousness of itself" (p. 547/783). Its "representations" are still obstacles. Thus, in being conscious of God as "absolute self-consciousness," it is conscious of its own self, but not "absolute," not self-sufficient; "for devout consciousness the absolute is *another*" (p. 547/783). It is not yet aware that God, the "abstract" absolute (Being), concretizes his own abstractness "to become a self" in the devotion community consciousness manifests (p. 548/783–84). The community is united with God, but because it is not aware that it *unites itself* with God, the union is "external" (p. 548/784). "Just as the *singular* God-man has a Father who is *in himself* and only an *actual* mother, so too the universal God-man, the community (*Gemeinde*) has its own *doing* and *knowing* as its father, but as mother the *eternal love* which it only feels, but which it does not contemplate in its own consciousness as an actual immediate object" (p. 548/784). The Spirit of the "community" (*Gemeinde*), then, is one whose religious consciousness is not fully identified with its self-consciousness; religious consciousness has not identified itself with the God of which it is conscious. It "speaks" of a union with God, but it is a union in which God is object for, but does not inhabit, its own spirit (p. 548/785).

Ultimately, then, Christian religious consciousness, in making God present to man, tells man a great deal about himself, but not all. It is all there in what it does tell him, but he is not aware of all that is there. He will not be aware of all that is there, of the dignity which is his as autonomous spirit, until he has plumbed conceptually the representations with which religious consciousness covers the divine Spirit present to it and in it. When this is achieved in "absolute knowing," the divine Spirit will not have departed— *Aufhebung* never means that—it will be present in man as the spirit which raises him to his fullest dignity—where his self-consciousness is the awareness of the thoroughgoing autonomy of his knowing.[26]

26 "Philosophy, so Hegel teaches, dissolves religion, just as religion dissolved art. In each case what is dissolved does not disappear but is no longer the highest. Nevertheless, the philosophy which here wins out over religion is the absolute knowing of the Hegelian system, and the religion over which that is victorious is the absolute religion, which is Christianity. According to Hegel, however, both absolute religion and absolute knowing have the same content and are distinguished from each other only in form, insofar as the form of religion is representation, that of philosophy, thinking. That, however, means that Hegel's interpretation of art is a Christian-theological one. That explains both the brilliance and the poverty of the interpretation. But that Hegel can identify Christian δικαιοσύνη διὰ πίστεως with Platonic λόγον διδόναι is based on the philosophical foundations of his Christian theology, neo-Platonism. Hegel consciously goes back from Kant to Plotinus and to Plotinus' disciple, Proclus, whom he particularly admires" (Walter Bröcker, *Auseinandersetzungen mit Hegel* [Frankfurt: Klostermann, 1965], pp. 35–36).

9

Absolute Knowing

AT THE OUTSET, in the Introduction to the *Phenomenology*, Hegel had said that, short of being "absolute," knowing could never lay claim to the august title of knowing in the full sense—a merely relative knowing is at least partially opinion. At that point, however, there was no way of telling either what absolute knowing could possibly be or whether absolute knowing is in fact a human possibility. No answer could initially be given to either question, because only a knowing which is absolute could give those answers. It should be clear, then, that we can be sure the phenomenological project introduced at the beginning was both possible and worthwhile only if, at the end of the project through which Hegel has guided us, the mere "phenomenon" of knowing has put aside all elements of non-knowing and has turned into knowing in the strictest sense. By the same token, only if the project actually has issued in a knowing which in an intelligible sense is absolute can we be in a position to comprehend what has been going on since the beginning. The present chapter, then, serves—at the very least—a double function: to show what has been arrived at as a result of the itinerary described and to serve as an introduction to a more intelligent—and indispensable—second reading of the whole *Phenomenology*.[1]

In a certain sense, at the end of the chapter on "Spirit," where moral consciousness has become "conscience," embodied in the "beautiful soul," there was already consciousness of what true knowing *has to be*, i.e., a consciousness dependent on nothing extraneous to itself for its content, a self-consciousness which both gives itself the content it has and is conscious of doing just that. For self-consciousness to know, however, that it can truly know a content for which it alone is responsible is not to know either what that content is or whether that content corresponds with the reality consciousness started out convinced that it was knowledge of. If, to go back to the dialectic of "force and understanding," it can be shown that the "appearing" of reality and the "consciousness" of reality are one and the same movement—objectively and subjectively designated—then an awareness, or self-awareness, which is truly complete will be the awareness of a reality

---

[1] To say this is to make no pretense that the present chapter—read either as the summation of the whole movement or as an introduction to a re-reading—will make sense by itself. If it is to make any sense at all, it will do so only when read in very close conjunction with the extremely dense and extremely illusive (and allusive) final chapter of Hegel's *Phenomenology*. Nor will that make sense unless the overall movement of the whole is kept in view.

which "appears" completely, and the second half of the last question has been answered. That, after all, is what the Hegelian "concept" shows itself to be: the oneness of the movement of thought and reality, and the consciousness of that oneness. But only if the content of the concept is "absolute," in the sense both that there is nothing in it which consciousness does not give to itself and that nothing is left out, is the second part of the question answerable. And short of religious consciousness, whose object is explicitly "absolute Being"—the grasp of which "absolute religion" provides—there is no "absolute" content of consciousness.

That it is necessary, then, to go beyond moral consciousness, model though it be of genuine human knowing, is clear. That a knowing which falls short of the absolute content which religion presents cannot be knowing in the full sense is also clear. Thus, our present task is threefold: (a) to recapitulate all the forms of consciousness which have paraded before us from the beginning; (b) to show that all these forms of consciousness are at the same time forms of self-consciousness and, ultimately, of spirit; and (c) to show both that the connection of each with the one which follows is necessary and that the list is complete. The last, incidentally, will be "shown," only to the extent that from the vantage point of absolute knowing both necessity and completeness are "seen." Whether or not "we" readers do "see" this will depend on the extent to which we identify with the human spirit coming to consciousness of itself, and that in turn will depend on the "second reading" to which this chapter is an introduction. One thing at least is clear: only after a second reading can we in conscience either go along with Hegel or part company with him.

Although the summit of religious consciousness is the human spirit's awareness of God, "the absolute," as its object and at the same time an awareness of itself as in some sense absolutized in order to correspond with its object, there is as yet no full realization that the consciousness of God and the consciousness of self are one and the same. Because God is "represented" in a number of figurative ways he is, so to speak, "presented to" consciousness but is not yet the very self of consciousness. What is needed, then, is a recognition on the part of the human spirit that in its "going out" (*Entäusserung*) to God, "the other," it finds itself, that "in its being other it is with itself" (p. 549/790). This is but another way of saying that the spirit's God-consciousness is its own movement, not something which is done to it; it is the summation of the moments of its own development (p. 550/790). Looking back over all the forms it has gone through, it can recognize that in each of them, including the highest, it is finding itself. "This sum total of its determinations makes *it* to be *essentially* (*an sich*) spiritual being, and it becomes this in truth consciously by grasping each and every one of these determinations as proper to the self,[2] or by spirit's

---

[2] The German here is *durch das Auffassen einer jeden einzelnen derselben als des Selbsts*. Grammatically speaking, then, Baillie's translation, "when the latter apprehends every individual one of them as self" (p. 790), is conceivably correct. Baillie takes *des Selbsts* to be in apposition with *einer jeden einzelnen*. Such a construction, however, is rather unusual. It seems better to take *des Selbsts* as "proper to the self."

already mentioned spiritual relation to them" (p. 550/790). *All* spirit's forms are products of its own spiritual activity. Along the way it was not possible to see this; now it is clear that none of the preceding forms could make sense except in the framework of the totality of them all.

[DYNAMIC UNITY OF CONSCIOUSNESS]

To *com-prehend* all these forms as the dynamic totality of self-movement is to know "absolutely." [3] The movement described turns out to be circular; only at the end is the beginning—and the whole movement—revealed in its true (spiritual) significance.[4] Here, of course, the reader of the *Phenomenology* runs into a difficulty which, perhaps, even a second reading will not eliminate: the *ways* in which spirit appears are the ways it has appeared to Hegel; what guarantee is there that they are either necessary or complete? None. It is simply up to the reader to judge, having examined them carefully, whether Hegel's account is convincing. The account can be neither convincing nor unconvincing if one has not gone through the total experience.

What Hegel asks us to do, then, is from the present vantage point to go back over the whole list of partial "manifestations" (*Gestalten*) to see what sense we can now make of them. The first three, in which being appeared first as independent, "out there," then as involving reflection on the part of the *perceiving* subject, and finally as having an objectively universal essence which only "understanding" could grasp, turn out to be forms in which consciousness, in knowing what is "other" than itself, is knowing itself. "As determined in these three ways, then, consciousness must know its object as itself" (p. 550/790). In going through this for the first time, of course, consciousness could not see itself in the framework of its own total-ity—only "we" who looked on from the sidelines could gather together the separate moments of both the object and consciousness of it (p. 550/791). If, Hegel assures us, the consciousness "we" have been observing now recalls *all* the forms it has gone through, *it* will find that the process reveals its own completeness. Consciousness will now recognize, for example, that when "observing reason" finds that knowing itself as "I" in objective reality is its own doing, it is in the process of discovering that according to its "con-cept" the living "I"—the "soul" which it has objectified—is in truth "spirit" (p. 551/791).

By the same token, consciousness has gradually come to realize that the "thing" of which it was conscious is a thing, only because the "I" made it so, and that the "usefulness" which the Enlightenment ascribed to things was but a partial recognition of the relativity of all reality to the self

---

[3] "Comprehensiveness here clearly serves as one of the synonyms of absoluteness. Affixed to the synoptic way of knowing, which results from the synthesis of the separate cognitive efforts, the label absolute seems unexceptionable" (Loewenberg, *Hegel's Phenomenology*, p. 358).

[4] "The circular movement which is spirit is the self which runs through this circle, and indeed the self revealed as spirit which in its moments never forgets itself and at the same time would never be for itself in them absolute spirit" (*Jenenser Metaphysik*, p. 185).

(p. 551/791–92), to the only self of which it can make sense, ultimately, to say that to it all things are relative. When, further, consciousness goes out of itself in "culture" and makes itself to be more than it is simply by nature, it is, in producing its own object, producing itself; the being which things have in consciousness is consciousness' own being, the self of which it is conscious; for consciousness to know is to be aware of what it creates. Only in "moral self-consciousness," however, which is a sort of model of what self-consciousness is to be, does consciousness "know" its object as essentially internal to itself, as a revelation of what it is to be a self (p. 551/ 792). Moral knowing and willing are the very "essence" of what is known and willed and thus "essentially" antecede the "actuality" produced (p. 552/ 792). This stage in the process of coming to know what "knowing" is is completed in "conscience," where consciousness of *what is to be done* finds only itself as responsible agent: "The objective element into which it projects itself as acting is no other than the self's pure knowledge of itself" (p. 552/792–93). It is, then, in knowledge oriented to action (practical knowledge) that the spirit begins to come to terms with what "being conscious" properly is (p. 552/793). When the spirit says to itself that it is certain that what it proposes to do is right because it corresponds to its "duty," it is saying that in knowing what is to be done it knows itself.

To know what is to be done, however, is not to do it. In fact, there is a tendency to preserve the purity of the knowing by refraining from doing, since the "actuality" of doing never corresponds with the "ideal" known. Thus, it becomes necessary to overcome "the iron hardness" of the "beautiful soul," wherein the "certainty" of self is opposed to the uncertainty of what action places outside the self. Only where there is consciousness that there is "forgiveness" for what is faulty in what is done need "knowing" not retreat from "doing," and only if the consciousness of "forgiveness" is a mode of self-consciousness can the opposition between knowing and doing be successfully removed—but only from the vantage point of "absolute knowing," which cannot be arrived at without passing through religious consciousness, can the consciousness of forgiveness be identified with self-consciousness.[5] What it comes down to is that an objective knowing, which is universal, and a knowing of self, which is presumably individual, are not opposed, because through religion consciousness becomes aware that to be conscious of the "absolute," the universal, and to be aware of self are one and the same consciousness, i.e., absolute consciousness.[6] "Knowing" is

---

[5] Not too much has been said about the importance of the consciousness of "forgiveness" in the movement of self-conscious reason. The notion is, perhaps, too religious to gain favor. It serves, however, as the link between knowing what is to be done and doing it which, as ideal and actuality, seem to be irreparably opposed; to actualize the ideal at all is to make it less than ideal. Whether one likes to call the consciousness which nevertheless permits action a consciousness of "forgiveness" matters little; what is important is that action get done—an "absolute" without "actuality" is forbiddingly empty.

[6] This contra Loewenberg, who seems to think that with religion has been introduced illegitimately an "absolute self-consciousness" which is "other" than human self-consciousness. "No superhuman subject need be invoked for the sort of experience the evolution of whose dialectic we are bidden to follow—the experience, for example, of

essentially an activity of the self, and it is essentially a self-knowing, a "positing" of the self and of all that the self knows. "Herein it is at the same time posited that the *third* moment, *universality,* i.e., the *essence* of both the opposed, makes sense *(gilt)* only as *knowing;* the two likewise ultimately transcend any remaining empty opposition and constitute the knowledge of I = I—this individual self which is immediately pure knowing, i.e., universal" (pp. 552–53/793).

For Hegel it is clear that a human consciousness which is comprehensive in the sense that its object comprehends all being (is "absolute") can be reconciled with human self-consciousness only through the mediation of religion, wherein spirit is first conscious of "absolute Being," upon which then follows spirit's consciousness of "being absolute" (p. 553/794). "We" observers, of course, could see prior to religious consciousness that the various forms which have passed before us are "moments" constituting one spiritual movement, but only with religion are all these recognized as moments of spirit's developing self-consciousness. "In the order in which its forms appeared to us, consciousness has long since come partly to the various moments of that order and partly to their union, before religion gave its object the form of actual self-consciousness" (p. 553/794).[7] The self-consciousness to which the human spirit could attain prior to religion is self-consciousness "from the point of view of its contentless form"; the "absolute content" of that self-consciousness is given only in religion. Only in "absolute knowing," finally, are "absolute content" and "absolute form" united; to know fully what knowing is is to know what knowing knows (p. 553/794). From this point of view, even "we" philosophers have a more concrete grasp of the implications of all the forms we have seen only from the vantage point of an "absolute knowing" whose object is "absolute spirit"—a knowing which is at once consciousness and self-consciousness.

Now, although the "union" of the various forms in which spirit has appeared has already taken place in religious consciousness—recall the recapitulation of all the forms under that heading—in the sense that what is there "represented" is self-conscious spirit, still the union has not taken place through "the movement of [human] self-consciousness" (p. 553/794). This it will be only when that movement is truly "concept": "The content, as well as the other aspect of self-conscious spirit, to the extent that it is the *other* aspect, is present and indicated in its completeness: the union which is still lacking is the simple unity of the concept" (p. 553/794). The concept

him who perceives or doubts, grieves over his divided self or rejoices in nature's adaptability to his reason, regards his personality neglected in a legalized society or feels alienated in the world of culture, acts in open rebellion against the established order or seeks absolute freedom in the inviolable sanctuary of conscience. It is the human psyche with which we are concerned at the level of consciousness preceding religion" (*Hegel's Phenomenology,* p. 365).

In fact, it is the "human psyche" with which we are concerned on the level of religion and on the following level, too. Without the last two, the full significance of the "experiences" Loewenberg has listed would not be revealed.

[7] So much for Loewenberg. What he failed to see was that, prior to the invoking of a "superhuman subject," the "dialectic" of whose experience is contained in the moments Loewenberg himself lists, the human spirit does not have adequate consciousness of itself precisely as spirit.

is there as a consciousness which finds all its truth in itself on the level of "the beautiful soul" but only a *"particular form of consciousness"* (p. 553/795), which is a "contemplation of the divine" but not a "self-movement of the divine." Thus prior to the "filling," the "positive outgoing (*Entäusserung*) and forward movement" which takes place in religion, it remains but a "self-consciousness without an object" (p. 554/795), i.e., self-consciousness does not really know what it is conscious of. The "conscience" of "the beautiful soul" is the last stop on the level of "moral spirit," a knowledge of what *ought* to be done; only if spirit moves forward to religion will it get anything *done*.[8] To *know* one's "duty" is not to know oneself; it is to know an "abstract essence" which falls short of the concrete self (p. 554/795).

One wonders, it is true, whether Hegel had to be so complicated in saying that a knowing divorced from action is not truly knowing, or that an action divorced from a consciousness of the divine guarantee will not succeed in healing the split between *ought-to-do* and *doing*. What is clear is that the "form" of self-consciousness, "the self itself," which is revealed in "conscience," must be combined with the kind of self-consciousness (absolute) which is "represented" but not fully present in religion, and that the middle term which permits the resolution of the "either/or" (*Entzweien*) is "action," wherein the concept ceases to be merely abstract (p. 554/795–96). What this comes down to is a recognition that *knowing* is an *action*, and in no sense a *being-acted-upon*. But as long as it is possible to consider even an absolute (divine) object as separated from the conceiving of it in the self-conscious spirit, the conceiving of it can be looked on as arrogating to the self a function which does not belong to it, a kind of "evil," consciousness making its own what is not its own (p. 554/795).

If, however, as we noted in reference to the dialectic of "force and understanding," the appearance of what appears is the consciousness we have of it, and if the consciousness we have is the activity of the self, then a knowing, even of the divine, is a *producing* or *re-producing* of the divine in a consciousness which is consciousness of self: "The very same which is already posited *in itself* repeats itself now as the knowledge which consciousness has of it, as a conscious doing" which is "consciousness' own doing" (p. 555/796). Neither the subject knowing nor the object known is independent of the other. When man knows God the knowing is an action the agent of which is the self and only the self and the object of which is the divine being as a self. Looking back we can see that all of this was "implicit" (*an sich*) from the beginning and that the successive negations of abstractness constitute one process in which not only consciousness but also its object are concretized until they are ultimately identified. Thus, the process in which the universality of the object is concretized, the "absolute" progressively revealing itself as what it is, is concomitantly the process wherein consciousness (self-consciousness) is universalized. In the process, then, the opposition between universality and particularity is progressively "transcended" in such a way that each side of the opposition is seen to be "self-transcending" (*sich selbst aufhebende*) (p. 555/796–97). "One of the two parts of the opposition is the dissimilarity between being *within itself,* in its singularity, and universality; the other, the dissimilarity of its [the object's] abstract universality in opposition to the self" (p. 555/797). Each needs the other in order to be what it truly is. Self-consciousness does this by relinquishing its self-enclosedness, getting outside itself; "it acknowledges itself." The object—implicitly the "absolute"—relinquishes "the rigidity of its abstract universality," "its lifeless self and static universality" (p. 555/797). Static universality has become dynamic, the universality of universal interrelation. The result is that self-consciousness "has augmented itself by means of the moment of universality, which is essence," and the object has augmented itself "by means of the universality which is self" (p. 555/797). The universality of objectivity can be dynamic only if subjectivity too is universal. The synthesis is achieved through a "movement" which is "activity" on the part of the spirit and a "thinking" which is "movement" on the part of the object: "as a pure universality of a knowing which is self-consciousness, and as a self-consciousness which is the simple unity of knowing" (p. 555/797).

Although in terms of the successive "forms" of consciousness in which spirit has manifested itself "absolute knowing" is not a "form" in the way the others are (not a "moment"), it can nevertheless be considered a "form of consciousness" in the sense that it is a *"gathering-together* of the singular moments, each of which in its principle manifests the life of the whole spirit" (p. 556/797). What is more, this "gathering" is "the *self's* own *doing*"; it is "knowing *this subject* as *substance*"; it is the concept precisely as concept (p. 556/797). The ultimate form in the dialectic of spirit has now been grasped as it truly is.[9] Where the *knowing* is absolute, the *spirit* knowing is absolute; and only a spirit which "comprehends the absolute" is itself absolute: "It is spirit knowing itself in the form of spirit, i.e., *comprehensive (begreifende) knowing*" (p. 556/798). For the self to know itself *as* absolute is for it to know itself *in* the absolute; the concept is the comprehensive form in which object and self are grasped as identical. "Thereby what has become the element of manifest being *(Daseins)* or the *form of objectivity* is the [absolute] essence itself, i.e., the *concept*" (p. 556/798).

[SELF-CONSCIOUSNESS AS CONSCIOUSNESS OF THE DIVINE]

There are, of course, those who will dispute that by "consciousness of the absolute" Hegel means "consciousness of God," but since it is difficult to

---

9 "Now, it is evident that absolute knowing as such is not a 'figure' *(Gestalt)* in the same way as, for example, observing reason or the artisan of the religion of nature. In it rather is expressed the transcending of every figure, understood as the singular reality which, in the overall syllogism, is still opposed to the universality of the spirit. But what is affirmed here is that absolute knowing is none other than the 'last figure of the spirit' (i.e., that of moral consciousness) comprehended in its truth. In this figure, then, the true and perfect content of the absolute essence is found to have attained to the form of the self, the same form expressed by the two consciousnesses in their experience of mutual forgiveness. . . . The spirit knows itself in this universal figure in the fullness of

see what else "comprehending the absolute" could mean, it seems safe to say that in some significant sense he means that self-consciousness and God-consciousness are identified in absolute knowing. A consciousness which is not consciousness of God is not a full consciousness of self; a consciousness of God which is not consciousness of self is not a consciousness of God—only a "representation" of him. Nor, in Hegelian language, does this mean that the only God there is is *self!* [10] In this, of course, there is nothing terribly new; St. Augustine said the same; and in their own way Fichte and Schelling were saying the same. Hegel, however, would seem to be closer to Augustine than to either of his two contemporaries. In any event, the "science" (*Wissen-schaft*) toward which the *Phenomenology* has been moving since its opening pages is a comprehensive grasp of the only comprehensive object there is. If to know is to produce—or re-produce (*hervorbringen*)—the object of knowing, then the spirit appearing in consciousness is the spirit "produced therein by consciousness," and this "*is science,*" i.e., knowing in the fullest sense (p. 556/798).

With the identification of "absolute knowing" (the absolute comprehending the absolute) and "science," the whole movement can once more be recapitulated as "the appearing of science." "The nature, the moments, and the movement of this knowing have, thus, manifested it as being the pure *being-for-itself* of self-consciousness" (p. 556/798). The "I" of which consciousness is conscious is at once "this I" and "universal" (p. 556/798). But because all this begins simply as "consciousness," the "I" is initially a content distinct from the conscious activity, and the elimination of that distinction is as much the movement of the content as it is the movement of consciousness; they are identified in the process of being "comprehended" (*begriffen*), i.e., the "I" finds itself as other only within itself. "This content, more determinately presented, is no other than the very movement just expressed; for the content is the spirit which runs its own course and, indeed, is *for itself*, in that it has the form of the concept in its objectivity" (p. 557/798). "Science," in fact, does not make its appearance until spirit has attained to this consciousness regarding itself, when it has become "the spirit which knows what it itself is," when by having taken on all the inadequate forms in which it appears "it has made itself for its own consciousness into the form of its own essence" (p. 557/799). Not until the self of which the spirit is conscious is coterminous with the object of which it is conscious is it truly spirit or is its knowing truly knowing. The comprehensive object of its knowing, however, is "substance" as the sum total of objectivity, the "absolute" object. But a substance which is not also subject would in no conceivable sense be absolute. If, then, a condition for knowing in the full sense be that its object be absolute and that its absolute object be also subject, it is equally

its spiritual existence (i.e., in the fully affirmed freedom of the object set forth as the self)" (Labarrière, *Structures et mouvement dialectique*, p. 223).

[10] "When there is question of philosophy as such it cannot be a question of *my* philosophy. In general, however, every philosophy is the comprehension of the absolute—and, therefore, not of something strange. By the same token, comprehending the absolute is the absolute's self-comprehension, as theology—when, of course, it was more theology than it now is—always said" (Letter to Hinrichs, Summer 1819; *Briefe*, II 216).

a condition for that same knowing that the subject knowing be absolute. Both the known object and the knowing subject, then, must in some sense be divine. How can we make sense out of that? Not, certainly, by a formal identification of the divine with the human spirit. But a dialectical identification is something else again. If knowing is the autonomous activity of a spiritual self, and the self-manifestation of the object is indistinguishable from that same spiritual activity, then there is only one activity, and subject and object are identified in that. The *being* of the subject is its activity, the *being* of the object is its activity, and the same *activity* is the being of both. More than that, the activity in question is not merely consciousness (*Bewusstsein*), it is self-consciousness, i.e., consciousness which has self as its object, and human consciousness of self is at the same time consciousness of a divine self. The "concept" in which both are grasped is the same (p. 557/799).

Although the movement from mere consciousness to self-consciousness occurs early in the overall dialectic of the *Phenomenology*, the "self" of self-consciousness is initially minimal; the "certainty" of self has little to be certain of. The consciousness of "substance" is richer, but as long as the moments of substance are merely abstract, the riches remain largely hidden. But if these same moments of substance constitute their own dialectic, then the movement of progressive self-consciousness and the movement of concretization of substance become one and the same movement. The movement of self-consciousness *begins* when consciousness recognizes that it produces its own object, which it takes to be other than itself; it *culminates* when it recognizes that what it has been producing all along is itself, that the process of concretizing its object is the object's process of self-concretization (p. 558/800).

Since the process is spiritual through and through, the culmination is there from the start, but uncomprehended (*unbegriffen*). It is for this reason that the spiritual process is one which takes place in *time*; it continues to be a temporal process until the process has been comprehended—in its *Begriff*, which cancels out time and allows for a non-temporal elaboration in the *Logic* (p. 558/800). "Because this concept has grasped (*erfasst*) itself, it transcends its temporal form, comprehends intuitively, and is a comprehended and comprehensive intuition" (p. 558/800). Spirit in process (in time) is necessarily incompletely spiritual. The process is complete when self-consciousness has justified to itself its initial self-certainty, i.e., when the self of which it is conscious is fully spirit (p. 558/800).

A new light has now been shed on the experiences through which spirit goes in coming to itself. They could not be skipped because the absolute which is the "truth" of consciousness has to be *experienced* in all possible ways if it is ever to be *known* and if the knowing of it is to be its revelation in self-consciousness. "For this reason it must be said that nothing is *known* which is not in *experience* or, as the same thing is also expressed, which is not present as *felt truth*, as the Eternal *interiorly revealed*, as the Holy which is *believed*, or whatever other expressions are employed" (p. 558/800). What is experienced in all these many ways is spirit which is "in itself substance and, thus, *object* of *consciousness*" (p. 558/800–801). What spirit is "in it-

self" (implicitly), however, is not enough; it must "become" explicitly all
that it is implicitly, and this *becoming* is its *being* and its *doing*; it becomes
what it truly is in "reflecting on itself" (p. 558/801). Thus and only thus is
substance transformed into *subject*, "the object of *consciousness* into the
object of *self-consciousness* . . . into *concept*" (pp: 558-59/801).

One of the objections which has frequently been raised against Hegel's
Phenomenology is that at the end it leaves us no place to go; all the experiences are in, and so consciousness can now take leave of experience. The
image which Hegel uses to illustrate the whole movement, however, dispels
this objection: the movement of consciousness is circular; its end is not an
end, because it is a return to the beginning, and it is complete not as termi-
nated but as constantly embracing all its moments. The realization that
all its experiences are moments of one continuous spiritual movement does
not render spirit static; spirit is the movement itself; it is self-movement in a
way in which no other vital movement is. Substance merely as substance, it
is true, is static, merely an object; it is vitalized, becomes dynamic in becoming subject, which is to say that as the *self* progressively becomes the
object of consciousness, the object of consciousness progressively becomes
self (p. 559/801). Nor is the process complete until it is the comprehensive
grasp of reality as a whole, "the world," a grasp which in turn is possible
only if the spirit is the "world-spirit." The consciousness of self and the
consciousness of the world are coterminous, but that is a never-ending
process; to be at the end is to be at the beginning.[11]

Because the human spirit is fully aware of what it is to be spirit only
when it is aware of the divine spirit, its series of experiences which permit
it to experience itself must include religious experience. But the images in
which religious experience is clothed must give way to the concepts proper
to knowing in the full sense, and to conceive is to know self as the source of
all knowing, even knowledge of God (p. 559/801). The process is "work,"
what spirit *does*, not what *happens* to it, and what it *does* is its "actual history." But its history would be incomplete if it did not make itself the source
of all its experiences, including its religious experience. Its work is not
done until it has "spiritualized" (*begeisten*) its world, until no facet of its
consciousness is not consciousness of itself. This "work" is more than the
"observing" which *finds* reality in rational thought or rational thought in
reality (p. 559/802); it is more than *finding* divine substance in nature, a
divine substance from which it finds its individual self alienated. Even
alienation must be its own doing, which it is in "culture." It is more, too,
than finding itself as the "I" which gives meaning to reality by "using" it.
Even the consciousness of the only comprehensive object there is, "the
absolute," must be its own doing (although the elaboration of that can be
left to the *Logic*) (p. 560/802-803). Finally, its work is more than setting up

11 It is for this reason that the Hegelian "system" could not terminate in a *Logic*,
which simply presents the complete framework in which what is to be thought is to be
thought—The Idea. Hegel must go on to show that the unity of the Idea is to be found
in nature, in man (spirit), in the work of man (history, morality, law), and in the
response of man to the Absolute (art, religion, philosophy).

an empty absolute whose content is either a "yawning abyss" or "introduced externally from sense perception" (pp. 560–61/803).

In the final analysis, then, the *doing* which is spirit is neither the withdrawal of self-consciousness into its own inner depths nor a plunge into the depths of a "substance" which swallows it up. It is "*this movement* of the self which goes out of itself, plunges into its own substance, and likewise as subject has emerged from that substance, making it an objective content by transcending the distinction between objectivity and content" (p. 561/804). The "I" which is to be genuinely identical with itself must put aside all Sartrean fear of being made an "object": "Nor does the I have to cling to itself in the *form* of *self-consciousness* in opposition to the form of substantiality or objectivity, as though it were afraid of going out of itself" (p. 561/804). Gone is any worry that if it goes out of itself it will cease to be in charge: "The power of spirit rather is in going out of itself to remain identical with itself" (p. 561/804). Neither its "independence" (*Fürsichsein*) nor its "scope" (*Ansichsein*) is at stake because both are only moments in its coming to its fullness (*das An- und Fürsichseiende*). Its self-assurance has become such that its work seems effortless: "Knowing consists rather in this seeming inactivity which merely observes how what had been distinguished from it moves itself in and returns to the unity of that knowing" (p. 561/804).

With knowing in the full sense, then, the series of forms which spirit has assumed along the way has been rounded out. In each of them it had found itself making some sort of distinction between consciousness and its object, a barrier to knowing which has now been overcome. In the "concept," which is totally its own, it has found both itself and all that it knows. Knowing is truly knowing because *what* it knows is necessary, and it is the completeness of the movement it has gone through in coming to this result which constitutes the necessity of that content. At the same time spirit has all along been moving toward autonomy, because the process is one in which it progressively determines itself. By the same token, what spirit knows is not an indeterminate manifold somehow tied together in self-consciousness; it is a completely integrated because totally interrelated manifold—all united in the "self" which spirit knows (p. 562/805). To know, ultimately, is to grasp interrelatedness, mutual implication.[12]

[CONCEPT AND BEING]

The Hegelian "concept," then, the "form" in which true knowing takes place, is the complete identification of the "appearing" of the object and the "thinking" of the subject; Aristotle's "mind" which "becomes" what it knows, because the "form" of both is the same, has been given dynamic vitality in Hegel's "concept." For both the result is "science." From the vantage point of this science, Hegel can now look back to see the stages along

---

12 "To know opposition in unity and unity in opposition, this is absolute knowing" (G. W. F. Hegel, *Vorlesungen über die Geschichte der Philosophie* I–III, ed. Hermann Glockner, Sämtliche Werke, XVII–XIX [Stuttgart: Frommann, 1928], XIX 689).

the way as more than simply "forms of consciousness" or even "moments" in the growth of spirit; they are "determinate concepts" whose movement has revealed itself as "organic" (p. 562/805). Along the way, however, it was constantly necessary to distinguish between the *knowing* at any stage and the *truth* of that knowing. In science the distinction is gone; united are "the objective form of truth and the form of the knowing self in an immediate union" (p. 562/805). Because the moments of spirit's growth are also the moments of developing science, the spirit's ultimate grasp of itself as spirit *is* science; the *Wissen-schaft* of *Wissen* is spirit's self-knowledge (p. 562/805–806).

To *know* "absolutely," then, is to recognize that the stages on the journey from sensation to science are necessary; thus the "forms of consciousness" turn out to be "moments of science": "To recognize the pure concepts of science in this form (*Form*) of manifestations (*Gestalten*) of consciousness constitutes the side of science's reality according to which its essence, the concept, which in its *simple* mediation as *thinking* is posited in science, separates the moments of this mediation, and presents itself as involving interior correlation (*Gegensatz*)" (p. 562/806). Only when the movement is complete can even "we" see that everything along the way was leading to this culmination. Each assurance that at any prior stage consciousness was genuine knowing has proved unsatisfactory, and that very unsatisfactoriness pushed it forward to a knowing which is in no sense other than spirit's own doing, where its object is its own because it has *re-produced* that object and because it knows itself in so doing. If the only knowing in the form of "concept" is self-knowing, then it follows that knowing reality in the form of "concept"—the "scientific" way—is self-knowing.

Science, then, demands that the whole process we have reviewed, which is the process of conceptualization, be set forth in such a way that spirit come to consciousness that this is its process. "Science contains within itself this necessity, to bring itself out in the form of pure concept and to bring about the transition of the concept into consciousness" (p. 563/806). When this is done there comes a realization that the very "sensory certainty" with which the whole process began was itself a form of self-knowing. But because that same certainty was directed toward an object other than the self, the self-knowing involved was not autonomous. It took time—a great deal of it—for spirit to recognize that what seemed to be a *taking in* from outside is in truth a *positing* from within. Thus, the initial self-knowing is also a knowing of its limitation (its negative). By the same token, to know its own limitation is to know how to "sacrifice itself," i.e., relinquish its spurious satisfaction. The stages of this "sacrifice" in turn are stages in positing itself externally, in the form of something "*happening freely and contingently*," in time and space (p. 563/806). Thus, when spirit seems to be *finding* itself in nature, it is in reality positing itself in its thinking of nature: "Nature, externalized spirit, is in its manifest being (*Dasein*) nothing but this eternal externalization of its *constancy*, the movement which the *subject* brings about" (p. 563/807). What spirit *knows* in nature is what it puts there.

Because this self-positing of spirit is not only spatial (in nature) but also temporal, the latter aspect of its becoming is its history, but this too does not just *happen* to it; "it is a *knowing*, self-*mediating* coming-to-be" (p. 563/807). The negating of spirit's merely natural being, a negation which is essential to its growth as spirit, is its own doing also. What can seem to be just a "succession" *(Aufeinanderfolge)* of one spirit after another, each of which the one spirit takes to itself, relinquishing one to take up another, retaining only the "memory" *(Erinnerung)* of it, is in fact a continuous "going-into-itself" *(Insichgehen)*, into the dark "night of its self-consciousness" (p. 563/807), holding on to each spirit so that it is reborn in "knowing" as "a new world and a new manifestation of spirit," i.e., a world in which spirit is manifest (p. 564/807). The human spirit has progressively canceled out a whole world of objectivity "out there" in order to re-create it within itself.

Once more we see how this final chapter of Hegel's *Phenomenology of Spirit* serves as an "introduction" to a second reading. Spirit returns to the "immediate" beginning to grow once more from there, as though it had missed the point of all the successive stages in its progress. When it does so, however, it finds that "memory [*Er-innerung* = "interiorization"] has retained them and is the inner, which is in fact the higher, form of substance" (p. 564/807–808). When spirit goes back and repeats the whole movement in the realization that that whole movement proceeds from itself, it begins again at a higher level; now it sees both the necessity and the completeness of the series of forms ("spirits") it has gone through. "The realm of spirits which in this way has constructed its existential framework constitutes a series in which one dislodged the other and each took over the realm of the world from the one preceding it" (p. 564/808). The mainspring of the whole movement is spirit's revelation of its own depths, "and this is *the absolute concept* [concept and only concept]": that it should be extended in time and space is its own "outpouring" of self. The path spirit travels is "the memory *(Erinnerung)* of the spirits as they are in themselves and as each accomplishes the organization of its realm" (p. 564/808).

None of these "spirits" is eliminated in the process; they all are retained. From the point of view of the various forms of spirit's seemingly "contingent" appearance, this retention is "history"; from the point of view of their "comprehended organization," it is "the *science* of *knowing as it appears*"; from both points of view, it is "history comprehended," where *Erinnerung* becomes the "calvary of the absolute spirit," from which follows its resurrection, "without which it would be lifeless and isolated." "Absolute knowing" is a science residing in the *human* spirit which in the process described has passed beyond all the limitations besetting it; out of all these "spirits" "its own infinity gushes forth," the infinity of a "reason" which acknowledges no barriers to its knowing, a *human* knowing which is also *divine*.[13] If the human spirit has successfully gone through all its stages, all necessary to its completeness, it need look only within itself for that explication of all being which takes place in Hegel's *Logic*, "the *presentation of God* . . . *as*

13 "This divine knowing in man is precisely universal reason, which is not my reason; nor is it a common or universal capacity but being itself, the identity of being and knowing" ("Aphorismen," *Berliner Schriften*, 1829, p. 310).

he is in his eternal being before the creation of nature or of a single finite spirit." [14] *The Phenomenology of Spirit* has become Hegel's justification for doing *logic* (or any philosophical investigation) the way he does.[15]

Human reason now knows what to know is. This does not mean that we have reached the end; rather we are at the beginning of philosophical knowing. What Hegel has provided here is neither a philosophy nor a methodology; he is saying what "knowing" will be in any area of philosophical investigation; only if it has the comprehensiveness here described will philosophy be a "knowing" at all. The consciousness in question is not some disembodied spirit; it is *human* consciousness whose self-awareness is comprehensive, whose growth in knowledge is growth in self-awareness, and whose growth in self-awareness is revelatory of the truth of reality.[16] The consciousness studied here is the concrete consciousness of concrete man; but man must be made conscious that he is not concrete—not completely human—in isolation from the world, in isolation from the human community, in isolation from God.

14 *Logik*, I 31.

15 "In the *Phenomenology of Spirit* (Bamberg & Würzburg, 1807) I presented consciousness in progress from the first immediate opposition between itself and its object up to absolute knowing. This path goes through all forms of the *relationship of consciousness* to its object and has as its result the concept of science" (*ibid.*, 29).

"Absolute knowing is the truth of all the manners of being conscious, because, as the aforementioned process brought out, only in absolute knowing has the separation of the *object* from consciousness' *certainty of itself* been completely dissolved, and the truth become equal to this certainty, just as the certainty has become equal to truth" (*ibid.*, 30).

16 One wonders how someone so perspicacious as Eric Voegelin ordinarily is could be so wrong in his estimate of Hegel's endeavor. "To imagine the search for truth not to be the essence of humanity but an historical imperfection to be overcome, in history, by perfect knowledge that will put an end to the search, is an attack on man's consciousness of his existence under God. It is an attack on the dignity of man. That is the attack Hegel commits when he replaces the consciousness of concrete man by the imaginary 'consciousness' that runs its dialectical course in time to the absolute consciousness of self in the System" ("On Hegel—A Study in Sorcery," 345).

10

Preface

APART FROM THE FACT that the Preface to the *Phenomenology of Spirit* was clearly written some months after the rest, referring as it does to the progressive manifestation of spirit as having already taken place, it equally clearly "belongs to the kind of pronouncement required to be read as an epilogue instead of as a prologue." [1] It is at once Hegel's manifesto of confidence in his own method, exemplified in the total movement of the *Phenomenology*, and his declaration of confidence in the human spirit—each and every human spirit. If, then, the final chapter, "Absolute Knowing," can legitimately be called an introduction to a second reading of the *Phenomenology*, the Preface can be seen as an introduction to his entire "System," the doors of which have been opened by the movement of the *Phenomenology*. All along, the spirit has been moving toward a comprehension of itself in "science." It now becomes abundantly evident that this is not science in the ordinarily accepted sense of that term, but in the only sense in which philosophical knowing can be said to be "science." [2] As Hegel sees it, he has presented the only method capable of penetrating to the very interior of reality rather than standing outside of it and *inferring* what that interior must be. He has laboriously sought to come to terms with reality's only locus of manifestation, i.e., consciousness, and now that consciousness has revealed its depths, Hegel feels confident that he can plumb the *Logic* of reality's self-revelation to consciousness. [3]

---

[1] Loewenberg, *Hegel's Phenomenology*, p. 2.

[2] It is, of course, the whole of the *Phenomenology* and not merely its Preface which serves as an introduction to the whole of the Hegelian "system." This does not mean that the *Phenomenology* is simply a propaedeutic, preceding, but not informing, the whole system. It is in this work, as presented in 1807, that the very concept of "philosophical science" finds its justification, a justification which must remain operative throughout all Hegel's subsequent philosophical investigations (see *Logik*, I 29–30).

[3] "What constitutes the peculiar significance of this Preface . . . is that, one can say, in writing it (immediately after completing the work) Hegel for the first time had before his eyes the whole of his philosophy. 'He had just finished the *Phenomenology of Spirit*; the elaboration of successive forms constrained him no longer, but the memory of the path traveled was still vividly alive within him. For the first time he found himself at his goal—then he looked back in order to express in summation what he had wanted. That is how the Preface came into being. If ever in the course of Hegel's whole life there was an instant where he was in a position to be at once rounded out and still constantly looking forward in complete possession of his philosophical thrust and thus to express himself, it was in the weeks when he was writing the Preface to the *Phenomenology of Spirit*. At that time he stood at the apex of his philosophizing'" (Hermann Glockner, *Hegel*, 2 vols. [Stuttgart: Frommann, 1929], II 419; quoted in Metzke, *Hegels Vorreden*, p. 140).

In looking back at what his examination of consciousness has revealed, then, Hegel finds that not only the consciousness of which consciousness has been aware but also the reality of which it is aware have been growing. In one sense they have been growing side by side, in another they have been growing together, into an identity. Aristotle's "the mind somehow becomes everything" has been rendered dynamic, and Hegel is convinced that he has unraveled the mysteries of the "somehow"—better still, that the mysteries have unraveled themselves. As consciousness concretizes itself in coming to know, reality concretizes itself in coming to be known—and the knowing is the same activity as the being known, the coming-to-be of spirit.

As he begins to write, Hegel asks himself a curious question: can a "preface" be written at all? Clearly he is speaking not of the preface to a book but of the preface to a philosophy—to philosophy itself. The question then becomes, can philosophy be presented any other way than philosophically, i.e., is it possible to *talk about* philosophy or only to *do* it? If the latter, then there is no *preface-to* philosophy, there is only doing it all over again. There is even a danger in attempting to write a preface, the danger that, since philosophy deals with the universal which subsumes the particular, it will seem possible to speak of the conclusions reached as though they had meaning apart from the way of arriving at them (p. 9/67). A second danger is that a preface will attempt to enumerate the parts of the endeavor as though they were static (the way of analysis) and thus miss the dynamic (living), organic interrelationship of all the parts to each other (the way of synthesis) (p. 9/67). Nor can synthesis simply follow upon analysis; if it did, both would be external to the intimate unity of what is developing; the whole would be an "aggregate" effected only by a subject knowing (p. 10/67). In this context "talking about" even such significant universal notions as "purpose" becomes a kind of narrative which lacks conceptual dynamism.[4]

Sometimes a preface will seek to show how this philosophical approach differs from other approaches to the same subject matter. In doing so it introduces an alien interest, and the search for truth is obscured. In being contrasted with each other, philosophies are presented as pursuits of truth "in-order-that," and truth is relegated to a subordinate role, to that of a *means*. It becomes a question of simply distinguishing the true from the false—and discarding the false. This, Hegel says, is a thoroughly unphilosophical procedure which, "instead of comprehending the diversity of philosophical systems as the progressive development of truth, sees in diversity only contradiction" (p. 10/68).[5] It is as though one were to see the

---

[4] The words Hegel uses are *historisch* and *begrifflos*. The "story" of philosophy cannot be *told*; it can only be *re-enacted*. "For this reason the lifting of natural consciousness to science is for Hegel not something which would be external to science itself; rather, it belongs to the very coming-to-be, the essence of science. In this introducing to science, then, there is no question of a conducting from without, which talks about philosophy and sets down principles regarding the teaching and learning of it. Rather, there is question of a movement of philosophy itself, which has its necessary focal point in the 'individual,' in the singular I and its certainty of itself" (*ibid.*, p. 175).

[5] One is reminded of Descartes' *Discourse on Method*—the Preface to his philosophy—where diversity of philosophical positions is evidence that they are all false!

diverse stages of growth in a plant—the shoot, the bud, the fruit—as simply contradictory phases not as parts of a dynamic organic whole. The unity of truth, too, is organic, and each moment in its growth, although apparently opposed to another as the true and the false, is necessary to the whole; "and this equal necessity alone constitutes the life of the whole" (p. 10/68). Despite common opinion, then, what contradicts a philosophical system is not to be refuted and discarded; we should eliminate the one-sidedness of contradictory positions, thus "recognizing in the form of conflicting and seemingly contradictory positions mutually necessary moments" (p. 10/68).

One does not improve this situation by granting a certain organic histori-cal growth in philosophy but insisting on the incompatibility of divergent positions in a given age; genuinely opposed positions are always dialectically related to each other, "for the matter is not exhausted in its *end*, but in the *exposition* of it, nor is the *result* the *real* whole, only the result together with its coming-to-be" (p. 11/69). Conclusions without the process of arriv-ing at them are not philosophy at all. "By itself the end is the lifeless uni-versal, just as orientation to the end is the mere impulse which lacks its actuality; and the naked result is the corpse which has left the orientation behind" (p. 11/69).

Differences, merely as differences and not as complementary, do not come near what really matters (*der Sache*) in philosophy, and, therefore, to dwell on differences is to refuse to dwell on what really matters; it is to insist on the superficial to the detriment of the essential.[6] To insist on the element of diversity (*Verschiedenheit*) is to miss the element of comple-mentarity. This sort of thing is easy, because one can quite readily stand outside and judge from there. "The easiest thing is to pass judgment on something which has import (*Gehalt*) and scope (*Gediegenheit*); it is more difficult to grasp it; most difficult—and this combines the two—to come up with a presentation of it" (p. 11/69–70).

To get into philosophy one needs the training to work oneself out of what one simply takes for granted. After beginning this way one can "ac-quire the knowledge of *general* principles and points of view" (p. 11/70). Then one can ascend to those thoughts where what matters resides; then too one can either confirm it or deny it on demonstrable grounds. Finally, and then only, one can comprehend the concrete and determinate fullness of what is in question, knowing how to judge with seriousness in its regard (pp. 11–12/70). When one does this one "experiences," not in the shallow sense of grasping sensibly but in the most profound sense of going through all the forms of consciousness implied in any act of consciousness. The "experi-ence," then, of truly philosophizing is not some least common denominator on which one puts the tag "experience"; it is a very special and very serious fullness of life, a profound experience of what is really in question, involv-ing all the seriousness of plumbing its depths conceptually (p. 12/70). The philosopher "experiences" in a way in which others do not.[7] To know how

6 The term Hegel uses for difference, *Verschiedenheit*, signifies "external difference" (see *Logik*, II 34–40).

7 Experience, it should be pointed out, is inseparable from the *decision* as to how one

he does we should have to go through once more all the headings of all the sections of the *Phenomenology of Spirit*. This is what Hegel means when he says, "The true form in which the truth exists can only be its scientific system" (p. 12/70). This too makes sense of his claim that what he seeks to do is to lift "philosophy" from a "love of knowing" into an "actual knowing." It is the nature of "knowing" (*Wissen*) that it necessarily become "science" (*Wissen-schaft*); and only philosophy can satisfactorily make this clear—by bringing it about (p. 12/70).

Corresponding to the *internal* necessity of the development he discovers in examining consciousness Hegel finds also an *external* necessity, in the sense that, historically speaking, the time is now ripe for precisely the sort of philosophical science—or scientific philosophy—the movement of which the *Phenomenology* sets out to trace (p. 12/70–71). There are, however, problems in this. It is Hegel's contention that the "element of truth's existence" is the "concept" alone, a contention which at this point can, like its opposite, only be stated not elaborated. But that contention is contradicted by the spirit of his own age, which will look for truth *anywhere* but there—in religious mysticism, in romantic intuitionism, in essentially finite understanding, in sound common sense—anything to avoid the *labor* involved in genuine conceptual comprehension. "Starting from there, then, what is at the same time demanded for the presentation of philosophy is rather the opposite of conceptual form"—truth is not to be "conceptually comprehended" but "felt" (p. 13/71).

It is as though, in Hegel's own age, the "self-conscious spirit" seeks to get beyond the solidly grounded life "which it otherwise led in the element of thought," which can only be finite, by means of a "feeling of the essence" which turns out to be not so much "insight" as "edification" (p. 13/72)—the "feeling" does little more than make one "feel good." The categories are "the beautiful" (Schiller), "the sacred," "the eternal" (Schelling), "religion" (Schleiermacher), "love" (Hölderlin and Hegel himself in his youth)—anything but "the concept": "Not the concept, but ecstasy, not the coolly progressing necessity of the matter itself, but open-mouthed (*gärende*) enthusiasm, is supposed to be the attitude and the progressive expansion of the wealth of substance" (p. 13/72). Anything to avoid work.

The excuse is that conceptual knowledge, with all its detailed efforts, comes up with only *trivial* truths. Even granted that in relation to the finite (the sensible) there is knowledge in the strictly scientific sense, in relation to the infinite (the suprasensible) something else is required, whether it be non-rational faith, romantic intuition, or just plain feeling. Either knowledge is thought to remain mired in the sensible with the concept or is con-

experiences and from the system of *relevances* within which experience takes on meaning. Neither is completely free, in the sense of being arbitrary; neither is completely determined, in the sense of being inscribed in a past over which one has no control; both are *historical*, in the sense that they can be understood only in the framework of significant and coherent antecedents. It is doubtful whether, apart from history in its fullest sense— on the macrocosmic scale—the discussion of experience can get beyond a kind of universalizing of what is peculiar to the one experiencing.

sidered as taking leave of the concept in order to achieve immediate contact with the absolute. What has happened is almost a reversal of history's course. It took a long, hard effort for spirit to turn its erstwhile heavenly gaze earthward "and to render both interesting and valid the attention to the here and now as such, which was called *experience*" (p. 14/73). Now the problem is the reverse: it requires some sort of violence to raise spirit above the sensible, the earthly in which it is immersed. The spirit has become so poor "that it seems only to thirst after revival in the shallow (*dürftigen*) feeling of the divine in general. By looking at what satisfies the spirit we can measure the magnitude of its loss" (p. 14/73).[8] In contrast to this Hegel sees the human spirit as incapable of being satisfied with anything less than science, and if philosophy is to be the highest form of human endeavor, it too cannot be less than science, and this means that it "must guard itself from wanting to be edifying" (p. 14/74).

By the same token, the spirit must beware lest it fall into the error of, so to speak, settling for science but granting that romantic enthusiasm is somehow superior to it, because the reflection proper to science is confined to the finite, as is the "necessity" proper to its "concept" (pp. 14–15/74). A profound but meaningless vocabulary does not make for superiority at all; empty profundity is no less empty than empty superficiality (p. 15/74), and the human spirit can be satisfied with neither.[9] Nor can the spirit satisfy its needs by taking refuge in the ineffability of the absolute: "The force of the spirit is only as great as its expression (*Äusserung*) and its depth only as deep as the confidence with which it extends and thus expends itself in its exposition (*Auslegung*)" (p. 15/74). Again and again the emphasis is on spirit's taking upon itself the responsibility for detailed conceptual elaboration, as against a pious surrender to some sort of "divine inspiration." The refusal of conceptual rigor is an evasion: "It hides from itself that instead of being dedicated to its God it rather, by scorning measure and determinateness, manages to preserve within itself only the contingency of its content and in God only its own arbitrariness" (p. 15/74). Rigorous thinking is what the spirit does when it is awake; pious acceptance of what God gives is what it does in sleep—and the gift is a dream! (p. 15/74–75).

After this scathing denunciation of the thoughtless romanticism of his own times Hegel would seem to be giving the lie to his own contention (cf. *supra*, p. 273) that the time is ripe for spirit to soar—authentically. He is, nevertheless, still convinced that his own age is one of transition, that in it the spirit is ready to surmount its own past "in the labor of its own transformation" (p. 15/75). He detects in it the restlessness of the fetus immediately before birth; the period of gestation has been slow, but now the spirit is on the brink of that sudden qualitative leap which, like the birth of a child, in a flash reveals a whole new world (p. 16/75). With that leap, however, the spirit is no more fully developed than is that newborn child: "Its first step is only its immediacy or its mere concept" (p. 16/75). At the be-

8 Hegel, once again, seems to be as good at prophecy as he is at criticism.

9 It is small wonder that Schelling, Hegel's erstwhile friend, who was certainly intelligent enough to see himself pilloried here, should have ceased to be friendly.

ginning it has only the barest "notion" of where it is to go—to the fullness of scientific philosophy—but it is pointed in the right direction.

For the spirit an arduous road lies ahead; it will have to labor to "transform" each and every one of its inadequate "forms": "The spirit is the whole returned back into itself out of that series and out of its own expansion (*Ausdehnung*); it is that same whole become *simple concept*" (p. 16/76). It must "take" the various "forms" [10] upon itself as "moments" in its development.

The image of the newborn child is a good one and, perhaps, justifies writing this as a prologue "preface." Just as the newborn child stands at the threshold of a host of experiences which will progressively unfold for him this new world into which he has been born, so at the beginning of the *Phenomenology* the human spirit stands at the threshold of a series of experiences, each of which will be revealed as a moment in its self-developing activity of unfolding its whole new world. The first appearance of its new world is "the whole enshrouded in its own simplicity" (p. 16/76). From the vantage point from which the Preface is written, however, all the forms which consciousness has taken in its journey "are present to it still in memory," but without both the detailed elaboration of its content, which belongs to the *Logic*, and "the development (*Ausbildung*) of the form whereby distinctions are determined securely and are arranged in their firm relationships" (p. 16/76). This is not to say that for every human individual, even after Hegel, "science" will be the term of his development; it does say, however, that at the term of the *Phenomenology* "science" will not be "the esoteric possession of a few individuals" (p. 16/76). It will not be "possessed" at all, but "the intelligible form of science is the way to it offered to all and made the same for all" (p. 17/76–77). The *Phenomenology of Spirit* is that "way." What is more, what consciousness comes to *know* scientifically by traveling along this "way" is what both scientific and non-scientific consciousness are aware of—by traveling the "way" the latter becomes the former (p. 17/77).

Even at the end of the *Phenomenology* the "science" of philosophy is just beginning; its development is the "system." Nor is there anything blameworthy in being at the end only at the beginning; what would be blameworthy would be the failure to recognize both the need for development and the content to be developed in the form which is science. Here, Hegel tells us, is the source of the present crisis: "One party [Fichte] insists on the wealth of material and on intelligibility; the other [Schelling], at the very least, scorns intelligibility and insists on immediate rationality and divinity" (p. 17/77). True science must satisfy both demands; it must grasp a comprehensive wealth of content, and its grasp must be profound.

Those who insist on a wide scope of knowledge are not going to be satisfied with lofty promises which never get down to determinate details. Still, those who insist on profundity in knowledge of the absolute have an easy task extending its content; they simply take all that is already known in

[10] The term Hegel uses here is *Gestaltungen* which adds to the notion of *Gestalt* the activity of the spirit in "forming" itself.

the sciences and find it all in the absolute *idea*. Not only is all scientific knowledge subsumed in knowledge of the absolute, but what is not yet scientifically known is known to be contained there also. What they have done, however, is not to elaborate the *idea* in detail, not to make its content determinate; they simply apply one and the same vagueness over and over again: "which is simply applied externally to a diverse material and takes on a boring semblance of diversification" (p. 18/78). Granted that in the absolute all is there—that is what "absolute" means—no one gets around to showing *how* it is there. "Instead it is a monochrome formalism which attains only to differences in the material, and that because the material is already prepared and familiar" (p. 18/78). It makes no contribution to knowing.

The sort of formalism here described is an attempt to unify all knowledge under the heading of an absolute whose universality is abstract and undiversified. Its proponents (Schelling) claim that failure to be satisfied with it bespeaks a failure to master the absolute point of view, the genuinely philosophical ("speculative") way of thinking (p. 18/78–79). All they are saying, however, is that *everything* is contained in the absolute, and that this constitutes the unity of all being and knowing. To say this, Hegel tells us, "is to present the absolute as the night in which . . . all the cows are black"—indistinguishable—"it is the naïveté of vacuity as far as knowledge is concerned" (p. 19/79). The remedy for this is that "the knowledge of absolute actuality have achieved complete clarity regarding its own nature" (p. 19/79). *What* knowing is must be made clear before the knowing can be elaborated in the "System," and this means eliminating a number of positions which have become so habitual as to constitute "an obstacle for philosophical knowledge" (p. 19/79).

[THE ABSOLUTE AS SUBJECT] [11]

It is here that Hegel makes a claim which, he contends, only the full-fledged presentation of the system will validate: that the identity of knowledge and self-knowledge will make sense only when "the true is comprehended and expressed not [merely] as *substance* but equally as *subject*" (p. 19/80). What is comprehended and expressed will be a dynamism of self-revealing activity, not merely an objective category. The affinity of thought and being, without which knowledge makes no sense at all, consists not in a correspondence of thought with the static being of "substance" but in a correspondence of being with the dynamic thought of "subject." This does not mean that substantiality is to be eliminated; it does mean that substantiality must be conceived as including within itself the dynamic universality proper to *knowing*. If God, who is being in the fullest sense, is conceived of simply as "substance," whose universality is abstract, static, merely objective, he is not conceived as "spirit," and thinking itself becomes a being-acted-upon, not a conceiving (p. 20/80).

11 Although in the table of contents of the *Phenomenology*, the Preface is elaborately subdivided, it seems less cumbersome in this text to provide only major subdivisions.

Because the term "subject" can call to mind merely that element of a proposition of which a predicate is "said" or the merely private subject of romanticism's self-awareness, there can be confusion here.[12] The subject of which Hegel speaks enjoys the same degree of universality (concretely) as substance does (abstractly). Thus, the self-positing, the self-objectification, the self-negation and reconciliation, which are recognized as characteristic of consciousness, must be seen as characteristic of what consciousness is conscious of. Consciousness is activity; being is activity; and the activity is one and the same. In this context the true "is its own becoming, the circle which presupposes its end as its purpose and has this as its beginning, which is actual only by being carried through to its end" (p. 20/81). The only truth is total truth, presupposed at the beginning, achieved at the end, but only by going through the whole movement.[13]

Properly speaking, the only total knowledge there is is divine knowledge; the only total dynamism, divine life. The all-embracing circle of which Hegel speaks is divine, and of this one *could* say (as Hegel himself did in his youth) that it is the self-creating "play" of love. To say this, however, is to make the whole enterprise look too easy; it is attractive, but it ignores the omnipresent thread of negativity, with its seriousness, its pain, its patient toil. It is an abstract way of seeing the all-embracing (universal) character of the divine; it makes God himself an abstraction, undifferentiated, an "essence," but not "Spirit" whose very being is *knowing* (pp. 20–21/81).

There is a very significant sense, then, in which what is *true* does not define what is known, but what is *known* defines what is true. In this sense there is no knowledge short of total knowledge, and there is no truth short of the totality of what is known. This means that wholeness is essential to both knowledge and truth, and only the divine essence in its development is whole; whatever else is known is known only as integrated into that whole. For consciousness, however, to integrate its multiple cognitions into that whole is to separate itself from all that is "familiar" (*bekannt*) in order to reproduce it as "known" (*erkannt*). It is true that what is present to consciousness is "in itself" the absolute. But since the absolute is "subject" (*Spirit*), what it is "in itself," indeterminately, is not adequately true. It will be true only by *becoming* true, in a process of self-determination which is identical with the process of consciousness coming to *know* it; only as the "result" of this process is the absolute truly absolute.

The point of all this, obscure as it unquestionably is, is to emphasize that *words* all too commonly used to designate the absolute, such as "divine,"

---

12 "Hegel's concept of subject has nothing at all to do with subject as individual person with its subjectively private vital experience (*Erleben*) (in romanticism's sense). The *Phenomenology* is opposed precisely to the philosophical claims of mere subjectivity" (Metzke, *Hegels Vorreden*, p. 162).

13 "The whole of modern philosophy is rooted in consciousness of self. Hegel went to the very end of this movement which had already attained to a point of culmination in Fichte and in Schelling. Hegel explained to consciousness its own nature, and he brought it up to absolute knowing. He did not, like Fichte, merely present a science of consciousness, but rather of the process in which subjectivity and substantiality interpenetrate; he made knowledge of self issue from absolute spirit" (Pöggeler, "Zur Deutung," 258).

"eternal," even "absolute," by themselves express no content, are essentially abstract, "say" nothing. If they are to say anything, at the very least a proposition is required, and that means "a *becoming other*, which must be recovered, and that is a mediation" (p. 21/82). This says both that knowledge of the absolute is mediated and that there is no knowledge in the strict sense which is not mediated. What apparently frightens the Romanticists is the thought that if there is no immediate knowledge of the absolute there is no absolute knowledge (p. 21/82). The fear, however, stems from a failure to understand the function of mediation in absolute knowing (*Erkennens*).[14] Mediation is the self-movement of that which remains identical with itself, the explicitation of the implicit, "immediacy coming to be and the immediate itself" (p. 21/82).

Knowing in the strict sense (*Erkennen*), then, is "re-cognition" in the sense that it contains "re-flection" (mediation) as a positive moment. "It is reflection which makes of the true a result, but at the same time overcomes (*aufhebt*) the opposition to the becoming of the true" (p. 21/83). In this way the true which is the result of the process, absolute truth, is not different from the true at the beginning. The process, in fact, is a re-turn to initial simplicity (pp. 21–22/83). Wherever there is process (e.g., the child becoming the adult), there is an opposition (of stages) which is not resolved by being ignored. Opposition is reconciled where the complementarity of opposed moments is recognized, such that they become moments of the one process which is the whole, the truth (p. 22/83). This, after all, is what "reason" is all about, the process of reconciliation which is not confined to the activity of a thinking subject over against a non-thinking world.

The whole thing can be looked at teleologically, i.e., as a vital process, wherein the end is present at the beginning, and the process of self-movement is the attaining of the end. From this point of view "reason is purposeful activity" (p. 22/83),[15] which has nothing to do with the "external finality" of serving a purpose other than its own development. It is characteristic of vital growth, e.g., of the organism, that its subject is at once at rest within itself and moving, i.e., self-moving. That is what process essentially is, and there is nothing paradoxical in saying that its result is the same as its beginning: "Its *beginning* is its *goal*" (p. 22/83); movement begins by having a goal toward which it moves. By the same token, there is nothing paradoxical in saying that the real is the same as its concept—which says simply that

---

[14] It is important to note the shades of difference in the cognates of *kennen*, "to know," in the sense of knowing someone. *Bekennen* is to know in the sense of being acquainted or familiar with; *erkennen* carries the connotation of "recognize." The single term *wissen* (of which, incidentally, *Bewusst-sein* is a sort of cognate) also carries these various connotations, but they must be gathered from the context.

[15] From one point of view, it should cause no difficulty at all to say with regard to any process that once the process has been gone through, the end of the process is recognizable as having been present from the beginning. The difficulty arises from looking at a process as though its end were determinately recognizable from the beginning. The aesthetic model, perhaps, could obviate the difficulty of this second way of viewing process. What needs to be remembered is that the inevitability proper to the work of art simply is not the inevitability proper to logic, mathematics, or the essentially repetitive teleology of mere nature.

knowing is knowing the real—the vital process of the real becoming actual is the same as the conceptual process of comprehending it. "The actual is the same as its concept only for this reason, that the immediate as purpose has the self or pure actuality in itself" (p. 22/83). What is "actualized" becomes what from the beginning it was to become, and the becoming is its own doing (act).

What reason does is comprehend this in concept. "The purpose effected or the existing (*daseiende*) actual is movement and unfolded becoming," a movement which is the movement of reason, "and precisely this restlessness is the self" (p. 22/83). To speak of actualization as self-development is to say of what is actualized what one says of a self: "That which is reflected back on itself, however, is precisely the self, and the self is identity relating itself to itself, simplicity" (p. 22/84). A self is *identical* with itself because it *identifies* itself with itself.[16]

Having come in a somewhat roundabout way to see that it makes sense to speak of the absolute, the whole, as "subject," there remains a risk, the risk of wanting to capture that truth in a proposition. The desire to "say" something about God issues in propositions such as "God is the eternal," "God is the moral order of the world," "God is love," etc.. God is made the "subject"—of a proposition—but he is not recognized as a self-mover; nor is the predicate recognized as his self-movement. Instead "God" is a meaningless sound, and the predicate "says" *what* he is (p. 22/84). There is, then, no point in speaking about God at all; it makes just as much sense to speak *about* "the eternal," "the moral order of the world"—or like the ancients, "the Idea," "Being," "the One"—such expressions serve equally well as subjects of propositions. God, then, is not a "subject" of which a predicate is "said" at all, not "being," not "essence," not "universal"; God is subject as self-reflecting process.[17] Quite obviously, if one reads Hegel's Preface as prologue and prologue only, one will anticipate in such a way as to fail to see the contradiction between a self-reflecting subject and the subject of a proposition. "The subject is taken as a fixed point on which predicates are hung as on a hook by a movement which belongs to the one who knows the point and which for this reason cannot also be looked on as belonging to the point" (p. 23/84). The subject of the proposition, then, is not a subject; it does not move. Speaking of God in propositions, then, is hopeless; the subject of a proposition has to be a motionless point. To speak of the absolute as subject in both senses, then, is to make of him both a motionless point and self-moving, a patent contradiction which makes the concept impossible (p. 23/83–84).

Hegel now draws two important consequences from the inadequacy of propositional language for expressing "absolute truth." (1) Absolute truth can reside only in systematic "scientific" knowing: "Knowing can be actual and be presented only as science or as *system*" (p. 23/85). (2) Philosophical

16 It should be noted that, although for Hegel "substance" must be "subject," in the sense that its articulation is self-differentiation, it is not "ego." Mere "ego" and mere "substance," however, are equally unarticulated.
17 The play on the term "subject" does become a bit bewildering.

"principles" are not true; they are only the "beginning" of a movement toward truth: "Furthermore, a so-called fundamental proposition or principle
of philosophy, if it is true, is for that very reason also false, insofar as it is
merely a fundamental proposition or principle" (p. 23/85). Such a principle
is readily refuted, precisely because it is only a principle, an abstract universal, a beginning; and the basic refutation is self-development itself. Refutation, however, is merely negative; the positive side must be seen, too
(p. 23/85).[18] But even the positive is also negative: the principle (beginning)
is positive as "*foundation of the system*"; it is negative because "in fact the
foundation of the system is only *its beginning*" (pp. 23–24/85).

Gradually we can begin to see why Hegel considered his own age as one
of transition to an adequate philosophical standpoint, despite the romanti-
cist aberrations he criticizes so violently. It is not, however, to the philosophy of his age that he gives credit for this, but to its *religion*.[19] The breakthrough comes with the conception of the absolute as "Spirit," and that is
initially a religious conception. It is "the most exalted concept, one which
belongs to the more recent period and to its religion. The spiritual alone
is the *actual*" (p. 24/85–86). As spiritual the absolute is both objectively
(*an sich*) and subjectively (*für sich*) absolute. Initially, however, i.e., on the
level of religion, it is that only "for us"; through the eyes of religion we
objectify God as "spiritual *substance*" (p. 24/86). Still, an object such as
this immediately transcends mere substantiality and is "just as immediately
as a transcended object reflected into itself" (p. 24/86). What spirit "is" is
what spirit "produces" in this movement of reflection, and this self-production is the pure concept. None of which, of course, makes sense if the "is" in
question is that of the mere proposition. For spirit, the pure concept is "at
the same time the objective element in which spirit has existence (*Dasein*),
and in this manner spirit is in its existence for itself object reflected into
itself" (p. 24/86).

What this is saying is that the self-consciousness of the divine Spirit,
initially only "spiritual substance," and the self-consciousness of the human
spirit come down to one process of self-consciousness. The statement, however, is far less startling if it is seen to mean that human knowledge of God
as absolute and human knowledge of self are coterminous. It will be even
less startling if we recall that, for Hegel, a knowledge of the part (human
self-knowledge) is truly "knowledge" only if it is also knowledge of the whole
(of the absolute) and that knowledge of the whole is itself truly "knowledge"
only if it is also knowledge of the part, in its determinateness—the lesson of
the whole diatribe against the indeterminate absolute of Schelling. In any
event, only if we grasp the significance of a knowledge which is at once a
knowing of the whole in the part and of the part in the whole shall we
grasp what Hegel means by "science." "The spirit which knows itself thus

---

[18] Cf. what Hegel has to say about "refutation" in *Einleitung in die Geschichte der
Philosophie*, ed. Johannes Hoffmeister (Hamburg: Meiner, 1940), p. 128.

[19] Cf. *Vorlesungen über die Geschichte der Philosophie* III (Sämtliche Werke XIX)
151–54, 200 on the significance of religion for the modern turn. Spirit speaks to spirit and
tells it what spirit is.

developed as spirit is *science*. Science is spirit's actuality and the realm which spirit builds for itself in its own element" (p. 24/86). The "actuality" of divine and of human knowing "is" the same, *Wissenschaft*.

God's self-knowledge is in fact creation, which is to say that the mode of divine creative activity is self-knowing. By the same token, human self-knowledge is re-creation, which is to say that human re-creation of the whole, human "science," is human self-knowing. Self-knowing is the foundation of all knowing: "Pure *self-knowing* in absolute other-being, this ether *as such*,[20] is the fundamental basis (*Grund und Boden*) of science, i.e., it is *knowing (Wissen) in general (im allgemeinen)*" (p. 24/86). This is but another way of saying "this is what *knowing* is all about." When "consciousness" is "in this element" it will be "knowing," but the "element" itself is complete and lucidly clear "only through the movement of its coming-to-be" (p. 24/86).

Once more it seems in order to attempt to put more clearly what Hegel expresses obscurely. There is "scientific" knowing only where there is "pure spirituality," i.e., self-activity (conceiving) with no element of "being-acted-upon." Because it is "knowing" it is simply universal; because it is "active" knowing it resides in Spirit and Spirit alone (pp. 24–25/86–87). Strictly speaking, then, knowing in its strictest sense is not the relationship of a subject to a world outside itself; it is its reflective relationship to a world within itself.[21] The comprehensiveness of concept consists in an activity which is totally spiritual, whose object is totally spiritual. This is *"transfigured essentiality* . . . the *being* which is reflection into itself"* (p. 25/87). If human self-consciousness can raise itself to this "ether"—climb the "ladder" of science—its very life will be its "absolute knowing," i.e., its consciousness of self as absolute.

Lest all of this seem to be a biography of "consciousness" which has left the human individual far behind, Hegel assures us that the individual has the "right" to expect that science will extend its ladder to him, i.e., let him know that he himself is the ladder. The basis for the individual's "right" is the presence within himself of the "form" of science, "his immediate certainty of himself," his "unconditioned being," i.e., the not-being-acted-upon, which is present in each of the "forms" of consciousness detailed in the *Phenomenology* (p. 25/87). In the individual there is, however, a resistance to science, and it stems from the prejudice of "objective" consciousness, the conviction that to be "objective" is to know "things" over against self and self over against things.[22] But this is to confuse *self* with mere individual *subjectivity* (ego), which science does not do. In fact, from the point of view of science we can recognize that for consciousness to know itself "all alone by itself" is to miss spirit entirely.

Naïve consciousness and scientific consciousness, then, are at odds with each other. For the former, science is as far removed from self-knowledge

20 "The ether is the absolute Spirit related to itself but does not know itself as absolute Spirit" (*Jenenser Logik*, p. 197; see also Hyppolite, *Phénoménologie*, I 24*n*44).

21 Even the "knowing" which is proper to "positive science" is achieved by reflection on its own concepts.

22 The common prejudice that to be objective is to leave self out of the picture.

as possible; in science the self loses itself. For the latter, on the other hand, to be scientific is to possess itself totally, i.e., to possess its *total self*. It is, thus, easy to see why naïve consciousness resists the latter concept of science; to surrender itself to that sort of science seems like "walking on its head," an unnecessary violence to itself which it is unprepared to undertake. Whatever genuine science may actually be, to merely immediate self-consciousness it *seems* perverse and unreal (p. 25/87–88).

[THE UNITY OF CONSCIOUSNESS AND SELF-CONSCIOUSNESS]

The problem of the *Phenomenology*, then, is to show that objective consciousness and self-consciousness are not at odds with each other, that a gain in one is not a loss in the other, that self-consciousness is inseparable from science (p. 26/88). What is more, Hegel tells us, where science is not actualized as self-consciousness, it is only implicitly science, a goal to be achieved, but achievable only when consciousness is conscious of itself as spirit, not merely of spirit as substance. Objective consciousness must make the implicit explicit; it must make itself one with self-consciousness, which it can do only as spirit, not as merely individual subjectivity (p. 26/88). "This becoming of *science in the strict sense* (*überhaupt*), i.e., of *knowing*, is what this *Phenomenology of Spirit* presents" (p. 26/88). It begins with a sensory consciousness which is "spiritless." The long road to "knowing proper" is the process of consciousness working through itself. What the *Phenomenology* is not, however, is a method of showing non-scientific consciousness how to be scientific (Kant); nor does it lay the foundations of science (Fichte); least of all is it an "enthusiasm" [23] for science (Schelling), which *begins* with absolute knowing, "as though shot out of a pistol," and handles other points of view by conveniently ignoring them (p. 26/88–89).

The real work of the *Phenomenology* is "that the universal individual, the self-conscious spirit, be examined in its process of training" (p. 26/89).[24] In this context each of the forms which pass in review is a particular form, and as they pass in review they are cumulatively taken up into each succeeding higher form (p. 26/89), so that one by one they constitute preparatory stages along the way (p. 27/89). As stages these are stages in the growth of the "universal spirit," such that, even though the single individual (presumably who reads the *Phenomenology*) must go through them, he does so as through stages "already passed through" (p. 27/89). The "passing through" is the process whereby substance which is universal "gives itself self-consciousness and, thus, produces its own coming-to-be and its own reflection into itself" (p. 27/90). In this way spirit's consciousness is universal, and the individual's realization that his consciousness of self is identified with this spirit universalizes individual consciousness.

---

[23] *Begeisterung*. The term is particularly important here, contrasting as it does with the true process of *Begeistung* ("spiritualization") (cf. *supra*, p. 265; *infra*, p. 284).

[24] In the present context "the universal individual" (*das allgemeine Individuum*) does not signify the individual who "is" the universal, which he is only at the end, i.e., having made the transition. It simply signifies the individual *as individual*, not as *any particular* individual, not this or that determinate individual.

What science does in all this is to manifest both the completeness of the process and the necessity of the development: "The goal is spirit's insight into what knowing is" (p. 27/90). The process forbids impatience; it is inevitable that the process should be long, both historically and in the growth of the individual; it is necessary that spirit linger at each stage along the way, not leaping to the next but waiting to be forced onward. What we who follow after on the path are spared is the successive "transcending of existential status"; what we must not escape is "representing the forms and familiarity with them" (p. 28/91); what must pass before our gaze in such a way that we become acutely aware of it is that the whole "is the activity of the *universal self* and the interest of thinking" (p. 28/92). What we progressively realize as we go along is that familiarity is not enough; knowledge is much deeper. In fact, familiarity can be an obstacle to knowing: "The familiar as such, precisely because it is familiar, is for that very reason not known" (p. 28/92).[25] This means that we must refuse to be satisfied with what is familiar; knowledge (*Erkennen*) is re-cognition or it is not knowledge at all. The most striking example of this is the use of familiar "words," whose very familiarity hinders knowledge; they retain their fixed meanings and there is movement only from one to the other. Strictly speaking, there is no movement, only a consistency in the employment of terms, which is at best superficial (p. 29/92).

Overcoming familiarity in order to promote knowledge, of course, is not particularly new or startling; "analysis," which is the work of "understanding," has always done that, and when it does, the elements of the analysis are "the immediate property of the self" (p. 29/92). Nor is it enough, even on this level, that analysis be the work of understanding; there has to be some sense in which the concrete which is analyzed "breaks itself up," is "self-moving." Just as the appearing of what appears is the consciousness of it, so the understanding's analysis of its object is the object's self-analysis—although it is not grasped as such at that level. The negativity of thought and the self-negation of the real are the same movement. "That, however, the accidental as such separated from its context, that what is bound to and is real only in connection with another gains an existence of its own and a detached (*abgesonderte*) freedom is the extraordinary power of the negative; it is the energy of thought, of the pure I" (p. 29/93). In thought the real becomes unreal and, in this sense, dies. Yet this sort of death is no obstacle to the life of spirit, precisely because spirit breathes new life into the lifeless unreal; it re-creates the concrete union in which it lived. "Not the life, however, which shrinks from death and keeps itself pure of corruption is the life of spirit; rather that life puts up with death and retains itself in death" (p. 29/93). Spirit can confront the negative and spend time with it. In fact, "this spending time is the magical force which transforms the negative into being" (p. 30/93). It brings about that change in "substance" whereby from the dead "object" which is analyzed it becomes the "subject" which differentiates itself, which "does not have mediation outside itself but is this

25 Kaufmann, whose translation of the Preface is for the most part illumining, here obscures the issue simply by reversing the order. His "what is familiar is not known simply because it is familiar" misses the force of the "because" (*Hegel*, p. 406).

[mediation] itself" (p. 30/94), i.e., this self-mediation is the very actuality of substance.[26]

What begins to come through now is the realization that it is not enough to recognize the conceptual elements of analysis as belonging properly to self-consciousness. This is no more than the recognition by naïve consciousness that universality is its own contribution. It was, says Hegel, the ancients who performed the arduous task of getting that across, and because they did, it is not today's task. Now the problem is to show that the very same process of universalization is "an emergence of the universal from the concrete and from the existing manifold . . . thoroughly to actualize and spiritualize (*begeisten*) the universal by transcending fixed, determinate thoughts" (p. 30/94). The task of the ancients was to make fluid the fixity of "sensible existence"; today's task is that of making fixed *thoughts* fluid, and it is the more difficult task (p. 30/94). It can be done, however, if thinking ceases to look upon itself as the only factor in the knowing process and recognizes itself as a moment in a larger conceptual process, if it "relinquishes the *fixity* both of its own self-positing and of the pure concrete which is I itself in contrast to its diversified content" (p. 31/95). With this, thoughts cease to be the "subjective" activities of the thinker and are identified with the "objective" movement of reality—provided, of course, that reality itself be permitted to be "conceptual." "By means of this movement pure thoughts become *concepts* and are for the first time what they truly are, self-movement, circles, what their substance is, spiritual essentialities (*Wesenheiten*)" (p. 31/95).

It is this movement of pure spiritual essentialities which constitutes the "scientificity" of genuine knowing. "Essentialities" are at once *objective* and *subjective*.[27] It is they which bring about "the necessary extension" of the content of consciousness "into an organic whole," i.e., the restoration of what was broken down in analysis to its pristine organic unity (p. 31/95). The necessity of the concept embraces both the world of reality and the consciousness of this world: "Through the movement of the concept this way will embrace the thoroughgoing world-ness (*Weltlichkeit*) of consciousness in the necessity of that world-ness" (p. 31/95).[28] Once spirit has attained to this knowledge of what it is to be spirit it will have achieved the *first* part of philosophical science. What distinguishes this part from the rest—Logic, Philosophy of Nature, and Philosophy of Spirit—is that it does not involve the actual return of spirit to itself in order to plumb its own depths; it is the pre-condition for all the rest. Now, "the very mention of this difference leads

---

[26] At the risk of being tiresome, we must insist that for Hegel *ist* is not the propositional copula.

[27] Hegel gives a detailed explanation of "essentialities" in the first part of his *Science of Logic*, "Doctrine of Essence," where he treats the objective contribution of subjectivity, a treatment which is only preparatory to the full "Doctrine of the Concept."

[28] I have chosen to translate *Weltlichkeit* by "world-ness" rather than "worldliness," because the latter term in English connotes "this-worldliness," which is certainly not what Hegel means (*pace* Kojève). The "world" is the totality of what is known, in knowing which consciousness knows itself—and vice versa.

to the exposition of a few of the fixed (fester) thoughts which in this context tend to emerge" (p. 31/96).

If we look at consciousness simply as a phenomenon, we find that it has two "moments," cognizing (subjectivity) and the cognized (objectivity). As related to each other, each is the negative of the other. What consciousness does not initially realize, however, is that subjectivity and objectivity both designate only what is contained in its "experience," and what is contained in experience shares the "spiritual" nature of experience: "Consciousness cognizes and grasps nothing other than what is in its experience, for what is therein is simply the spiritual substance, and that indeed as *object* to *itself*" (p. 32/96). As object to itself, however, spirit is somehow "other" in relation to itself. Experience, then, is a "movement" whereby whatever is experienced makes itself "other" in becoming "the property of consciousness" (p. 32/96). Now, if knowing is to be an *identity* of the knowing and the known, the dissimilarity between them—between "the I and the substance" —would seem to be an obstacle to knowing. If knowing is, rather, a process of *identification*, then dissimilarity is essentially the moving force, the "soul" Hegel calls it, likening it to the "void," as the condition of movement, in the philosophy of the ancient atomists (p. 32/97).[29] What is not comprehended at this initial stage of consciousness is that the moving force is going to turn out to be "the self," the very source of differentiation. Nor is consciousness initially aware that "substance," as the unified totality of objectivity, must differentiate itself, i.e., contain "dissimilarity" within itself. Now, if self-differentiation is essentially a function of "subject," the self-differentiating substance is also subject, and the identification of knowing and the known is accomplished in "spirit," which in "comprehending" objectivity comprehends its own spiritual activity. The process of identification is "the concept." "Being is absolutely mediated—it is substantial content which is just as immediately property of the I, has the character of a self, i.e., is concept" (pp. 32–33/97). The full realization of this last is the term of the *Phenomenology of Spirit*, the "knowing" which spirit has been working toward all along. "What spirit prepares for itself in the *Phenomenology* is the element of knowing" (p. 33/97).[30]

All the stages which spirit has been working through in the long process

29 "The 'soul,' we might say, is the vital principle of the mere 'I,' which like mere 'substance' is initially undifferentiated. In *Encyclopedia*, par. 318–319 (1817), Hegel makes it clear that the soul is life on the margin of consciousness, that it primitively feels its bifurcation, its antagonism with otherness. It is subjectively anchored to its future self-conscious career and yet mired in the blind universality of nature. On the other hand (par. 323), the opposition is productive and necessary. Here is the primary internal opposition in the genesis of the human condition" (Kelly, "Hegel's 'Lordship and Bondage,'" in MacIntyre, *Hegel*, pp. 203–204).

30 "Phenomenology is the science of consciousness, 'insofar as consciousness is in general the cognizing of an object, interior or exterior.' In a broad sense, then, consciousness has three degrees, according to the nature of its object. The object is either the exterior object, the I itself, or finally something objective pertaining to the I (thought). The science of consciousness, then, is divided into: consciousness, consciousness of self, reason" (Hyppolite, *Phénoménologie*, I 31–32n60; cf. Hegel, "Phänomenologie," *Philosophische Propädeutik*, Nos. 5, 6, 9).

leading to the term of the *Phenomenology* turn out to be "moments" in the *unification* of "being" and "knowing." Now that the "element" of this *unity* has been elaborated, "the movement" of its diversified content, "which organizes itself into the whole, is *logic* or *speculative philosophy*" (p. 33/97). It should be noted, incidentally, that Hegel employs "speculative" in its original sense: "speculative philosophy" is a philosophy which "looks within."

To say that all this is a "process," however, poses a problem, especially since it is a process of spirit "appearing." If at any stage of the process toward a science which has "truth" as its goal, spirit is only "appearing," then its very appearance would seem to be other than true, i.e., false (not true), and therefore not worthy of consideration. To pose this as a problem, of course, presupposes a clear distinction between "the true" and the "not true" (the false), which would seem to be a very arbitrary distinction prior to the attainment of "the true." [31] What is more, says Hegel, the very notion of "the false" upon which the objection is based is an obstacle to "entry into truth" (p. 33/98). It demands that philosophical knowing be modeled on mathematical (non-philosophical) knowing, where true and false can be antecedently distinguished (by postulate).

In this view it is taken as given that true and false are simply contradictories which mutually exclude each other; if true, not false; if false, not true. But truth is not a "given" value, the way a coin whose value is "stamped" upon it is given and can be put in one's pocket. Even less is "the false" a given; if it were, there would be an "absolutely false," which could only be the non-existent (or, perhaps, "the devil"!). As a universal term covering whatever is not true, "false" has, of course, its distinct intelligibility—but only as *abstraction* (pp. 33–34/98). In the concrete the true is also not true, i.e., not completely true, and the false is also not false, i.e., not completely false. Thus, even if we grant that a part isolated from the whole (substance) is negative and therefore false in relation to the whole, we must also admit that this is an abstract way of speaking. As concrete, the whole (substance) contains its own negative, "partly as distinction and determination of the content, partly as *simple* distinguishing, i.e., as self and knowing in general" (p. 34/98). One might say, if it is necessary to introduce distinction (negativity) in order to get to truth, it is necessary to introduce falsity to get at the truth.

It is in this way that we must try to understand Hegel's startling statement, "one can know falsely" (p. 34/98), i.e., one's *knowing* can be inadequate to *what is known*. The inadequacy, however, is an essential moment in the movement toward adequate knowing, i.e., truth. Nor is the inadequacy of partial knowing simply discarded when truth is known; it remains present in the truth as known, which is to say that the path to truth is integral to truth. Lest this seem, however, to contradict the very notion of "absolute knowing," it should be added that Hegel is not saying that "the false" is a

---

[31] One is again reminded of Descartes' procedure in the *Discourse*: prior to establishing what is *true* Descartes knew that the divergent opinions of his predecessors were "false" (errors).

component of "the true." As false, i.e., as isolated from the dialectical process, "the false" cannot be integral to "the true"; but all this says is that "true" cannot be "false" according to the meanings which the terms have outside the dialectical process: "As false"—i.e., isolated—"the false is no longer a moment of the true" (p. 34/99).[32] In the abstract "the false" is the contradictory of "the true"; in the concrete they are complementary.

[THE NATURE OF PHILOSOPHICAL TRUTH]

Here it is that the danger of "dogmatism" comes in. It is the conviction that vital truth can be fixed in a proposition, a "dogma," which proposition can be immediately known and held onto for all eternity. A statement of historical fact or a mathematical equation may be eternally true, even after the process of arriving at them has been discarded, i.e., without the "mediation" involved. The same cannot be said of philosophical truth or philosophical knowing.[33] The *Phenomenology* may be an "introduction" to the system, "the first part of the system"; nevertheless, it plays an active role throughout the system.

The difference between philosophical knowledge and knowledge of historical facts can be handled quite briefly. Historical facts are contingent events; as events they either happened or they did not; nor is there any necessary connection between the events and the knowledge of them. It should be noted, of course, that the term for "historical" here is *historisch*, which pertains to the kind of knowledge derivable from a record of the events and has no connection with what Hegel calls a philosophical comprehension of the significance of "history" (*Geschichte*). Still, even establishing the truth or falsity of the record of historical events requires, he tells us, the mediation of self-consciousness, in the sense that careful research is necessary, and research demands reflection (p. 35/100).

The treatment of mathematical knowledge could well seem more controversial, especially since it evidences no profound understanding of mathematics. It should be noted, however, that Hegel is not impugning mathematics; he is simply rejecting it as a model for philosophical knowledge because it is superficial, in no pejorative sense of the term—it tells us a great deal about the surface of reality, nothing about its inner dynamism. As with regard to the knowledge of historical facts, however, Hegel begins his discussion of mathematical knowledge by pointing out that knowing answers is not

---

32 The relationship of dialectical "moments" is simply not that of mutually exclusive abstractions.

33 "In particular Hegel summarily rejects the opinion that in the *Phenomenology* there is question only of a 'negative' preparatory stage which is supplanted—and thus can appear as possibly false—by true knowing, which has gone beyond the opposition of consciousness and object. Precisely the path consciousness has trod remains essential for the understanding of being; it is not eliminated, but 'transcended,' i.e., for Hegel too; it is not simply negated but as a negated moment at once retained and lifted to a higher level. It is clear that here stubborn dogmatism, which swears on a single principle and reckons with 'true' and 'false' like minted coins, fails completely and from beginning to end misconstrues the 'nature of philosophical truth'" (Metzke, *Hegels Vorreden*, p. 185).

knowing mathematics; the former can be learned by rote (*auswendig*), the latter only by an inner appropriation (*inwendig*) of mathematical processes, proofs. Immediately, then, an important difference crops up: the mathematical proof is not dictated by the movement of the mathematical content; the process is extrinsic to what is being proved. It is the activity of the mathematician which reveals the truth of his theorem; the construction he employs is external to the "matter" with which he deals (p. 35/100–101).[34] There is no *knowing* the answer without knowing the process—as in philosophical knowledge—but in mathematics the process, the movement, is all in the knower; in it there is missing the double movement which integrates subject and object, where both are "moments" in the process (p. 36/101).

In a sense, then, the geometrical construction "falsifies"; the figure in question is broken up by the mathematician into other figures and then reconstructed in order to reach a conclusion.[35] What is more, Hegel tells us, not only is the matter of mathematics deficient as object of true knowing, even the *knowing* is faulty. (*a*) The necessity of the construction employed is not evident, which is to say that the construction is not dictated by the problem but by the established rules for "doing" mathematics; and (*b*) the end, what is to be proved, is related to the means of proving "externally"—there is no genuine integration of means and ends (p. 37/102). To which, one might reply, "so what, so long as the answer is correct?" But that is exactly Hegel's point; mathematics with its "correct" answers must stay on the surface of reality, and that is not enough for philosophy.

Hegel does not at all question the exactness of mathematical knowledge; his point is that the exactness of its knowledge is based on the limitedness of its *purpose* and the triviality of its *subject matter*. Its purpose, i.e., the "concept" it seeks to establish, is a relationship of "magnitude" (not necessarily spatial), a relationship which is singularly "inessential" and foreign to "the concept" in the deeper sense. Mathematical thought is essentially abstract and can, therefore, never issue in a comprehensive grasp of reality. That which mathematical thought does grasp, its "matter," Hegel tells us somewhat enigmatically is "space and the *one*," presumably extension and number, every number being a unity (p. 37/103).

Although it is doubtful that anyone today needs to be convinced that mathematics is a tool affording an extremely partial grasp of reality, what Hegel has to say about it negatively does serve to highlight what he looks for in philosophical knowledge. Thus, when he says that mathematics exhibits no organic unity of truths, that its connections are not necessary, based on the nature of its subject matter, he points to the total interconnectedness of the reality with which philosophy is concerned. When he says that the

---

[34] The objection might be raised that Hegel's discussion of mathematics is confined to geometry, but since he is not concerned with mathematics as such but only with a mathematical way of philosophizing, he may be excused for confining himself to the most conspicuous example of that, Spinoza's *more geometrico*.

[35] It should be pointed out that Hegel, who was mathematically unsophisticated, by present standards at least, seems unaware that mathematical concepts are constructs to begin with and that the further constructs employed to "prove" them belong to the logic of these concepts.

propositions of mathematics are simply expressions of equality and hence "dead," he is emphasizing once more the dynamic character of the "is" in the "speculative" proposition (p. 37/103). When he insists that mathematics as such even fails to see the significance of incommensurability (e.g., of diameter and circumference of a circle), he is illustrating the infinitude of the conceptual relationship which mathematics cannot fathom (p. 38/104). Finally, he is saying quite simply that to take mathematical knowledge as the model for "scientific" philosophy is to impoverish philosophy immeasurably (p. 38/104).

It might be argued, of course, that while pure mathematics, which Hegel claims simply ignores the relationship of time and space, may be susceptible to his criticisms, applied mathematics is not. In mechanics, physics, astronomy, cosmology, etc., it is precisely the mathematicizing of the time–space relationship which has produced such remarkable results. Hegel is not about to deny that the results are remarkable or significant; he does say, however, that what this sort of mathematics involves is an application of formulas to the objects of sensible experience, which may ultimately show us how to blow up the universe but not how to find meaning in existence. Somewhat ironically he adds that mathematics even shows the importance of "proofs" for knowledge, "since, where it has nothing better, it prizes even the empty illusion of proof" (p. 38/104). What is more, a critique of mathematical proofs in regard to the space–time relationship will show how necessary another, higher form of knowledge is. Time, for example, is "the existential concept itself" (p. 38/104),[36] about which mathematics can tell us nothing. In fact, mathematics turns the self-movement of reality into a motionless content—points, lines, surfaces, instants (p. 39/105).

With mathematics out of the way as a contender to the title of "absolute knowing," Hegel turns once more to philosophical knowledge.[37] Like any science—like mathematics—philosophy is concerned with what characterizes the reality it knows. Unlike other sciences—particularly mathematics—it is concerned only with the "essential" characteristics of reality, and what characterizes reality essentially is its own self-determination, the "concept" wherein reality is "the self-positing, having its own life in itself" (p. 39/105). This, of course, makes sense only if reality as a whole is an organic totality, which is precisely what Hegel claims that it is. It is a whole made up of essentially interrelated and mutually complementary parts, and the life of this whole, like the life of consciousness as spirit, is its "concept." This, incidentally, does not mean that there is only one concept; it does mean that no part of the whole is conceptually comprehended except as integrated in the conceptual framework of the whole.

---

[36] A somewhat terse way of saying, it would seem, in a "speculative" proposition that the actualization of reality in its concept necessarily has temporal dimensions, or that time is the "element" in which knowledge as a process takes place.

[37] It might be argued, of course, that mathematics never was such a contender; those who exalt the claims of mathematics do not believe in "absolute knowing." Quite true; but the claim that the philosopher must come up with proofs which are acceptable to the mathematician is not too uncommon, and more than one philosopher has had to handle it.

An organism for Hegel is a process which generates its own moments, and as such it is the positive reality which contains its own negative, i.e., it constantly becomes, thus negating what it is (in conceptual terms, "falsifying"). The process, then, which is the "appearing" corresponding to the "conceiving," is the enduring dialectic of constancy and inconstancy, which is life itself. "Appearing is the coming-to-be and passing-away which itself does not come-to-be or pass-away, but rather is in itself and constitutes the actuality and movement proper to the life of truth" (p. 39/105). If truth, then, has a life of its own, the method of scientific hypothesis—setting up a proposition, finding "grounds" for it, refuting its opposite with other "grounds"—"is not the form in which truth can make its entrance" (p. 40/106). Such a method is one "employed" by the thinker but "external" to the reality it seeks to probe —good for day-to-day coming to terms with reality or with historical events (facts) but affording no "knowledge" of reality (p. 40/107); conviction, perhaps, but not knowledge (p. 41/107).

This does not mean that knowing can dispense with method. It does not, above all, mean that either the loose kind of "ratiocination" (*Räsonnieren*) which characterizes conversation or debate, or the more rigid process which characterizes scientific pomposity, is to be replaced by the "non-method" of conjecture, of enthusiasm, of the arbitrariness proper to prophetic utterance; any such non-method excludes science entirely (p. 41/107). Nor will the Kantian triadic *schemata,* so conspicuous, for example, in the table of categories, guarantee scientific knowing. Precisely because these triads are static rather than dynamic they can serve at best as a pre-condition for science, not as authentically scientific.[38] The *schema* (particularly in the hands of Kant's followers) is lifeless and thus becomes more properly a "scheme," wherein the organization of the material is imposed from without; a "table" of categories manifests no internal structuration of reality (it is, in fact, applicable only to "appearance") (p. 41/108).

This sort of "formalism" pretends to come to terms with the "life" of what appears (*einer Gestalt*) when it can attach to it a predicate out of the *schema.* Where, however, there is no internal self-structuring of the material, order in predication is arbitrary, no authentic interrelationship is forthcoming, and there emerges only "a circle of mutual contrast (*Gegenseitigkeit*) which does not permit one to experience what the matter in question itself is, neither what the one nor what the other side of the contrast is" (p. 41/108). Where there is no dynamic complementarity, no genuine mutual implication, "the real" (*die Sache*) does not reveal itself. Available predicates, then, are partly sensible determinations "drawn from common intuition" (pp. 41–42/108), predicates which *say* very little but are supposed to *mean* more than they say, e.g., strength, weakness, expansion, contraction. Partly they are

---

[38] "Hegel's fundamental complaint, then, is that Kant analysed the categories as functions of thought, not when they were functioning in actual knowing, but only in their status as necessary conditions for knowing contained in the formal structure of the understanding for the purpose of providing the ground on which objectivity is based" (John Smith, "Hegel's Critique of Kant," *The Review of Metaphysics,* 26, No. 3 [March 1973], 443). Cf. *Enzyklopädie,* No. 41.

equally meaningless determinations belonging to the level of thought, e.g., subject, object, substance, cause, universality, none of which gets to the heart of the matter, "with the result that such a metaphysics is as unscientific as are the aforementioned sensory images" (p. 42/108). Multiplying predicates which are applied to reality at the behest of the thinker provides no secure approach to science—it provides only a readily memorized jargon, in which everything is taken care of with a convenient but severely limited vocabulary, permitting a "crystal-clear account of the organism of the universe" (p. 43/110).[39] A pat terminology not too concerned to be meaningful serves only as a cover-up for an undifferentiated absolute wherein distinctions are *de facto* eliminated (p. 43/110). It is unfortunate, but perhaps inevitable, that the lofty title of "science" should have been applied to this sort of superficial universalism (p. 44/111).

The mistake would seem to lie in the very attempt to lay down the pre-conditions for the possibility of scientific knowledge instead of allowing reality to reveal its own organic structure of interrelation. "Science ought to organize itself only through the concept's own proper life" (p. 44/111). Predicates are not to be "pasted on" as though the content of knowledge were a surface susceptible to this kind of determination; determination is "the self-moving soul of the teeming (*erfüllten*) content" (p. 44/111). The language here, to be sure, is metaphorical, but it serves to emphasize the dynamic character of reality whose inner movement of self-determination is identical with the inner movement of consciousness knowing it.[40] The movement, which the *Phenomenology* examines only as the movement of consciousness on its way to a scientific comprehension of the real, is a move-ment of distinguishing self from self ("self-othering") in order to make pos-sible a movement of return to self—of self-identification rather than im-mediate self-identity. This comes down to saying that the very being of reality, like the being of consciousness (*Bewusst-sein*), is to be a whole which must articulate itself in order to re-integrate itself. The total experience of consciousness, which is a process of re-cognition of an original *an sich* unity, is the total articulation of reality, which re-integrates itself into its original *an sich* unity—to know self in its wholeness is to know reality in its whole-ness, and vice versa; to know one without the other is not to *know*. "In this way the content shows that its determinateness is not received from an-other, is not something pasted on; rather the content gives itself its own determinateness, makes of itself a moment which has its place in the whole" (p. 44/111).

All this bespeaks the function of consciousness (self-consciousness) as "reason," which is to penetrate to the very heart of self-determining reality —is to be in fact the very self-determining of reality—as opposed to "under-

---

[39] The allusion, as Kaufmann rightly remarks (*Hegel*, p. 433n15; cf. p. 375n13), is to Fichte's *Sonnenklarer Bericht an das Publikum über das eigentliche Wesen der neuesten Philosophie* (1801) (unfortunately Kaufmann's "Sun-clear Report" is un-English) and seems to indicate that Hegel accuses Fichte as well as Schelling of a formalistic employ-ment of empty jargon.

[40] The extent of this identification is revealed only in the *Science of Logic*.

standing" which simply *imposes* order on an independent manifold and, thus, "only gives the table of contents but does not deliver the content itself" (p. 44/112). This latter is all that understanding can do, since it insists on remaining in control of what it *says*. Precisely for this reason "understanding" "looks over (*übersieht*) the whole" but "does not see (*sieht*) it at all"—all it can do is talk *about* it (p. 45/112).[41] Only reason, then, not understanding, can be "scientific" in the full sense. "Scientific knowing, then, demands rather that knowing surrender (*übergeben*) itself to the life of its object, or—what amounts to the same—that it have before itself and express the interior necessity of its object" (p. 45/112). As scientific, self-conscious reason immerses itself in its content, from which it returns back into itself, but not before the content has returned back into itself and thus raised itself to a higher level of truth—of wholeness. "Thereby emerges the simple whole with a comprehensive view of itself (*sich übersehende*) out of the wealth [of objectivity] in which its reflection seemed to have been lost" (p. 45/112–13). The disinterested, self-forgetting research of the scientific spirit turns out to be self-discovering.

There is here a remarkable insight into the role of the non-self in the revelation of the self to itself, and it works both ways. A self-identity which is only that, involving no non-identity, is static and abstract, amounts to $A = A$ which, in fact, says nothing. If the self of which consciousness is aware is just *there* to be grasped immediately, it is a static, abstract, contentless self. If it is to have a content, it must make itself other and then appropriate itself in that other. This is what consciousness does when it knows reality; it appropriates the other of itself and thus appropriates itself. By the same token, if substance, as the unified whole of objectivity, is simply identical with itself, substance = substance, it is as empty as $A = A$ (or $I = I$). If, on the other hand, substance as actualized, i.e., as self-actualizing, is subject, then it too must other itself in being thought and thus appropriate itself. Substance *becomes* all that it initially (*an sich*) is in being thought; thought (consciousness) *becomes* all it initially (*an sich*) is in thinking (articulating and appropriating) substance (p. 45/113). This comes down to saying that the determinations which distinguish the object of thought, i.e., *being*, are at once its self-determinations and thought-determinations: "Being is thinking" (p. 45/113). The object of thought *becomes* what it is in being thought, but it is the object which *becomes*; what it is (becomes) is not imposed on it from without (p. 45/113).

Thus, what Hegel is advocating here is not some form of subjective idealism, substituting for the "dogmatism" which tries to contain truth within a proposition an equally insidious "dogmatism of self-certainty" (p. 46/113). The activity of knowing in the strict sense is not an empty self-knowing which arbitrarily finds all other knowledge in self-knowing; it is thoroughly "immersed in its content, since the activity is the immanent

---

[41] The German language permits a significant play on words here which is impossible to render in English. The verb *übersehen* can mean "overlook," "look over," or "view comprehensively." At this point a combination of the first two connotations is intended. A few lines down, the third connotation will be emphasized.

self of the content and at the same time turned back on itself" (p. 46/113–
14). There is even, so to speak, a certain "trickery" (*List*) at work here.[42]
When consciousness turns back upon itself, it could seem to be withdrawing from its objective stance and adopting a subjective one; it is actually
doing the opposite, dissolving its mere self-certainty and turning it much
more significantly into a moment of the total process which embraces all
objectivity and subjectivity alike (p. 46/114). As a result, just as the articulation effected by understanding is significant for the determinate consciousness—self-consciousness—of substance, so too is it significant for the
way substance is. The manifest being (*Dasein*) is a qualification of substance itself, a determination of its being as simple and self-identical, but it
is a determinateness inseparable from thought thinking substance. A realization of this serves to explain why Anaxagoras could see νοῦς (reason?) as the
essence of reality or why later Socrates and Plato could express the
same insight more determinately by assigning to εἶδος or ἰδέα (containing the
determinate universality of *species*) the essence of the real. The *idea* of
something expresses the specific objective class to which that something belongs and in so doing "determinately designates a concept," i.e., the something *as* conceived (p. 46/114).

[ANALYSIS AND SYNTHESIS]

Conceiving any reality, then, involves breaking it up in thought (understanding) and putting it together again in thought (reason). The species to
which the reality in question belongs is at once simple, constantly identical
with itself, and distinguished from others (p. 46/114). A breaking up and
putting together again, however, is surely rather arbitrary, if reality itself
has no part in the act; it is external to the reality and, in fact, leaves it
intact. If, on the other hand, we recognize that the very self-identity of
anything involves its distinction from what is other, that in being itself it
distinguishes itself from what is other, we can begin to see a network of
interrelationships which are essential to the self-identity of anything, relationships which are, it is true, articulated in thought, but which are
meaningless if they are not relationships inherent in reality itself. Thus conceiving is itself meaningless, unless the inner reality of that which is conceived is conceptual; in fact, says Hegel, the concept of anything is "the
proper interiority" of that which is conceived (p. 47/115). *What* is thought
has its being; the *thought* of it has its being; but neither is independent of
the other, since both are "moments" in the one process, which Hegel calls
"concept." To say that reality is rationally grasped is to say that it is "intelligible" (*verständig*). Its "intelligibility" (*Verständigkeit*), however, is not
some static quality which characterizes it but a process of "becoming, and
as this becoming it is *rationality* (*Vernünftigkeit*)" (p. 47/115). The reason

---

[42] Those familiar with Hegel will recognize this metaphor which he employs a number
of times, most strikingly in the *Philosophy of History*, where he speaks of the "trickery
of reason." In history each individual thinks he is promoting his own interests but is, in
fact, promoting the overriding ends of reason in its march through historical events.

which comprehends is rational; the reality comprehended is rational; but neither is rational except in the dialectical identification of both.

"In general, logical necessity consists in what is the nature of what is, i.e., to be its concept in its being" (p. 47/115). Reality is an "organic" whole, all of whose parts are dynamically interrelated; hence, to speak of "logical necessity" is to speak of (*a*) *knowing* a content; (*b*) the content as essentially *concept*; (*c*) thought as "speculative," i.e., a "seeing-into" (p. 47/115). By the same token, to speak of reality in the concrete as "appearing" is to speak of reality as (*a*) self-moving, (*b*) being determinate, (*c*) having a "logical" form, i.e., that which the content is "essentially" (p. 47/115). The concrete existence of any reality, what it *really* is, is its logical existence, what it *essentially* is. The form of reality, therefore, which belongs to it *in* thought is not a form imposed on it *by* thought. The concrete content of thought *actualizes itself* in this form, "because the form is the innate becoming of the content itself" (p. 47/115). The form which the content has in rational thought is its own proper form. The task of the entire *Phenomenology* is to show that, when thought is truly rational, this is so.

One might well ask, of course, if there is any term to this sort of rationality; can reason ever rest assured of its own rationality, or must it be a never-ending striving to be more rational? Hegel would seem to be constrained to assert the latter, yet he seems, in fact, to be asserting that at the end of the *Phenomenology* reason has attained rationality. This second interpretation would be possible, were it not for two things: (*a*) the constant assertion that the very rationality of reason is nothing apart from the process of striving toward it; and (*b*) that the scientific method is constantly described as a method of moving *toward* rationality never as a resting *in* rationality; the "movement" described in the *Phenomenology* never ceases to play its role. What Hegel is at pains to emphasize is that "speculative philosophy"—not *his* philosophy but philosophy as the perennial activity of the human spirit—is the scientific method in operation as (*a*) inseparable from its content, and (*b*) having its own rhythm of self-determination. How this is to be worked out remains to be seen; here it is merely asserted, and it is called concept—and, admittedly, it can be denied with equal ease (p. 47/116); in fact he sees denial as the common reaction in his own day (pp. 47–48/116).

Whether the Preface is to be read as prologue or as epilogue, its task cannot be to work out the whole system and thus concretely to justify the method. What it can do, however, is to insist that the study of philosophical science demands that one "take upon oneself the rigorous efforts (*Anstrengungen*) of the concept" (p. 48/116). This in turn requires careful *attention* to the dynamic character of such determinations as "*being-in-itself, being-for-itself, self-identity,* etc." (p. 48/116). It demands that these be seen as inner movements of what is known (metaphorically they could be called "souls," but that is an inadequate metaphor). To be avoided at all costs are (*a*) the use of sensible images to express pure thought determinations; (*b*) a "ratiocination" which functions independently of the content of thought, as though it were indifferently applicable to any content.

Indispensable is the *effort*—and effort it surely is—to relinquish this independence, this being in control, and allowing content to reveal itself in all its richness. The philosopher must be willing to give up the arbitrariness of his own "bright ideas" *(Einfälle)*; giving them up is "an essential moment of attention to the concept" (p. 48/117).

"Attention to the concept" is what Hegel in the same context calls "thinking comprehensively" *(das begreifende Denken)*. This sort of thinking is diametrically opposed to the attitude of "ratiocination" which he finds characteristic of contemporary subjective idealism, which is but a *purely* negative attitude toward the content of philosophical thought, a "reflection on the empty I, the vanity of its knowing"—and it is doubly vain, empty of content and relying on unmediated "insights." In this sort of thinking, negativity is essential to the thought itself but not to what is thought. In "thinking comprehensively," on the other hand, the negative "as its *immanent* movement and determination, and as the *whole* of that, is the *positive* . . . , the *determinate* negative and therefore a positive content" (p. 49/118). It is important to reiterate here that for Hegel a thinking which has *only* the self as content has no content or, to put it in other terms, in such thinking the self becomes only a "notional *subject*[43] to which a content is related as an accident or predicate" (p. 49/118). But authentic predicates are not "accidents" of a "substance"; they are "activities" of a "subject," where "is" is not simply the *copula* in a proposition but expresses *action*. In "ratiocination" the *self* does all the moving, whereas in "conceptual thinking" "the concept is the object's own self, presenting itself as the object's coming-to-be" (p. 49/118). Such an object (or "substance" as an objective whole) is not a static "bearer" of accidents; "it is the self-moving concept which appropriates its own determinations" (p. 49/118).

In this context there is no room for a knowing subject standing over against a known object; to be subject is to constitute the determining and distinguishing movement of the content known. "With this the content is, in fact, no longer predicate of a subject; rather, it is the substance, the essence and concept of that which is in question" (p. 50/119). What in a proposition has the form of a predicate "is substance itself" as passage from subject to predicate, i.e., acting. In true thinking, then, there are no static subjects to which an external thinking, "acting as ratiocination," attributes an arbitrary number of predicates (p. 50/120). "Knowing rather still has to do with the self of the content; it should not be independent of but joined with that self" (pp. 50–51/120). It may, of course, seem arbitrary to speak of an object as a "self"—just as to Kant it seemed arbitrary to speak of a self as "object"—and perhaps the language is a bit out of the ordinary.[44] But if we reflect on what Hegel is trying to emphasize, the terminology may be less shocking. Where, as in the "formal proposition," the predicates of a subject signify what is "attributed" to the subject by someone thinking, strong language is needed to indicate that in the "speculative proposition"

[43] Subject of a proposition.
[44] To say of the object that it is a "self" is not to say that it is an "ego," but that its determinations are its own.

predicates are activities (Hegel translates Aristotle's ἐνέργεια by *Tätigkeit*) [45] of the subject *itself*. It is for this reason, too, that knowledge of objects is revelatory of *self* to the knower.

In any event, Hegel is at pains to insist over and over again that philosophical statements signify neither a static identity of subject and predicate nor a "pasting" of predicates on a subject. In fact, the speculative "identification" of subject and predicate does not at all cancel out their distinction; "rather, their unity should emerge as a harmony" (p. 51/120). The attribute named in the predicate is substance's own self-expression; the subject *universalizes* itself in the predicate (p. 51/121)—through the mediation of the knowing subject, to be sure.

To illustrate what he is saying, Hegel here gives two examples of "speculative" statements. If we say "God is Being," the predicate has "substantial significance," in the sense that being is the "outpouring" of God. God ceases to be a *fixed* subject of which the predicate "being" is *said*. In one sense the predicate says something of the subject; in a more important sense the subject says the predicate of itself and thus reveals the significance of the predicate (p. 51/121). If, secondly, we say with Hegel, "the *actual* (*das Wirkliche*) is the *universal*," we are saying that the "actualization" of the subject is its "universalization"—"the actual as subject vanishes (*vergeht*) in the predicate" (p. 51/121). What the statement says, then, is not "the actual is universal," but "the universal is to express the essence of the actual" (p. 52/121). Once again, in saying the predicate of itself the subject says as much of the predicate as the predicate says of the subject. The "speculative" proposition says what it says only because it says it of *this subject*, not of *any subject*. In the example given, by becoming the universal the actual becomes real; in universalizing itself it becomes what it really is.

It is because of language such as this that the complaint is leveled against philosophical writing that it has to be read more than once to be understood (p. 52/122). This, says Hegel, is as it should be; it is the first reading which makes the second reading possible, which does not mean that philosophical writing is "esoteric"; it means only that, because it must express itself in propositions, it can be understood only if its propositions are not read in the ordinary way. "The philosophical proposition, because it is a proposition, evokes the opinion that what it states is the customary relationship (*Verhältnisses*) between subject and predicate and the customary attitude (*Verhaltens*) of knowing" (p. 52/122). Overcoming the customary demands effort; because the content of the proposition is "philosophical," it destroys "this attitude and the opinion which goes with it" (p. 52/122). Such a proposition is not "intended" (*gemeint*) in the way "opinion" (*Meinung*) "thought" (*meinte*) it was. Thus, the proposition has to be read again: "This correction of its opinion imposes on knowing the necessity of coming back to the proposition and of interpreting it in another way" (p. 52/122). [46]

---

45 Cf. *Geschichte der Philosophie* II (Sämtliche Werke XVIII), 321.

46 No one will debate Hegel that a constant effort is required to understand his statements the way he intends them to be understood.

The temptation to confuse "the speculative and the ratiocinative manner" of speaking is constant. To say *concept* of subject is not to say *predicate* of subject; the two ways of "saying" are mutually exclusive, but it is easy to confuse them. Philosophical language must be dynamic, and to be that it must studiously exclude "the manner of the customary relationship of the parts of the proposition" (p. 52/122).[47] It is not philosophical, however, simply to eliminate the non-speculative proposition without showing how this is done; nor will the mere content (subject-copula-predicate) of the proposition show that (p. 52/122–23). Thus, it is not enough to show *that* the non-speculative proposition is too restrictive; the converse movement has to be "expressed": "This return of the concept into itself must be presented" (p. 53/123). What must be shown is that "the dialectical movement of the proposition itself" replaces ratiocinative "proof," and the showing itself must be dialectical.[48] "The *proposition* should express *what* the true is, but essentially the true is subject. As such it is only the dialectical movement, this process which is self-generating, progressing, and returning into itself" (p. 53/123). When this is being done it should at the same time be made clear that "proof" in the ordinary sense is not being used (p. 53/123).

It would, of course, be ridiculous to attempt to philosophize by not using propositions at all; they are inescapable, and confusion would seem to be unavoidable. If we are to ground propositions, we must employ other propositions, and that would seem to make an infinite regress inevitable. This, Hegel tells us, is precisely the case when the customary form of the proposition is employed in "proofs." "This form of grounding and conditioning, however, belongs to the sort of proving from which the dialectical movement is different; the former belongs, then, to cognition from outside" (p. 53/123). In "dialectical movement," on the other hand, the content is not made up of "subjects" to which "predicates" are added. But since the propositional form is as such empty, its content must be supplied. Ordinarily this is done by taking as subject either a sensibly intuited "this" or a mere "name" (p. 53/124). If the subject is the sensibly intuited, it remains outside the concept; if it is a name, it hides from the user of it the fact that he does not *know* the subject, e.g., God, because the mere word is not immediately the concept. The predicates which are said of such a nominal subject, on the other hand, are immediately conceptual, e.g., "being," "oneness," "singularity," "subject," etc. (p. 54/124). To use the word "God," then, apart from the concept is to say nothing, and to pile on conceptual predicates does not change matters—unless "edification" is what is aimed at. It might even be better to avoid using the term "God."

In any event, philosophical language demands extreme care. "True to the insight into the nature of the speculative, the presentation must retain the dialectical form, introducing nothing except to the extent that it is

[47] One might illustrate this in a very homely way. If we say "grass is green," the adjective "green," which is attributable to innumerable other objects, is said of the "grass." It tells us something, but it does not deliver to us the "greening" precisely of grass.

[48] Hegel tries to do this with meticulous care in the *Logic* (Part II), by describing the dynamic articulation of thought in "concept" (*Begriff*), "judgment" (*Urteil*), and "syllogism" (*Schluss*).

conceptualized and is concept" (p. 54/124). By the same token, the obstacle to speculative thinking would be just as great if its truths were looked upon as acquired once and for all, never in need of re-examination. If, then, one is to think philosophically and avoid the pitfalls indicated, constant practice is necessary, just as it is in any of the sciences, arts, techniques. No more than one is an adept in other disciplines, is one a philosopher just because one has a head to think with; "native reason" is not adequate equipment. Philosophy is not a formal discipline which can either dispense with contents or understand its contents without *comprehending* them, i.e., keeping them always in the context of the whole (p. 55/125).

Philosophizing, in short, is hard work; nor can an appeal to some sort of immediate revelation of the divine or to sound common sense be a substitute for the long hard path of "discipline" (*Bildung*) or for the extensive as well as profound movement of spirit along the road to knowledge—any more than chickory can be a substitute for coffee! One of the difficulties to be overcome is the all-too-attractive temptation to look upon the inability to come to terms with abstract propositions as "freedom of thought" or as "genius" (p. 55/126). Moreover, lack of discipline not only produces bad philosophy; it also produces prosaic poetry and inflammatory rhetoric. But, says Hegel, we are told that what is needed is "natural philosophizing," which is not thought but imagination and which produces "images which are neither fish nor flesh, neither poetry nor philosophy" (p. 55/126). Sound common sense is armed with a rhetoric suited either to trivial truths—they are in the heart (p. 55/126)—or to "ultimate truths"—which are in the catechism (p. 56/127). As long as it keeps its truths vague enough, its task is easy, just as it is easy to call rigorous thinking "sophistry," "a motto of sound common sense in its opposition to disciplined reason" (p. 56/127). It simply rejects whatever disagrees with its own opinions and in so doing treads under foot the very roots of humanity, "for it is the nature of humanity to press for agreement with others, and its existence (*Existenz*) is to be found only in the established community of consciousness" (p. 56/127). To reject that and rely on feeling is animalistic.

As attractive as the prospect might be, there is no "royal road to science." If one wants to limit oneself to reading reviews of philosophical books—or their "prefaces"—one can enjoy being an armchair philosopher, but "true thoughts and scientific insight are to be gained only in the labor of the concept" (p. 57/128). What the philosopher needs is not natural talent but hard work, which will enable him to come to terms with "truth which has attained to the form proper to it, truth which is capable of being the property of every self-conscious reason" (p. 57/128).[49]

Because the prevailing mood is what it is, Hegel is under no illusions that his dynamic conception of science will meet with a generally favorable

---

[49] The term for "property" is *Eigentum*. Hegel is not here contradicting what he said earlier about truth's not being a "possession"—like a minted coin one can put in one's pocket. He is simply saying that truth can—and should—become "one's own" (*eigen*); each "self-conscious reason" should *appropriate* it. It is "proper" to self-conscious reason to know truth.

reception. Still, he recalls, there were periods, "which are even called periods of wild enthusiasm," when Aristotle's philosophy was highly regarded for its speculative profundity, and Plato's *Parmenides* was looked upon as the unfolding and the positive expression of divine life,[50] when even mystical ecstasy, despite its obscurity, was in fact held to be what the pure concept is (p. 57/129). What is more, says Hegel, even our own age, however inadequate its conception of it may be, has a high regard for the scientific character of philosophy (p. 58/129). He has reason to hope, then, that his own attempt to render philosophy scientific will by virtue of the intrinsic truth of the "matter" (*Sache*) gain entry. When the time is ripe, when there is a public ready for it—despite what that public's official spokesmen may be saying—the true philosophy will establish itself. The official spokesmen simply do not know that they are already dead. Hegel closes, nevertheless, with an admission that no one individual will make an enormous contribution to the desired result—a disclaimer which has been belied by the enormous influence his work has had, even had during his own lifetime.

[50] One is reminded of Aristotle's characterization of "first philosophy" as the "divine science," both because its ultimate object is God and because it is a "divine" way of knowing. See *Metaphysics* 1, 983A5–10.

Bibliography of Works Cited

NOTE: Rather than give here an exhaustive bibliography which would be merely repetitive of bibliographies readily available elsewhere, it seems more economical to list only those works actually cited in the present volume. That a host of other books were consulted in the process of preparing the text goes without saying.

For those who seek a more extensive bibliography there is an excellent list of works in English in Frederick G. Weiss, "Hegel: A Bibliography of Books in English, Arranged Chronologically," in *The Legacy of Hegel: Proceedings of the Marquette Hegel Symposium 1970* (The Hague: Nijhoff, 1973). There are excellent bibliographies in Henry Harris, *Hegel's Development: Toward the Sunlight,* and in Walter Kaufmann, *Hegel.*

Adorno, Theodor W. *Drei Studien zu Hegel.* Frankfurt: Suhrkamp, 1963.

Andler, Charles. "Le Fondement du Savoir dans la *Phénoménologie de l'Esprit* de Hegel." *Revue de Métaphysique et de Morale,* 38 (1931), 317–40.

Baillie, J. B., trans. *The Phenomenology of Mind.* New York: Humanities Press, 1949.

Becker, Werner. *Hegels Begriff der Dialektik.* Stuttgart: Kohlhammer, 1969.

Bloch, Ernst. *Subjekt–Objekt: Erläuterungen zu Hegel.* Berlin: Aufbau-Verlag, 1952.

Boey, Conrad, s.j. *L'Aliénation dans la Phénoménologie de l'Esprit.* Paris: Desclée De Brouwer, 1970.

Bröcker, Walter. *Auseinandersetzungen mit Hegel.* Frankfurt: Klostermann, 1965.

Findlay, J. N. *The Philosophy of Hegel: An Introduction and Re-examination.* New York: Collier, 1962.

Gadamer, Hans Georg. *Hegels Dialektik.* Tübingen: Mohr, 1971.

Garaudy, Roger. *Dieu est mort: Étude sur Hegel.* Paris: Presses Universitaires de France, 1962.

Gauvin, Joseph. "Le 'Für uns' dans la Phénoménologie de l'Esprit." *Archives de Philosophie,* 33, No. 4 (December 1970), 829–54.

Glockner, Hermann. *Hegel.* 2 vols. Stuttgart: Frommann, 1929.

Grégoire, Franz. *Études Hégéliennes: Les Points capitaux du système.* Louvain: Presses Universitaires de Louvain; Paris: Beatrice-Nauwelaerts, 1958.

Häring, Theodor. "Die Entstehungsgeschichte der Phänomenologie des Geistes." *Verhandlungen des dritten Hegelkongresses* (Tübingen, 1934), 118–38.

Harris, Henry. *Hegel's Development: Toward the Sunlight.* Oxford: Clarendon, 1972.

Hartmann, Nicolai. *Hegel* (Die Philosophie des deutschen Idealismus). 2 vols. Berlin & Leipzig: Grünter, 1927.

Hegel, Georg Wilhelm Friedrich: see appended listing.

Herder, Johann Gottfried. *Schriften.* Ed. Walter Flemmer. Munich: Goldmann, 1960.

Hyppolite, Jean. *Genèse et structure de la Phénoménologie de l'Esprit de Hegel.* Paris: Aubier, 1946.

————, trans. *La Phénoménologie de l'Esprit.* 2 vols. Paris: Aubier, 1939, 1941.

Kaufmann, Walter. *Hegel.* New York: Doubleday, 1965.

Kojève, Alexandre. *Introduction à la lecture de Hegel: Leçons sur la Phénoménologie de l'Esprit, professées de 1933 à 1939.* Ed. Raymond Queneau. 2nd ed. Paris: Gallimard, 1947. Partial English version: *Introduction to the Reading of Hegel.* Trans. James Nichols, Jr. New York & London: Basic Books, 1969.

Labarrière, Pierre-Jean. *Structures et mouvement dialectique dans la Phénoménologie de Hegel.* Paris: Aubier-Montaigne, 1968.

Lauer, Quentin, s.j. "Hegel on Proofs for God's Existence." *Kantstudien,* 55, No. 4 (1964), 443–65.

————. "Hegel on the Identity of Content in Religion and Philosophy." *Hegel and the Philosophy of Religion.* Ed. Darrell E. Christensen. The Hague: Nijhoff, 1970. Pp. 261–78.

————. "Phenomenology: Hegel and Husserl." *Beyond Epistemology: New Studies in the Philosophy of Hegel.* Ed. Frederick G. Weiss. The Hague: Nijhoff, 1974. Pp. 174–96.

Loewenberg, J. *Hegel's Phenomenology: Dialogues on the Life of the Mind.* La Salle, Ill.: Open Court, 1965.

Lukacs, Georg. *Der junge Hegel.* Zurich & Vienna: Europa, 1948.

MacIntyre, Alasdair, ed. *Hegel.* New York: Doubleday, 1972.

McDermott, John J., ed. *The Philosophy of John Dewey.* 2 vols. New York: Putnam, 1973.

Metzke, Erwin. *Hegels Vorreden.* Heidelberg: Kerle, 1949.

Niel, Henri. *De la Médiation dans la philosophie de Hegel.* Paris: Aubier, 1945.

Pannenberg, Wolfhart. *The Idea of God and Human Freedom.* Philadelphia: Westminster, 1973.

Pöggeler, Otto. "Zur Deutung der Phänomenologie des Geistes." *Hegelstudien,* 1 (1961), 255–91.

Purpus, Wilhelm. *Die Dialektik der sinnlichen Gewissheit bei Hegel.* Nuremberg: Seitz, 1905.

Sartre, Jean-Paul. *L'Être et le néant.* Paris: Gallimard, 1949.

Seeberger, Wilhelm. *Hegel oder die Entwicklung des Geistes zur Freiheit.* Stuttgart: Klett, 1961.

Smith, John. "Hegel's Critique of Kant." *The Review of Metaphysics,* 26, No. 3 (March 1973), 438–460.

Taylor, Charles. *Hegel.* London: Cambridge University Press, 1975.

Vermeil, Edmond. "La Pensée politique de Hegel." *Revue de Métaphysique et de Morale,* 38 (1931), 421–510.

Voegelin, Eric. "On Hegel—A Study in Sorcery." *Studium Generale,* 24 (1971), 335–68.

Wahl, Jean. *Le Malheur de la conscience dans la philosophie de Hegel.* Paris: Rieder, 1939.

Wallace, William. *Prolegomena to the Study of Hegel's Philosophy.* New York: Russell & Russell, 1968.

Weiss, Frederick G. *Hegel's Critique of Aristotle's Philosophy of Mind.* The Hague: Nijhoff, 1969.

Hegel, Georg Wilhelm Friedrich.
    Aesthetik. Ed. Friedrich Bassenge. 2 vols. Frankfurt: Europäische Verlagsanstalt, 1955.
    Berliner Schriften. Ed. Johannes Hoffmeister. Hamburg: Meiner, 1956.

Briefe von und an Hegel. Ed. Johannes Hoffmeister. 4 vols. Hamburg: Meiner, 1952.

"De orbitis planetarum." Ed. Hermann Glockner. Sämtliche Werke I. Stuttgart: Frommann, 1927.

"Differenz des Fichteschen und Schellingschen Systems der Philosophie." *Jenaer kritische Schriften.* Edd. Hartmut Buchner and Otto Pöggeler. Hamburg: Meiner, 1968.

Dokumente zu Hegels Entwicklung. Ed. Johannes Hoffmeister. Stuttgart: Frommann, 1936.

Einleitung in die Geschichte der Philosophie. Ed. Johannes Hoffmeister. Hamburg: Meiner, 1940.

Enzyklopädie der philosophischen Wissenschaften. Edd. Friedhelm Nicolin and Otto Pöggeler. 6th ed. Hamburg: Meiner, 1959.

Glauben und Wissen. Ed. Georg Lasson. Hamburg: Himmelheber, 1962.

Grundlinien der Philosophie des Rechts. Ed. Johannes Hoffmeister. Hamburg: Meiner, 1955.

Jenenser Logik, Metaphysik, und Naturphilosophie. Ed. Georg Lasson. Hamburg: Meiner, 1967.

Phänomenologie des Geistes. Ed. Johannes Hoffmeister. 6th ed. Hamburg: Meiner, 1952.

Philosophische Propädeutik. Ed. Hermann Glockner. Sämtliche Werke III. Stuttgart: Frommann, 1927.

Schriften zur Politik und Rechtsphilosophie. Ed. Georg Lasson. 2nd ed. Leipzig: Meiner, 1923.

Theologische Jugendschriften. Ed. Hermann Nohl. Frankfurt: Minerva, 1966.

Vorlesungen über die Geschichte der Philosophie. Ed. Hermann Glockner. 3 vols. Sämtliche Werke XVII–XIX. Stuttgart: Frommann, 1928.

Vorlesungen über die Philosophie der Geschichte. Ed. Hermann Glockner. Sämtliche Werke XI. Stuttgart: Frommann, 1928.

Vorlesungen über die Philosophie der Religion. Ed. Georg Lasson. 2 vols. Hamburg: Meiner, 1925.

Wissenschaft der Logik. Ed. Georg Lasson. 2 vols. Hamburg: Meiner, 1963.